T0213939

Lecture Notes in Computer Science 12327

More information about this series at http://www.springer.com/series/7408

Maurice H. ter Beek · Dejan Ničković (Eds.)

Formal Methods for Industrial Critical Systems

25th International Conference, FMICS 2020
Vienna, Austria, September 2–3, 2020
Proceedings

 Springer

Editors
Maurice H. ter Beek (iD)
ISTI, Consiglio Nazionale delle Ricerche
Pisa, Italy

Dejan Ničković (iD)
AIT Austrian Institute of Technology GmbH
Vienna, Austria

ISSN 0302-9743 ISSN 1611-3349 (electronic)
Lecture Notes in Computer Science
ISBN 978-3-030-58297-5 ISBN 978-3-030-58298-2 (eBook)
https://doi.org/10.1007/978-3-030-58298-2

LNCS Sublibrary: SL2 – Programming and Software Engineering

This Springer imprint is published by the registered company Springer Nature Switzerland AG
The registered company address is: Gewerbestrasse 11, 6330 Cham, Switzerland

Preface

This volume contains the papers presented at the 25th International Conference on Formal Methods in Industrial Critical Systems (FMICS 2020), virtually held during September 2–3, 2020. This year the conference was organized under the umbrella of QONFEST, alongside with the 31st International Conference on Concurrency Theory (CONCUR 2020), the 17th International Conference on Quantitative Evaluation of Systems (QEST 2020), and the 18th International Conference on Formal Modeling and Analysis of Timed Systems (FORMATS 2020).

FMICS this year reached its 25th edition, providing for a quarter of a century a forum for researchers who are interested in the development and application of formal methods in industry. FMICS celebrated its 25th birthday with a panel in which the founders and previous chairpersons of the FMICS working group of ERCIM acted as panelists. They recalled the original motivation and beginning of FMICS, shared some success stories, and presented an extensive survey on the past, present, and future of formal methods in research, education, and industry. The detailed report of this study, included in these proceedings, presents an analysis of the opinions of 130 renowned experts in formal methods, as well as thought-provoking position statements on formal methods of 111 of them.

This year we received 26 submissions. Each of these submissions went through a rigorous review process, and as a result each paper received at least three reports. We selected 11 papers for presentation during the conference and inclusion in these proceedings, an acceptance rate of 42%. The conference featured invited talks by Roderick Bloem (Graz University of Technology, Austria, joint keynote with CONCUR and FORMATS), Thomas Henzinger (IST, Austria, joint keynote with CONCUR and QEST), and Stefan Resch (Thales, Austria).

Following a tradition established over the years, Springer provided an award for the best FMICS paper. This year, the reviewers selected the contribution "Verifiable and Scalable Mission-Plan Synthesis for Multiple Autonomous Agents" by Rong Gu, Eduard Enoiu, Cristina Seceleanu, and Kristina Lundqvist for the FMICS 2020 Best Paper Award.

We are grateful to all involved in FMICS 2020. In particular the Program Committee members and subreviewers for their accurate and timely reviewing, all authors for their submissions, and all attendees of the conference for their participation. We thank the general chair of QONFEST, Ezio Bartocci, for providing the logistics that enabled and facilitated the organization of FMICS. We are very grateful to QONFEST platinum sponsor Interchain Foundation, gold sponsors Vienna Center for Logics and Algorithms (VCLA) and Vienna University of Technology, and bronze sponsors ERCIM and Springer.

August 2020

Maurice H. ter Beek
Dejan Ničković

Organization

FMICS Program Chairs

Maurice H. ter Beek   ISTI-CNR, Italy
Dejan Ničković   AIT Austrian Institute of Technology, Austria

FMICS Program Committee

Bernhard Aichernig	TU Graz, Austria
Jiri Barnat	Masaryk University, Czech Republic
Davide Basile	ISTI-CNR, Italy
Carlos Budde	University of Twente, The Netherlands
Rance Cleaveland	University of Maryland, USA
Thao Dang	VERIMAG, France
Michael Dierkes	Rockwell Collins, France
Georgios Fainekos	Arizona State University, USA
Alessandro Fantechi	University of Florence, Italy
Wan Fokkink	Vrije Universiteit Amsterdam, The Netherlands
Maria Del Mar Gallardo	University of Malaga, Spain
Ichiro Hasuo	University of Tokyo, Japan
Klaus Havelund	NASA, USA
Thierry Lecomte	CLEARSY, France
Alberto Lluch Lafuente	Technical University of Denmark, Denmark
Axel Legay	UC Louvain, Belgium
Gabriele Lenzini	University of Luxembourg, Luxembourg
Florian Lorber	Aalborg University, Denmark
Tiziana Margaria	University of Limerick and LERO, Ireland
Radu Mateescu	Inria, France
Franco Mazzanti	ISTI-CNR, Italy
Stefan Mitsch	Carnegie Mellon University, USA
José N. Oliveira	University of Minho, Portugal
Jaco van de Pol	Aarhus University, Denmark
Adam Rogaliewicz	Brno University of Technology, Czech Republic
Markus Roggenbach	Swansea University, UK
Matteo Rossi	Polytechnic University of Milan, Italy
Bernhard Steffen	TU Dortmund University, Germany
Stefano Tonetta	FBK, Italy
Jan Tretmans	TNO, The Netherlands
Andrea Vandin	Sant'Anna School of Advanced Studies, Italy
Tim Willemse	Eindhoven University of Technology, The Netherlands
Kirsten Winter	University of Queensland, Australia
Lijun Zhang	Chinese Academy of Sciences, China

Additional Reviewers

Lukas Armborst   Vojtěch Havlena
Tomáš Fiedor   Iraklis Symeonidis

FMICS Steering Committee

Alessandro Fantechi   University of Florence, Italy
Hubert Garavel   Inria, France
Stefania Gnesi   ISTI-CNR, Italy
Diego Latella   ISTI-CNR, Italy
Tiziana Margaria   University of Limerick and LERO, Ireland
Radu Mateescu   Inria, France
Jaco van de Pol   Aarhus University, Denmark,
                       and University of Twente, The Netherlands

Abstracts of Invited Talks

A Survey of Bidding Games on Graphs

Guy Avni and Thomas A. Henzinger

IST Austria

Abstract. A graph game is a two-player zero-sum game in which the players move a token throughout a graph to produce an infinite path, which determines the winner or payoff of the game. In *bidding games*, both players have budgets, and in each turn, we hold an "auction" (bidding) to determine which player moves the token. In this survey, we consider several bidding mechanisms and study their effect on the properties of the game. Specifically, bidding games, and in particular bidding games of infinite duration, have an intriguing equivalence with *random-turn* games in which in each turn, the player who moves is chosen randomly. We show how minor changes in the bidding mechanism lead to unexpected differences in the equivalence with random-turn games.

Keywords: Bidding games · Richman bidding · Poorman bidding · Mean-payoff · Parity

Extended Abstract

This is an extended abstract of [3].

Two-player zero-sum games on graphs games have deep connections to foundations of logic [14] as well as numerous practical applications, e.g., verification [9], reactive synthesis [13], and reasoning about multi-agent systems [2]. The game proceeds by placing a token on one of the vertices and allowing the players to move it throughout the graph to produce an infinite trace, which determines the winner or payoff of the game.

Several "modes of moving" the token have been studied. The most well-studied mode is *turn-based* games, in which the players alternate turns in moving the token. Other modes include *stochastic games* and *concurrent games*.

We study the *bidding* mode of moving. Abstractly speaking, both players have budgets, and in each turn, we hold an "auction" (bidding) to determine which player moves the token. In this survey, we consider several concrete bidding mechanisms and study the properties of the bidding games that they give rise to.

We emphasize that bidding is a mode of moving the token and bidding games can be studied in combination with any objective. We focus on three objectives: *reachability*, *parity*, and *mean-payoff*. We start by surveying results on reachability games that

This research was supported in part by the Austrian Science Fund (FWF) under grant Z211-N23 (Wittgenstein Award).

were obtained in two papers in the 1990s [10, 11]. We then turn to summarize more recent results on infinite-duration games. Our most interesting results are for mean-payoff games. In a nutshell, reachability bidding games with a specific bidding mechanism called *Richman bidding* were shown to be equivalent to a class of games called *random-turn games* [12]. We show a generalized equivalence between mean-payoff bidding games and random-turn games. While the equivalence for finite-duration games holds only for Richman bidding, for mean-payoff games, equivalences with random-turn games hold for a wide range of bidding mechanisms.

In all mechanisms that we consider, both players simultaneously submit "legal" bids that do not exceed their available budgets, and the higher bidder moves the token. We focus on three orthogonal distinctions between the mechanisms:

Who Pays: We consider *first-price* bidding in which only the higher bidder pays his bid, and *all-pay* bidding in which both players pay their bids.

Who is the Recipient: Two mechanisms were defined in [10]: in *Richman bidding* (named after David Richman), payments are made to the other player, and in *poorman bidding* the payments are made to the "bank" thus the money is lost. A third payment scheme called *taxman* spans the spectrum between Richman and poorman: for a fixed constant $\tau \in [0, 1]$, portion τ is paid to the bank and portion $1 - \tau$ is paid to the other player.

Which Bids Are Allowed: In *discrete bidding* [8], the budgets are given in coins and the minimal positive bid a player can make is one coin. Unless stated otherwise, we consider *continuous bidding* in which bids can be arbitrarily small.

To state our results we need several definitions. The central quantity in bidding games is the *ratio* between the players' budgets. For $i \in \{1, 2\}$, let B_i denote Player i's budget. Player i's ratio is then $B_i/(B_1 + B_2)$. The random-turn game that corresponds to a bidding game G w.r.t. $p \in [0, 1]$, denoted $\mathrm{RT}(G, p)$, is similar to G only that instead of bidding, in each turn, the player who moves is chosen according to a (biased) coin toss that favors Player 1 with probability p and Player 2 with probability $1-p$. When G is a mean-payoff bidding game, then $\mathrm{RT}(G, p)$ is a mean-payoff stochastic game, and its value is the expected payoff under optimal play. We focus on strongly-connected games in which the value does not depend on the initial vertex.

In this survey we summarize the main results of the following sequence of papers:

- In [4], we show that mean-payoff first-price Richman bidding games are equivalent to un-biased random-turn games: the optimal payoff a player can guarantee in a bidding game G does not depend on the initial ratio and equals the value of $\mathrm{RT}(G, 0.5)$.
- In [5], we show that contrary to Richman bidding, the initial ratio matters in mean-payoff first-price poorman bidding games: the optimal payoff a player can guarantee in a bidding game G w.r.t. an initial ratio $r \in (0, 1)$ equals the value of $\mathrm{RT}(G, r)$.
- In [6], we unify the previous two results and show that the optimal payoff a player can guarantee in a mean-payoff first-price taxman bidding game G with taxman parameter $\tau \in [0, 1]$, and initial ratio $r \in (0, 1)$ equals the value of $\mathrm{RT}\left(G, \frac{r + \tau \cdot (1-r)}{1+\tau}\right)$.

- In [1], we study qualitative infinite-duration discrete Richman bidding games and study tie-breaking mechanisms that guarantee determinacy.
- In [7], we study reachability all-pay poorman bidding. Even though they are technically significantly more challenging than reachability first-price bidding games, we can still obtain simple yet powerful results on this model.

Acknowledgments. We would like to thank all our collaborators Milad Aghajohari, Ventsislav Chonev, Rasmus Ibsen-Jensen, Ismäel Jecker, Petr Novotný, Josef Tkadlec, and ore Žikelić; we hope the collaboration was as fun and meaningful for you as it was for us.

References

1. Aghajohari, M., Avni, G., Henzinger, T.A.: Determinacy in discrete-bidding infinite-duration games. In: Proceedings of the 30th CONCUR, LIPIcs, vol. 140, pp. 20:1–20:17 (2019)
2. Alur, R., Henzinger, T.A., Kupferman, O.: Alternating-time temporal logic. J. ACM **49**(5), 672–713 (2002)
3. Avni, G., Henzinger, T.A.: A survey of bidding games on graphs. In: Proceedings of the 31st CONCUR, LIPIcs, vol. 171 (2020)
4. Avni, G., Henzinger, T.A., Chonev, V.: Infinite-duration bidding games. J. ACM **66**(4), 31:1–31:29 (2019)
5. Avni, G., Henzinger, T.A., Ibsen-Jensen, R.: Infinite-duration poorman-bidding games. In: Christodoulou, G., Harks, T. (eds.) WINE 2018. LNCS, vol, 11316, pp 21–36. Springer, Cham (2018). https://doi.org/10.1007/978-3-030-04612-5_2
6. Avni, G., Henzinger, T.A., Žikelić.: Bidding mechanisms in graph games. In: Proceedings of the 44th MFCS, LIPIcs, vol. 138, pp. 11:1–11:13 (2019)
7. Avni, G., Ibsen-Jensen, R., Tkadlec, J.: All-pay bidding games on graphs. In: Proceedings of the 34th AAAI (2020)
8. Develin, M., Payne, S.: Discrete bidding games. Electron. J. Comb. **17**(1), R85 (2010)
9. Emerson, A.E., Jutla, C.S., Sistla, P.A.: On model-checking for fragments of μ-calculus. In: Proceedings of the 5th CAV, pp. 385–396 (1993)
10. Lazarus, A.J., Loeb, D.E., Propp, J.G., Stromquist, W.R., Ullman, D.H.: Combinatorial games under auction play. Games Econ. Behav. **27**(2), 229–264 (1999)
11. Lazarus, A.J., Loeb, D.E., Propp, J.G., Ullman, D.: Richman games. Games No Chance **29**, 439–449 (1996)
12. Peres, Y., Schramm, O., Sheffield, S., Wilson, D.B.: Tug-of-war and the infinity laplacian. J. Amer. Math. Soc. **22**, 167–210 (2009)
13. Pnueli, A., Rosner, R.: On the synthesis of a reactive module. In: Proceedings of the 16th POPL, pp. 179–190 (1989)
14. Rabin, M.O.: Decidability of second order theories and automata on infinite trees. Trans. AMS, **141**, 1–35 (1969)

Applying Formal Methods in Industrial Railway Applications at Thales

Stefan Resch

Thales Austria GmbH, Vienna, Austria
stefan.resch@thalesgroup.com
www.thalesgroup.com

1 Introduction

The application of formal methods is intended to improve software quality. While common tools that perform static code analysis such as Coverity [3] are well known and applied in the industry, this talk presents three use cases at Thales that leverage formal methods and the according tools to an even larger extend.

The conditions for applying formal method tools for safety critical software in the railway domain are defined by the CENELEC EN 50128 [2] standard. This standard highly recommends the use of formal methods for safety relevant projects for the highest safety integrity levels (SIL) of SIL3 and SIL4. The CENELEC EN 50128 categorizes tools into three different types from T1 to T3 depending on whether they can introduce faults into the safety critical software. Here tools related to formal methods usually are of type T2, since they are used for verification and may fail to identify a fault, but cannot introduce them themselves. This requires that, when used in a safety relevant project, (1) the selection of the tool and its assigned category are justified, (2) potential failures are identified, as well as measures to handle such failures, (3) the tool has a specification or handbook, (4) it is ensured that only justified versions of the tools are used and (5) this justification is also performed when switching versions of the tool.

Each of the use cases presented in the following sections has a different focus, illustrating the vast potential of formal methods. They demonstrate that while formal methods may pose a significant overhead at design time they provide an overall benefit when used in the right context.

2 Use Case: ERTMS Hybrid Level 3

ERTMS Hybrid Level 3 is a concept that enables an increase of track capacity in the railway network by reusing regular signaling and interlocking interfaces to integrate into existing systems while benefiting from the continuous supervision of the trains in network via radio. [4] The specification of this concept was analyzed and validated using a formal model in B [1] and executed at runtime in Pro-B [7]. It was subsequently successfully used in a field demonstration controlling real trains.

3   Use Case: Checking ETCS Level 1 Line Side Data

One of the challenges when deploying the new European Train Control System (ETCS) lines lies in the complexity of the configuration data. We use the tool Emerald for checking the ETCS Level 1 lineside configuration data against rules derived from a customer specific "Book of Rules". Emerald internally uses B and Pro-B and is developed and maintained by Thales, since it is a highly specific application. The advantage of Emerald's approach is that many data preparations errors can be caught early on during development, before starting the verification phase of the projects. This tool is actively being used in the current projects.

4   Use Case: TAS Control Plaform

The method of model-checking was used to model and develop fault-tolerant and safety-critical modules for TAS Control Platform, a platform for railway control applications up to safety integrity level (SIL) 4. [8] By model-checking modules in TLA+ [5] and PlusCal [6] core safety and liveness properties of a distributed fault-tolerant protocol were analyzed. A translator from PlusCal to C bridges the gap between model and code.

References

1. Abrial, J.R.: The B Book - Assigning Programs to Meanings. Cambridge University Press, August 1996
2. CENELEC: EN 50128-Railway Applications: Software for Railway Control and Protection Systems. European Committee for Electrotechnical Standardization (2011)
3. Coverity Scan. https://scan.coverity.com/
4. Hansen, D., Leuschel, M., Körner, P., Krings, S., Naulin, T., Nayeri, N., Schneider, D., Skowron, F.: Validation and real-life demonstration of ETCS hybrid level 3 principles using a formal B model. Int. J. Softw. Tools Technol. Transf. 1–18 (2020)
5. Lamport, L.: Specifying systems: the TLA+ language and tools for hardware and software engineers. Addison-Wesley Longman Publishing Co., Inc. (2002)
6. Lamport, L.: The PlusCal algorithm language. Theoretical Aspects of Computing-ICTAC 2009, pp. 36–60 (2009)
7. Leuschel, M., Butler, M.: ProB: an automated analysis toolset for the B method. Int. J. Soft. Tools Technol. Transf. **10**(2), 185–203 (2008)
8. Resch, S., Paulitsch, M.: Using TLA+ in the development of a safety-critical fault-tolerant middleware. In: 2017 IEEE International Symposium on Software Reliability Engineering Workshops (ISSREW), pp. 146–152. IEEE (2017)

Safe Reinforcement Learning using Probabilistic Shields

Nils Jansen[1], Bettina Könighofer[2,3], Sebastian Junges[4],
Alexandru Serban[1], and Roderick Bloem[2]

[1] Radboud University, Nijmegen, The Netherlands
[2] Graz University of Technology, Institute IAIK, Austria
[3] Silicon Austria Labs, TU-Graz SAL DES Lab, Austria
[4] RWTH Aachen University, Aachen, Germany

Abstract. We target the efficient construction of a safety shield for decision making in scenarios that incorporate uncertainties. Markov decision processes (MDPs) are prominent models to capture such planning problems. This paper concerns the efficient construction of a safety shield for reinforcement learning. We specifically target scenarios that incorporate uncertainty and use Markov decision processes (MDPs) as the underlying model to capture such problems. Reinforcement learning (RL) is a machine learning technique that can determine near-optimal policies in MDPs that may be unknown before exploring the model. However, during exploration, RL is prone to induce behavior that is undesirable or not allowed in safety- or mission-critical contexts. We introduce the concept of a probabilistic shield that enables RL decision-making to adhere to safety constraints with high probability. We employ formal verification to efficiently compute the probabilities of critical decisions within a safety-relevant fragment of the MDP. These results help to realize a shield that, when applied to an RL algorithm, restricts the agent from taking unsafe actions, while optimizing the performance objective. We discuss tradeoffs between sufficient progress in the exploration of the environment and ensuring safety. In our experiments, we demonstrate on the arcade game PAC-MAN that the learning efficiency increases as the learning needs orders of magnitude fewer episodes.

1 Introduction

A major open challenge for systems employing reinforcement learning (RL) is the *safety* of decision-making. In particular during the exploration phase – when an agent chooses random actions in order to examine its surroundings – it is important to avoid actions that may cause unsafe outcomes. The area of *safe exploration* investigates how RL agents may be forced to adhere to safety requirements during this phase. A suite of methods that deliver theoretical guarantees are so-called *safety-shields*. Shields prevent an agent from taking unsafe actions at runtime. To this end, the performance objective is extended with a constraint specifying that unsafe states should *never* be visited. This new safety objective ensures there are no violations during the exploration phase.

We propose to incorporate constraints that enforce safety violations to occur *only with small probability*. If an action increases the probability of a safety violation by more than a threshold δ with respect to the optimal safety probability, the shield blocks the action. Consequently, an agent augmented with a shield is *guided* to satisfy the safety objective during exploration (or as long as the shield is used). The shield is *adaptive* with respect to δ, as a high value for δ yields a stricter shield, a smaller value a more permissive shield. The value for δ can be changed on-the-fly, and may depend on the individual minimal safety probabilities at each state. Moreover, in case there is not suitable safe action with respect to δ, the shield can always pick the optimal action as a fallback. We base our formal notion of a probabilistic shield on MDPs, which constitute a popular modeling formalism for decision-making under uncertainty and is widely used in model-based RL. We assess safety by means of probabilistic *temporal logic constraints* that limit, for example, the probability to reach a set of critical states in the MDP. In order to assess the risk of one action, we (1) construct a behavior model for the environment using model-based RL. By plugging this model into any concrete scenario, we obtain an MDP. To construct the shield, we (2) use a model-based verification technique known as *model checking* that assesses whether a system model satisfies a specification. In particular, we obtain precise *safety probabilities of any possible decision* within the MDP. These probabilities can be looked up efficiently and compared to the threshold δ. The shield then readily (3) augments either model-free or model-based RL.

2 Problem Statement

Setting. We define a setting where one controllable agent (the *avatar*) and a number of uncontrollable agents (the *adversaries*) operate within an *arena*. The arena is a compact, high-level description of the underlying model. From this arena, the potential states and actions of all agents may be inferred. For safety considerations, the reward structure can be neglected, effectively reducing the state space for our model-based safety computations. Some (combinations of) agent positions are safety-critical, as they e.g., correspond to collisions or falling off a cliff. A safety property may describe reaching such positions, or use any other property expressible in (the safety fragment of) temporal logic. To encode a *performance criterion*, we associate edges of the arena with a *token* function, indicating the status of some edge. Tokens can be (de-) activated and have an associated *reward* earned upon taking edges with an active token.

Application. We designed the setting to be applicable to a series of scenarios. As an example, take a factory floor plan with several corridors. The nodes of the arena describe crossings, and the edges the corridors with machines. The adversaries are (possibly autonomous) transporters moving parts within the factory. The avatar models a service unit moving around and inspecting machines where an issue has been raised (as indicated by a token), while accounting for the behavior of the adversaries. Corridors might be to narrow for multiple (facing) robots, which poses a safety critical situation. Several notions of cost can be induced by the tokens, either as long as they

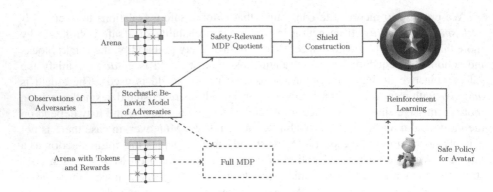

Fig. 1. Workflow of the Shield Construction

are present (costs of a broken machine) or for removing the tokens (costs for inspecting the machine).

Problem. Consider an environment described by an arena as above and a safety specification. We assume stochastic behaviors for the adversaries, e.g, obtained using RL in a training environment. The underlying model is then an MDP: the avatar executes an action, and upon this execution the next exact positions (the state of the system) are determined stochastically.

We compute a δ-shield that prevents avatar decisions that violate this specification by more than a threshold δ with respect to the optimal safety probability. We evaluate the shield using a model-based or model-free RL avatar that aims to optimize the performance. The shield therefore has to handle an intricate tradeoff between strictly focussing on (short and midterm) safety and performance.

3 Constructing Shields for MDPs

We outline the workflow of our approach in Figure 1. We employ a separation of concerns between the model-based shield construction and potentially model-free RL. First, based on observations in arbitrary arenas, we construct a general (stochastic) *behavior model* for each adversary. Combining these models with a concrete arena yields an MDP. At this point, we ignore the token function (and necessarily the unknown reward function), so the MDP may be seen as a quotient of the full MDP that models the real system within which we only assess safe behavior. We therefore call the MDP the *safety-relevant quotient*. The real scenario incorporates the *token function*. Rewards may be known or only be observed during learning. The underlying *full MDP* including tokens constitutes an *exponential blowup of the safety-relevant quotient*, rendering probabilistic model checking or planning practically infeasible. In the workflow, using the safety-relevant MDP, we construct a *shield* using probabilistic model checking. RL now aims to maximize the reward according to the original scenario, while unsafe actions are blocked by the shield.

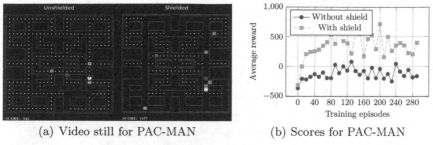

(a) Video still for PAC-MAN   (b) Scores for PAC-MAN

Fig. 2. Scenario and results for PAC-MAN

4 Implementation and Experiments

For our experiments we consider the arcade game PAC-MAN. The task is to eat *food* in a *maze* and not get eaten by *ghosts*. We model each instance of the game as an arena, where PAC-MAN is the avatar and the ghosts are adversaries. The safety specification is that the avatar *not gets eaten* with a high probability. Tokens represent the food at each position in the maze, such that food is either present or already eaten. We learn the ghost behavior from the original PAC-MAN game for each ghost. Transferring the resulting stochastic behavior to any arena (without tokens) yields the safety-relevant MDP. For that MDP, we compute a shield via the model checker Storm for a horizon of 10 steps. Our implementation uses an approximate Q-learning agent (using $\alpha = 0.2$, $\gamma = 0.8$ and $\varepsilon = 0.05$) with the following feature vector: (1) how far away the next food is, (2) whether a ghost collision is imminent, and (3) whether a ghost is one step away. Figure 2(a) shows a still of a series of *videos* we created[1]. Each video compares how RL performs either shielded or unshielded on a PAC-MAN instance. In the shielded version, we indicate the risk of potential decisions by the colors green (low), orange (medium), and red (high). Figures 2(b) depict the *scores* obtained during RL. We see a large difference in scores due to the fact that PAC-MAN is often saved by the shield.

5 Conclusion and Future Work

We developed the concept of shields for MDPs. Utilizing probabilistic model checking, we maintained probabilistic safety measures during reinforcement learning. We addressed inherent scalability issues and provided means to deal with typical trade-off between safety and performance. Our experiments showed that we improved the state-of-the-art in safe reinforcement learning. For future work, we will extend the applications to more arcade games and employ deep recurrent neural networks as means of decision-making. Another interesting direction is to explore (possibly model-free) learning of shields, instead of employing model-based model checking.

---

[1] http://shieldrl.nilsjansen.org

Contents

Temporal Logic and Model Checking

FMICS 25th Anniversary

The 2020 Expert Survey on Formal Methods

Hubert Garavel[1]($\boxtimes$), Maurice H. ter Beek[2]($\boxtimes$) (iD), and Jaco van de Pol[3,4]($\boxtimes$) (iD)

[1] Univ. Grenoble Alpes, Inria, CNRS, Grenoble INP, LIG, 38000 Grenoble, France
hubert.garavel@inria.fr
[2] ISTI–CNR, Pisa, Italy
maurice.terbeek@isti.cnr.it
[3] Aarhus University, Aarhus, Denmark
jaco@cs.au.dk
[4] University of Twente, Enschede, The Netherlands

Abstract. Organised to celebrate the 25th anniversary of the FMICS international conference, the present survey addresses 30 questions on the past, present, and future of formal methods in research, industry, and education. Not less than 130 high-profile experts in formal methods (among whom three Turing award winners and many recipients of other prizes and distinctions) accepted to participate in this survey. We analyse their answers and comments, and present a collection of 111 position statements provided by these experts. The survey is both an exercise in collective thinking and a family picture of key actors in formal methods.

Keywords: Cybersecurity · Education · Formal method · Modelling · Safety · Software engineering · Software tool · Specification · Survey · Technology transfer · Verification

1 Introduction

FMICS, the international conference on Formal Methods for Industrial Critical Systems, is celebrating its 25th anniversary. The FMICS community recognised the revolutionary potential of verification technology quite early on. Its members devoted their energy to evolve this technology, and to apply it to the verification of complex industrial critical systems. These 25 years have brought numerous highlights, like better specification languages, more efficient verification algorithms, landmark tools, and academic recognition in the form of awards. But also many successful industrial applications, the rise of "verification engineer" as a new job title, and the advent of industrial laboratories that focus on formal verification technology.

After decades of glory, formal methods seem at a turning point. In industry, many engineers with expertise in formal methods are assigned new priorities, especially in artificial intelligence. At the same time, the formal verification landscape in higher education is scattered. At many universities, formal methods courses are shrinking, likely because they are deemed too difficult. The transmission of our knowledge to the next generation is not guaranteed. So we cannot lean back.

The original version of this chapter was revised: The structuring of the author names with regard to the particle has been corrected. A correction to this chapter can be found at
https://doi.org/10.1007/978-3-030-58298-2_14

M. H. ter Beek and D. Ničković (Eds.): FMICS 2020, LNCS 12327, pp. 3–69, 2020.
https://doi.org/10.1007/978-3-030-58298-2_1

As part of the celebration, and in order to address this turning point, we have conducted a survey among a selection of internationally renowned scientists that have played a big role in formal methods, either within the FMICS conference series, or outside of it. We report on their collective vision on the past, present, and future of formal methods with respect to research, industry, and education. What did we achieve? What did we miss? Where should we go?

Related Work. Early introductions to the application of formal methods are those by Wing [22] and Rushby [19]. The 1996 survey by Clarke and Wing [8] illustrates many case studies in specification, theorem proving, and model checking. Other classical texts that reflect on the industrial application of formal methods use the metaphors of seven myths [15] or ten commandments [6].

We list a few more recent historical overviews of formal methods. A 2009 survey [23] reports about the application of formal methods in 62 industrial projects; that paper also provides an interesting overview of 20 earlier surveys on formal methods in industry from 1990 to 2009. The handbook [14] published by the FMICS community in 2012 presents applications of formal methods in various domains of industrial critical systems. An 2013 study [11] provides a synthetic account of the diverse research in formal methods, including a list of 30 carefully selected, well-documented case studies that illustrate the progress in formal methods during the period 1982–2011. A history of 40 years of formal methods [5] includes an analysis of some obstacles to their application, while [17] focuses on their history in the UK.

Other papers examine the adoption and industrial strength of formal methods. Three recent surveys with stakeholders [4] investigate what are the most prominent formal methods styles used in the railway domain and the expectations railway practitioners have from formal tools [3]. In a follow-up experimental study [10], a panel of experts judges the suitability of nine formal methods for the specification and verification of (sub)systems in that domain. Barriers to the adoption of formal methods in aerospace are considered in a survey [9] among 31 individuals from nine organisations: the top three barriers stem from education, software tools, and the industrial environment. Multiple contributions have been made for lifting these respective barriers: [7] proposes a coherent formal methods curriculum in higher education; [12,20] reflect on the development of software tools to make it more efficient and relevant, while software competitions [2] help to enhance the quality and visibility of tools; [18] provides economical evidence by demonstrating the benefits of the application of formal methods to industrial-strength problems. Finally, a recent position paper [16] discusses some obstacles and enablers for the application of formal methods, and translates them to actionable recommendations for industry, academia, and policy makers, to improve the situation.

Outline. The present report is organised as follows. Section 2 exposes the methodology used for our survey. The next five sections present and discuss the responses, which are organised in five themes: assessment of formal methods (Sect. 3), formal methods in research (Sect. 4), formal methods in industry (Sect. 5), formal methods in education (Sect. 6), and the future of formal methods (Sect. 7). Finally, Sect. 8 gives concluding remarks and Sect. 9 presents the 111 position statements collected during the survey.

2   Survey Methodology

This section presents the main decisions concerning the organisation of the survey.

2.1   Participants

Initially, the plan was to centre our survey around FMICS, from its origins to our times, by asking all FMICS working group chairs, all FMICS programme committee chairs, and all FMICS invited speakers to participate in the survey. This gave a list of 94 names, much longer than that of the 1996 survey on formal methods [8], which involved 27 participants. But it became clear that our survey would benefit from an even larger panel of experts. We then started adding further names of key players in the field, based upon personal knowledge, discussions with colleagues, and taking the extensive 92-page bibliography of [11] as a source of inspiration. This resulted in a list of 230 names, which, unfortunately, was too long, since we wanted to offer each participant the possibility to write a 10-line position statement, but had only a limited number of pages in the present LNCS volume. We then devised a thorough selection procedure, based on individual scores and other criteria, in order to retain only 170 names from the list of 230. Doing so, we tried to achieve a good coverage of academia and industry, hardware and software, global corporations and technology startups, etc., as well as a fair balance between the various styles of formal methods and a suitable geographical diversity, making sure to invite experts from most countries with a notable activity in formal methods. As the three survey organisers, we decided to exclude ourselves from the list of participants.

2.2   Questions

Through a long iterative process, we progressively elaborated a set of 30 questions for our survey. These questions are divided into 5 themes: *assessment* of formal methods (5 questions), formal methods in *research* (6 questions), *industry* (9 questions), and *education* (5 questions), and the *future* of formal methods (5 questions).

Concerning the content, most of the questions derived from our own professional experience in developing software tools, collaborating with various industries, and teaching formal methods at several universities. We also drew inspiration from other sources, among which [11,12,16,20]. For each question, we proposed a set of predefined, Likert-scale[1] answers and, whenever possible, we added an *Others* alternative in case these answers would not be found relevant. We deemed many of these questions to be difficult, in the sense that we had no obvious answers for them; instead, we were curious to see all the answers given by our colleagues to figure out what was the opinion of the formal methods community on such matters. Some questions were even intentionally provocative, in order to push reflections out of the comfort zones.

---

[1] https://en.wikipedia.org/wiki/Likert_scale.

Concerning the form, we chose to use the open-source LimeSurvey[2] software, an instance of which was already installed and freely available on an INRIA server, because this choice provided the best privacy guarantees for the experts. We thus implemented our 30 questions as an online LimeSurvey questionnaire to be filled in by the experts. For each question, we used the most appropriate LimeSurvey template, depending on whether the question had mutually exclusive answers (represented with round buttons) or multiple-choice answers (represented with square buttons). In the latter case, we often imposed a higher bound on the number of answers that experts could select, thereby forcing them to exclude approximately 33% (at least) of the proposed answers and keep only the most relevant ones. Also, whenever possible, the lists of answers were proposed in random order to eliminate option order bias (i.e. the tendency to pick the first or last answer option).

We prepared four successive beta-versions of the questionnaire and had it pretested by nine reviewers from four different countries. Their feedback helped us to improve the questionnaire through successive iterations.

2.3 Survey

To ease the practical management of the survey, we split the list of 170 experts into two groups of 100 and 70 people, respectively. Both groups were invited to fill in the LimeSurvey questionnaire within two successive time frames (June 3–14 and June 17–28, 2020). Each expert received one invitation and, possibly, two reminders by e-mail. In addition, intensive e-mail exchanges took place between the three survey organisers and certain experts, to provide them with more information about the survey, adapt their position statements to formatting constraints, and/or recover from technical issues with LimeSurvey (eventually, no input data was lost),

We received 130 responses after sending 170 invitations. Such a response ratio of 76% seems particularly high for an online survey. A few experts declined participation in the survey, while others remained silent. Some experts initially promised to participate in the survey, but eventually did not because they were too busy with students or peer reviews. After expiration of the deadline, in July, we also received, from a few experts, offers to participate, which we unfortunately had to decline.

In spite of the 40 missing responses, we are most happy to count, among the high-profile participants to our survey, three Turing Award winners: Hoare (1980), Emerson (2007), and Sifakis (2007); all the three recipients of an FME Fellowship Award: Jones (2015), Broy (2018), and Meseguer (2019); thirteen CAV Award winners: Alur (2008), Dill (2008), Rajamani (2011), Rushby (2012), Larsen (2013), Wang Yi (2013), Godefroid (2014), Peled (2014), Valmari (2014), Grumberg (2015), Abdulla (2017), Biere (2018), and Cimatti (2018); as well as the recipients of many other awards and distinctions that we do not list here exhaustively.

2.4 Answers

In total, 130 experts replied to our 30 questions. Most of them also answered a 31st additional question, which was a request to (optionally) provide a short (10-line)

---

[2] https://en.wikipedia.org/wiki/LimeSurvey.

position statement (cf. Sect. 9). The statistics recorded by LimeSurvey indicate that the mean time spent by each expert on the questionnaire was 90 min (and 36 s), while the median value was 56 min (and 24 s). Actually, the real durations are probably longer, for at least three reasons: (i) due to LimeSurvey problems, a few experts had to restart their questionnaire from scratch, and their initial attempts are not counted; (ii) many experts chose to complete their 30 answers first, and write their position statement offline to send it later by e-mail; (iii) there have been iterations with many experts to finalise their position statements. In any case, the aforementioned timing statistics represent an important collective effort from the formal methods community.

Using the LimeSurvey features, the answers of all experts were aggregated to produce, for each question, cumulative statistics, which are presented in Sects. 3–7. Because it was specified that all answers to the 30 questions would remain anonymous, we considered each question in isolation and made no attempt at tracking or correlating the answers of a given expert across different questions. For the same reason, we did not try to analyse the answers using personal information about the respondents, such as country, place of work, hardware or software background, teaching activities (if any), etc.; in particular, our questionnaire did not ask for any information about the profile of participants.

2.5 Comments

For most questions, the questionnaire proposed a comment field in which the experts could input some text to express their opinions in more detail. Our idea was that such comments would be extremely valuable, and we intended to use them as a basis for discussing the findings of the survey, thus avoiding the pitfall of presenting statistical results only.

Such a possibility was greatly appreciated by the experts, and we received a large volume of comments (namely, 5000+ lines of 80 characters, corresponding to 111 pages of text in LNCS format) that exceeded our expectations by far. Given that all these comments could not be quoted in the present report, we had to make a selection, which raised a triage problem. A careful examination of comments led us to dispatch them into several categories:

- A *critical comment* expresses the dissatisfaction of the expert with the question and/or its proposed Likert-scale answers. For instance: "just a weird question".
- An *explanatory comment* gives the justification for the particular answer chosen by the expert. For instance: "too much irrelevant 'nice' theory".
- A *restrictive comment* defines the conditions in which the proposed answer is valid. For instance: "depends on the industry".
- An *alternative comment* provides an alternative answer (typically associated with the *Other* answer) and/or justifies this choice. For instance: "governments/states (through regulations)" to answer a question asking who can best drive the adoption of formal methods in industry.
- A *redundant comment* does not provide new information. Example: the answer "yes" accompanied by the comment "there is no doubt about this".

- A *conflicting comment* introduces a contradiction with the answer it accompanies. For instance: "I chose 'probably not' but I have no opinion in fact". In such cases, we kept the answer as it was and discarded the conflicting comment. Such situations were rare and, thus, statistically negligible.
- A *misplaced comment* does not address the current question, but another question discussed elsewhere in the survey. Most often, "elsewhere" means "later", i.e. the respondent has anticipated on a question yet to come. In such cases, we either discarded the comment or moved it to the most appropriate question.

Such a classification was not always easy, especially for long comments (e.g. from 5 to 10 lines of text) that contained different ideas. But we did our best to process all comments and quote many of them in Sects. 3–7. Some contents are ironic, or even sarcastic; mentioning them does not mean that we necessarily endorse their point of view.

The analysis of comments revealed an issue that we had not anticipated. Most questions of the survey deal with general topics such as past, present, and future of formal methods, as well as human factors, economical considerations, impact on industry and society, etc. The answers to such questions cannot be fully formal; instead, they are subjective opinions, reflected in the proposed Likert-scale options ("definitely", "probably", "probably not", "to a limited extent", etc.). Moreover, to keep the survey short and knowing that the invited experts are busy people, we tried to provide concise questions, without a lengthy set of preliminary definitions, taking as granted a number of common expressions. After submitting the questionnaire, we got some negative reactions, as the imprecision of our questions was antithetic to the culture, based on mathematical rigour, of formal methods experts. In particular, the first two questions, which we expected to be easy, made certain experts unsure and raised criticisms due to missing definitions ("what is the meaning of 'trustworthy'?"; "how do you interpret 'quality'?"; "what is the exact difference between 'partial failure' and 'partial success'?"; etc.). We believe that these questions discouraged a few experts to further consider the questionnaire.

2.6 Terminology

The term *formal methods* progressively evolved over time, starting from a narrow initial definition to a broader meaning that covers a plethora of methods and tools applied all along the design life cycle, from the elicitation of requirements and early design phases to the deployment, configuration, and run-time monitoring of actual systems. At present, formal methods encompass multiple, diverse artefacts, such as the description of the environment in which the system operates, the requirements and properties that the system should satisfy, the models of the system used during the various design steps, the (hardware or software) code embedded in the final implementation, etc. Formal methods can be used to specify these artefacts and express conformance relations between them.

Being aware of this evolution, we gave a definition of formal methods on the welcome page of the LimeSurvey questionnaire, to make sure that all respondents would agree on a common definition before answering the 30 questions of the survey. We adopted a modern, inclusive point of view by defining formal methods as "mathematics-based techniques for the specification, development, and (manual or automated) verification of software and hardware systems". However, when analysing the comments received (this is also manifest when reading some of the position statements in Sect. 9), we observed at least four different interpretations of the perimeter and scope of formal methods:

- The *extensive mathematical interpretation* assumes that any use of mathematics in computer science is part of formal methods. To us, this definition is too wide; for instance, the use of linear algebra in computer graphics is usually not considered to be formal methods.
- The *extensive theoretical interpretation* considers as "standard basic formal methods" all the concepts of formal languages, grammars, finite-state machines and automata, lexer and parser generators, etc. To us, this definition is also too wide, even if formal methods borrow many ideas from the (pre-existing) language and automata theories; for instance, the construction of a "traditional" compiler cannot be called formal methods.
- The *lightweight interpretation* considers as formal methods all those language features introduced for defensive programming (type checking, library interfaces, program assertions, loop invariants, pre- and post-conditions, etc.), as well as all related verifications, from simple compiler checks to advanced static analyses. Even if some concepts predate formal methods (e.g. types were already present in Algol-60), we agree that such "lightweight" techniques, which are increasingly successful in industry, are indeed part of formal methods.
- The *heavyweight interpretation* recognises as formal methods only those approaches that are fully mathematical and based on proofs. We consider that such a definition is too restrictive, both for design needs (in the early phases of system design, the requirements are rarely fully formal) and for practical use ("heavyweight" techniques have a clear potential, but their success stories are isolated).

Although such diverging interpretations might have affected several answers to our questionnaire, we do not see them as a serious threat to validity, given the large number of participants in the survey. But this is an important problem for the community, as it is more difficult to promote formal methods if experts do not agree on their definition. The same issue occurs at various places, e.g. in the arXiv classification[3] where formal methods must fit either under "cs.LO" (logics in computer science) or "cs.SE" (software engineering); yet, many aspects of formal methods (e.g. executable specification languages, concurrency theory, or hybrid systems) cannot easily be reduced to logics, while the numerous applications of formal methods in hardware design do not belong to software engineering. We thus call for a standalone category of formal methods, whose perimeter should be considered inclusively. As one comment wisely pointed out: "we should act as a community".

---

[3] https://arxiv.org/corr/subjectclasses.

3 Assessment of Formal Methods

3.1 System Design

With this first question, we wanted to query the experts about the necessity of formal methods for system design, i.e. whether or not they are dispensable or replaceable by alternative approaches.

Is it possible to design trustworthy (hardware or software) systems without using formal methods?				
Definitely: 16.2%	Probably: 21.5%	Probably not: 33.1%	Definitely not: 29.2%	N/A: 0.0%

The answers are scattered, with no clear majority. Only the analysis of the 90 comments received may provide better insight.

Several comments display some criticism, since the answer depends on the definition/scope of formal methods (cf. Sect. 2.6), the complexity of the system, and the definition of *trustworthiness*. The latter is a valid point: many comments mention that a system is trustworthy only if there is an objective justification of its reliability. This interpretation introduces a substantial overlap with the next question (quality assessment). Most comments seem to agree that the question is about real systems, which are complex. We note that the answers *probably not* (for complex systems) and *probably* (for simple systems) actually express the same opinion. Five comments contradict the selected answer (maybe due to the implicit negation in *without*). In hindsight, a better formulation would have been: *is using formal methods necessary to design well-functioning complex (hardware or software) systems?*

The comments that explain that designing trustworthy systems is (definitely or probably) impossible, fall into two broad classes. The first class (14 comments) explains that formal methods are necessary to handle the inherent system complexity: "it is the size and the complexity that matter", and, consequently, that informal methods are incomplete: "it is so easy to make bugs with informal methods and extensive testing is so difficult, that adequate formal methods do help a lot in the end". The other class (14 comments) explains that trustworthy systems require some form of objective argumentation, involving unambiguous requirements. This was actually the topic of the next question. One argument was by analogy with (general) engineering. The following comment summarises these positions nicely: "The answer depends on the size, nature and complexity of software, and on the notion of 'trustworthy' you are interested in. Certainly, it is not possible to trust complex, safety critical software, built without recurring to any formalisation of its functions".

Several comments indicate that not using formal methods is possible, but infeasible or costly. "There is a very important trade off between costs, time to delivery, quality". The comments that explain that designing trustworthy systems is (definitely or probably) possible, fall into two categories: 15 comments mention counterexamples of systems that we generally trust, but that did not use formal methods in their design, such as airplanes, while four comments even apply this to the majority of systems: "there are many examples of systems such as airplanes that are produced without the use of formal methods and in general these are still considered 'trustworthy'". Another 16 comments claim that it is possible to build trustworthy systems by alternative methods, such as simulation and testing, or building in redundancy, but seven comments state this is the case only for simple or non-critical systems: "properties of systems can be fully verified by exhaustive simulation if they are sufficiently small", and provided that our expectations on their reliability are sufficiently low.

3.2 Quality Assessment

This question also aimed to query the experts on the necessity of formal methods but, this time, for assessing the quality of complex systems.

Is it possible to assess the quality of complex (hardware or software) systems without using formal methods?

| Definitely: 15.4% | Probably: 26.9% | Probably not: 36.9% | Definitely not: 20.0% | N/A: 0.8% |

A majority of 56.9% deemed the use of formal methods important for quality assessment.

This question received 73 comments. Eight of them state that *quality* is a too broad notion that possibly includes performance, usability, process, etc., for which formal methods are not the most appropriate tool. The comments also indicate that the position of experts depends on whether systematic testing is considered to be part of formal methods or not.

There are mainly two arguments in favour of using formal methods to assess system quality. The first is that, in order to be scalable, assessment requires the use of tools, which need to rely on proper semantics: "Complex systems need scalable methods, scalable methods need a degree of automation, and such automation cannot be trusted if there is no mathematical notion of 'quality' and a model of the system supporting it". The second, more frequent, argument is that an assessment of quality requires to demonstrate the conformance of the product to an unambiguous specification: "a complex system's quality needs to be checked against well-specified requirements, and this again involves formal methods". One comment indicates that such an argument could be phrased in natural language, in principle. Another comment states: "the only way of assessing quality is by examination of the code itself, which is best conducted by specialised software based on sound theory".

Twenty-five comments mention alternative methods that can, at least, increase the confidence in digital systems: testing, simulation, statistical fault analysis, quality metrics, user interviews, and analysis of system logs. On the other hand, several comments state that alternative methods would be incomplete for complex systems, or that applying them exhaustively would be very costly ("the testing costs would be huge!"). One comment indicates that assessing the quality of the process is insufficient, although "certification institutions base their opinion mainly on criteria concerning the development process". Some comments mention certain systems considered reliable, despite not being assessed by formal methods, e.g. "Linux" and "Isabelle/HOL". Some comments distinguish quality assessment of brand new versus long-existing systems: "some military applications do surprisingly well without using formal methods. However, these are almost exclusively new variants of previously deployed systems. Assuring the behaviour of a brand new system without using formal methods would be, in my judgement, very challenging".

3.3   Expected Benefits

This question provided the experts with a list of promises often associated to formal methods, so as to query whether these promises are actually kept.

Do you believe that formal methods, together with the rigorous use of formal analysis tools, can deliver the promise of:

	Definitely	Probably	Probably not	Definitely not	N/A
Better software quality	81.5%	16.9%	0.8%	0.0%	0.8%
Improved system safety	92.3%	7.7%	0.0%	0.0%	0.0%
Enhanced cybersecurity	65.4%	31.5%	0.8%	0.0%	2.3%
Higher performance systems	27.7%	46.2%	19.2%	0.0%	6.9%
Cheaper software development	19.2%	40.8%	30.0%	5.4%	4.6%
Reduced time to market	19.2%	37.7%	31.5%	4.6%	6.9%
Easier certification	61.5%	35.4%	2.3%	0.0%	0.8%
Easier long-term maintenance	60.0%	36.9%	2.3%	0.0%	0.8%

Quasi unanimously, the experts confirmed that formal methods deliver quality, safety, security, easier certification, and easier maintenance. With weaker, yet clear majorities, the experts estimated that formal methods lead to better performance (73.9%), lower costs (60%), and faster development (56.9%).

One critical comment expresses that the proposed scale (*definitely*, *probably*, etc.) was too coarse. We received no other comment for this question, presumably because it already asked for many inputs from the experts.

3.4   Relation to Cybersecurity

This question sought confirmation from the experts concerning the need for formal methods to properly address cybersecurity issues.

In your opinion, are formal methods an essential part of cybersecurity?

No: 0.8%	Marginally: 16.9%	Yes: 74.6%	N/A: 7.7%

The large majority of experts recognised an important role for formal methods in cybersecurity.

This question attracted 57 comments. Several experts (including those with *no opinion*) indicated not to be cybersecurity experts. Note that, indeed, the question was addressed to an audience of, primarily, formal methods experts.

Among the 13 comments for *marginally*, eight indicate fundamental problems, half of them because one cannot foresee and formalise all possible threats, such as side channel attacks ("the problem is how to formally specify and analyse the huge variety of possible attacks"), others because cybersecurity is very broad, involving, for instance, social aspects. Five comments see this as an opportunity to apply formal methods more widely, but similar arguments are also found quite often among the *yes* comments.

Many comments for the *yes* answer indicate opportunities in code analysis (e.g. avoiding memory leaks) and protocol analysis: "many cybersecurity issues involve code with memory issues, issues with access control and faulty security protocols. These would, I'd say, be typical issues that can be (and are being) addressed by formal methods". Other comments point to programming languages offering strong guarantees. Another opportunity is mentioned: "cybersecurity is particularly interesting because there are so many social factors, like social engineering, that can override verified algorithms. The challenge of how to model and verify, e.g. properties of social networks, represents an interesting frontier for formal methods".

Two comments indicate that there is much low-hanging fruit that should be harvested before applying formal methods, e.g. "programming language, architecture, development processes". There were relatively few concrete case studies mentioned, the most concrete one being the "network access restrictions [...] checked using formal methods in Azure [to] both ensure security (e.g. prevent configurations where SSH ports are opened) and avoid customer issues (detect and prevent common misconfigurations that block services)".

3.5 Missed Opportunities

To complete the assessment of formal methods, we wanted to know from the experts whether they believe academics have sufficiently applied formal methods.

Do you think the academic community has missed some opportunities to apply formal methods in industry, in other sciences, and/or in society at large?				
Definitely: 40.0%	Probably: 42.3%	Probably not: 10.8%	Definitely not: 0.0%	N/A: 6.9%

Clearly, most experts (82.3%) believe that some opportunities must have been missed, although, when analysing the 73 comments received, very few concrete examples are given.

Many comments put the blame either on academic practice (in particular its publication culture and its focus on theoretical results), or on industrial practice. A few comments acknowledge that the required multidisciplinarity is difficult, since academia and industry have conflicting goals. One comment describes "a healthy tension" between "on the one hand, to do as much as we can to bring formal methods to industry; but on the other, to develop intrinsically better technologies". Another comment wonders about the apparent brakes on change in industry: "why is it that we still are fighting to get accepted as a mainstream (software engineering) discipline? Why is C still the most dominant implementation language in the world?"

The *probably not* answer is explained in most comments by the fact that applications have been in the focus of formal methods research from the beginning: "I think there have been many serious attempts to transfer formal methods ideas to industry". Therefore, 10 comments explicitly blame industry for underestimating formal methods, e.g.: "the choice not to use formal methods can be based on silly things, such as not having the IDE one is used to".

On the other hand, several comments state that formal methods have been over-sold: "it may be the case that formal methods have been sold to industry while they were still immature". Many other reasons why we have *probably* or *definitely* missed out on opportunities were mentioned, such as the lack of standard notations, service providers, whole-system engineering approaches, support of design processes, and data-driven approaches.

Finally, only a few concrete missed opportunities are mentioned, like: "we have probably missed an opportunity to introduce formal methods in the design of medical devices"; "there are so many domains with domain-specific languages that could greatly benefit from the formal methods toolkit"; and "the formal methods community should have shown that formal methods can fit modern agile development".

4 Formal Methods in Research

4.1 Overall Evaluation

This first question polled the experts concerning the degree of success, from an academic perspective, of formal methods.

How would you evaluate the achievements of formal methods in academia?		
A failure: 0.8%	A partial failure: 6.9%	N/A: 1.5%
A partial success: 62.3%	A success: 28.5%	

The experts almost unanimously agreed that formal methods are a *success* or a *partial success*; only 7.7% stated the contrary, while a tiny minority had *no opinion*.

Analysing the 73 comments received, the question was largely misunderstood and criticised. One reason for this was the imprecision of the term *academia* (two comments mention this explicitly, e.g. "I am not sure what is meant by 'in academia'"). When drafting the question, we were interested in the perceived success of formal methods in research, but some respondents considered a different scope: 19 comments evaluate the success as partial, because of the limited success of formal methods in education ("I refer here to education, not research") and/or their lack of impact in industry. Other comments consider a *partial failure* and a *partial success* to be indistinguishable options.

The few comments from experts who consider the outcome to be a failure can be summarised as follows: "nice theory", but a lack of impact in industry "to drive formal methods into actual design, analysis, and deployment processes", and even in curricula. Note that the impact of formal methods in industry and education is addressed later in this survey using specific questions.

Further criticism, explicit or implicit, concerns how to measure success. Such ambiguity created a lot of variability in the comments, especially those considering formal methods to be a *success*. The most frequently used measures of success, mentioned in 12 comments, are based on objective data, such as the size of the formal methods community (considered to be an active community), the number of conferences embracing formal methods (e.g. FM, FMICS, iFM, CAV, POPL), the number of associations and working groups (e.g. FME and FMICS), the number of ERC grants, the number of formal methods researchers hired by industry, and (less objective) the sheer diversity of techniques and tools.

Eight comments attribute the success of formal methods to some of its specific sub-fields (e.g. formal verification or SMT solving) or to a few success stories. Another nine comments call for more success stories (especially on real-world systems) and improved visibility of the existing ones. Indeed, formal methods have a "nice corpus of theories and techniques, many good tools, a few impressive applications", "but many researchers program and verify as if they never heard of formal methods", and students often believe that "producing (buggy) code and then fishing for bugs is the 'best practice' and the grown up way to design and implement". But another comment recalls, in software and hardware design, the existence of "achievements nobody can question, everybody takes for granted, and we forget to be proud about". Finally, a few comments also mention geographic differences, with more success in Europe than in China and the US.

4.2 Foundational Nature

This question wanted to know from the experts whether they believe formal methods are one of the scientific backbones of computer science.

In your opinion, do formal methods provide mathematical foundations for many branches of computer science?			
No: 0.8%	To a limited extent: 36.9%	Yes: 61.5%	N/A: 0.8%

Nearly all the experts agreed that formal methods do form the foundation for many branches of computer science, but only *to a limited extent* for just over one-third of them. Only one expert answered *no* and another one had *no opinion*.

This question received 56 comments, all of which for the *yes* or *to a limited extent* answers. There was some criticism on the question, basically boiling down to what is to be understood by *formal methods*. Although we gave a preliminary definition in our survey (cf. Sect. 2.6), seven comments mention that their answer strongly depends on the chosen definition. As one comment states: "depending on what you mean by 'formal methods,' the question could be tautological in that mathematical foundations are formal methods". Three comments actually claim the reverse, i.e. many other "branches of computer science provide mathematical foundations for formal methods". A couple of comments go as far as stating that "it establishes computer science as a science" and "by definition". One comment contains a more pondered variant: "I do believe that formal methods, or rather mathematical logic, is as essential to computer science as mathematical analysis is to physics".

A few comments put forward that knowledge of formal methods provides one with a competitive edge in industry. The opinion is substantiated in 12 comments, which note that formal methods are fundamental for understanding software and hardware (typically citing programming languages and compiler design).

Finally, one comment (from an expert who answered *yes*) points out some exceptions: "soft subjects like human-computer interaction rely more on psychology and sociology. Formal methods for artificial intelligence hardly exist". However, this might (need to) change, since another comment notes that "the 'explainable artificial intelligence' movement [...] cannot decently succeed without formal methods". Six comments of experts who answered *to a limited extent* also mention exceptions: "human-computer interaction", "speech recognition, computer graphics, computer vision", "data science", "machine learning", and "complexity theory"; yet, another comment specifically mentions complexity theory as one of the branches for which formal methods do provide foundations.

4.3 Main Criticisms

This question tried to weigh to what degree the experts agree with frequently heard criticism concerning misplaced efforts of academic researchers in formal methods.

Would you agree with the criticism that most academic researchers in formal methods are:	
Not investing enough effort to develop software tools that are usable and robust?	66.9%
Too much novelty-driven and not enough interested in the consolidation of existing results to make them available to a wider audience?	60.8%
Too much focussed on the most difficult and challenging problems, while neglecting the development of broader approaches applicable to "real world" issues?	53.8%
Other criticism	33.1%

(multiple answers allowed; answers sorted by frequency)

The three frequently heard types of criticism suggested by the proposed answers created consensus among a large number of experts, namely 87, 79, and 70 experts (in the order of frequency displayed in the table). One-third of the experts had (also) other criticism concerning academic researchers in formal methods.

This question generated the remarkable amount of 170 comments. The experts who answered *other criticism* had quite varying opinions, ranging from not agreeing with the proposed answers to criticising the question, typically because they believe it is difficult to generalise or because they believe neither of the suggestions belongs to the task of academic researchers. Most, however, share two general beliefs that also featured very frequently in the comments provided by those experts who did choose one of the proposed answers. Basically, the effort and interest to develop more usable and robust tools, to consolidate results and approaches and make them more widely applicable and available—clearly perceived by the experts as improving the transfer of technology to industry—is hindered by two current realities in academia: (i) a lack of academic recognition (criteria for publications and thus career promotions are based on novelty); and (ii) a lack of funding for industrial application (requiring tool advancement and maintenance). Several comments nicely summarise this belief. Some picks: "even though industry participation is sought, in essence academia creates its own bubble where criteria for success are mostly within the bubble"; "there is no business case for long term support of (academic) tools; industry needs stability and performance, academics need to innovate"; and "at the end of the day, researchers do not get much credit (nor funding) for building and maintaining tools and high-quality software, despite the enormous effort involved; instead, publications are more rewarded and are often what counts". This opinion recurred in 67 comments.

Finally, it is worth mentioning that two comments are positive on artefact evaluations, which "have at least accomplished that reported results are reproducible, but this is still miles away from a tool that is mature enough to be used by industry". However, one comment is convinced of the contrary: "the current practice of 'artefact evaluation' is harmful as it rewards building prototypes that are not really used by anyone, but give the illusion of building tools".

4.4   Topic Relevance

With this question we simply wanted to know whether the experts still consider formal methods a hot topic.

Do you believe that formal methods are still a major topic today for academic research in computer science?				
Definitely: 71.5%	Probably: 20.0%	Probably not: 7.7%	Definitely not: 0.0%	N/A: 0.8%

The vast majority of experts claimed that formal methods are indeed still a major research topic; only ten thought this is *probably not* the case, while one expert had *no opinion*. Interestingly, not a single expert thought this is *definitely not* the case.

This question attracted 67 comments. The seven experts who commented their choice for *probably not* constitute two groups of more or less equal size. One group believes that "the momentum has gone elsewhere", in one case attributing this to the fact that "industry has chosen a different direction". The other group actually seems to be convinced that formal methods are *(definitely) not* a major topic for research ("most computer science departments at major universities do not have anyone specialising in formal methods currently"), partly criticising the question: "still? It has been a marginal activity at most universities for a while".

Several of the 14 experts who commented their choice for *probably* mention that formal methods *should* still be a major research topic, but that it is currently "under pressure of other 'hot' topics such as artificial intelligence and machine learning". Half of the 93 experts who believe that formal methods *definitely* are still major research topic today added a comment, mostly explaining their choice: "though there are always certain hypes, formal methods are an important and solid basis for the development of safety-critical systems"; "in fact, formal method papers are appearing in major conferences, even outside the community. Look at the latest POPL and PLDI conferences"; and "as more and more aspects of human societies rely on some computing system, formal methods are more relevant than ever". But, there is room for improvement: "we have to learn to switch from an 'individual problem view' to a global view which exploits the power of the various methods, i.e. like going from 'post mortem verification' to 'correctness by design', which allows us to exploit the strength of many formal methods disciplines". Interestingly, one comment contradicts the opinion expressed in a previous comment: "in some public institutions the number of research teams dedicated to formal methods is relatively significant".

4.5   Research Priorities

Assuming that resources for supporting research in formal methods are limited, this question asked the experts to establish a ranking between various research topics.

Which should be the most urgent priorities of researchers working in formal methods?	
Scalability: design more efficient verification algorithms	70.0%
Applicability: develop more usable software tools	68.5%
Acceptability: enhance integration into software engineering processes	65.4%
Discovery: explore new classes of problems and application domains	44.6%
Theory: search for the next fundamental breakthroughs	35.4%
Languages: design more expressive and user-friendly notations	31.5%
Other	16.2%

(from 1 to 4 answers allowed; answers sorted by frequency)

Analysing the three most selected answers, one observes a strong wish that formal methods are applied to real problems, especially industrial ones. In this respect, the importance of *scalability* can be explained as the desire to overcome major obstacles to practical applications. Also, the big difference between both extremes, namely *scalability* and *languages*, might lay in the perception that the former addresses hard, objective problems deeply rooted in complexity theory, whereas the latter deals with softer, subjective issues that are largely a matter of human conventions. Such an explanation perhaps ignores the fact that languages are a key factor for industrial acceptability, and that poorly-designed languages may significantly increase the cost of formal analyses.

This question received 19 comments. Six of them refuse to define priorities, pointing out that "all the above problems are important and should be addressed" or that "science should not be priority-driven"; instead, one "should encourage researchers to follow their inspiration" and "focus on the task they are best in". One comment on *scalability* stresses the importance of modularity, with "compositional and reusable verification of code fragments and libraries". Two comments on *acceptability* point out that the formal methods community should ensure explainability (i.e. provide "a justification for the diagnostic/result" computed by software tools) and "influence standards and regulations to make sure formal methods are required where it makes sense". Three comments on *languages* mention that they should be "co-developed" with verification tools and methodologies, suggesting to "design more deterministic and analysable languages (which will likely be less expressive)" and to build "good code generators" for specification languages, so as to enhance their "integration with existing programming languages". Five other comments propose alternative research priorities: validation of requirements, code synthesis, process mining, and connections to artificial intelligence, such as "artificial-intelligence-driven invariant discovery".

4.6   Software Development

This final question on formal methods in research tries to poll expert opinions on the role and responsibility of academia with respect to the delivery of professional tools.

Which one of these two statements do you like best?	
Public research in formal methods should only develop prototype (proof-of-concept) tools, while leaving the development of professional tools to industry	36.2%
Formal methods are too involved and their market is too small for most companies, so academia should invest effort to develop and consolidate usable tools	38.5%
Other answer	25.4%

This question apparently divided the experts: while one-fourth did not like either of the two statements best, we note an almost perfect distribution of the remaining experts among the two statements. The outcome thus provides little guidance as to where the effort concerning professional tool development should come from.

This question received 80 comments, most of which are insightful. The 34 comments provided with *other answer* actually show a remarkable variety of opinions. Ten comments believe (to a certain extent) in both: "the tools we develop should be usable (and extensible) by researchers in our own community, and should therefore go beyond the proof-of-concept stage. However, we should not spend time on polishing the things that matter for acceptance in industry, such as user interfaces, have round-the-clock available help desks, liability, etc.". Ten comments (strongly) believe in neither of the two statements. Five comments believe in a "combination of the two statements": "neither fully, both partially". Another ten comments believe something similar, namely that developing formal methods tools should be a collaborative effort by academia and industry, but four of them note that academia should be leading the development, and five of them that academic prototypes "should go beyond the current state of proof-of-concept tools". A couple of comments, finally, mention that "effort should be devoted to open-source community efforts".

The 16 comments provided by those experts who best like the first statement are very much in line, mainly indicating two (related) reasons. First, eight comments claim that tool development is "not the role of academia" and "most academic institutions are not equipped to maintain professional level tools, even if they manage to develop a first version". Second, four comments claim there is a lack of "funding to develop industrial-strength tools".

The 30 comments provided by the experts preferring the second statement are less in line, but there are two recurring reasons in support of this statement. First, eight comments state that "good research groups tend to work on one tool, for decades, which brings about solid tools"; CADP, UPPAAL, and Z3 are explicitly mentioned as examples. Second, six comments state that "this is the only way to provide technological transfer to industry, [as] in most cases efficient implementation requires to know a bit about the underlying theory".

5   Formal Methods in Industry

5.1   Impact Evaluation

This first question asked from the experts to evaluate the degree of success of formal methods in industry.

How would you qualify the impact of formal methods on industrial software development practices?		
A failure: 2.3%	A partial failure: 29.2%	
A partial success: 63.8%	A success: 3.1%	N/A: 1.5%

According to most answers, the impact is neither a complete success nor a complete failure, but in between, and clearly more of a success than a failure.

This is confirmed by the 79 comments, which are distributed as follows among the proposed answers: 0 for *failure*, 24 for *partial failure*, 51 for *partial success*, 3 for *success*, and 1 for *no opinion*. Eighteen comments mention "a few great achievements" of formal methods in CAD and "EDA tools for hardware design and embedded software", "in a few enlightened industries (aerospace, railway, nuclear)", "in some fields like avionics, distributed algorithms, and now security", and in "many of the most successful companies", which "develop and adopt formal methods for [their] own use"—with mentions of Airbus, AMD, ARM, ASML, AWS, Facebook, Google, Huawei, IBM, Intel, Microsoft, Philips Healthcare, and Siemens, "just to name a few". Building a global picture is difficult however, since "some of the work is being done by secretive companies who do not publish/highlight their successes": formal methods are often used "behind the scenes" and "unfortunately, once a formal-methods tool becomes successful, it [is] usually renamed to something else".

Twelve other comments list "ideas of formal methods [that] found their way into modelling and programming languages", e.g. "typed languages (in spite of the current Python frenzy)", "type checking" and "type inference", "interfaces for libraries", "assertions in programs", "pre- and post-conditions of functions", but also "techniques that improve the code production", e.g. "model checking", "automatic test case generation", "lightweight verification tools (runtime verification, 'linters', etc.)", "static analysis and other embedded analyses, [which] are accepted and included in industrial toolchains", and "now routinely used for systems software and open-source software", sometimes "without people even realising it".

On the critical side, forty comments express almost the same idea: "formal methods are [...] used only to a limited extent, and not where it would be required"; "in a few industries it has been a success but in the majority of industries not"; "there are some successes to celebrate, but they are at the moment too few to have impact". One comment underpins this general opinion: "there are some ways to measure this impact: the offers to hire professionals with formal-methods background, the investment of software licenses for formal-methods-based tools, the contracts with research institutions or companies to solve specific projects, etc. I do not see a big impact with these parameters".

Some comments justify the fact that many companies are not using formal methods either for financial reasons ("too little of a cost reduction in return for too great an investment of time and skill"; "company cultures [are] particularly hostile to things that give no immediate product, but merely add quality to a product"), or due to human factors ("the inertia of industrial software development practices is enormous"; "the somewhat heavy emphasis on having a rich math background [...] is not going to be mainstream"), or by historical after-effects ("formal methods may have gotten a 'bad reputation' [since they] in some cases have become associated with

'1980s style formal methods' such as VDM, Z, B method and the like; even though such approaches would be considered outdated today, they are still mentioned in applicable standards in some industries, and this in effect delays introduction of more modern formal methods").

Nonetheless, the majority of comments remains optimistic, as many "prefer to see the glass as half full rather than half empty: formal methods are making their way [...] maybe not as widely as we would like, and probably not in their most theoretical or full-blown strength, but they make an impact".

5.2 Technology Readiness

With this question we wanted to learn about the perceived readiness of formal methods for technology transfer.

Do you believe that formal methods are now ready to be used extensively in industry?			
No: 3.8%	Only to a limited extent: 67.7%	Yes: 26.9%	N/A: 1.5%

Two-third of the experts answered that formal methods are, *to a limited extent*, ready for industry, while another quarter expressed that formal methods can already be used extensively. Only a few experts indicated *no* or *no opinion*.

When analysing the comments, it appears that many *yes* answers are nuanced and should be interpreted as *yes, but*. The twelve most outspoken *yes* answers point to successful projects that have demonstrated that formal methods are ready and their application is beneficial: "there are plenty of academic case studies that appear to scale well enough for industrial application" and "formal methods are already widely used in industry in existing tools". Four of these comments explicitly mention hardware: "formal methods have been used extensively for quite a few years now in hardware design verification". The reasons why formal methods are only ready to a certain extent are often related to application domains, tool maturity, or people's skills and willingness.

Nineteen comments restrict the readiness of formal methods tools to certain *application domains*, in particular "domains with high standards for safety and cybersecurity, where requirements are well understood". Even in such cases, "industrial researchers need to do the work to fit this into existing development flows". For instance, "we need to show how formal methods can be used to explore system design alternatives much faster".

Concerning *software tools*, fourteen comments indicate that the maturity of the current tools is not acceptable for industry: "[formal methods] tools are in general much lower quality than programming language tools"; "the existing tools are, for the most part, too brittle and hard to use"; and "the industry should be involved in developing tools that meet industrial standards". Yet, thirteen comments point out that particular lightweight tools can be applied in continuous integration pipelines and, thus, readily deployed: "I think that we are getting close with tools like hybrid fuzzers (that combine fuzzing with symbolic execution), test-case generators, [and] bounded model check[ers]. I think that these would make a measurable difference in productivity and quality". "They can be a useful bug finding tool. Ideally, they will be integrated into IDEs and compilers and operate in the background".

Fifteen comments note that formal methods are only ready to be applied by sufficiently *skilled and willing people*: "there is probably still a lack of trained engineers and of will" and "it also requires scientific skill and attitude". There are conflicting comments around "being modest". On the one hand: "it may still be too early for a wide-spread roll-out of formal methods in industry. We run the risk of over-promising", but, on the other hand: "how many whip lashes should you self-apply before you have the permission to venture out in the world?"

5.3 Return on Investment

This question asked the experts to make an informal cost-benefit analysis over time.

In your opinion, are formal methods profitable enough to outweigh their costs?		
No return on investment: 2.3%	Profitable in the long term only: 12.3%	N/A: 11.5%
Immediately profitable: 15.4%	Profitable in medium and long terms: 58.5%	

A small majority judged that the application of formal methods is *profitable in medium and long terms*. Another 15% (resp. 12%) indicated that they pay off *immediately* (resp. *in the long term*). A few experts answered that formal methods do not pay off, while a relatively large group has *no opinion*.

This question received 73 comments. In the *no opinion* category, two comments criticise the question as ill-posed: "your scale is very unhelpful", or even: "your question is part of the problem". The other ten, however, indicated that the answer depends too much on the specific circumstances.

The comments justifying immediate pay-off are very diverse. Some see the pay-off in the added value, either "to explore and analyse design-time problems", or as an alternative to "more ad-hoc methods such as testing", or in "added security and safety". Others justify the pay-off by the huge costs of errors in critical software. Three comments condition an immediate pay-off on the proper alignment with software development processes, for instance: "the key is to align the formal methods [...] with incremental software development".

Ten comments explicitly mention that initial investment costs prevent an immediate return on investment: "as for any technology move, one needs to adapt methods and tools, to train and educate, to practice". One comment concludes that "the initial cost is really high, and a critical research focus should be on how we can provide lightweight formal methods that are more proportional in their effort/value ratio", while another expects that "if smoothly integrated into the development process, the extra cost will be amortised by the savings gained from better quality". Indeed, several comments point out that "the real savings [come] later with improved product quality and reduction of errors".

But "a clear problem is that the benefits cannot be quantified clearly", especially when "companies get away with the consequences of their bad development", "as long as states/governments do no enforce strict regulations with proper penalisation". Four further comments explain that the real cost savings appear only later, with less and cheaper maintenance due to fewer failures. Another fifteen comments note that the return on investment "is really depending on the context, and the right choice of technique and problem".

Another argument justifies long-term-only benefit after considerable invest-ment: "we should think of formal methods as a 'disruptive technology'. Such tech-nologies have the potential to change the way things are done and generate a process of 'creative destruction' in Schumpeter's sense; but this of course generates resis-tance and requires investment, more than of money, investment on people".

5.4 Most Effective Framework

This question polled the experts to know in which companies formal methods can be most efficiently deployed.

Which kind of company is best suited for using formal methods?	
Large companies, because they have the budget and time frame needed to experiment with formal methods	23.8%
Small companies, because they are agile enough to prototype with non-standard languages and software tools	6.9%
Any kind of company, whatever its size	63.8%
N/A	5.4%

The majority of the experts (around 70%) did not select a clear advantage for either *large* or *small companies*, when it comes to the application of formal methods. The number of experts that expect a fruitful application from *large companies* was three times larger than the number of experts who expect this from *small companies*.

Looking at the 61 comments received, 20 of them indicate that the presence of skilled and enthusiastic people is more important than company size. Another 13 comments express that the application domain is more important than com-pany size. These reasons can explain why many experts did not choose any of the extremes: "the size of the company does not matter. What matters is their implicit motivation (to be the best in the business), the ability of a local champion (to carry the torch, overcome internal hurdles, motivate other people), and an obvious business opportunity where the application of a formal technique is of paramount benefit".

The comments provide further insights in the perceived difference between small and large companies. On the one hand, eight comments indicate that *large com-panies* are more suited, as they can devote time and budget to formal methods: "large companies are typically willing to invest in pilot projects to study the feasi-bility of using formal methods. They have the financial means to do so". On the other hand, eight comments indicate that *small companies* are more agile to adopt formal methods quickly: "small companies can decide faster and are more dependent on quality"; "the actual killer case would be a startup company formed of people who are already highly trained in formal methods and have a killer app for which for-mal methods gives them overwhelming advantage". Three other comments discuss examples of formal methods deployed in small or big companies.

What are the limiting factors for a wider adoption of formal methods by industry?	
Engineers lack proper training in formal methods	71.5%
Academic tools have limitations and are not professionally maintained	66.9%
Formal methods are not properly integrated in the industrial design life cycle	66.9%
Formal methods have a steep learning curve	63.8%
Developers are reluctant to change their way of working	62.3%
Managers are not aware of formal methods	57.7%
Many companies do not pay enough attention to software quality and security	56.2%
Formal methods are not properly integrated in standard certification processes	46.9%
Formal methods focus on relevant problems, but only on a small part of all problems	36.9%
Benefits of formal methods are not marketed enough	36.9%
There are too many formal methods, with a lack of independent comparison	28.5%
Formal methods are too costly, with no perceived immediate added value	26.9%
Formal methods are too slow to meet current time-to-market constraints	17.7%
Professional tools are too expensive because of the small market for them	14.6%
Other approaches to software quality outperform formal methods	13.1%
Industrial software development practices change too often and too quickly	8.5%
Formal methods focus on the wrong problems	7.7%
Other	13.8%

(from 1 to 12 answers allowed; answers sorted by frequency)

5.5   Limiting Factors

This question asked the experts to rank a large number of potential barriers and obstacles that may prevent formal methods from being accepted in industry.

Interestingly, obstacles arising from human factors predominate, as the 1st, 4th, 5th, and 6th most selected answers reflect educational problems, namely a lack of knowledge from managers and developers, and their difficulties to learn and deploy formal methods. Technical factors appear in the 2nd and 3rd answers, whereas financial factors underlie the 7th answer.

This question attracted 17 comments, most of which are attached to the *other* answer but actually correspond to answers already present in the above list (namely, the 1st, 2nd, 4th, 5th, and 8th most selected answers). For instance, five comments echo the 1st answer (*engineers lack proper training in formal methods*), one of them regrets that "education in formal methods frightens off students and puts them off for life rather than showing potential benefits". Two comments, somewhat related to the 5th answer (i.e. *developers are reluctant to change their way of working*), raise concerns about misguided applications of formal methods: "formal methods people are too stubborn; they advocate that everything should be formal", but "trying to apply formal methods everywhere is a non-sense", as "formal methods have to be sold [only] to people with problems". Two other comments reinforce the 8th answer (i.e. *formal methods are not properly integrated in standard certification processes*), regretting that "professional bodies do not encourage best practices, like they do in other disciplines" and that "regulation often focuses on process quality, not product quality". Another comment draws a critical eye on those limiting factors: "it is like benefits that show in the long-term, they are trumped by short-term obligations".

5.6   Research-Industry Gap

This question tried to evaluate the distance, and its growth trend, between the problems actually faced by industry and the solutions brought by academic researchers.

Which one of these assertions do you consider to be the most appropriate?	
There is no gap between academic research in formal methods and industry	2.3%
There is currently a gap, but it is narrowing	68.5%
There is currently a gap and it is growing	20.0%
N/A	9.2%

Most experts agreed upon the existence of a gap between academic research and industry, and they are also positive that this gap is getting smaller.

This question received 54 comments distributed as follows among the proposed answers: 3 for *no gap*, 33 for *narrowing gap*, 13 for *growing gap*, and 5 for *no opinion*. One comment indicates that "a general response" to such "a very open question" is impossible. Three comments point out that "in hardware companies there is virtually no gap", as these "companies are long-time users of formal methods"; so, most of the discussion focuses on software and systems development. A large majority of comments consider that the gap is narrowing, since "technology transfer is visibly increasing", but five comments notice that "progress is slow" or "very slow", and "there is a huge work to be still done". Other comments make a clear distinction between "a few elite companies" (Amazon, Facebook, Google, Microsoft, and Thales Railways are cited in four comments as "examples of the gap narrowing"), certain application domains ("in hardware design, communication protocols, critical applications like avionics, and formal system testing, [the] gap seems to be narrowing"), and the rest, for which "the situation is heterogeneous", as "more industries get interested" in formal methods, "but few do more than experiments". Formal methods are also successful in domains such as "cryptocurrencies, [where] any bug can cause an enormous financial loss". The market size, in itself, does not seem to be a criterion: "the gap is narrowing in safety-critical robotics [but] growing in Android mobile-phone apps; both are multi-billion dollar industries".

The explanations given for a growing gap are threefold: complexity of industrial projects and agility of industrial processes ("industry is moving forward very fast, and academia has a hard time to catch up"), fragmentation of formal methods ("too many competing approaches with too little distinguishing impacts in practice", as well as increasingly complex "extensions of [...] computational models that are only relevant to increasingly smaller audiences"), and lack of properly trained personnel ("the education of software professionals seems to contain less and less hard topics such as logic"). This latter point is deemed crucial, as "the dismal lack of mathematical abilities of the iPhone generation and the dismantling of theoretical courses [...] even in top universities" prevents the gap from being filled ("if you always need the academic doctor working in formal methods for a real industrial project, then something is wrong").

Six comments confirm that "there is a gap" but one "cannot tell whether it is narrowing or growing", because "while formal methods are becoming more mature and capable to handle larger problems, problems are also becoming more complicated". Finally, a comment suggests that the gap is perhaps different from what one would expect, as "Google, Facebook, and Amazon have stronger formal-methods research than most academic groups", whereas another comment recommends that academic research "should make progress regardless of industry, as long as there are realistic applications".

5.7 Design Life Cycle

It has often been stated that formal methods are best applied all the way, step by step, from the initial requirements to the final executable code. However, many publications report successful uses of particular formal methods in particular phases of the design life cycle. This question tries to explore and quantify the discrepancy between the ideal expectations and the practical achievements.

In which phases of the design life cycle are formal methods likely to be the most useful?	
Generating test cases, especially for corner cases	77.7%
Capturing and formalising requirements	75.4%
Checking whether models are correct	69.2%
Building models of the system	64.6%
Validating the requirements	53.8%
Generating code from models	53.1%
Certifying correctness of the final code	45.4%
Monitoring deployed software at run time	43.1%
Maintaining consistency between models	42.3%
Detecting mistakes in handwritten code	39.2%
Evaluating the test results	20.0%
Other	10.8%

(from 1 to 8 answers allowed; answers sorted by frequency)

The presence of test-case generation at the top of the list is significant, as it contradicts the ideal vision of a fully formal design flow, where refinement is used at each step to ensure that the final code satisfies the initial requirements. Indeed, in such a design flow, tests would be no longer necessary or, at least, their importance would decrease. Instead, the stated relevance of formal methods for test-case generation indicates that formal methods fit well with conventional design flows, in which testing efforts often represent more than a half of the total development costs. Cutting down such efforts (e.g. by generating tests automatically and/or by generating tests of a better quality) is thus a promising target for formal methods. The next answers in the list show that different methods can be beneficially used during the various phases of the design life cycle. All in one, the answers suggest that formal methods can be evolutionary, rather than revolutionary.

This question received 13 comments, all associated with the *other* answer. A first group of comments stresses that formal methods should be used in all phases of the life cycle to maintain some consistency from requirements to code. A second group of comments suggests other specific uses of formal methods: "certified compilation", "deployment configuration", analysis of "legacy systems", assurance that "certain classes of bugs" are "absent [from] the final code", and development and verification of "concurrent and distributed systems" and "systems of systems".

5.8 Dissemination Players

The next question tried to determine who, in the stakeholder network that exists between academia and industry, can contribute most to the industrial deployment of formal methods.

Who could best drive a more widespread application of formal methods in industry?	
Universities and engineering schools	63.8%
Research and technology institutes	63.8%
Large industrial companies	50.0%
Tool-vendor companies	46.2%
Dedicated service companies	30.0%
Others	14.6%

(from 1 to 4 answers allowed; answers sorted by frequency)

The answers make it clear that all stakeholders have a role to play, perhaps at a different level and with a different impact factor. Somewhat paradoxically, the respondents show greater confidence in public (or non-for-profit) institutions than in private companies, although the goal is to trigger methodological changes in entities belonging to the private sector—a trend that is in line with former answers, such as those of Sect. 4.6.

This question attracted 131 comments distributed as follows among the proposed answers: 29 for *universities and engineering schools*, 27 for *research and technology institutes*, 24 for *large companies*, 20 for *tool-vendor companies*, 13 for *dedicated service companies*, and 18 for *others*.

Concerning *universities and engineering schools*, their most important mission is, according to 17 comments, to "create the necessary critical mass of talent-pool" by "delivering more graduates who know and like formal methods". Yet, five comments point out that "these institutions should be doing it better" and "definitely enhance their commitment in formal methods". Four comments list research-oriented missions, such as "illustrating novel ideas", "demonstrating the state-of-the-art via prototypes", and "develop[ing] and maintain[ing] formal methods tools".

Concerning *research and technology institutes*, four comments cite the examples of Fraunhofer (Germany), GTS (Denmark), INRIA (France), IRTs (France), MPI (Germany), MSR (worldwide), and SRI (California). Six comments point out that such institutes "can play an important role in industrial take-up of formal methods" since "they are at the interface between researchers and industry" and, thus, "have more chance to be closer to the problem domain". Ten comments expect them to "play a crucial role" in "devising user-friendly formal methods, designing efficient analysis methods, and developing robust tools", and in "taking up larger challenges" to "demonstrate the value of formal methods on actual systems". Two comments claim that such institutes "are better at long-term investment than individual universities", but "they have to realise the missions set to them by their paymasters".

Concerning *large companies*, seven comments mention Airbus, Amazon Web Services, Facebook, Google, Intel, Microsoft, and Thales, as well as "organisations in general that build critical software systems". Eleven comments consider such companies and organisations as ideal hosts for formal methods: "they have the money, they have staff to spare, they have problems at scale, and they have the visibility that when they speak up, others listen"; this latter point references their capacity to "champion formal methods" and "boost the[ir] widespread application" by "commit[ting] their suppliers" and "provid[ing] a market for tool vendors". However, two comments warn that large companies "do have the resources, but are often slow to react", so that "we keep seeing companies on the brink of bankruptcy due to catastrophic errors that formal verification could catch".

Concerning *tool-vendor companies*, two comments stress the importance of software: "without tools, no application of formal methods". Nine comments state the missions expected from such companies: "transfer academic ideas and prototypes to industrially applicable software tools", "sell and maintain [these] tools" and "make [them] appealing" by "working on usability issues", "provide tutorials and courses", and "offer consultancy" services. Two comments consider tool vendors as "companies that are quite successful", while three other comments predict that such companies "have the heaviest resources and motivation to promote formal methods", and that "tool vendors that open up the market can make a difference" and "will ultimately decide the acceptance of formal methods".

Concerning *dedicated service companies*, five comments discuss the business model and genesis of such companies, which can be either "started up by academics" or spun off from larger companies that "prefer outsourcing this activity, at least temporarily". Seven comments define such companies as arrays of "consultants", who "concentrate a critical mass of expertise" and "specialised knowledge" to "help choosing the most appropriate approach" and deliver "formal methods as a service".

Concerning *others*, five comments do not give a precise answer, while other comments suggest further stakeholders who could contribute to the industrial adoption of formal methods: governments/states (through regulations), certification authorities (through quality standards), funding agencies, alliances for open source and open APIs, non-for-profit associations, and communities of software developers.

5.9 Academic Policies

The last question of this group reviewed the concrete actions academia can do to improve the transfer of formal methods results to industry.

Which academic policies can contribute most to the adoption of formal methods in industry?	
More collaborative projects between research and industry	78.5%
Increased support for academic researchers developing tools	68.5%
Construction of benchmarks and datasets for formal methods	53.1%
Construction of learning resources for formal methods	48.5%
Dedicated engineers to increase the quality and TRL[a] of academic tools	45.4%
Databases of case studies showing the applicability of formal methods	44.6%
Collaborative software platforms integrating tools from different institutions	35.4%
Economic studies to estimate the return on investment of formal methods	34.6%
Increased resources and scientific credits to software competitions	26.9%
Others	10.8%

(from 1 to 7 answers allowed; answers sorted by frequency)

[a]Technology Readiness Level (http://en.wikipedia.org/wiki/Technology_readiness_level).

The analysis of the most selected answers shows three main lines of action for academia: (i) *collaborative projects* with industry, the number of which should be increased; (ii) *software tools*, for which academia should receive greater financial and human support—notice that such a confirmation of the manifest role of academia in tool development corroborates the prior results of Sect. 4.6; and (iii) *scientific data*, by producing benchmarks, datasets, case studies, and learning resources.

This question received 14 comments, most of which associated with the *others* answer. Four comments recommend to "invest in long-term collaboration with industry" (as opposed to the usual short-term projects supported by funding agencies), with "academic reward structure changes", "increased support and scientific credit for researchers involved in collaborative projects with industry", and "programs for PhD theses to be done in collaboration between academia and industry". However, another comment warns that "formal methods will [only] succeed in industry when a CEO decides it is a priority", a possible reminiscence of Bill Gates's famous memo on security [13]. Two other comments evoke the "inclusion of formal methods in regulatory regimes", with "standards and regulations that demand the kind of guarantees that only formal methods can provide". Finally, four other comments mention educational issues (specifically addressed in Sect. 6 below), with the suggestions of "updating curricula in ICT professionals at bachelor level" and "teaching students on a large scale", with a "compulsory formal methods module" and "better courses that speak to students' needs rather than professors' passions".

6 Formal Methods in Education

6.1 Course Level

Our first question concerning education was to ask the experts about the most suitable place for formal methods in an ideal teaching curriculum.

When and where should formal methods be taught?	
In master courses at the university	80.0%
In bachelor courses at the university	79.2%
In professional (software) engineering schools	70.8%
In continuing education for professionals	70.0%
During doctorate studies	31.5%
Others	3.8%

(from 1 to 4 answers allowed; answers sorted by frequency)

The main lesson is that formal methods should be taught early, in *bachelor* and *master* courses. Waiting until *doctorate* studies would be a mistake, as the PhD students would not have enough time to acquire a proficiency level in formal methods sufficient to survive on the international research scene.

There were only five comments on this question, all associated with the *others* answer. Most of them indicate that formal methods should be taught in all the proposed answers. Another comment points out that non-specialists should be taught "mathematical thinking and the capacity of abstraction, not formal methods per se".

6.2 Importance Level

This question asked the experts about the current situation of formal methods in computer science teaching. In order to avoid *no opinion* answers from respondents lacking a global overview of universities, we added a restriction to familiar schools.

What is your opinion on the level of importance currently attributed to teaching of formal methods at universities? (If you feel that the question is too general, restrict your answer to the universities you know best.)	
Not enough attention	50.0%
Sufficient attention, but scattered all over	31.5%
Right level of attention	6.9%
Too much attention relative to other skills	1.5%
No opinion	10.0%

Exactly half of the experts indicated that formal methods do *not* receive *enough attention* in university curricula, while roughly one-third expressed it does, but in a *scattered* way. Only nine experts responded that universities attribute the *right level of attention* to teaching formal methods, while two experts answered it receives *too much attention*. Thirteen experts had *no opinion*.

This question received 47 comments. The four comments expressing *no opinion* mention that the answer varies too much "from country to country and institution to institution". Four of the six experts commenting on the *right level of attention* base their opinion only on their personal situation. These two types of comments are also common for the *not enough attention* and *sufficient attention, but scattered* answers.

Another recurring comment is that education in formal methods is often isolated. Five comments indicate that applications of formal methods should occur in other courses, like databases, algorithms, concurrency, distributed systems, operating systems, security, compilers, and programming languages. A few comments also mention that the role of formal methods in the software development process and in actual engineering practice should be taught. Another comment explicitly mentions that formal methods should be given "the same relevance as programming".

Finally, the comments also point to some causes of the under-representation of formal methods in curricula: unawareness among staff and management, emergence of new hypes (e.g. heuristic and agile approaches), computer science curricula getting more and more crowded with other topics, and students of an increasingly variable entrance and abstraction level.

6.3   Course Format

This question investigated the target audience and the most appropriate contents for formal methods courses.

Which of the following course formats is preferable?	
Intensive courses on formal methods, targeted to a small number of good students, so as to ensure that the research in formal methods remains strong	6.9%
Non-specialist courses giving a flavour of formal methods combined with other topics (software engineering, distributed systems, embedded systems, etc.)	5.4%
Both: specialist courses taught to a limited number of students, and gentle introduction to formal methods for a larger number of students	83.8%
Other answer	3.8%

The answers show a clear consensus of the experts on the 3rd answer (*both*), with an overwhelming majority.

This question received 32 comments, distributed as follows among the proposed answers: 4 comments for *intensive courses*, 2 comments for *non-specialist courses*, 21 comments for *both*, and 5 comments for *other answer*. Three comments decline to answer the question, arguing that "it very much depends on the level and of the kind of students" and that "each instructor has to figure this out". Five comments state that "every bachelor in computer science/informatics should know about formal methods" and "be trained in applying [them]". Four comments stress that "intensive courses [taking] the matter seriously are the only way to truly educate people", whereas "overview courses (gentle introductions)" giving "just a flavour [are] more likely to lead to disappointment than to something good". Another comment warns, however, that "students (and practitioners) will avoid intensive courses as long as [...] they are too complex". Eleven comments support the two-level approach proposed by the 3rd answer (*both*), putting forward the need to educate a few specialists, who will design new methods and tools, as well as a majority of software engineers and future managers, who will adopt these methods and tools in their professional practice. Finally, one comment recommends to "spread the word" about the excitement of formal methods: "it is not a religion, but treating it as such may help".

6.4   Course Organisation

The next question asked about the best manner to set up formal methods courses.

How should formal-method courses be organised?	
Top-down: primarily focused on theory, starting from theoretical results and possibly illustrating them with applications	6.9%
Bottom-up: starting from concrete problems, and later introducing theory as a means to solve these problems	40.8%
Alternative way, possibly with a combination of top-down and bottom-up (you can explain your vision in the comment field)	44.6%
Other answer	7.7%

Only nine experts answered a *top-down* setup would be best, but the vast majority was divided between a *bottom-up* setup and an *alternative way*.

Fortunately, the analysis of the 58 comments provides more detailed information. Ten experts chose *other answer*, but six of them actually suggested an *alternative way* in their comments, often even a mixture of top-down and bottom-up. Besides, two experts who opted for *bottom-up* also added such comments. This means that just over half of the experts consider an *alternative way* to be the best choice for organising a formal methods course.

As could be expected from our suggestion in the option, a majority of 36 comments came from experts who opted for an *alternative way*. Nine comments indeed favour a combination of the two extremes, but 11 comments also mention that the answer depends on factors, such as the context, the lecturer, the course ("foundational courses [...] can be top-down; more applied courses [...] should be bottom-up"), and the students ("bottom-up at the BSc level, [as] young students want to solve problems [...], top-down at the MSc level, [as] more mature students like to learn new theories [...]"). A few comments suggest to take inspiration from how we teach mathematics and programming.

From the comments, one can distil a fundamental motivation for the *bottom-up* approach, namely: we need to teach students to understand the problem and the requirements before selecting a particular tool or solution. More than half of the 13 comments from experts opting for *bottom-up* agree that "starting from examples is important", since "a good theory always comes with a good practical motivation". Six of the experts opting for an *alternative way* also mention a need for appealing running examples and non-trivial applications. Ironically, the only comment received by an expert opting for *top-down* is: "no good tools without theory!"

6.5 Tool Usage

This question asked the experts whether, and to which extent, students should be exposed to software tools when being taught formal methods.

Which role should software tools play in formal-methods courses?	
No role at all, as they obscure or divert from theoretical concepts	0.0%
Marginal role: their existence should be mentioned to show that theoretical concepts can be implemented	3.1%
Fair role: students should be told to learn by themselves about a few selected tools	19.2%
Major role: lab exercises on concrete applications should be assigned to students	75.4%
No opinion	2.3%

An overwhelming majority of answers judged the use of tools essential when teaching formal methods. Moreover, nobody supported the idea that tools should be kept away from formal-methods lectures; this is one of the very few questions where one of the proposed answers has been chosen by none of the respondents. This confirms a high consensus about the usefulness of tools in teaching.

This question received 55 comments distributed as follows: 0 for *no role at all*, 3 for *marginal role*, 10 for *fair role*, 39 for *major role*, and 3 for *no opinion*. Most comments claim that tools "need to be integral part of the courses", since "many students enjoy working with tools", "exercises on paper are not convincing", "without tools you will not be able to convince students that things are applicable, i.e. in their minds: worth studying", and "unless students are able to apply the concepts they learn to concrete examples, theory will not stick". Other comments put forward that "if you want people to use tools, you have to get students to use some", because "if students get a feel of formal methods tools, they are more likely to apply them in practice during their professional life". Thus, "hands-on courses are needed" and "not only lab exercises but also almost all homework should involve tools". One comment suggests that "another option is to have students implement tools".

A few comments express various reservations: (i) tools should be carefully chosen, because "if students negatively perceive a tool, this also reflects on the applicability and usefulness of the theory"; (ii) tools are only part of a larger problem, as "formulating a good model is a huge challenge in many cases" and students should "understand what the tools are saving them from having to do themselves"; (iii) there should be a correct balance between theory and practice, as "theoretical aspects [are] not always taught best with tools only"—a comment notices that "this is the same as the debate about teaching things that can be used immediately vs. teaching foundations that will be valid in 25 years from now".

7   Future of Formal Methods

7.1   Future Dissemination

This first question on the future of formal methods aimed to evaluate the long-term industrial uptake of formal methods.

Do you believe that formal methods will eventually spread more widely in industry?				
Definitely: 37.7%	Probably: 52.3%	Probably not: 6.9%	Definitely not: 0.0%	N/A: 3.1%

A huge majority of 90% thinks the use of formal methods will likely become more widespread in industry, while only nine experts doubt this and four have *no opinion*.

This question received 57 comments. From the experts who doubted an increasing use of formal methods in industry, two comments base their expectation on what happened in the past; one comment thinks that "industry is just too conservative for that"; one comment urges the formal methods community to "radically change the way we 'sell' formal methods"; and one comment displays a general disappointment with society, concluding that "it does not look like that the humankind will be interested in software quality".

Fifteen comments justify an increase of the application of formal methods by an expectation for a growing demand, either because "the risk induced by (cyber-physical) systems [...] will be omnipresent", or because "with the increased advent of certification regulations, industry companies having their products certified will have a competitive advantage". Several comments mention the growing complexity of systems, which "get so complex and hardly predictable that they need all type of computer-aided support to assure safety and correct functioning". One comment identifies a new mission for formal methods: "because [unmanned, autonomous] systems cannot rely on a human operator to act when a serious problem occurs, developers of autonomous systems want high assurance that these systems behave safely and securely and that they are functionally correct".

A few comments believe that the tools will become easier to use in the future. Yet, successful technology transfers might remain confidential, since a comment reports that "once a formal method tool achieves success, it is usually given a new name, probably to avoid the stigma of being a 'formal method'". Finally, another comment expresses careful optimism: "the word is getting out! More companies are hiring formal methods engineers".

7.2 Future Users

This question aimed at predicting the target audience for the future applications of formal methods.

Who are most likely to use formal methods in the future?	
A large number of mainstream software engineers	42.3%
A small number of skilled experts	43.8%
Others	13.8%

The experts were quite divided on this question, since the first two proposed answers attracted nearly the same number of proponents (55 vs. 57 experts).

The analysis of the 65 comments received provides more insight. From the 18 experts who selected *others*, actually 12 indicate in the comments that they believe that the answer is *both*: "a large number will make small, rote usage of the tools, [while] a small number of skilled experts will be heavy users".

Two comments express the belief that *domain experts* will be the power users of formal methods. One comment wonders how hardware experts fit in the question, but another comment confirms their role: "within hardware development, it has been standard practice to perform Logical Equivalence Checks for some time; this is a specialised use of SAT to check equivalence of two circuits and it is used for translation validation and sometimes to check manual optimisations".

Many comments further distinguish between various kinds of formal methods. Mainstream software engineers are expected to use lightweight formal methods, particularly the automated ones, which are hidden in standard development tools. This idea is present in at least 22 comments. On the other hand, specialists will always be needed to advance tool development; several comments also claim that the explicit use of formal methods will require experts, whenever skills like modelling, specification, abstraction, and interactive proof generation are involved.

It is encouraging that many experts envision a wide audience of mainstream software engineers as future users of formal methods. The fact that this is still not happening is attributed by some to the low quality of (automated) tools: "until enough progress is made to make formal methods accessible to mainstream programmers, only trained experts will be able to use the tools". Others explain the issue by a lack of appropriate scientific/technical education.

7.3 Promising Applications

This question tried to list all domains in which formal methods may have impact.

Do you foresee promising upcoming applications of formal methods?	
In other branches of computer science	69.2%
In finance (digital currencies, smart contracts, etc.)	61.5%
In other sciences (biology, etc.)	58.5%
In politics (e-voting, e-government, etc.)	43.8%
In other parts of society	31.5%

(multiple answers allowed; answers sorted by frequency)

The experts appeared rather optimistic (60–70%) concerning new applications of formal methods in hard sciences (including biology), but less convinced (30–40%, which is still important) by applications in social/human sciences and other parts of society. A pessimistic expert added one missing option: "I see them nowhere".

The question attracted 144 comments. Many of them explicitly suggest applications in *other branches of computer science*, among which (i) software engineering: program synthesis, legacy software, aspects, product lines, human interfaces, business process modelling, etc.; (ii) networking and distributed systems: internet of things, sensor networks, security, etc. (iii) safety-critical systems: embedded systems, robotics, cyber-physical systems, control software for infrastructure systems, etc.; (iv) data science, machine learning, and artificial intelligence; and (v) traditional fields such as compilers, databases, algorithms, numerical computing. As one comment observes: "all those communities realise their problems are too hard to solve just by brute force, and growing calls for reliability in these fields are forcing investigation into and adoption of formal methods".

Among *other sciences*, the most frequently cited ones are biology, epidemiology, surgery, and medicine: "I am excited by the work in model checking of biological systems! Maybe we can even help with drug development?" Chemistry and physics are also mentioned ("one can perfectly well see a hydrogen atom as a state machine"), as well as engineering disciplines such as automotive, transportation, traffic control, aerospace, power or energy control, and the verification of numerical simulations. Social sciences, including law, are also considered as potential application areas.

The comments are optimistic about applications in *finance*, in particular to make transactions more secure. One comment phrases the urgency as: "we sit on a financial bomb". This raises many interesting challenges: "highly complicated cryptography and contracts need formalism". Several comments point to recent successes in formalising blockchains and smart contracts. There are also grander visions, such as developing "formal models of the entire financial service industry, banks, [and] stock exchanges".

Several comments mention that more research on *e-voting* is required, since "trust is really required in that domain". As a comment predicts, "formal methods will show that we have to be careful with e-voting". More ambitious expectations consider a much larger scope: "Perhaps more formalisation of laws and regulations" is needed, and "I would like to see formalised notions of fairness, causality, justice, etc.". Finally, the comments addressing *in other parts of society* largely overlap with the aforementioned ones.

7.4 Potential Competitors

This question polled the experts whether other rising approaches that are increasingly in competition with formal methods to get research funding, to capture industry interest, and to attract students might eventually overshadow formal methods.

Do you believe that alternative approaches (e.g. artificial intelligence or quantum computing) will eventually replace formal methods?				
Definitely: 0.0%	Probably: 3.1%	Probably not: 41.5%	Definitely not: 51.5%	N/A: 3.8%

A vast majority (93%) of the experts stated that formal methods will *(probably or definitely) not* be replaced by alternative methods. No expert believed that this will *definitely* happen. Five experts indicated they have *no opinion* on this matter.

Analysing the 72 comments received, 26 of them indicate that formal methods are incomparable or complementary to the proposed alternatives. A few comments criticise the question for this reason. Interestingly, 38 comments stress that formal methods and artificial intelligence can strengthen each other. Only 10 such remarks were made for quantum computing. No comment mentions another alternative than the two proposed ones.

Several comments explain why neither artificial intelligence nor quantum computing can replace formal methods. Many of them argue that only formal methods can provide guarantees about correctness, e.g. "artificial intelligence is wrong in 10 to 25% of the cases and must be hand-tuned. What is formal there?" and "artificial intelligence will need to be certified. What methods will be used to certify it?".

A quite different reason is provided in two comments that praise the crucial role of formal methods in requirements specification: "at the end of the day, both the ambiguous setting and the mapping to the unambiguous setting are characteristic of human activities. I have a hard time imagining that these creative aspects can be fully automated".

Other comments see fruitful interactions between both fields. Formal methods may help understand artificial intelligence, generate explanations, assist the certification of machine-learned components, or complement them with safety supervisors. In turn, artificial intelligence can improve formal methods by providing heuristics for guiding proof search: "I have seen artificial-intelligence-guided first-order provers that can learn from manual interactive proofs". Another comment adds: "we need approaches that combine model-driven and data-driven techniques".

Although less frequent, similar comments appear for quantum computing: "of course, quantum computing could provide a big hammer", but "there will still be a place for formal methods to study the computational models and perform reasoning about quantum computing" and "formal methods have also been investigated to show correctness of quantum programs".

Finally, we mention a few diverging opinions. Two comments recall that certain parts of formal methods (in particular, symbolic reasoning) were originally a branch of artificial intelligence. Two other comments fear that, in the perception of the public, artificial intelligence could replace formal methods: "but in terms of 'branding', formal methods might disappear from the perception of users who may think of these things more as artificial intelligence. This will require active intervention".

7.5 Major Breakthroughs

This last question on the future of formal methods wanted to know whether a scientific breakthrough can be expected any time soon.

Do you expect that a major breakthrough ("game changer") will happen in formal methods?		
Not really: 33.8%	Within 2 years: 0.0%	Within 5 years: 12.3%
Within 10 years: 17.7%	Within 25 years: 6.9%	N/A: 29.2%

The answers listed in this table are better understood by examining the 46 comments received for this question. We first discuss those comments arguing that a breakthrough is *not really* expected. Ten comments foresee a more gradual, evolutionary progress of the techniques tending to their widespread adoption. Five comments point to external factors, e.g. "societal and economic factors" and "the cultural barrier to the use of formal methods". Another comment shows some hope: "the only game changer I would see, if more and more standards, certifications, and regulations demand the kind of guarantees that only formal methods can provide".

From the comments that, sooner or later, expect a breakthrough, three of them see it coming from killer applications, six others from a particular combination of methods, and four others from a single technical development that could be a game changer. Interestingly, the advances in SAT/SMT solvers are mentioned, in those three sets of comments, as the example of the most recent game changer.

An example of such a potentially groundbreaking combination is given: "just as tools (e.g. solvers) in formal methods have grown tremendously over the past few decades, so too have tools in other areas: most obviously in machine learning, but also in fields like stochastic optimisation. Putting together all these in meaningful ways may lead to dramatic improvements in all of them".

Three examples of individual advances that could lead to a breakthrough are also given: "synthesis of correct-by-construction control components for critical systems", "serious use of models instead of programs, coupled with automatic generation of code", and applications of "big data" or "quantum computing".

8 Conclusion

Formal methods are now more than 50 years old, and after half a century of sustained research, development of new techniques, and continuous enlargement of the perimeter of formal methods, it was high time to review the situation: the 25th anniversary of the FMICS conference was a suitable opportunity to do so.

The present survey is an unprecedented effort to gather the collective knowledge of the formal methods community. Not less than 130 internationally renowned experts agreed to participate in the survey and spent significant time to express their views, through answers to our questionnaire, through detailed comments accompanying these answers, and through position statements that deliver the personal opinions of these key actors in formal methods.

Many lessons can be learned from all these contributions, the collective ones are synthesised in Sects. 3–7, while the individual ones can be found in Sect. 9. The general opinion is that formal methods achieve many technical successes, but are not yet mainstream to their full potential. There is still much to be done and, among all the pending tasks, we wish to highlight three action points more particularly:

- The results of the survey indicate a consensus about the essential role of *education* to give the next generations of students a sufficient background and practical experience in formal methods. Unfortunately, it appears that the current situation is very heterogeneous across universities, and many experts call for a standardisation of university curricula with respect to formal methods. A recent white paper [7] provides a good starting point for such an undertaking. Also, one should not neglect continuing education and make sure that industry professionals who did not attend university classes can learn about formal methods from alternative channels (online courses, tutorial videos, etc.).
- The results of the survey also make it clear that formal methods are no longer a paper-and-pencil activity: like other fields such as logic and computer algebra, formal methods have shifted their orientation, and their progress now closely relies on *software tools*. A majority of experts considers that universities and research institutes have a central role to play in the construction of such tools. However, software development is often underrated by standard academic evaluation, which primarily measures excellence in terms of publications in scientific conferences and journals. Thus, many experts call for a revision of the current academic reward system to better encourage long-term investment in the development of innovative, high-quality software. Researchers are also invited to join forces to build common platforms that can become part of mainstream development practices.
- Computing takes an ever-growing importance in modern societies but is still much less regulated than other sectors (transportation, real estate, healthcare, etc.), even though software or hardware bugs may have dire consequences in an increasingly connected digital world. The industrial dissemination of formal methods really progresses when companies that produce software or software-intensive systems decide to protect the safety, security, and privacy of their customers—thereby protecting their own assets and reputation at the same time.

The current incentives for such virtuous behaviour are probably not enough, and many experts call for a greater *regulation* of software quality (beyond the traditionally supervised sectors of aerospace, nuclear energy, and railways), with stricter standards that examine the final product rather than its development process, and a stronger promotion of best practices by professional bodies. Such measures (together with, e.g. finer risk assessment of software products by insurance companies) would turn formal methods into a profitable investment.

We hope that this survey will highlight the potential of formal methods to the numerous stakeholders (policy makers, regulators, company managers, research funding agencies, professionals, students, etc.) and encourage industry to use these methods more intensively.

9   Position Statements

Each expert who answered all 30 questions of the survey was then warmly invited (yet not required) to write a short statement (not exceeding 10 lines) about formal methods. Guidelines were given in the form of three questions, with the expectation that each position statement would address these questions, or a subset of them:

1. Personally, what do you consider to be the next challenges for formal methods?
2. How are you currently contributing to these efforts?
3. Which of your contributions could be most beneficially picked up and carried forward by the next generation?

It was stated that each position statement would be nominally attributed to its author, the intention being to confront individual visions from many high-profile experts—contrary to the 30 questions of the survey, whose answers would be anonymised to distil the collective opinion of the formal methods community.

Nearly 60 acronyms occur in the position statements. In below tables, we only expand those needed to understand ideas; we neither detail acronyms defined before being used in position statements, nor well-known acronyms (OS, PC), nor names of computer languages (UML, VDM), software tools (CADP, SPIN), universities (ECNU, RWTH), organisations (ISO, NASA), and conferences/workshops (FMICS, MARS).

Acronym	Signification	Acronym	Signification
AI	Artificial Intelligence	IT	Information Technology
CPS	Cyber-Physical System	JSON	JavaScript Object Notation
CTL	Computation Tree Logic	LTL	Linear Temporal Logic
DSL	Domain-Specific Language	ML	Machine Learning
FM(s)	Formal Method(s)	PLC	Programmable Logic Controller
GPU	Graphics Processing Unit	PR	Public Relations
GUI	Graphical User Interface	REST	Representational State Transfer
HMI	Human-Machine Interface	SAT	Boolean Satisfiability Problem
HW	Hardware	SMT	Satisfiability Modulo Theories
IP	Intellectual Property	SW	Software

Please note that each position statement reflects only its authors' views, and not necessarily the opinions of the authors of this report, nor those of their employers.

The scope of FMs extends beyond program and model verification. FMs are applied in Workflow and Business Process Management, and recently in data-driven approaches like process mining. This reconfirms the importance of concurrency theory, a subfield of FMs rooted in early work of Carl Adam Petri. Petri's guiding principle was "Concurrency should be a starting point for system design and analysis and not added as an afterthought (locality of actions)". Operational processes are inherently concurrent, and the availability of event data allows to discover such processes. I anticipate FMs and data science to converge. We need FMs to describe real-world phenomena, and the abundance of data offers a unique opportunity. Thus, the practical applicability of FMs will continue to increase. It is vital that students learn to abstract and structure, and FMs are the tool for this. Edsger Dijkstra once said "Beauty Is Our Business". I would like to add "...and business is good".

Wil van der Aalst

The pioneering works of Clarke, Dijkstra, Emerson, Hoare, Milner, Pnueli, Sifakis, Vardi, and many others set the stage for an exciting area that lays the foundations of computer science. In the early days, program semantics and verification were restricted to small idealized calculi, but there has been a rise in rigorous engineering methods to elucidate and analyze real-life problems of processor architecture, programming languages, computer networks, database systems, etc. Formal methods also play an essential role in education by teaching students abstract thinking, problem solving, and the ability to communicate new ideas in an articulate manner. Thus, integrating formal methods in under- and post-graduate education is vital to make students more prepared to their academic or professional careers regardless of their areas of specialization.

Parosh Abdulla

Being addicted to the beauty of math, I look back to two decades of joyful time to develop and connect mathematically rigorous approaches for the modeling and analysis of various types of systems. In the area of fast rising new technologies for autonomous and learning systems, the formal methods community enthusiastically adapts, extends and creates new ways to contribute to the development of correct and safe systems. But our achievements unfold their full potential only if there are people who are willing to as well as able to use the developed methodologies and tools. We should put the strongest possible weight on education, explaining elegant formal methods algorithms, which are perfectly suited to awake interest, train precise analytical thinking and to prepare to use formal methods tools.

Erika Ábrahám

Formal methods should be uniquely those which are concerned with *proofs*. This eliminates many activities pretending to be formal methods. Companies give formal methods a mixed reception: some industries (e.g., railways) are fervent adopters while others (e.g., aerospace) firmly resist, often because managers are reluctant to introduce new approaches that disrupt current work methodologies that took much effort to install. Such resistance is likely to stay for the next thirty years. Teaching formal methods in academia is fundamental. Unfortunately many teachers are reluctant because they do not want to put sufficient effort into competence in proving. I am currently contributing to these efforts by teaching, developing tools, and cooperating with Chinese universities like ECNU.

Jean-Raymond Abrial

Emerging machine-learning algorithms are enabling new generations of autonomous systems in robotics, medicine, and transportation. Two challenges are that (1) safety is of paramount importance in these applications, and (2) it is unclear how to integrate data-driven models generated by machine-learning algorithms in complex software systems. Their combination offers promising opportunities for formal methods, both in terms of academic research and integration in industrial practice. At the intersection of formal methods and machine learning, there are many research problems ranging from integrating formal specifications in training algorithms to formally verifying systems that include, say, a neural-network-based controller. These are all challenging problems, and progress is likely to be achieved by focusing on specific case studies first.

Rajeev Alur

The overwhelming complexity of systems critical to our society emanates not from complicated computations, but from latent combinatorics of the potential interactions of their parts. It is notoriously hard to carve a protocol out of such an exponentially large interaction space to correctly manifest the desired behavior of a system. It is even more difficult to ensure that such a protocol simultaneously excludes other unforeseen slices of that vast space that constitute undesired behaviors that, e.g., compromise privacy, safety, or security. Reo is a language for compositional construction of protocols, based on a model of concurrency that treats interaction as its only first-class concept. In Reo, protocols become concrete software constructs independently specified and compiled, which one can separately verify and reuse, or compose into more complex protocols.

Farhad Arbab

In my experience, there is a lot of progress in formal languages to express data, basically types, such as JSON Schema. Engineers use these languages in practice, but struggle constructing more complex type definitions. Far too often I have seen "string" as a type with a comment that this string should contain a date or similar. This shows a lag between academia, for which this is no longer an issue, and industrial practice. By automatically generating test cases for such type definitions, we contribute to improved specifications and more reliable code. Expressing behaviour is even more of a struggle in practice. General languages to express such behaviour are not widely accepted. But embedded in patterns (like REST) they widely exist. Formal methods should use the semantics embedded in patterns to assist developers.

Thomas Arts

With a PhD in mathematics, I have devoted a large part of my scientific life to the mathematical underpinnings of computer science, thus contributing to the science of "computer science". I am happy to have played a part in this. I view formal methods as the application of these mathematical underpinnings to the practice of computer science. I am not so satisfied with the achievements I have been able to make in formal methods, and hope others in the community can do better. I find that convincing IT companies to adopt formal methods is more difficult than convincing companies making other products (that are software-intensive). I find mechanical engineering students more interested in learning and using formal methods than computer science students. Therefore, maybe the best way forward is to work in systems engineering rather than software engineering.

Jos Baeten

For me, the main challenges are better formal specification and programming languages, simpler general verification assistants, more powerful automatic methods and software, and, above all, more widespread tools and education with respect to these subjects. I used to be quite active in academia and industry on the development of formal synchronous languages, which reconcile concurrency and determinism while supporting fully formal verification and compiling technologies: Esterel v5 for embedded software, and Esterel v7 for hardware microarchitecture, with semantics-based links between these languages and formal verification techniques. I did it first in academia with strong links to software and hardware industry, then as chief scientist of the Esterel Technologies company. I finally taught this, among other things, as a professor at Collège de France.

— Gérard Berry —

The biggest challenge is to put formal methods into a language and software process that is easy to access and similar to existing approaches. One has to make sure that such a new formal approach is combined with other important parts of system design, particularly testing, fuzzing, debugging, coverage etc. The next most important aspect is how to combine inductive and deductive reasoning for rigorous design of systems with a learning component. Third, there are still huge potentials for improving logical reasoning tools, which then will allow to tackle larger problems. This last challenge is of course the one on which I focus most, also because I have witnessed a steady increase in scalability of for instance SAT and SMT solvers, which led to a wider adoption of formal methods in academia and industry.

— Armin Biere —

In formal software development, one should first understand and describe the domain, then analyse and prescribe the requirements, before finally specifying and designing the software itself. Descriptions, prescriptions, and specifications should be mathematical entities, formulated in one or more languages (e.g. VDM, Z, B, Alloy, CASL, CafeOBJ, Maude, or RAISE), which have formal syntax, a mathematically expressed semantics, and one or more proof systems that (more or less) cover the entire language. Formal software development involves a series of iterated domain descriptions, requirements prescriptions, and software specifications, where mathematical properties can be expressed and reasoned upon for each of these phases, and where correct transformations between them can likewise be formally argued.

— Dines Bjørner —

There is no shortage of next challenges for formal methods. The emergence of large-scale cloud-based systems presents one such opportunity; and many challenges. They are the ultimate dream/nightmare of IT administrators obsessed with solutions to capture *intent*, driving systems to *goal states* in *day two* of deployments that integrate many interoperating pieces. It is an opportunity to build foundations for semantic interoperability, interfaces and tools to ensure security and reliability. It also presents opportunities to add formal methods value to systems driven by a continuous life-cycle involving measurement, synthesis, optimization and deployment. I contribute to this line by deploying the SMT solver Z3 and other formal tools in the Azure cloud.

— Nikolaj Bjørner —

Recently, NASA looked for a "formal methods engineer". We should always present formal methods explicitly and consistently as an engineering discipline within computer science: "formal methods" alone is a too generic term. Underlining the engineering aspect in research and education clarifies their practical role. We should teach "FM engineering" as a specialisation of software engineering. FM engineering applies formal methods to improve software reliability, but also involves software development to support the application of formal methods. Underlining the engineering aspect in research would counter-balance the limited understanding of formal methods as a purely theoretical research topic. Hopefully, underlining the engineering aspect will help promote formal methods in academy and industry, and the term "formal methods (software) engineering" will broaden the understanding and appreciation of formal methods.

Frank de Boer

Given that my main occupation in the past ten years has been in university management, I prefer to formulate my position in terms of two general principles. First, the next challenge for formal methods is always to remain relevant, i.e. to develop methods and tools to design systems with desirable properties in the context of new computational paradigms. Current examples are machine learning, big data, probabilistic programming, quantum-inspired computing—I am sceptical about quantum computers, but very interested by novel hardware architectures faking them. Second, always try and combine good theories with real applications, and try to contribute to both. This entails developing and adapting theory, systematic tool development, and having in-depth knowledge of relevant application domains.

Ed Brinksma

Industrial critical software and cyber-physical systems need formal techniques to guarantee correctness, safety, security and long-term quality. We need scientific progress in techniques to model critical aspects, progress in practical methods and tools to deal with large, complex systems, and integration through experimentation. While we have seen a lot of progress, we are far from a satisfying situation. Scientific research and results in formal modelling and verification often do not address the most relevant issues from practice, just like interesting scientific approaches often are not really evaluated by practitioners and commercial tools do not integrate them. Reasons include insufficient education and insufficient understanding by managers. I would like to see much more intensive collaboration between science and practice, supporting also the development of effective and powerful tools.

Manfred Broy

Our society's safety and well-being depend on our software infrastructure, and current inspiring perspectives for robotics and autonomous systems will increase such reliance. Industry has applied formal methods for software engineering successfully, but we need that to become standard practice. It is possible to develop useful systems without formal methods, but if software engineering is to be truly an engineering discipline, based on mathematics, then we have to cater for the theory that explains practice. Formal methods are the scientific backbone of software engineering and can be used to improve quality and to reduce costs. To maximise this potential impact, we have to deal with usability via palatable notations and effective tools. We have done a lot as a community. We have a lot of very exciting work still to do.

Ana Cavalcanti

A large part of research on automated symbolic verification has been focusing on developing dedicated engines for model checking. This has led to huge progress in scalability, thanks to SAT-based methods for the finite-state case, and to SMT-based methods, in combination with automated abstractions, for the infinite-state case. There are equally important problems that deserve attention, in order to increase the penetration of formal methods in the standard process for system design: requirements modeling and validation; provably correct contract-based design; safety assessment, i.e. methods to analyze a system's response under faults; design-space exploration of parametric models for the identification of configurations meeting the desired requirements.

Alessandro Cimatti

I believe the great future challenge for formal methods is for users to stop being pleasantly surprised when they work, as is typically the case currently, and instead to be irritated when they do not! Achieving this vision requires notational, methodological, technological and outreach-focused advances. Notations need to be standardized within domains and, together with analysis tooling, embedded in design processes. New technologies such as quantum and machine learning need formal support. Students and professionals also need exposure to formal methods. My contributions currently are focused on approaches for inferring system properties from observations of system behavior, to provide a bridge to formal methods for engineers who are not versed in them.

Rance Cleaveland

Expanded use of formal methods in aircraft software is crucial due to the high cost of verification and certification activities, as well as the extremely high potential cost (both financial and human) of design defects that escape into service. Our experience shows that formal methods can both reduce costs (through automation and reduced rework) and eliminate hard-to-find defects. However, we are not starting with a blank slate but face huge process inertia. We are working now to incorporate formal methods into model-based system engineering environments. This presents a great opportunity to use a common system design model throughout the life-cycle to drive safety/security analysis, system development, verification, infrastructure code generation, and certification evidence.

Darren Cofer

Within the formal methods spectrum, I mainly worked on fully automated verification, which either restricts itself to decidable cases, or requires sound (but sometimes incomplete) approximations. I specialized on the latter approach, working on theory (abstract interpretation), practice (static analysis), and education of students, designers, and end-users. This led to Astrée [1], a successful tool for proving the absence of runtime errors and invalid concurrent behaviour in safety-critical software written or generated in C. The next challenges for automated formal verification are threefold: *scope* (coping with a variety of specification and programming languages), *scalability* (analysing programs of millions of lines with reasonable resources and sufficient precision), and *applicability* (designing formal methods that can be inserted in industrial development methodologies at an acceptable cost).

Patrick Cousot

The challenge of the formal methods community is to have them properly included in the system development process. Today, most companies are not willing to adopt formal methods as they believe it is costly and time demanding. Since the software industry process is not properly regulated, companies bluntly cross the ethics boundaries. Thus, it is my belief that we need public policies that properly regulate software industry, forcing companies to include rigorous and mathematically based techniques and to properly document it in the different stages of the development process. Cost and time might be an issue at the beginning, but once formal methods are normally adopted they will have a positive impact in both aspects. For this, we need that governments really understand the consequences of a bad software product.

Pedro R. D'Argenio

I have believed for several decades that the primary barrier to widespread adoption of formal methods is not educating engineers, friendly notation, or better GUIs. It is the value and productivity of the methods in expert hands. We need to be able to develop demonstrably superior systems at a cost that is significantly less than the benefit of applying the methods. The only path I can see is co-development of formal methods, tools, system design methods (including languages, programming patterns, etc.) to maximize the benefit and minimize the cost of developing high-quality systems in particular application areas. It will require an iterative effort and a single-minded focus on optimizing the value of the method, with creativity and without dogma.

David L. Dill

Most of the work on formal methods so far has been contending against *stupidity*. It is so easy for humans to commit programming or design mistakes that the supply of stupidity is almost infinite and we will never run out of issues to work on. Although the poet and philosopher Friedrich Schiller wrote: "Against stupidity the gods themselves contend in vain", formal methods are valuable and effective enough to prevent or detect certain classes of mistakes. But more work on formal methods is now needed to contend against *malevolence*. It is much too easy for attackers to exploit software vulnerabilities, such as buffer overflows, dangling pointers, and race conditions. Our techniques can also address such issues, and the area of formal methods for cybersecurity should definitely receive more attention.

E. Allen Emerson

As most mainstream programming languages have not been designed to be analyzed formally, the adoption of formal methods in industry should be addressed by developing tools that operate at scale on legacy and existing programming environments. One should also pave the way to a better future by inventing languages with sound bases for formal analysis, and equip these languages with effective development tools, including comprehensive libraries and code profilers. Concurrency remains a major challenge, especially with the rise of general-purpose GPU computing, from data centers to mobile devices. The programming models of such heterogeneous systems may have underspecified concurrency aspects (such as scheduling fairness, which is the focus of my current research at Google) that formal methods help to clarify and verify.

Hugues Evrard

The next challenges for formal methods are related to the pervasive use of artificial intelligence (machine-learning engines) in safety-critical applications: formal methods will be called in to help certifying the safety of such systems, which is a very hard job due to the extremely vague notion of "correctness" that can be ascribed to this kind of systems. For the latter challenge of certifying the safety of such systems, which has very recently emerged as really important, I conjecture that the notion of a *safety envelop* for a moving object will need to be extended to objects moving in an uncertain environment. My own recent contributions on formal modelling and formal verification of various kinds of railway signalling systems can be fruitfully considered for such systems, and extended outside the railway domain.

Alessandro Fantechi

Traditionally, formal methods have focussed on functional correctness, but the Meltdown and Spectre attacks demonstrated that it is not enough: even in processor designs where each individual execution is correct, it may be possible for an attacker to obtain secret information by comparing multiple executions. Formal methods need to treat concerns like information-flow security and privacy (and other non-functional requirements, such as robustness and perspicuity) with the same level of rigour as functional correctness. In my opinion, a central role in this new class of formal methods will be played by hyperproperties, which generalize trace properties to relations between multiple traces and can express many non-functional properties of interest. We recently developed algorithms that monitor, verify, and even synthesize systems from hyperproperties: this shows great promise, but plenty of interesting questions are still open.

Bernd Finkbeiner

As computing technology becomes integrated into our physical and social fabric, formal methods can help create systems on which billions rely, from secure data networks to sustainable water supplies. Such projects require *collaborative* methods, tools that mesh with those of other disciplines, and researchers and practitioners who can create and use them. Our work at Newcastle University envisions collaborative modelling, co-simulation and co-verification. There are challenges not only in laying the foundations of these techniques, but in integrating robust methods and tools at the level of systems and systems-of-systems. Meeting these challenges requires a generation of formalists who can work across traditional divides between disciplines and departments—and that means a more open, intellectually and socially diverse formal methods community.

John Fitzgerald

At Eindhoven University of Technology we cooperate with Rijkswaterstaat, which is responsible for development and maintenance of infrastructure in the Netherlands. A wide range of companies make the control software of bridges, waterway locks, tunnels in a variety of ways, leading to software that cannot be easily maintained. We turn system requirements into PLC code automatically by means of supervisory control synthesis. We are now involved in the design process of several infrastructural systems. Recently, a bridge was operated in real life by software generated automatically from the requirements. PhD students on the projects have pushed the boundaries of supervisory control synthesis by developing novel specification and verification techniques that have been pivotal in scaling this method to real-life applications.

Wan Fokkink

My area of research is the verification of cyber-physical systems, where continuous variables evolve with time and interact with control software. The proliferation of artificial intelligence (AI) in perception and decision-making poses a formidable verification challenge, e.g., in robotics and autonomous vehicles. We investigate how formal methods can assist such that safety is guaranteed both during training and operation. We enhance the learning algorithms and add a supervisor (shield) that interferes in time to avoid critical behavior. Our work on efficient yet precise set propagation and abstraction can help to ensure that such checks are fast, while at the same time being accurate enough to provide the required guarantees without being overly cautious.

Goran Frehse

Software-intensive systems increasingly behave as autonomous entities living in the physical world, augmenting it, collaborating with humans, and offering new advanced functionalities. Novel opportunities and challenges arise for formal methods, to support both development and operation of such systems. Design often requires multi-disciplinary, domain-specific competences. In addition, design decisions must often be made in the presence of high levels of uncertainty about the embedding physical world. Formal modeling notations and validation methods must be revisited and engineered to effectively comply with these issues. Formal models and verification must also live at run-time to support dependable support to autonomy. In particular, they should allow software to self-adapt to detected changes in the environment's behavior and offer support to co-evolution with humans.

Carlo Ghezzi

Whole system assurance I see as a next challenge for formal methods: a coordinated verification effort covering the entire chain from hardware and operating systems to selected user applications. Proving liveness properties, saying that systems will do what they are meant to do, is a high priority for me. A lot of work has been done on safety and security, but often separated from checking functional correctness. I see good prospects to address functional correctness in combination with safety and security properties. To ensure the sustained application of formal methods, we need forums and repositories for showcasing the fruits of formal modelling and verification. I am proud to be one of the founders of the MARS workshop and repository, which focuses on the formal modelling of real systems.

Rob van Glabbeek

The next challenges for formal methods are in their pervasive application in the development of more and more sophisticated cyber-physical systems, such as for example autonomous systems, to assure their dependability, safety, and security. One aspect of these challenges concerns the early formalisation phase. In this area, I have recently focussed on methods and tools to remove defects in natural language requirements and to avoid possible misinterpretations. The design of critical systems can benefit from the paradigm of software product lines, which allows developing families of systems starting from the same initial model. In this field, we have provided a behavioural and logical framework for modelling and analysis of safety-critical systems, such as railway control systems.

Stefania Gnesi

Formal specification and verification methods have made tremendous progress over the last decades. Some have by now been adopted in many industrial software and hardware domains. In the software world, type checking is probably the most widespread use of formal verification. As another example (dear to my heart), our SAGE project at Microsoft has tested and verified memory safety of large parts of the Windows OS and of Office applications using formal program analysis techniques like symbolic execution, constraint generation and solving, by formalizing x86 semantics and leveraging SMT solvers; as a result, a billion users world-wide now enjoy their PCs more safely and securely. Of course, much is still to be accomplished to have even more impact.

Patrice Godefroid

With the end of Moore's law, we face extreme parallelism leading to data races and the inexorable costs of data movement. There is a dire need for race checkers based on formal principles, that handle irregular computations, and are usable. Reduced-precision floating-point is fundamental to reducing data movement. Rigorous and scalable error analysis methods are essential to licensing the use of reduced precision. Our research is contributing to the development of race checkers for OpenMP. They have caught multiple data races in large-scale projects. Our research is also contributing to rigorous floating-point error analysis that has pushed the boundary up by several orders of magnitude. We expect both our race checking methods and error estimation methods to be perpetuated.

Ganesh Gopalakrishnan

Currently, I see the following two challenges. 1) How do we learn to use formal methods and formal modelling in a practical context such that we can reap the benefits of formal methods (i.e. verification of properties and overall correctness; modelling for verification). This aspect hardly received attention, because so few researchers model substantial systems. 2) How do we change the (industrial) society such that they will incorporate formal methods within their production processes on a large scale. This is hardly scientific, as it requires tool builders, service providers, willing managers, probably changes of the law regarding software responsibility, etc.

Jan Friso Groote

A main challenge in formal methods is to keep advancing the theory, methodologies and tools for handling new problems arising in the real-world, as well as new application areas. My work is aimed at developing new approaches to new problems while exploiting and incorporating established "old" knowledge into the novel ones, as well as combining ideas from other disciplines. Another important challenge is education, to make sure that mainstream software engineers are aware of formal methods, understand them and are willing to apply them. I teach a yearly large undergraduate course on formal methods to software engineering students, which then carry the knowledge into industry. They apply formal methods and develop industrial verification tools. My research students join academic research or lead verification groups in industry.

Orna Grumberg

Formal methods are well established in a few specialized sectors in industry where risk is very high, financially or even in the form of endangering people. In these cases, formal methods are most often used by domain and method experts. It is a big challenge to evolve formal methods in such a way that they can be used successfully in other sectors as well. For several years, I used formal methods in different sectors: safety critical systems, hardware verification, software model checking and cryptocurrencies. Now, my main goal is teaching students to make them aware of the possibilities of using formal methods, to write formal specifications, and to use formal analysis tools on real problems. I deem it very important to give a realistic view of advantages but also limits of formal methods.

Matthias Güdemann

The main challenge for formal methods is very basic: how to discover loop invariants. We still can't get around that barrier. I do, however, see some reasons to believe that this problem will get more focus: the introduction of programming languages supported by proof systems. I do expect it to become more common with programming language implementations being born with program verifiers of various kinds. This can bring formal methods in the hands of software developers, and put pressure on the research community to address the right problems. It is a pleasure to see modern programming languages to an increasing degree look and feel like well known formal specification languages. There is a convergence it seems, of formal methods and programming language design and implementation.

Klaus Havelund

If formal methods should have a future, it is now time to focus more on their industrial adoption: More collaboration projects with industry are needed. In these projects, methods and tools should be industrialised and cost-benefit analyses should be carried out. It should be investigated how formal methods can be integrated into existing software life cycles and made simpler to use, e.g. by the provision of professional tools encapsulating the use of formal methods. First Movers (companies providing or applying formal methods) should help drive the marketing and spreading of formal methods to industry. In courses, we should not only teach theory and show toy examples, but also show how formal methods can be integrated into existing life cycles and used in industrial applications.

Anne Haxthausen

In the past, our research and most other formal methods research has focused on verifying, or detecting defects in, formal models of critical software systems. While such research was extremely valuable, ultimately, assurance is needed that the executable system code satisfies critical properties, such as safety and correctness. One relatively new application of formal methods, called run-time verification, aims at formally verifying the system code. This code will often rely on AI techniques, such as machine learning, to perform its functions. The aim of our recent research is to develop a comprehensive set of new formal methods and robust, usable tools that support run-time verification and provide assurance of machine-learning systems. This new technology will be used throughout the system development process to ensure that requirements are satisfied, with a focus on the safety and correctness of the important and steadily growing class of autonomous systems.

Constance L. Heitmeyer

I would like to put forward a reasonable conjecture that the next virus to threaten civilisation will be an infovirus. It may be accidental (due to software error), or due to rumour (misinformation), or to unsubstantiated but deeply held beliefs (e.g. about chloroquine or measles), or to an extreme political agenda (disinformation), or it may be due to malice (malware). To imagine the consequences, think of something like the present coronavirus attack, in which all connected computers, both public and private, have closed down. The closure could be permanent, because each component relies on another component to restore it to a stable state.

I would like to make an urgent plea that researchers from the entire computer science community should participate in a project to reduce the risks and consequences of a potential infovirus pandemic. Research into formal programming methods should aim to reduce the risk of accident, and increase the likelihood of recovery. We also need to define and verify security properties of basic hypervisors, supervisors, and other critical basic software. Finally all programmers should lobby their professional organisations, their employers, and their elected political representatives to establish and implement verifiable standards that keep the reproduction rate of the infovirus low.

Tony Hoare

I believe that there is considerable benefit in the further development of formal methods based tools that can perform analyses in real-time, interactively. In my own work, I have tried to develop two types of methods that can achieve this. The first concerns a swarm verification strategy that is aimed at large cloud computing environments, where we launch large numbers (up to millions) of very small, and very quickly executing search engines in the cloud, to jointly deliver a verification result with high confidence of full coverage of a complex problem domain. The second concerns the development of the Cobra tool (github/nimble-code) to perform interactive static analysis on large code archives, including, most recently, new analyses for cybersecurity vulnerabilities. More research in this area of interactive formal analysis is needed.

Gerard Holzmann

How to make software reliable is an important open challenge, and formal methods will play a crucial role in this. To address this challenge, it is essential to close the gap that currently exists between industrial practice and the academic state-of-the-art. This means that we have to make formal methods usable for engineers developing large-scale software. However, this is a challenge that will not be solved from one day to the other: it is a long-term process, and requires serious investment from both sides. As a scientific community, we can help this process by giving academic rewards for investing in (long-term) collaborations with industry, adapting tools to make them practically usable, and by providing good training material that can help engineers to apply suitable formal methods to their products.

Marieke Huisman

The future use of formal methods for the development of hardware/software systems depends on demonstrated cost reductions. Microprocessor vendors have been able to save tens of millions of dollars of development costs annually by proving the correctness of parts of their designs. A mathematical proof run on a single small machine can replace millions of hours of simulation run on thousands of machines. Formal specifications provide designers with clear targets, both for engineers implementing such specifications and for users of precisely-defined IP blocks and subroutines. My recommendation for the formal-methods community is to continue demonstrating and emphasizing the cost savings, quality improvements, and shortened time-to-market, that a formal-methods-based process can provide.

— Warren A. Hunt Jr.

Formal methods have made tremendous progress in foundational underpinnings and tool development! But formal methods, as a School of Thought, may look alien to software developers who use Jira and Github, do Sprint plannings and Sprint reviews and, think of Epics, User Stories, and Tasks. Getting adoption and impact in that world means being able to support these activities and ways of thinking. "Formal methods" also needs to cultivate its branding and do some effective PR. It has a lot of—almost invisible—but lasting and far reaching impact, e.g. in modern programming languages. These are missed PR opportunities. At present, I work in a startup for privacy-preserving collaborative AI—designing efficient protocols. Future generations may appreciate that I have a nuanced and humble view of the place of formal methods.

— Michael Huth

I am convinced that formal methods are the only means to tackle the ever growing complexity of systems, whether it is software or hardware or a combination thereof. I am not sure that we have already reached the point where the benefits really overcome the costs (except in specific domains, such as hardware), but I continue to try making formal methods percolate to industry. Formal methods will also probably be the only way to gain confidence in systems embedding machine-learning algorithms. This is actually a new and fantastic challenge, surely requiring new formal techniques. I sincerely hope that the current hype about AI, and the general movement of people (including students) and industry towards that direction will not end-up marginalizing even more the effort towards the industrialization of formal methods.

— Eric Jenn

I believe that formal methods are best suited to express, analyze and organize models, and that interesting application domains for formal methods may be found not only in software engineering and computer science, but anywhere in science or society where correct models matter. I also believe that to increase the impact of formal methods, it may be useful to frame them as powerful extensions of simulation, which is a technique that everyone understands and accepts. In my work on the ABS modeling language, focus has always been on formal methods as executable high-level programs with clearly defined semantics and additional analysis support.

— Einar Broch Johnsen

To me, the challenge is to get formal methods used all the way from formal specification through a verified design process: although it is possible to analyse code and detect classes of errors, it is more cost-effective to detect mistaken design decisions before further development is undertaken. For sequential programs, methods such as VDM and (Event-)B have shown that this can be done. Concurrency has proved to be more challenging, but ideas like the rely/guarantee method have shown that compositionality can also be achieved for concurrent programs. Tool support is essential if methods are to be used widely.

Cliff B. Jones

Formal methods developed enormously in the last 25 years. They led to various international standards and influenced more recent ones, such as ISO 26262, which prescribes formal methods for the automotive domain. Software tool capabilities made incredible progress, and major software and hardware companies invest considerably in making formal methods industrially applicable. To be successful in the future, I believe that we need much more emphasis on "lightweight" formal methods: techniques that can be applied on a daily basis by system engineers in the same way as they use compilers and debuggers. This requires orchestrated efforts by the research community and industry. Examples of such efforts at RWTH Aachen are the COMPASS toolset for AADL (developed together with FBK since 2008 with ESA funding) and an IC3-based software model checker (joint work with Siemens).

Joost-Pieter Katoen

Recall the parable of the Blind Men and an Elephant: e.g., an elephant is like a snake if we touch only its trunk. Thus, formal methods may seem to be automatic equivalence checking if we only compare related hardware models, but may seem to be interactive theorem proving (ITP) if we only verify deep properties. Let's embrace the entire elephant! Note that many ITP systems—including the one I know, ACL2, which is used daily at several companies—support the use of automatic tools in human+machine proof development. As hardware and software continue to grow in complexity, their successful verification will demand further education and research on a variety of mechanized formal methods.

Matt Kaufmann

It has been amply demonstrated that even deep formal methods like interactive proof can be used to good effect on real, deployed systems. The challenge is to make these methods scale to larger systems and at the same time make their application cheaper, to reach the point where deep formal methods are economically preferable to normal software development. Our projects such as the seL4 microkernel verification are within a cost factor of less than 4 compared to standard high-quality software development, and work on proof engineering, better tools, and better methods looks promising to overcome this factor in the future.

Gerwin Klein

Formal methods should become a more ecumenical community, as it is now understood that each approach has it own strengths and weaknesses, so that no formal method alone can be a silver bullet. One must thus combine several approaches by connecting modelling languages to the various verification engines available. I am addressing this long-term objective in the particular area of model checking. Specifically, I explore *adaptive* model checking, which tries to dynamically select the most appropriate algorithms and heuristics for a given model under verification and a given property to verify. Software competitions are helpful for this purpose, as they allow a fair comparison of tools and algorithms on a common set of benchmarks, and encourage the development of gateways between different software implementations, or even between different formal methods.

Fabrice Kordon

My vision, after more than 25 years in this field, is still that formal methods will become a "natural" part of industrial software and systems engineering like compiler and simulation technology already is today. This requires appropriately adapted methods, user-oriented tools, and solid integration into engineering curricula, such that these methods can be applied by engineers with only a basic understanding of the underlying concepts but without deep knowledge of theoretical results. I believe that making formal methods applicable is a research topic of its own which has been neglected in the past. It has to be different than the usual formal methods research, e.g., by involving user studies instead of theorems and proofs. But it is key for the future of our field.

Stefan Kowalewski

A major challenge confronting formal methods is usability. For too long we have ignored it entirely, and research shows this was ill-advised. Researchers still have very naive views of what "usability" even means: e.g., they assume one is speaking of slapping a GUI on a tool. Rather, human factors methods need to be applied to all parts of the pipeline, from the languages and notations we use for specifying problems, to the methods we use for presenting output, the modalities we offer for working, and so on.
I focus on two aspects. One, I am explicitly applying human factors to formal methods tools to tackle the issues listed above. Second, I am also applying education research methods to the way we teach formal methods, understanding what problems students actually confront and devising teaching methods and tools to address those.

Shriram Krishnamurthi

Formal methods are unavoidable when concurrency is at stake, but they often face the complexity wall of state-space explosion. I am confident that such limits can ultimately be overcome by using well-defined concurrent languages, together with compositional verification techniques based on divide-and-conquer approaches exploiting property-preserving reductions. To this aim, I contribute to the design and implementation of LNT, a next-generation language combining the best traits of imperative languages, functional languages, and process calculi. I am also advancing the effectiveness and user-friendliness of compositional verification, whose implementation in the CADP toolbox successfully tackled all the CTL and LTL parallel problems proposed at the RERS 2019 competition.

Frédéric Lang

Industrial impact requires an evolution of both their methods and our tools, potentially in several iterations of collaboration with academia. Formal methods tools must fit development methodology applied by industry, and it may be necessary to create domain specific formalisms for maximal impact. Sustained industrial use needs repeated committed collaboration. For increased impact it is important that more academic tools become available on commercial terms from spin-out companies. As a next important step I envisage that synthesis of correct-by-construction control components of critical systems will disrupt the way that such systems are currently constructed. The complexity of such synthesis may even benefit from the use of machine-learning techniques.

Kim G. Larsen

Personally, I think that the main challenge for the industrial application of formal methods at large is that 1) it generally requires highly skilled formal methods champions, 2) it takes too long to produce and analyse formal models and 3) the formal methods tools are much less user friendly than conventional programming language tools. In my own research, I also target the 2nd and 3rd of these, trying to combine such formal methods models based on discrete mathematics with models from different kinds of mathematics, for example representing physical elements in cyber-physical systems (for example in a digital twin context). I see many future possibilities for using formal approaches in this context in the future.

Peter Gorm Larsen

The main challenge is to ensure that systems, whether legacy, current or under design, meet their requirements by modelling the reasoning explaining why they are/were designed that way. This approach is universal, allows to capitalize knowledge and to improve (safety/security) when reusing/modifying/improving, by keeping track of the design decisions. This is particularly important for the (critical) infrastructures that are expected to survive decades—especially when their designers left or retired. Formal proofs of correct interoperability and correct design have been performed over the last 5 years on real railway systems under exploitation, with quite a number of safety-related findings. Other domains would benefit from this approach.

Thierry Lecomte

The key challenge is understanding the role of formal methods in engineering. It is not, as is often stated, to prove a system correct. Formal proofs are statements about relationships between models, not statements about some physical-world realization of a system. And, as George Box famously said, "all models are wrong, but some are useful". What makes a model useful? To a scientist, a model is useful if it reasonably accurately describes some physical-world system. To an engineer, however, a model is useful when a useful physical-world system can be constructed that reasonably accurately behaves like the model. From the engineering perspective, all physical-world systems are wrong, but some are useful. Formal methods shine when they make statements about models that are accurately emulated by useful physical-world systems.

Edward A. Lee

Formal methods have reached a milestone in the last 15 years: the formal verification of functional correctness (not just safety) for the actual source code (not just models) of general-purpose, reusable systems software, such as the seL4 microkernel, the FSCQ and BilbyFS file systems, the miTLS secure communication library, and the CompCert and CakeML compilers. Much future work remains to verify infrastructure software. One challenge is to convince industry to pick up the effort, which goes beyond what academics can do. Another challenge is to better integrate specification and proof with programming, preferably at the level of programming languages and tools. Finally, it may be time to re-think priorities in formal methods research, with less emphasis on abstraction and automation and more emphasis on compositionality and reuse of verifications.

Xavier Leroy

Formal methods are the key to building dependable systems, but formal methods are mainly used in domains like cryptocurrencies, avionics or railways. Why are formal methods not used more often? In my opinion, their use is often not cost-effective. Potential software failures can typically be mitigated by simple updates without spending the extra effort for using formal methods. But when financial loss is huge or when faulty software threatens life, the situation is different. Does this mean formal methods cannot be applied in the majority of software system projects? In my opinion, no. But we have to make their application more cost-effective, i.e. cheaper. Formal methods research has mostly concentrated on developing new methods. Now that we have a variety of powerful methods and tools, research should rather focus on methodology, on applicability in the software engineering process, and on education of software engineers.

Martin Leucker

Formal models can help understanding critical systems and mastering their complexity. One challenge is helping humans understand the formal models better, e.g., by visualizations, interactions or automated extraction of knowledge. This is of particular importance for domain experts, who may not be familiar with the particular formal notations and concepts being used. If successful, formal models can play the role of interactive requirement or specification documents. Another challenge is to put formal models into the loop at runtime. This allows to use formal models embedded in a real-life system, either as a demonstrator or for test and certification purposes. This could also pave the way for more intelligent systems making predictions based on the formal models.

Michael Leuschel

When I was a graduate student I spotted a deadlock. The program was taken from a book ("books never lie!", I thought) and the deadlock was hard to reproduce. I spent days figuring out how all those threads could get stuck, up to the point I was able to convince my course mates and my teacher that the book was wrong. A few months later I met the SPIN model checker; I was able to find the deadlock in milliseconds! I was so excited that I decided to use SPIN for my Ph.D. and shortly after that I was having fun spotting bugs with AI algorithms (and earning a Ph.D. for it). Now that we talk about programming everything (including life!), we need new generations of students excited about novel ways to apply and extend formal methods. Life can't get stuck!

Alberto Lluch Lafuente

Formal methods, to me, is a very broad term: any technique that provides a logical and computational lens to the study of systems falls within its purview. Thus, it is difficult to summarize all the challenges in the field. I shall thus confine myself to one challenge: a better understanding of temporal behavior of continuous-state, continuous-time dynamical systems. Dynamical systems arise naturally when we study computational systems interacting with the physical world. My current research focuses on the application of formal methods principles, such as abstraction and composition, and tools, such as logics and automata, to the analysis of dynamical systems. I believe these principles and tools will be crucial to building high-confidence, autonomous, cyber-physical systems.

Rupak Majumdar

Beating the same path, trying to push complicated methods and manual approaches, is not likely to lead to fundamentally different results. The significant paradigm change that uses formal methods to power a transformational change is to start using models and DSLs instead of programs; properties and property analysers (even general purpose model checkers) instead of testing; and code generation (through certified or verified compilers) to generate correct by construction and optimised code that nobody needs to "maintain" anymore. If something changes, the action is on the models, the properties or the generation toolchain, and a new generation and deployment occur. See tools like CINCO, DIME and earlier jABC. This makes the effect of programming available to the masses, bypassing legions of handcoders and eliminating costly code maintenance.

Tiziana Margaria

I believe that formal methods will become an essential piece in the design process of industrial systems. But, for this to happen, it is crucial to increase the scalability of analyses by designing better algorithms and tools, and to devise user-friendly formalisms, which are easier to learn and use. My current efforts towards these goals are focused on the extension of MCL, a temporal specification language for concurrent, value-passing, and probabilistic systems, together with the design of model-checking algorithms for MCL, which are made available as part of the CADP toolbox and used in many industrial applications. I also believe that greater efforts are needed to instill a "formal methods culture" to university students, especially in courses on software engineering, distributed systems, and hardware design.

Radu Mateescu

Formal methods have a long record of success in terms of algorithms, academic papers and tools, and relevant applications. This research community also contributed to other areas where concurrency and real-time are critical aspects. However, such level of maturity in research in the last 40 years did not impact as expected mainstream tools and practices to develop software. The use of rigorous methods for design and testing software is still rare. In my opinion, expanding the use of formal methods and tools to capitalize on the huge knowledge is not a role for the research community. Expanding software skills is for universities updating their bachelor degrees, and for companies creating the software development kits. Teaching formal methods only at master's and doctoral level for years gives the wrong impression that only few selected people will be ready to use them and they will never become general software engineering tools. Are we are still on time?

Pedro Merino

Handling formally the domain knowledge in design models is a challenge in system and software engineering. Domain knowledge is mainly related to the domain expert and the system under construction is in fact manipulating concepts that are valid according to knowledge. When developing justifications in the proof process, one can request knowledge that is known only by the expert. A formal and effective link should be defined between formal methods and knowledge-based techniques. Currently we are considering the definition of reusable mathematical theories for HMI or CPS. Moreover, we develop specific lectures for training master students using effective formal techniques together with case studies borrowed from our past and current scientific projects, while focusing on domain engineering.

Dominique Méry

In my opinion, research in formal methods focuses too much on methods and notations. I believe that the main benefit comes from clearly documenting algorithms and designs at a suitable level of abstraction, above the code level. The skills of mathematical thinking and rigorous reasoning are important: notation and support tools should help express and analyze/verify precise specifications in a way that corresponds to the problem rather than forcing users to shoehorn their thinking into a narrow formalism. An important challenge for researchers in formal methods is to provide useful and highly automated feedback for expressive formalisms.

Stephan Merz

Future developments in formal methods should broaden its impact. Rather than focusing mostly on verification, they should support system design, validation, evolution and maintenance from the earliest stages. For this, use of executable formal specifications for fast system modeling and analysis before implementation are crucial. In my own experience, formal executable languages like Maude have shown how this can be done for designing new web browsers, new cloud storage systems, correct-by-construction distributed real-time systems, or for fully specifying languages like Java or C. This supports what I call the "system specification" part, which is already scalable. The "property verification" part supports formal verification of properties specified in the logics of theorem provers and model checkers. Increasing verification's scalability is a key challenge ahead.

José Meseguer

Today formal methods consist largely of algorithms and tools for the automated analysis of system and software models. Many such tools are incorporated in software development environments for "behind the scenes" analysis and are routinely used with great success. Unfortunately, these applications are often given new names, probably to avoid the perception that formal methods are difficult to use. Formal verification tools have recently been used to verify important safety properties of models used to generate code for critical systems. While failure of these systems can expose a company to crippling liabilities, formal verification is still not seen as a valuable complement to testing. Since bottom-up technology transfer is not working, emphasis needs to be put on convincing senior management to make the use of formal verification a priority.

Steve Miller

As the co-founder of the startup TrustInSoft, I am developing formal-methods-based tools for the software industry. These tools perform advanced static source-code analysis, with comprehensive mathematical analyses that formally guarantee the absence of complete families of software flaws. Thus, our users know exactly in which conditions their software can be trusted. The main breakthrough of our approach is: "be modest with formal methods". We train our users to gain trust incrementally, on limited parts of their software first, but with a very precise plan to reach, depending on their time constraints, the largest possible perimeter of trust. This is the only path to success in commercializing formal methods: adapt the tools to non-specialists and fit within the time constraints of the industry.

Benjamin Monate

My research has focused on automated tools that do not require formal method expertise from end users, though designing and implementing these tools requires that expertise. I worked on the Astrée static analyzer: though it helps if the end user understands invariants, no advanced abstract interpretation expertise is needed. I am now working on improving the CompCert formally certified compiler with optimizations. Certified high-level synthesis tools are promising: the user specifies the design in a suitable high-level language, and target code is generated by formally proved compilation or optimization phases. This could be much safer and less human-intensive than the manual approaches still commonly used. One could for instance wish to synthesize concurrent communication structures automatically.

David Monniaux

Let's identify an important subset of formal methods...and stop calling it formal methods. Teach it early, between "programming introduction" (for all) and "harder-core" formal methods (for eventual specialists only). Start it with assertion-labelled flowcharts (Floyd style); call assertions "comments"; and name it "programming continuing". Teaching that would improve significantly the quality of the IT industry at its intermediate levels, where most programmers work and which affects our everyday lives so much. I teach such "(in)-formal methods" at roughly second-year level (6 times now); and the course has been picked up by other institutions. Lessons from where that has worked, and the effect it has had, and how it could be improved: they are concrete things that could be passed on.

Carroll Morgan

We have witnessed some very successful applications of formal methods in a number of different fields and industrial sectors; these include applications in medical and healthcare devices, and railway and automotive industry. We must recognise and celebrate these success stories, but also draw some conclusions from our failures. In my opinion, some of our failures were due to our obsession with developing sophisticated linguistic constructs, rather than focussing on usability and scalability of verification techniques for those aspects that the domain experts deem most relevant. To replicate and amplify the success stories of formal methods, we need industrial-strength tools and integration of various verification techniques with a focus on usability and scalability. We should be ready to embrace scalable and possibly non-exhaustive formal verification methods to deal with the heterogeneous complex systems of the future.

Mohammad Reza Mousavi

A growing number of companies is looking for formal methods to adopt in order to develop safe and secure software systems. Thankfully, many automated reasoning tools and analysis platforms are now available to all as open source projects. For program proof, the future is bright. Industrial tools for program proof should consider partial verification as the norm, allowing for different levels of assurance; strive to include executable specifications in the programming language as some form of contracts; distinguish specification-only and verification-only code, also known as ghost code; and consider manual proof as a programming activity in the auto-active style of manual proof. Rustan Leino once said: "Program verification is unusable. But perhaps not useless". Program verification will remain hard. But definitely useful.

Yannick Moy

It is disappointing that computer science and cyber security have taken over the language of biology—in particular the word "virus"—to indicate malign agents. In biology researchers are struggling to understand how building blocks operate and to deal with the complexities of scale. In computer science and (largely) cyber security we do understand how building blocks operate and are at most left with the complexities of scale. The use of terms from biology to discuss the vulnerabilities of IT systems risks putting expectations too low—to the extent that managers and policy makers remain unaware of what formal methods (full blown or "light weight") might achieve. If the language of biology cannot be avoided, formal methods should perhaps be explained as a "vaccine" deployed during software development.

Flemming Nielson

I see the next challenge for formal methods as the modelling and verification of autonomous systems. The challenges include dealing with the autonomy, learning and adaptation present in such systems, as well the fact that they do not operate in isolation and often in unknown environments with human interaction. My current work is focused on formal models for stochastic games. Such games combine nondeterminism, representing the adversarial, cooperative and competitive choices, stochasticity, modelling uncertainty, and concurrency, representing simultaneous execution of interacting agents. This research is still in its early stages, but a critical direction to carry forward is model partial observability.

Gethin Norman

We need to build formal methods tools that can scale and are accessible to non-experts. Among such tools are model checkers and theorem provers. Almost all model checkers available do not scale very well. Theorem provers have several tasks left for humans, such as lemma conjecture. It is hard for non-experts to construct proof scripts for theorem provers. We have been working on some techniques that may make model checking scale better and building a tool that supports the technique. We also have been working on a flexible way to construct proofs and building a tool that produces proof scripts from such proofs and scales well. I would like to pass on my experiences of case studies on formal methods and my knowledge accumulated through the experiences to younger generations.

Kazuhiro Ogata

No mature technology has ever dispensed with a formal basis in its evolution. The founding fathers of software engineering very early emphasized the need for software to be based on theoretical foundations playing a role similar to those of other established branches of engineering (Garmisch NATO conference, 1968). Fifty years are, at best, 'childhood' in the life of any technological field. Wait and see what comes with 'adulthood'. With software taking over all fields of (what used to be) human activity, the challenges are enormous. Insecurity, risk of malfunction/failure in increasingly complex systems will reach unprecedented levels, opening up a great opportunity for formal methods.

José Oliveira

Time is ripe for formal methods in mainstream software development, since: the "winner-takes-all" nature of the software industry justifies up-front investment into system quality; industry is realizing that standard validation techniques are insufficient; and industrial success stories on using formal methods are emerging (e.g., at Amazon). Achieving this goal requires modeling languages and analysis methods that scale to today's systems, and developers who appreciate formal methods. I try to contribute to this goal by: (i) developing simple and intuitive modeling languages for complex real-time and cyber-physical systems (using Maude and AADL); (ii) developing complexity-reducing formal patterns where verifying a CPS is reduced to simpler problems; and (iii) writing an introductory formal methods textbook and teaching a second-year formal methods course with 50 students.

Peter Csaba Ölveczky

Application of formal methods to learning-enabled systems, i.e. systems that use machine learning (neural networks) is a big challenge due to the approximate nature of machine-learning algorithms. It is difficult to write formal specifications for such systems. Perhaps probabilistic properties can be written but there is very little work in that direction. I am personally working on property inference and also probabilistic analysis of neural networks, that will hopefully address some of these challenges.

Corina Pasareanu

We need to focus on performing simple verification tasks: integrate (even hide!) backend light formal methods in graphical tools (in Bell Labs, we had such a success with analyzing message sequence charts), monitor executions to perform run-time verification, allow lightweight automatic verification tasks that can be run by programmers or engineers during system development; such tasks should be performed automatically in the background, or as a simple extension to hardware or software development tools. I am currently concentrating on run-time verification, developing algorithms and tools that are immediately applicable for system development. I also worked on making model checking more efficient (e.g. partial order reduction and LTL translation) and integrated it in automatic genetic synthesis of code from specification.

Doron Peled

Formal methods have enjoyed many areas with successes. But it is still difficult to use them to get a real system safe. Admittedly, getting real systems working, let alone safe, is exceedingly difficult and time-consuming, no matter what approach is used. Formal methods have an opportunity to help with this challenge, however, but only if they broaden their scope to cover full systems.

Resting on the logical foundations of cyber-physical systems, my research is pursuing this question in multiple complementary ways: 1) Forming logical links between models and reality with ModelPlex; 2) Verified compilation to executables that inherit safety theorems from verified models; 3) Formally supported development processes for incremental development that benefit from formal results about prior designs.

André Platzer

The challenge of FMs as a science is to contribute to a fundamental question: How can one use computers not only to solve a problem (say, autonomous driving) but also to build the solution to the problem. The problem may be complex, but building the solution is an even more complex problem. A science is a language, and the challenge lies in finding the language that allows us to translate aspects of practical issues into concrete research questions. Until now, the lingua franca in FMs has been logic; what is the language for the kind of systems we will have to deal with in the future? FMs is an attractive research area since it offers many variations of self-reflection, a theme dear to computer scientists from the very beginning. A typical example is the question whether the requirements on a system are correct. What are the requirements for system requirements, and how can we check them? What are the requirements on a system, say, for autonomous driving?

Andreas Podelski

Rather than coming up with more powerful formalisms and better tools, one of the biggest challenges—and opportunities—in formal methods is still to get very basic formal notions into the minds of our students, so that it becomes natural for them to tackle problems thinking in concepts such as finite state machines and grammars, or in terms of object invariants and types when coding. The bulk of all security problems is due to hand-written parsers of overly complex and poorly specified input formats and protocols, in long prose documents with odd, informal diagrams. This is downright embarrassing, given that formal languages and parser generation are some of the oldest formal methods around. This is something I hope to improve as part of the LangSec community.

Erik Poll

Computer systems have become pervasive in all walks of our lives. Formal methods have contributed to both foundational understanding and construction of tools for practical analysis and validation of computer systems. While we should continue to be critical of how we frame problems and introspect about the impact we are having, we should also be happy that formal methods researchers have won Turing awards, and every major SW and HW company has groups developing, building, and deploying tools based on formal methods. Looking to the future, systems are getting larger and more complex and diverse. We have systems driven by AI and ML in their core, cyber-physical systems, and autonomous systems, and will have quantum and biological computers. We should continue work in foundational understanding of such systems, develop tools and techniques that work at industrial scale, and constantly strive to close the gap between theory and practice.

Sriram Rajamani

The foremost challenge for formal methods remains to demonstrate their applicability in industry. The second challenge for formal methods is to educate students. Yet the standard computer science graduate leaves the university with either no knowledge of formal methods or, even worse, a hatred for them. The third challenge for formal methods is to find ways of combining them with ML and AI techniques. With companies, I work on applying formal methods to their challenges. With colleagues, I have written a book "Formal Methods for Software Engineering", I have organised the "1st International Workshop on Formal Methods—Fun for Everybody". I am collaborating with colleagues from the ML/AI community. I would very much hope all three of my contributions would be picked up ☺

Markus Roggenbach

Formal methods, despite the significant progress in recent years, are still not yet readily available to average engineers. I believe that the main challenges are: the creation of robust, open and usable infrastructures for research and industrial application; the design of a standard formalism to exchange benchmarks and models; and the creation of adequate and attractive teaching material. Finally, widen the application to emerging areas (e.g. trustworthy AI). My main contribution was taking an active part in the development of the NuSMV open source model checker. NuSMV and its derivatives have been integrated in several commercial and academic verification tools, and are used in other domains (AI planning) as a reasoning framework. Finally, it is widely used as a teaching tool in several formal methods courses at different levels.

Marco Roveri

The next frontier in formal methods is to make them *usable* and *practical*. Our main challenge is still the specification bottleneck: formal methods are highly dependent on specifications. We must know where we get specifications from, how we measure their quality, and how we best organize and maintain them. If we support non-experts to semi-automatically extract unambiguous, analyzable specifications, then formal methods are *usable*. Formal methods must also be *practical*: such as reasoning under constraints on time, memory, knowledge, and other resources. How do we create living, changing, hierarchical models and specifications that tie formal verification to the real system, at different levels of abstraction, throughout its lifecycle? How do we build formal verification into systems, and build formal verification tools so they become one with the systems they are meant to specify, validate, and verify?

Kristin Yvonne Rozier

Formal methods allow us to calculate properties of computational systems, just as computational fluid dynamics allow us to calculate the flow of air over a wing. The challenge is, and always has been, to automate this efficiently. With modern SMT solvers that can deal with quantified formulas, nonlinear arithmetic, and complex data types, we are almost there.

The next challenge is effective use of these capabilities and here I see two big opportunities. First is to embed them, invisibly, inside every tool for software, hardware, and system development with a view to improving their fault detection and, consequently, their productivity and the quality of the artifacts produced. Second is to find contributions to the predictability and safety of modern autonomous systems largely driven by machine learning and AI.

John Rushby

Formal methods are the only way to develop high-quality software and hardware. There are still difficult problems to be tackled: performance, scalability, usability, etc. The main challenge, in my opinion, is to make these methods become mainstream. To this aim, I have been working with companies (Naver, Nokia, and Orange) to show how such methods could be used to solve industrial problems. I have been developing tools supporting the development and verification of component-based software, business processes, and IoT applications, where formal methods are hidden within software development platforms. Such press-button approaches are a promising solution, which allows formal methods to be used by anyone without requiring a high level of expertise.

Gwen Salaün

The advancement of modern formal methods and their successful industrial applications have been a consequence of some key factors: automation, continuous education, the "hidden formal methods" approaches, and integration with other areas like natural language processing, (semi-formal) graphical notations and system testing. There are several challenges for an even more significant industrial insertion; I single out scalability as a major concern. My research focus has been on compositional analysis in the context of model checking, and industrial applications of formal strategies for test case generation from natural-language requirements, in a partnership with Motorola/Lenovo and Embraer. More recently, I have been exploring formal modelling, simulation and analysis of autonomous systems.

Augusto Sampaio

The challenge for formal methods is to be integrated in system design flows to enhance their rigorousness. The objective is to break with the promise of "absolute correctness" and focus on understanding and accountability. Design flows should be model-based, to allow semantic coherency achieved by translation into a single host language. Additionally, they should be component-based, meaning that they rely on a common and general component model and theory for building systems bottom-up from components. The third requirement is correctness by construction, achieved by property-preserving source-to-source transformations and extensive use of architecture patterns. I have played a leading role in the BIP project of Verimag. My efforts focus on the design of dynamic reconfigurable systems, autonomous systems in particular.

Joseph Sifakis

Some of the future challenges for formal methods include verification of algorithms and systems developed for quantum computers which is a long term challenge, verification of systems developed using artificial intelligence such as autonomous vehicles and verification of applications in security and privacy. I am currently working on—(i) automated methods for verifying privacy and accuracy properties of differential privacy mechanisms, (ii) verifying properties of autonomous vehicles controlled by AI techniques. For verifying differential privacy mechanisms the challenges include wider applicability, speed of verification as well as handling inputs of all sizes. For autonomous vehicles, we are exploring run-time verification of safety properties. Here the challenges include handling deep neural networks and modeling the environment.

A. Prasad Sistla

We have to move from thinking in terms of individual methods and tools to thinking in terms of adequacy for solution: which methods fit where and under which paradigm? CINCO, our meta-tooling suite, has morphed into a DSL-driven correctness-by-construction environment in this way, where language design has become a prime means for guaranteeing system correctness. The corresponding rich meta models require strong formal methods-based support for static semantics checking. Required analysis tools are in turn built automatically within our environment, establishing a bootstrapping-based continuous improvement cycle. Our experience suggests that this way of DSL-driven development may well become a popular new style of system development.

Bernhard Steffen

I'm quite optimistic about formal methods: type checking is now standard, model checking is heavily used in hardware verification, model-based testing is daily practice, and Simulink, UML and SysML are rooted in formal methods. To achieve ambitious goals, we should get really serious about software tools: there are far too many tools. Rather than everyone working on her own research prototype, we should, as a community, work on joint tools. On tools that have impact. On tools that come with excellent GUIs and visualization features. On tools that have decent user manuals, training sessions and even customer support. We should not wait for a start-up company to commercialize one of the research prototypes. No, if we really want formal methods to have impact, we must change the way we handle tool development. This requires communication, coordination and courage, but that is what science needs.

Marielle Stoelinga

I believe formal methods are most useful as a mindset, i.e., a systematic, rigorous way of approaching and solving problems. Being trained in formal methods, I often find it easier to see what a problem really is, how to generalize it and how to approach it. My students on the contrary can't seem to differentiate the problem/concept from the implementation. The challenge is thus to install the mindset of formal methods early in the mind of the students. Beyond working as a mindset, formal methods tools and techniques apply only if the return (in terms of improved safety and security) outweighs the cost of applying formal methods. It thus implies that all we have to do is to drive down the cost and demonstrate the return on real-world systems.

Jun Sun

Based on my decades-long experience, I think that one of the most serious impediments to the adoption of formal methods in industry is a generalized lack of education and training in formal specification and reasoning, especially in the US. Few companies employ computer scientists and engineers who have a working knowledge of logic beyond propositional logic. This usually makes it hard to even convey what a formal methods tool can offer, let alone how to use it. I am convinced that to go from its current technical successes to a wide adoption of formal methods, the formal methods community needs a concerted and sustained effort aimed at making the teaching of logic and formal specification an integral part of computer science and engineering curricula. Until then, we are condemned to developing wondrous tools that the majority of our intended user base will not be able to use.

Cesare Tinelli

During my last visit to Oded Maler, in Oct. 2017, he was even more philosophical than usual. Maybe he knew he would not live much longer (he passed away on Sept. 3, 2018). To create industrial impact, Oded argued, we need to come up with *simple ideas*. Most of the research in the formal methods community is just way too complex. He mentioned his work on verification and synthesis of timed/hybrid systems. Mathematically appealing, but with limited practical impact due to the decision algorithms' complexity. In contrast, Oded argued, his results on signal temporal logic are mathematically trivial, but the industrial impact is the highest from all his work. Of course, it is not always clear what simple means: while the functionality of SAT solvers is simple, sophisticated algorithms are used underneath. Still, there is much wisdom in Oded's words, and I use them to guide my research.

Frits Vaandrager

Systems should do the right things and do them right. Much of the work goes into finding out and understanding what are the right things. It requires understanding user needs and their consequences much better than how users express them. Computers obey instructions precisely, no matter how stupid the outcome is from the human point of view. To prevent stupid outcomes, software professionals must understand both the computers' and the end users' worlds, and build a bridge between them. Formal methods can be a good tool here. However, good analysis and reasoning skills in the informal side are a must. Unfortunately, teaching thinking is difficult. Software education seems to more and more focus on blind use of ready-made components and prescribed methods. I find it worrying.

Antti Valmari

Formal methods offer a promising path towards building reliable systems; there exist numerous examples that highlight the benefits. From my own personal experience at ESA (European Space Agency), the main obstacle to the widespread adoption of formal methods is that they tend to address limited aspects of the design space, using notations that require expert knowledge, which imposes significant upfront investment. Industrial users often perceive the proliferation of notations as a risk. The integration of formal and informal techniques, and their embedding in process standards, is crucial for successful industrial adoption; it would help if scientists spent time in an engineering setting to understand these challenges. To capitalise on the positive impact that formal methods have had in niche applications to date, industry requires long-term support for professional formal tools, with stability and performance guarantees.

Marcel Verhoef

In my opinion, formal methods will become essential to successfully handle the ever increasing complexity of software systems, their design, construction and maintenance, at a much larger scale than they are now. However, it is not only academia that will make the spread of application of formal methods happen. Also industry will foster the uptake of formal methods as soon as this will be economically beneficial and I expect that it will. Therefore, academia should focus on its own agenda, of course keeping in touch with developments elsewhere. Top priorities are the development of a theory of formal methods, encompassing and integrating the myriad of approaches, and the building of a community or a society of researchers and practitioners that goes beyond scattered conferences and journal publications.

Erik de Vink

I see two primary challenges for formal methods over the next years. 1) Be able to document requirements specifications formally so that all stakeholders can be involved and understand the specification, and also then use that to improve validation of requirements. 2) Use formal methods to produce effective and fully integrated model-based engineering tool chains, that help us build complex systems and also assure properties of those systems with a high enough degree of confidence. Currently assurance and development are not integrated well enough. They will have to be in order for us to produce safe, secure and dependable complex systems. Our group is working on modeling this integration.

Alan Wassyng

Among all the challenges for formal methods, the analysis for worst-case execution time (WCET) is a very difficult one, which must be performed on executable code, as instruction semantics, memory allocation, machine-register use, and compiler optimizations heavily influence the execution times. This analysis must search for the longest path in an enormous space of combined program paths and architectural paths. Thus, sound WCET analysis is only feasible through appropriate abstraction of the execution platform. We used Abstract Interpretation to obtain a reliable, precise, and scalable analysis method, which was implemented by the spin-off company AbsInt and instantiated for many architectures. The resulting tools are the only ones widely used in industry, and are validated by EASA (European Aviation Safety Agency) for time-critical tasks in several Airbus plane generations [21].

Reinhard Wilhelm

Scalability and usability of model checking and model-based testing remain major challenges in formal methods, and, in particular, in their adoption in practice. While breakthroughs in the past (e.g. symbolic methods) have paved the way to analyse systems of immense complexity, there is a huge gap between our academic languages and solutions, and the languages used in industry, offering fancy data types, language constructs, etc. Bridging this gap is among the most important challenges in formal methods research. Through case studies, I identify weaknesses and strengths in our academic solutions, often in the context of our mCRL2 tool set, and also expose situations when this gap is minimal. I believe research into languages, (fixpoint) logics and game theory are needed to narrow this gap.

Tim Willemse

Trustworthy AI: We are seeing an astounding growth in deployment of AI systems in critical domains such as autonomous vehicles, criminal justice, healthcare, and public safety, where decisions taken by AI agents directly impact human lives. Can these decisions be trusted to be correct, reliable, fair, and safe, especially under adversarial attacks? Just as for trustworthy computing, formal methods could be an effective approach for building trust in AI-based systems. However, we need to extend the set of trust properties to include fairness, robustness, probabilistic accuracy under uncertainty, and other properties yet to be identified. Further, we need new specification and verification techniques to handle new kinds of artifacts, e.g., data distributions and machine-learning models.

Jeannette M. Wing

Formal methods are a cornerstone of computer science. They form the scientific basis for the design, validation and verification of software systems. Formal methods have been, are and will continue to be the starting point for many successful companies. Artificial intelligence and novel computing paradigms such as quantum and molecular computing are the next challenges for formal methods. How can we make AI systems safe and secure? How can we build reliable mixed systems that combine quantum and molecular components with conventional hardware and software?

Currently, I am working on safe machine-learning algorithms and how to integrate them into a rigorous development process for collective adaptive systems. But there are many other pressing research questions for formal methods. May formal methods live and prosper!

Martin Wirsing

Today, the functionality as well as economical value of most industrial systems and products, such as cars, airplanes, and medical devices, is defined and realized by software as embedded system. The ability to deploy software updates dynamically is critical for security, new features, and customization of next-generation embedded systems. But such deployments are not possible today because we lack the techniques to guarantee that the updated system remains safe. In 2019, I received an ERC advanced grant for the CUSTOMER project (Customizable Embedded Real-Time Systems). The mission of CUSTOMER is to develop a new paradigm supported by powerful model-based tools for building embedded systems which can be updated on demand dynamically, safely, and securely over their operational life-time.

Wang Yi

I am working on a new model of the domain of networking, called "compositional network architecture," with networking expert Jennifer Rexford at Princeton University [24]. We believe it will have a major long-term impact on education, practice, and especially verification in the field of networking. For education, we are writing a textbook based on the terminology, patterns, and principles derived from our model. We are also engaged in a research project to embody the model in an implementation, so we can explore model-driven design, development, and verification of networks. The biggest benefit of our model for network practitioners is that it explains layering in a completely new way that is realistic, precise, and offers strong modularity to exploit for reuse and verification.

Pamela Zave

We live in a revolutionized digital era: smartphones, self-driving vehicles and online education turn the planet into a global village. Guaranteeing correctness of such products is a cornerstone for modern society. Formal methods is arguably the most convincing methodology to achieve both performance and dependability; interdisciplinary in nature, it integrates established disciplines like control theory and language processing and promising new directions like machine learning and quantum computing. I am contributing to developing tools for learning models and verifying probabilistic systems, and I am excited to witness the birth of new fundamental theories and advanced tools. Formal methods still have a long way to be standardized in industry, familiarized in universities and popularized in society: this will happen and needs the efforts of us all. Long live formal methods, congratulations to FMICS 25th anniversary and looking forward to the next 25 years!

Lijun Zhang

Acknowledgements. We heartily thank all our colleagues who participated in the survey. This includes all those whose position statement appears in Sect. 9. Thanks also are due to those experts who took the time to answer our questionnaire, but did not provide a position statement, namely Bernhard Aichernig, Roderick Bloem, Arne Borälv, Rocco De Nicola, Cindy Eisner, Dimitra Giannakopoulou, Georges Gonthier, Susanne Graf, Aarti Gupta, Thomas Henzinger, Holger Hermanns, Michael Hinchey, César Muñoz, Tobias Nipkow, Joël Ouaknine, Charles Pecheur, Alastair Reid, Ina Schieferdecker, and Jim Woodcock. Finally, we are grateful to Nicolas Amat, Pierre Bouvier, Alessio Ferrari, Arnd Hartmanns, Ajay Krishna, Rom Langerak, Lina Marsso, Franco Mazzanti, and Wendelin Serwe, who tested four successive beta-versions of our questionnaire and provided us with many wise observations; Pierre Bouvier, Alessio Ferrari, Dejan Ničković, and Wendelin Serwe also proof-checked the author version of the present report.

References

1. AbsInt: Astrée software (2020). http://www.absint.com/astree
2. Bartocci, E., et al.: TOOLympics 2019: an overview of competitions in formal methods. In: Beyer, D., Huisman, M., Kordon, F., Steffen, B. (eds.) TACAS 2019. LNCS, vol. 11429, pp. 3–24. Springer, Cham (2019). https://doi.org/10.1007/978-3-030-17502-3_1
3. Basile, D., et al.: On the industrial uptake of formal methods in the railway domain: a survey with stakeholders. In: Furia, C.A., Winter, K. (eds.) IFM 2018. LNCS, vol. 11023, pp. 20–29. Springer, Cham (2018). https://doi.org/10.1007/978-3-319-98938-9_2
4. ter Beek, M.H., et al.: Adopting formal methods in an industrial setting: the railways case. In: ter Beek, M.H., McIver, A., Oliveira, J.N. (eds.) FM 2019. LNCS, vol. 11800, pp. 762–772. Springer, Cham (2019). https://doi.org/10.1007/978-3-030-30942-8_46
5. Bjørner, D., Havelund, K.: 40 years of formal methods: some obstacles and some possibilities? In: Jones, C., Pihlajasaari, P., Sun, J. (eds.) FM 2014. LNCS, vol. 8442, pp. 42–61. Springer, Cham (2014). https://doi.org/10.1007/978-3-319-06410-9_4
6. Bowen, J.P., Hinchey, M.G.: Ten commandments of formal methods. IEEE Comput. **28**(4), 56–63 (1995). https://doi.org/10.1109/2.375178
7. Cerone, A., et al.: Rooting formal methods within higher education curricula for computer science and software engineering: a white paper. In: Cerone, A., Roggenbach, M. (eds.) FMFun 2019. CCIS, vol. 1301. Springer (2020)
8. Clarke, E.M., Wing, J.M.: Formal methods: state of the art and future directions. ACM Comput. Surv. **28**(4), 626–643 (1996). https://doi.org/10.1145/242223.242257
9. Davis, J.A., et al.: Study on the barriers to the industrial adoption of formal methods. In: Pecheur, C., Dierkes, M. (eds.) FMICS 2013. LNCS, vol. 8187, pp. 63–77. Springer, Heidelberg (2013). https://doi.org/10.1007/978-3-642-41010-9_5
10. Ferrari, A., Mazzanti, F., Basile, D., ter Beek, M.H., Fantechi, A.: Comparing formal tools for system design: a judgment study. In: Proceedings of the 42nd International Conference on Software Engineering (ICSE), pp. 62–74. ACM (2020). https://doi.org/10.1145/3377811.3380373
11. Garavel, H., Graf, S.: Formal methods for safe and secure computer systems. BSI Study 875, Bundesamt für Sicherheit in der Informationstechnik (2013). https://www.bsi.bund.de/DE/Publikationen/Studien/Formal_Methods_Study_875/study_875.html
12. Garavel, H., Mateescu, R.: Reflections on Bernhard Steffen's physics of software tools. In: Margaria, T., Graf, S., Larsen, K.G. (eds.) Models, Mindsets, Meta: The What, the How, and the Why Not?. LNCS, vol. 11200, pp. 186–207. Springer, Cham (2019). https://doi.org/10.1007/978-3-030-22348-9_12

13. Gates, B.: Trustworthy computing, January 2002. https://www.wired.com/2002/01/bill-gates-trustworthy-computing. e-mail memo to Microsoft employees
14. Gnesi, S., Margaria, T. (eds.): Formal Methods for Industrial Critical Systems: A Survey of Applications. Wiley (2013). https://doi.org/10.1002/9781118459898
15. Hall, A.: Seven myths of formal methods. IEEE Softw. **7**(5), 11–19 (1990). https://doi.org/10.1109/52.57887
16. Huisman, M., Gurov, D., Malkis, A.: Formal methods: from academia to industrial practice. A travel guide. CoRR abs/2002.07279 (2020). https://arxiv.org/abs/2002.07279
17. Jones, C.B., Thomas, M.: The development and deployment of formal methods in the UK. CoRR abs/2006.06327 (2020). https://arxiv.org/abs/2006.06327. Submitted to IEEE Ann. Hist. Comput.
18. Miller, S.P.: Lessons from twenty years of industrial formal methods. In: Proceedings of the 20th High Confidence Software and Systems Conference (HCSS 2012) (2012). http://cps-vo.org/node/3434
19. Rushby, J.: Formal methods and the certification of critical systems. Technical report SRI-CSL-93-7, Computer Science Laboratory, SRI International, December 1993. http://www.csl.sri.com/papers/csl-93-7/. Also issued under the title "Formal Methods and Digital Systems Validation for Airborne Systems" as NASA Contractor Report 4551, December 1993
20. Steffen, B.: The physics of software tools: SWOT analysis and vision. Int. J. Softw. Tools Technol. Transfer. **19**(1), 1–7 (2017). https://doi.org/10.1007/s10009-016-0446-x
21. Wilhelm, R.: Real time spent on real time. Commun. ACM (2020, to appear)
22. Wing, J.M.: A specifier's introduction to formal methods. IEEE Comput. **23**(9), 8–22 (1990). https://doi.org/10.1109/2.58215
23. Woodcock, J., Larsen, P.G., Bicarregui, J., Fitzgerald, J.: Formal methods: practice and experience. ACM Comput. Surv. **41**(4), 19:1–19:36 (2009). https://doi.org/10.1145/1592434.1592436
24. Zave, P., Rexford, J.: The compositional architecture of the Internet. Commun. ACM **62**(3), 78–87 (2019). https://doi.org/10.1145/3226588

Quantitative Analysis
and Cyber-Physical Systems

Verifiable and Scalable Mission-Plan Synthesis for Autonomous Agents

Rong Gu$^{(\boxtimes)}$, Eduard Enoiu, Cristina Seceleanu, and Kristina Lundqvist

Mälardalen University, Västerås, Sweden
{rong.gu,eduard.enoiu,cristinase.celeanu,kristina.lundqvist}@mdh.se

Abstract. The problem of synthesizing mission plans for multiple autonomous agents, including path planning and task scheduling, is often complex. Employing model checking alone to solve the problem might not be feasible, especially when the number of agents grows or requirements include real-time constraints. In this paper, we propose a novel approach called MCRL that integrates model checking and reinforcement learning to overcome this limitation. Our approach employs timed automata and timed computation tree logic to describe the autonomous agents' behavior and requirements, and trains the model by a reinforcement learning algorithm, namely Q-learning, to populate a table used to restrict the state space of the model. Our method provides means to synthesize mission plans for multi-agent systems whose complexity exceeds the scalability boundaries of exhaustive model checking, but also to analyze and verify synthesized mission plans to ensure given requirements. We evaluate the proposed method on various scenarios involving autonomous agents, as well as present comparisons with two similar approaches, TAMAA and UPPAAL STRATEGO. The evaluation shows that MCRL performs better for a number of agents greater than three.

1 Introduction

Autonomous agents are systems that usually move and operate in a possibly unpredictable environment, can sense and act on it, over time, while pursuing their goals [16]. As this kind of systems bear the promise of increasing people's safety, as well as industrial productivity, by automating repetitive tasks, autonomous technologies are drawing growing attention from both researchers and practitioners. In order to realize their functions, autonomous agents need *mission planning*, including path planning and task scheduling, which is most critical to solve [9]. As path-planning algorithms focus just on calculating collision-free paths towards the destination, they do not cover requirements concerning logical and temporal constraints, e.g., delivering goods in a prioritized order, and within a certain time limit. In addition, when considering a group of agents that need to collaborate with each other and usually work alongside humans, the job of synthesizing correctness-guaranteed mission plans becomes crucial and more difficult.

© Springer Nature Switzerland AG 2020
M. H. ter Beek and D. Ničković (Eds.): FMICS 2020, LNCS 12327, pp. 73–92, 2020.
https://doi.org/10.1007/978-3-030-58298-2_2

In our previous work [17], we have proposed an approach based on Timed Automata (TA) and Timed Computation Tree Logic (TCTL) to formally capture the agents' behavior and requirements, respectively, and synthesize mission plans for autonomous agents, by model checking. Our approach is successfully implemented in a tool called TAMAA, and shown to be applicable to solving the mission-planning problem of industrial autonomous agents. However, TAMAA alone does not scale for a large number of agents, as the state space of the model explodes when the number of agents grows.

The state-space-explosion problem is one of the most stringent issues when employing model checking [10] for verification, therefore many studies have explored ways of fighting it [24]. In this paper, we propose a novel method called **MCRL** that combines model checking with reinforcement learning [25] to restrict the state space, in order to synthesize mission plans for large numbers of agents. Our method is based on UPPAAL [5] and leverages the model of autonomous agents generated by TAMAA. Instead of exhaustively exploring and storing the states of the model, MCRL utilizes random simulations to obtain the execution traces leading to the desired states or deadlocks. Note that in TAMAA timing uncertainties are modeled by non-deterministic delays bounded from below as well as above, rather than by probability distributions. Therefore, the simulation is used just to sample execution traces randomly. Next, a reinforcement learning algorithm, namely Q-learning [27], is employed to process the execution traces, and populate a Q-table containing the state-action pairs and their values. The Q-table is recognized as the mission plan that we aim to synthesize, so we inject it back into the old TAMAA model, forming a new model. As the Q-table regulates the behavior of the agent model, the state space is greatly reduced, which makes it possible to verify mission plans for large numbers of agents. Moreover, MCRL enables the model equipped with Q-tables to make best decisions when the task execution time and duration of movement are uncertain, which is not supported by TAMAA. As MCRL is based on formal modeling, it complements classic reinforcement learning algorithms with means to verify the synthesized mission plans against safety requirements, for instance.

We select relevant scenarios involving autonomous agents in a construction site, and conduct experiments with MCRL, as well as TAMAA, and a similar tool called UPPAAL STRATEGO [13]. The experimental results show that MCRL performs much better than the other two, when the number of agents is greater than three. The time of synthesizing mission plans using MCRL increases linearly with the number of agents, whereas for the other two methods it increases exponentially.

To summarize, the contributions of this paper are:

- A novel approach called MCRL for synthesizing mission plans of large numbers of autonomous agents, by reinforcement learning, combined with verifying the synthesis results by model checking.
- An evaluation of the scalability of MCRL, via experiments conducted with the latter, as well as the TAMAA, and UPPAAL STRATEGO tools, on relevant scenarios involving autonomous agents.

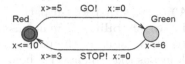

Fig. 1. An example of a timed automaton of a traffic light (Color figure online)

The remainder of the paper is organized as follows. In Sect. 2, we introduce the preliminaries of this paper. Sect. 3 describes the problem that we attempt to solve and its challenges, whereas in Sect. 4, we introduce our approach for taming the scalability of model checking, which combines the latter with reinforcement learning. In Sect. 5, we explain the experiments and their results on TAMAA, UPPAAL STRATEGO, and MCRL, and in Sect. 6 we discuss the open issues of our approach. In Sect. 7, we compare to related work, before concluding the paper in Sect. 8.

2 Preliminaries

In this section, we introduce the background knowledge of this paper.

2.1 Timed Automata and UPPAAL

A *timed automaton* (TA) is a finite-state automaton extended with real-valued variables, called *clocks*, suitable for modeling real-time systems [2]. UPPAAL [5] is a tool for modeling, simulation, and model checking of real-time systems, which uses an extension of TA as the modeling formalism. Figure 1 depicts a simple UPPAAL TA model of a traffic lights example. Two circles labelled Red and Green, called *locations*, model the two colors of the traffic light. A clock variable x that measures the elapse of time is used in the *invariants* (Boolean expressions over clocks) on locations (e.g., x<=10) to enforce an upper bound of delaying in each location, respectively. The directed lines used to connect locations are called *edges*, and can be decorated by *guards*. Guards are Boolean conditions over clocks or discrete variables, and enable traversing the respective edge once they evaluate to true. In UPPAAL, locations denoted by encircled c are called *committed* locations, and require that time does not elapse in those locations and the next edge to be traversed must start from one of them. Clocks can be reset over edges, e.g., x:=0 in Fig. 1, whereas discrete variables can be assigned values, accordingly, via updates on the edges, or via functions that are implemented in the declaration of the TA, by a subset of the C language. A *network* of TA, $B_0 \parallel ... \parallel B_{n-1}$, models a parallel composition of n TA that can synchronize via *synchronization channels* (i.e., a! is synchronized with a? by handshake). In Fig. 1, the edges are labeled with channels named STOP and GO, which synchronize this TA with other TA of the model.

The UPPAAL queries that we verify in this paper are properties of the form: (i) **Invariance**: $A\square p$ means that for all paths, for all states in each path, p is satisfied, (ii) **Liveness**: $A\Diamond p$ means that for all paths, p is satisfied by at least one state in each path, (iii) **Reachability**: $E\Diamond p$ means that there exists a path where p is satisfied by at least one state of the path, and (iv) **Time-bounded Leads to**: $p \rightsquigarrow_{\leq t} q$, which means that whenever p holds, q must hold within at most t time units thereafter; it is equivalent to the property: $A \Box (p \Rightarrow A \Diamond_{\leq t} q)$.

2.2   UPPAAL STRATEGO

UPPAAL STRATEGO [13] is a tool that integrates UPPAAL with two of its branches, i.e., UPPAAL SMC [12] (statistical model checking) and UPPAAL TIGA [4] (policy synthesis for timed games). UPPAAL STRATEGO is designed to synthesize strategies for stochastic priced timed games. A game is a mathematical model of a system consisting of several players that compete in a common environment and aim to achieve their independent goals. Since it is based on UPPAAL, its modeling language is an extension of timed automata, which differentiates actions into two types: controllable and uncontrollable. The former is controlled by the players, whereas the latter is controlled by the environment. We refer readers to the literature [13] for details of this tool.

2.3   Reinforcement Learning

Reinforcement learning is a branch of machine learning aiming to calculate how agents should take actions in an environment, in order to maximize the accumulated reward obtained from the environment [25]. In this paper, we use one of the model-free reinforcement learning algorithms called *Q-learning* [27], which is usually adopted to learn policies that indicate agents what actions to take at different states. A policy is associated with a state-action value function called *Q function*. The optimal Q function satisfies the Bellman optimality equation:

$$q^*(s,a) = \mathbb{E}[R(s,a) + \gamma \max_{a'} q^*(s',a')], \tag{1}$$

where $q^*(s,a)$ represents the expected reward of executing action a at state s, $\mathbb{E}$ denotes the expected value function, $R(s,a)$ is the reward obtained by taking the action a at state s, γ is a discounting value, s' is the new state coming from state s by taking action a, and $\max_{a'} q^*(s',a')$ represents the maximum reward that can be achieved by any possible next state-action pair (s',a'). The equation means that the expected reward of the state-action pair (s,a) is the sum of the current reward and the discounted maximum future reward. As the learning process iterates, the Q-value of each state-action pair converges to the maximum Q-value, i.e., q^*. Although Q-learning is a model-free algorithm, the learning process often relies on a simulation that depends on the form of the model. In this paper, we use the simulation query in UPPAAL to gather the information of state-action pairs, and invoke the Q-learning algorithm to populate a Q-table.

3   Problem Description: An Autonomous Quarry

In this section, we introduce an industrial use case of an autonomous quarry provided by VOLVO CE, to illustrate our research problem. The quarry contains various autonomous vehicles, e.g., trucks, wheel loaders, etc. For instance, as shown in Fig. 2, we consider the mission of transporting stones in a quarry site, where a wheel loader digs and loads stones, and trucks transport stones. They need to first carry the stones from the stone piles to the so-called primary crushers, where stones are crushed into fractions, and then proceed to carry the crushed stones to the secondary crushers, where the destination is. During this process, the vehicles must avoid static obstacles (e.g, holes and rocks on the ground, larger than given sizes) and go to the charging point when their battery level is low. In an autonomous quarry, all the operations are performed automatically, without human intervention, and the vehicles are autonomous agents that we call *agents* for short, in this paper. To achieve their goals, respectively, the agents need to be able to calculate collision-free paths and schedule their tasks efficiently. Hence, our research problem involves task scheduling, path planning and following, and collision avoidance for multiple agents. In our previous work [18], we have proposed a two-layer framework for the design of formal models of agents, where task scheduling and path planning belong to the so-called *static layer*, whereas the path following and avoidance of dynamic obstacles, including the case of overlapping paths of multiple agents, is being dealt with in the *dynamic layer*. In this paper, we focus on the static layer, to synthesize verifiable mission plans, while assuming that the collision avoidance of dynamic obstacles functions correctly.

3.1   Problem Analysis

For simplicity, henceforth, we call the problem of path planning and task scheduling for autonomous agents as *mission planning*. Path planning deals with computing collision-free paths that visit all required target positions (a.k.a. milestones), via efficient algorithms such as Theta* [11] and RRT [20]. We adopt the Theta* algorithm in this paper, since the environment in the problem is a 2-D map, and the algorithm is especially good at generating smooth paths with any-angle turning points in 2-D maps. After the paths are calculated, the

Fig. 2. An example of an autonomous quarry

autonomous agents need to follow the assignment and execution order of tasks. For instance, digging stones must be carried out at stone piles before the stones are unloaded into the primary crushers. In this case, digging stones and unloading stones are two tasks, and their execution places and order must be correct. Additionally, as the agents must guarantee a certain level of productivity, the work has to be completed within some given time. As our solution aims to be general, regardless of the exact type of agents, we formulate the requirements generically, and categorize them as follows:

- *Milestone Matching.* Tasks must be performed at the right milestones.
- *Task Sequencing.* The task execution order must be correct.
- *Timing.* Tasks must be done within a prescribed time limit.
- *Event Reaction.* Some tasks are triggered by events, e.g., when the battery level is low, the agents must go to charge themselves.

The task-scheduling problem in this paper is similar to a classic scheduling problem called the *job-shop* problem [15]. The problem is NP-hard, so even a simple instance with very restrictive constraints remains difficult to solve [1]. Although the task scheduling in this paper shares many similarities with the job-shop problem, e.g., tasks are non preemptive, our problem poses some unique challenges, as described below.

3.2   Uncertainties and Scalability of Mission Planning

The classic job-shop problem is deterministic as the information is known and fixed a priori. However, the task-scheduling problem in this paper contains two types of uncertainties, i.e., the uncertain execution time of tasks and uncertain duration of agent movement.

- *Uncertain execution time of tasks.* The execution time of tasks is modeled by time intervals between the BCET (best-case execution time) and WCET (worst-case execution time), which are usually different.
- *Uncertain movement time.* The traveling time between milestones is not fixed for any agent, due to the fact that the destination milestone can be occupied at some time, and thus the agent that is approaching it has then to wait until the destination is available, and the waiting time is uncertain.

These features make our problem more difficult than the classic job-shop problem. Moreover, when the number of agents increases, the complexity of the problem grows exponentially.

In our previous work [17], we propose a timed-automata-based approach called TAMAA to solve the mission planning problem. On the one hand, although the approach manages to generate mission plans that satisfy complex requirements, and is able to handle up to 100 milestones and tasks, the synthesized mission plans are restricted to the fastest, shortest, or random strategies, as they are the diagnostic traces resulting from the UPPAAL-based verification. In addition, when the number of agents increases to 5, model checking the TAMAA model exhausts the physical memory due to the notorious state-space explosion problem of model checking [10]. On the other hand, a similar existing approach supported by UPPAAL STRATEGO [13] is able to synthesize strategies considering all possible task execution time and movement time. However, UPPAAL STRATEGO is only able to generate results when the number of agents is less than 3 (see Sect. 5), as it depends on UPPAAL TIGA that uses exhaustive model checking. In a nutshell, task scheduling for multiple autonomous agents, as an NP-hard problem, remains unsolved when the number of agents is large.

4   MCRL: Combining Model Checking and Reinforcement Learning in UPPAAL

In this section, we introduce our proposed approach, namely MCRL, for mission planning of multiple autonomous agents, which combines model checking with reinforcement learning to alleviate the state-space-explosion problem. The TA model in MCRL originates from TAMAA, therefore, we first briefly introduce TAMAA to lay the foundation of this method. The formal definitions of the movement and task execution, as well as the model generation algorithms are described in our previous work [17], which readers are referred to for details.

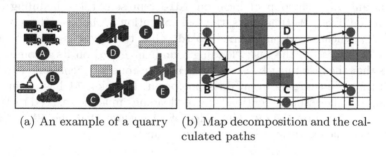

(a) An example of a quarry   (b) Map decomposition and the calculated paths

Fig. 3. An example decomposing a map of a quarry and calculating paths in it

4.1   Timed-Automata-Based Model for Mission-Plan Synthesis

We elaborate the TA model in TAMAA by an example illustrated in Fig. 3(a). In this quarry, there are four autonomous trucks starting from milestone A, which aim to transport stones from milestone B, to the primary crusher at milestone C or D, and eventually go to the secondary crusher at milestone E. There are also autonomous wheel loaders working at milestone B, digging stones and loading them into the trucks. A charging point is located at milestone F, where all the vehicles go for charging when their battery-level is low.

Initially, the environment is decomposed into a Cartesian grid and the Theta* algorithm [11] is executed to calculate the shortest paths among milestones A - F (See Fig. 3(b)). Note that the trucks only need to choose one primary crusher at position C or D, to unload stones. Next, a TA model is automatically generated by TAMAA, based on the decomposed environment. For brevity, in Fig. 4(a), we show a part of the TA model describing the movement of the autonomous trucks between milestones A and B. The outgoing edge from the initial location to location A indicates that the trucks start from milestone A. Locations A2B and B2A are created to measure the duration of traveling between A and B. Variable $TT[m_1][m_2]$ denotes the travelling time between milestones m_1 and m_2. Locations G0 and G1 are used to diverge the movement to multiple targets. Since some of the milestones are exclusive, the guard function occupied is utilized to judge if the milestones are occupied or not. When the function returns *false*, the edge is enabled but not triggered, which means that the agent can stay at this location rather than go to the target. Therefore, the channel go[id] is used to synchronize the transitions in this TA with the task execution TA (Fig. 4(b)) so that the moving actions are triggered periodically. The updating functions move and reach simply change the values of integers representing the agents' positions and the status of the milestones, respectively. The movement to other milestones is modeled in a similar way.

When an agent is at a milestone, it has three options for the next motion: staying, moving, or executing tasks. TAMAA generates tasks execution TA that model these motions. One such TA is partly depicted in Fig. 4(b), where location Idle represents the status of no operation, when the agent is allowed to move. The invariant and self loop of location Idle represent the scheduling of the moving action. Every MW time units, the task execution TA informs the movement TA, via the synchronization channel go[id], that the agent is ready to move. Location T1 represents the task "loading", and the guard on its incoming edge regulates that the task must be carried out at milestone B, when Task 2 finishes, provided that the charging event does not occur. Location T1 has an invariant indicating that the actual execution time of "loading" must not exceed its WCET. Similarly, the guard on the outgoing edge of T1 ensures that the TA leaves the location when the execution time is greater than BCET.

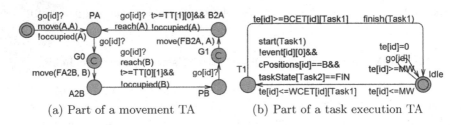

(a) Part of a movement TA   (b) Part of a task execution TA

Fig. 4. The TA models of agent movement and task execution

Besides the TA for movement and task execution, TAMAA also generates monitor TA in order to supervise some time-related variables in the systems, e.g., battery/fuel level. Therefore, for each of the autonomous agents in the environment, three TA are generated by TAMAA. After the resulting TA model is generated and verified in UPPAAL, execution traces indicating the order of visiting milestones and operating tasks are generated. Since UPPAAL provides three types of execution traces, that is, the shortest, the fastest, and random ones, respectively, we can generate mission plans that take the least number of steps (shortest), or the shortest time (fastest), or are random. However, the verification is based on exhaustive model checking, which means that the entire state space is built and stored during the process. The number of states of the model grows exponentially with the number of agents, hence the computation time and memory consumption increase dramatically. In the following, we show how we alleviate this shortcoming, by applying Q-learning and simulation to explore the state space of the TA model.

4.2 MCRL Method Description

Figure 5 depicts the process of MCRL. First, in the *data-gathering* phase, we obtain the execution traces of the model by the simulation function in UPPAAL. We assign rewards to the state-action pairs of the execution traces that satisfy the desired properties, and penalties to the ones containing deadlocks. The traces that neither hold the properties nor contain deadlocks are ignored and not used in the next phase. In the *model-training* phase, we adopt Q-learning to process the traces and populate a Q-table, which is then used to form a new model whose state space is restricted.

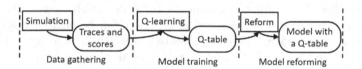

Fig. 5. The process of creating a model using a Q-table

Model Design and Data Gathering. To differentiate between the state of TA and the state of Q-tables, we define a *Q-state* and a *Q-action* as follows:

Definition 1 (Q-state). *A Q-state is defined as the following tuple:*

$$QS = <TP, MATCH>,$$

where TP is a real number denoting the time point of leaving the state, and MATCH is a tuple $<RT, CT, CP, EV, ST>$, where:

- *RT is an integer denoting the number of rounds for finishing all tasks,*
- *CT is an integer denoting the index of the current task,*
- *CP is an integer denoting the index of the current milestone,*

– *EV is a set of Boolean values of events, i.e., occurred or not,*
– *ST is a set of integers of EST (execution statuses of tasks) of all the agents.*

□

Definition 2 (Q-action). *A Q-action is defined as the tuple below:*

$$QA = <BT, WT, MT, TT>,$$

where

– *BT is a real number denoting the BCET of the action,*
– *WT is a real number denoting the WCET of the action,*
– *MT is an integer denoting the type of motion,*
– *TT is an integer denoting the target of the motion.*   □

"*TP*" in Definition 1 is created to distinguish "meaningless" execution traces of agents that simply move around but complete no tasks. The Q-states that have the same values of other attributes but own a much larger value of "*TP*" can be omitted. "*ST*" in Definition 1 represents the execution status of tasks (*EST*), for all agents in the environment. It has three possible values, i.e., 0: unfinished, 1: finished, or 2: will be finished by the time the current agent arrives at the milestones where other agents are located. As each agent owns a Q-table, respectively, when it needs to make a decision of where to go, it must be aware of the *EST* of other agents to avoid unnecessary waiting. "*MT*" in Definition 2 has two possible values, that is, 0: movement, 1: execution. Correspondingly, "*TT*" can be the index of the target milestone, or the index of the next task.

All the attributes of a Q-state and a Q-action can be elicited from the TA model generated by TAMAA, hence, we create a 2-dimensional array in the global declaration of the TA model in UPPAAL to represent the Q-table for each of the agent models. The state-action pairs and their values are calculated and stored in the array during the random simulation. UPPAAL 4.1.22[1] provides a new function of simulation that prints information only when certain predicates are true. For instance, in the query below, the model is simulated for R rounds and T time units in each round. Only when the predicate following the simulation query is true, i.e., the Boolean variable `taskAllFinish` turns true, the information within the curly parentheses ({...}) is printed.

$$\texttt{simulate[<=T; R]\{...\} : taskAllFinish == true} \qquad (2)$$

By using this function, we can control the simulation to print the array of the Q-tables when all tasks are finished (good traces), or any of the agents is stuck in a deadlock (bad traces). At the end of each simulation round, if the predicate is satisfied, rewards (positive values) are assigned to the state-action pairs in the trace by the functions in the TA model; if a deadlock occurs, penalties (negative values) are assigned to them in a similar way. More precisely, the reward has a value of $(T - C)^2$, where T is the entire simulation time as used in Query (2),

---

[1] UPPAAL 4.1.22 was published in March 2019 on http://www.uppaal.org/.

C is the time point of finishing all tasks, whereas penalties have the same fixed value. In this way, the traces that reach the states that satisfy the predicates faster get higher rewards and are thus enhanced by Q-learning.

There are several things about the simulation that deserve further explanation. In UPPAAL, the simulation query subsumes Monte Carlo simulation to simulate the model, which is originally designed for statistical model checking [12]. However, in this paper, we do not adopt this feature of UPPAAL but only utilize the simulation to explore the state space of the model, and the only two uncertainties in the problem, e.g., uncertain task execution time and movement time, are modeled as time-bounded delays that follow a uniform probability distribution. One can change it to an arbitrary choice of time-bounded delays or other probability distribution, and still use MCRL to solve the problem. Additionally, the simulation time of each round should not be shorter than the shortest time needed to finish the entire mission, otherwise the predicate remains false, hence no good trace can be obtained in the simulation. The number of simulation rounds should be set properly so that the gathered data is not only enough for training the model, but also not too large, which would entail unnecessarily long time to process it. When the simulation finishes, the state-action pairs and their values are printed into files, which are parsed and used in the next phase.

Model Training and Reforming. After the state-action pairs are gathered in the simulation, we input these data into the Q-learning algorithm, which is implemented as a Java program, to populate a Q-table. The Q-table is a two-dimensional array of a data structure in the following form:

$$\{AgentID\}|\{Q\text{-}state, Q\text{-}action, Q\text{-}value\},$$

where *Agent ID* is the first dimension of the array, whereas *Q-state*, *Q-action*, and *Q-value* are the elements of the data structure. After running the Q-learning algorithm, the Java program produces C-language code of this array, which is then injected back to the TA model. Equation 1 guarantees that the Q-values of the state-action pairs are accumulated and converged.

In the *model-reforming* phase, a new TA model, which we call *conductor*, is designed for each of the autonomous agents; it looks up the agent's Q-table and sends controlling commands. Since there is no centralized control in the environment, each agent model is equipped with one conductor, respectively. However, the conductor contains the Q-tables of all agents in order to decide which one has the priority to act, when multiple agents intend to perform some concurrent actions. Figure 6 depicts the TA model of conductors. The initial location `Init` is urgent to ensure that whenever the agent is ready, it is scheduled immediately. The function `makeDecision` looks up the Q-table and chooses the action that owns the highest value among those that match the current Q-state of the agent. Note that we only need to compare the attributes in "*MATCH*" but not "*TP*", as the latter has infinite values and the former is enough to represent the states of the agent and environment. If the chosen action is "execution", the conductor sends an "executing" command to the task execution TA via channel

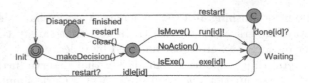

Fig. 6. The conductor TA in the new model equipped with a Q-table

exe[id]. If the chosen action is "movement", the conductor looks up other agents' Q-tables to obtain their intentions of actions. If they also intend to go to the same milestone where agents are mutually exclusive, the one with the highest value of state-action pair is allowed to move, whereas others have to wait until the former finishes scheduling. Whatever the command is, the conductor TA transfers to the location Waiting to wait until the agent finishes its action when it responds to its conductor via the synchronization channel done[id].

The fact that all other locations, except locations Disappear and Waiting, are either urgent or committed guarantees that all agents are scheduled simultaneously. Meanwhile, UPPAAL sets the order of running the conductors to be arbitrary, which means agents could act in any order. However, the formal verification of the model equipped with Q-tables can prove that no matter what the acting order is, agents are guaranteed to satisfy the desired properties. This is what traditional RL algorithms alone cannot provide.

Consequently, the original TA of movement and task execution (see Fig. 4(a) and (b) as examples) need to be slightly adjusted. In the movement TA, channel go[id] is replaced by a new channel, namely run[id], as the movement TA is now scheduled by the conductor TA instead of being synchronized with the task execution TA. Similarly, the task execution TA is synchronized with the conductor TA via channel exe[id] when it starts tasks, and the self-loop of location Idle is omitted, since it does not need to trigger the moving transitions any more. In the functions move() and start(), a Boolean variable idle[id], which is also used in the conductor TA, is turned to *false*, indicating that the agent is scheduled to start working. However, if the target position is exclusive and occupied at the moment, the movement TA should not transfer. Hence, the channel run[id] is broadcast so that it does not block the transition in the conductor TA, and the variable idle[id] remains *true* since the function move() is not invoked. In this case, the conductor TA needs to be informed when the position is released in order to re-schedule the agent. However, as the time of carrying out tasks is not determined, the conductor does not know when to restart, hence the non-deterministic delay at location Waiting in Fig. 6. Therefore, the channel done[id] is used to synchronize the task execution TA and movement TA with the conductor TA, so that whenever an agent completes an action, its conductor restarts. The conductor TA could also go back to its initial location via the edge labelled with broadcast channel restart? and guard idle[id], indicating that another agent has finished something and changed its state, so if the current agent is idle, it can be re-scheduled. A Boolean variable finished is used in the conductor TA. When the agent finishes the requested rounds of work, this variable turns to *true* on the edge to location Disappear, and the milestone occupied by this agent is released, indicating that it has left the site and stopped. This edge is also labelled with the channel restart! to inform other agents for re-scheduling.

Mission Plan Synthesis and Analysis. By introducing the conductor TA, the behavior of the autonomous agents is restricted by the Q-table. Hence, if the Q-table is formed by using the state-action pairs satisfying certain predicates, the reformed model is supposed to satisfy the predicates. For example, in the data-gathering phase, the simulation query is designed as follows:

$$\texttt{simulate[<=T; R] }\{...\}\texttt{:forall(i:int[0,N-1]) work[i]} \geq \texttt{X}, \quad (3)$$

where T is the simulation time of each round, R is the number of simulation rounds, N is the number of agents, and X is the requested rounds of work. In the case of autonomous trucks, one round of work means starting from the stone pile and eventually unloading stones at the secondary crusher, as shown in Fig. 2. The predicate specifies that if the N agents accomplish X rounds of work, then the information between parentheses ({...}), i.e., the state-action pairs and their rewards/penalties, is printed into text files. Next, the text files are parsed by our Java program, which also implements the Q-learning algorithm and populates Q-tables. Finally, the Q-tables are used by the newly built conductor TA to govern the movement and task execution TA.

By verifying queries of the forms below, we can prove that the synthesized mission plans satisfy our requirements described in Sect. 3. In these queries, $\texttt{te}_n$ and $\texttt{move}_n$ are the task execution TA and movement TA of agent n, respectively. tasks is a two-dimensional integer array of agents' task execution status, e.g., finished, or unfinished, event is a two-dimensional Boolean array of events' status, and x is a clock variable.

- *Milestone Matching*. Query (4) checks that agent's n position is always at milestone P_i, when it is executing task T_i.

$$\texttt{A}\square \texttt{ (te}_n\texttt{.}T_i \texttt{ imply move}_n\texttt{.}P_i\texttt{)} \quad (4)$$

- *Task Sequencing*. Query (5) checks if agent's n precedent task T_{i-1} is always finished (FIN means finish), when agent n is executing task T_i.

$$\texttt{A}\square \texttt{ (te}_n\texttt{.}T_i \texttt{ imply tasks[n][i-1]==FIN)} \quad (5)$$

- *Timing*. Query (6) checks if agent n can always finish all its tasks within TL time units, where M indicates the last task and TL is an integer of time limit.

$$\texttt{A}\square \texttt{ ((forall(i:int[0,M-1]) tasks[n][i]==FIN) imply x<TL)} \quad (6)$$

- *Event Reaction*. Query (7) checks if agent i can always reach milestone P_k within EL time units if event j occurs, where EL is an integer of time limit.

$$\texttt{event[i][j] --> (move}_n\texttt{.}P_k \texttt{ \&\& x} \leq \texttt{EL)} \quad (7)$$

These queries are impossible to be verified by traditional model checking alone in cases containing large numbers of agents, due to the exponentially grown state space.

5 Experimental Evaluation

In this section, we evaluate MCRL by comparing it with TAMAA and UPPAAL STRATEGO in several experiments. This experimental evaluation is conducted in UPPAAL 4.1.22 and UPPAAL STRATEGO 4.1.20-7, on a laptop running an Intel Core i5 processor with 16 GB of RAM and a 64-bit Windows OS. The environment model used in this experiment is depicted in Fig. 3(a), and contains 4 static obstacles, 6 milestones, several autonomous trucks and 1 autonomous wheel loader. For comparing TAMAA and UPPAAL STRATEGO, we vary the number of agents from 2 to 6.

Experimentation Using TAMAA. After configuring the environment, agents, and tasks in the TAMAA tool, we obtain the TA model of task execution, movement, and monitor for the battery-low event. To synthesize the mission plan that carries all the stones with the minimum time consumption, we verify the model in UPPAAL and select the fastest diagnostic trace. The TCTL query designed for the verification is as follows:

$$E\Diamond \ (\texttt{stone==0 \&\& x} \leq \texttt{LIMIT}), \tag{8}$$

where variable "stone" represents the volume of the stone pile, whose value is updated in the function "finish()" in the task execution TA, and "$x \leq$ LIMIT" regulates the time limit of finishing the job. The verification results[2] show that TAMAA can generate mission plans that avoid static obstacles and carry all the stones to the destination. However, this approach can only synthesize a certain type of mission plans, e.g., fastest, shortest, or random, as UPPAAL provides these three types of diagnostic traces. When the respective execution time of tasks is uncertain, these types of mission plans are not sufficient to handle all situations.

Experimentation Using UPPAAL STRATEGO. In order to synthesize mission plans in UPPAAL STRATEGO, the TA model in TAMAA needs to be adjusted slightly. As an example, in Fig. 4(a), edges from location A2B to location B, and from location B2A to A in the movement TA are changed to "uncontrollable" ones, as they are controlled by the environment. Similarly, in the task execution TA, the incoming edges of location Idle are changed to "uncontrollable". Thereafter, we verify the model against queries as follows:

$$\texttt{strategy MP = control: A}\Diamond \ \texttt{stone==0} \tag{9}$$

$$E\Diamond \ (\texttt{stone==0 \&\& x} \leq \texttt{LIMIT}) \ \texttt{under MP} \tag{10}$$

---

[2] Further visual information on the missions plans in TAMAA can be found at http://doi.org/10.5281/zenodo.3731960.

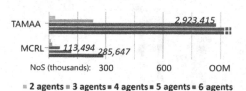

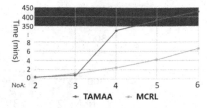

(a) The number of explored states for checking Query (8) by using TAMAA and MCRL

(b) The computation time of checking Query (8) by using TAMAA and MCRL

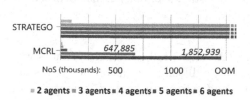

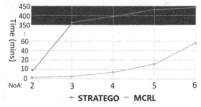

(c) The number of explored states for checking Queries (6) and (9) by using MCRL and UPPAAL STRATEGO, respectively

(d) The computation time of checking Queries (6) and (9) by using MCRL and UPPAAL STRATEGO, respectively

Fig. 7. Experimental result of the algorithm performance of synthesizing mission plans for different numbers of agents using three methods

Query (9) utilizes a special syntactical keyword of UPPAAL STRATEGO, namely "control", to synthesize strategies (i.e., "strategy MP", where "MP" stands for mission plans) that enable the model to transfer all the stones to the destination under any circumstances (i.e., "A◊"). Query (10) verifies the model to see whether the agents are able to transfer stones within a time limit, when their behaviors are restricted by the strategy (i.e., "under MP"). These queries provide a means of synthesizing and optimizing mission plans that handle the uncertain time of task execution and movement, respectively, which is better than TAMAA. However, as UPPAAL STRATEGO still replies on exhaustive model checking to generate strategies by queries like Query (9), the state-space explosion problem is inevitable when the system is large and complex.

Experimentation Using MCRL. In this experiment, we train and reform the TA model of TAMAA in the way described in Sect. 4.2. Then, we synthesize mission plans for 2 to 6 autonomous agents. Fig. 7(a) and 7(c) show the comparison of the number of explored states in the verification, using different methods, where "NoS" means the number of explored states, and "OOM" means that the verification runs out of memory and fails to generate a result. MCRL is able to generate a result for all the cases and explores much less states than the other two methods (see Fig. 7(a) and (c)). Figure 7(b) and (d) depict the computation time of different methods, where "NoA" means the number of agents. Since the difference between the computation time is significantly large, in order to show the data in one graph, the Y-axis is not entirely equidistant, and we skip some

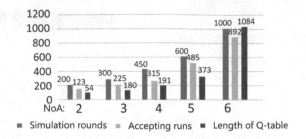

Fig. 8. The rounds of simulation and lengths of Q-tables for different numbers of agents

numbers. Since TAMAA and UPPAAL STRATEGO fail to generate results when agents are more than 4 and 2 respectively, the black portions of the graphs indicate that the methods exhaust memory and return an "out of memory" error, even after large amounts of time.

The computation time of MCRL is the sum of two phases, namely *data gathering* and *model training*, as *model reforming* currently is done manually. Figure 7(b) shows that as the number of agents grows, the increase of computation time of MCRL verifying reachability properties is nearly linear. In case of 3 agents, TAMAA costs the least time, as UPPAAL STRATEGO and MCRL consider all the situations of uncertain task execution and movement time, which are not dealt with in TAMAA. In case of 4 agents, TAMAA costs more than 5 hours, whereas MCRL only needs about 3 min. However, when we compare the performance of MCRL and UPPAAL STRATEGO for verifying liveness properties (see Fig. 7(c) and (d)), we discover that, although MCRL is able to handle up to 6 agents, while UPPAAL STRATEGO can only manage less than 3 agents, the increase of both the number of states and computation time of MCRL is still dramatic. This is because checking liveness properties of the form "A◊" requires exploring all paths of the model, and the complexity of the problem is high.

In addition, we record the minimum number of simulation rounds and accepting runs that are needed to generate Q-tables, as well as the lengths of the Q-tables. Fig. 8 depicts the results of our experiments for different numbers of agents. The numbers of simulation rounds and accepting runs, as well as the lengths of Q-tables grow exponentially as the number of agents increases. This can be explained by the fact that the number of states considered during model checking increases exponentially when the TA of multiple agents are composed and verified together. Hence, the time of searching Q-tables also increases dramatically, which influences the verification time, and explains why the computation time increases rapidly when the number of agents is more than 5 (see Fig. 7(d)). In a nutshell, the experimental results demonstrate that the new approach is applicable and scalable to solve the mission-planning problem for larger numbers of agents than TAMAA and UPPAAL STRATEGO are able to handle. However, as the number of explored states and length of generated Q-table still grow significantly, most probably MCRL still has an upper bound on the number of agents it can scale with. To address this problem, future work includes experimenting with more than 6 agents in even more complex environments.

6 Discussion

Despite the promising result of MCRL handling larger numbers of agents, there are still some issues regarding accounting for rare events and designing the reward functions, which are worth mentioning in this section.

Rare Events. In our experiments, we observe that if the agents need to repeat their tasks for a large number of rounds, the number of simulation rounds needed to obtain successful traces grows quickly. For instance, in case of 6 agents, if the iteration time of tasks increases from 1 to 5 for all agents, and the number of simulation rounds keeps the same in Query (3), the number of accepting runs becomes insufficient to properly populate a Q-table. This happens because the agents are allowed to move freely in the environment, even if not executing any tasks. Therefore, when the agents are asked to repeat their tasks for multiple rounds, finishing their entire missions becomes a rare event [8], which is hard to achieve when using random simulations. Some algorithms extend statistical model checking, in order to provide a solution to this problem, by using *Importance sampling* and *Importance splitting* [19]. Another direction of solving this problem is to integrate the Q-learning algorithm into the process of simulation in UPPAAL. Currently, the *data gathering* and *model training* are separated into two phases in MCRL. If the Q-values of state-action pairs are calculated and accumulated in each step of the simulation, UPPAAL can exploit the Q-values to avoid unnecessary exploration of the state space, and reach the desired state quicker.

Reward Functions. As the mission-planning problem of autonomous agents concerns multiple factors (e.g., safety, travelling time, etc.), and needs to take into account uncertainties in the environment model, the design of reward functions that comprehensively reflect the considered requirements is important and a difficult task during the modelling phase [14]. In this paper, we use an algebraic formula (i.e., $Reward = (T - C)^2$) to construct the reward function, which only reflects the time to accomplish all tasks. Other important factors such as distances to obstacles, energy consumption, and others need to be considered when constructing a comprehensive reward function. Formulating the reward function as a UPPAAL TA can be used to compose multiple sources of rewards, while also providing the ability of verifying that reward function [22].

7 Related Work

Recently, there has been a rising interest in policy synthesis for autonomous systems. Wang et al. [26] propose a novel Partially Observable Markov Decision Processes (POMDP) formulation to the synthesis of policies over a vast space of probability distributions. Bouton et al. [6] also employ POMDP for modeling, and their solution enables the autonomous vehicles to adapt to the behavior of other agents. Nikou et al. [23] propose an automata-based solution for controller synthesis of multi-agent path planning, where Metric Interval Temporal Logic (MITL) is used to describe each agent's individual high-level specification. Compared with these studies, our approach combines model checking and reinforcement learning so that both methods' strengths benefit our solution that proves to be accurate and, to the extent of our experiments, scalable.

The combination of formal methods and learning algorithms is a recent trend that attracts a large body of research work. Li et al. [21] utilize the expressiveness of formal specification languages to capture complex requirements of robotic systems, and construct reward functions of reinforcement learning, so that they are interpretable. Bouton et al. [7] propose a generic approach to enforce probabilistic guarantees on agents trained by reinforcement learning. As aforementioned, UPPAAL STRATEGO is a new branch of UPPAAL designed by David et al. [13], which adopts reinforcement learning algorithms to refine the synthesized strategies for winning priced timed games. However, as different from these studies, our approach focuses on using reinforcement learning to replace exhaustive model checking for mission-plan synthesis of multi-agent systems, so that the state-space explosion is alleviated. To the best of our knowledge, the first attempt to solve the state-space-explosion problem of model checking using reinforcement learning is done by Behjati et al. [3]. These authors propose a bounded rational verification approach for on-the-fly model checking. However, this method is limited to non-timing LTL properties.

8   Conclusions and Future Work

In this paper, we present a novel mission-plan synthesis method called MCRL, which can handle large numbers of autonomous agents. The method adopts formal modeling to capture the behavior of autonomous agents, and Q-learning to train the model and synthesize mission plans in the form of Q-tables.

We demonstrate MCRL's ability of handling multiple agents by an experiment, and compare the result with TAMAA and UPPAAL STRATEGO. The computation time of MCRL increases linearly with the number of agents, whereas the other two approaches show an exponential increase of their computation time, respectively. MCRL is also able to cope with uncertain task execution and movement time, which is not supported by TAMAA. We present means for verifying and analyzing the synthesized mission plans using model checking to ensure safety-critical requirements. Future work will focus on integrating Q-learning directly into the generation of the state space with UPPAAL, and possibly on applying other machine learning or AI algorithms to tame verification scalability or guide the model checking. Synthesizing mission plans of agents working for much longer time will be another direction, which would complicate the problem even more.

Acknowledgement. The research leading to the presented results has been undertaken within the research profile DPAC - Dependable Platform for Autonomous Systems and Control project, funded by the Swedish Knowledge Foundation, grant number: 20150022.

References

1. Abdeddaı, Y., Asarin, E., Maler, O., et al.: Scheduling with Timed Automata, vol. 354. Elsevier, Amsterdam (2006)
2. Alur, R., Dill, D.: Automata for modeling real-time systems. In: Paterson, M.S. (ed.) ICALP 1990. LNCS, vol. 443, pp. 322–335. Springer, Heidelberg (1990). https://doi.org/10.1007/BFb0032042
3. Behjati, R., Sirjani, M., Nili Ahmadabadi, M.: Bounded rational search for on-the-fly model checking of LTL properties. In: Arbab, F., Sirjani, M. (eds.) FSEN 2009. LNCS, vol. 5961, pp. 292–307. Springer, Heidelberg (2010). https://doi.org/10.1007/978-3-642-11623-0_17
4. Behrmann, G., Cougnard, A., David, A., Fleury, E., Larsen, K.G., Lime, D.: UPPAAL-Tiga: time for playing games!. In: Damm, W., Hermanns, H. (eds.) CAV 2007. LNCS, vol. 4590, pp. 121–125. Springer, Heidelberg (2007). https://doi.org/10.1007/978-3-540-73368-3_14
5. Bengtsson, J., Yi, W.: Timed automata: semantics, algorithms and tools. In: Desel, J., Reisig, W., Rozenberg, G. (eds.) ACPN 2003. LNCS, vol. 3098, pp. 87–124. Springer, Heidelberg (2004). https://doi.org/10.1007/978-3-540-27755-2_3
6. Bouton, M., Cosgun, A., Kochenderfer, M.J.: Belief state planning for autonomously navigating urban intersections. In: Intelligent Vehicles Symposium, pp. 825–830. IEEE (2017)
7. Bouton, M., Karlsson, J., Nakhaei, A., Fujimura, K., Kochenderfer, M.J., Tumova, J.: Reinforcement learning with probabilistic guarantees for autonomous driving. arXiv preprint arXiv:1904.07189 (2019)
8. Bucklew, J.: Introduction to Rare Event Simulation. Springer, New York (2013). https://doi.org/10.1007/978-1-4757-4078-3
9. Chandler, P., Pachter, M.: Research issues in autonomous control of tactical UAVs. In: Proceedings of the 1998 American Control Conference. ACC (IEEE Cat. No. 98CH36207). IEEE (1998)
10. Clarke, E.M., Klieber, W., Nováček, M., Zuliani, P.: Model checking and the state explosion problem. In: Meyer, B., Nordio, M. (eds.) LASER 2011. LNCS, vol. 7682, pp. 1–30. Springer, Heidelberg (2012). https://doi.org/10.1007/978-3-642-35746-6_1
11. Daniel, K., Nash, A., Koenig, S., Felner, A.: Theta*: any-angle path planning on grids. J. Artif. Intell. Res. **39**, 533–579 (2010)
12. David, A., et al.: Statistical model checking for stochastic hybrid systems (2012)
13. David, A., Jensen, P.G., Larsen, K.G., Mikučionis, M., Taankvist, J.H.: UPPAAL STRATEGO. In: Baier, C., Tinelli, C. (eds.) TACAS 2015. LNCS, vol. 9035, pp. 206–211. Springer, Heidelberg (2015). https://doi.org/10.1007/978-3-662-46681-0_16
14. Dewey, D.: Reinforcement learning and the reward engineering principle. In: 2014 AAAI Spring Symposium Series (2014)
15. Fisher, H.: Probabilistic learning combinations of local job-shop scheduling rules. In: Industrial Scheduling, pp. 225–251. Prentice Hall, Englewood Cliffs (1963)

16. Franklin, S., Graesser, A.: Is it an agent, or just a program?: a taxonomy for autonomous agents. In: Müller, J.P., Wooldridge, M.J., Jennings, N.R. (eds.) ATAL 1996. LNCS, vol. 1193, pp. 21–35. Springer, Heidelberg (1997). https://doi.org/10.1007/BFb0013570

17. Gu, R., Enoiu, E.P., Seceleanu, C.: TAMAA: UPPAAL-based mission planning for autonomous agents. In: The 35th ACM/SIGAPP Symposium On Applied Computing SAC2020, Brno, Czech Republic, 30 March 2020 (2019)

18. Gu, R., Marinescu, R., Seceleanu, C., Lundqvist, K.: Towards a two-layer framework for verifying autonomous vehicles. In: Badger, J.M., Rozier, K.Y. (eds.) NFM 2019. LNCS, vol. 11460, pp. 186–203. Springer, Cham (2019). https://doi.org/10.1007/978-3-030-20652-9_12

19. Larsen, K.G., Legay, A.: On the power of statistical model checking. In: Margaria, T., Steffen, B. (eds.) ISoLA 2016. LNCS, vol. 9953, pp. 843–862. Springer, Cham (2016). https://doi.org/10.1007/978-3-319-47169-3_62

20. LaValle, S.M.: Rapidly-exploring random trees: a new tool for path planning. Technical report (1998)

21. Li, X., Serlin, Z., Yang, G., Belta, C.: A formal methods approach to interpretable reinforcement learning for robotic planning. Sci. Robot. **4** (2019)

22. Mallozzi, P., Pardo, R., Duplessis, V., Pelliccione, P., Schneider, G.: MoVEMo: a structured approach for engineering reward functions. In: 2018 Second IEEE International Conference on Robotic Computing (IRC), pp. 250–257. IEEE (2018)

23. Nikou, A., Boskos, D., Tumova, J., Dimarogonas, D.V.: On the timed temporal logic planning of coupled multi-agent systems. Automatica **97**, 339–345 (2018)

24. Pelánek, R.: Fighting state space explosion: review and evaluation. In: Cofer, D., Fantechi, A. (eds.) FMICS 2008. LNCS, vol. 5596, pp. 37–52. Springer, Heidelberg (2009). https://doi.org/10.1007/978-3-642-03240-0_7

25. Sutton, R.S., Barto, A.G., et al.: Introduction to Reinforcement Learning, vol. 2. MIT press Cambridge, Cambridge (1998)

26. Wang, Y., Chaudhuri, S., Kavraki, L.E.: Bounded policy synthesis for POMDPs with safe-reachability objectives. In: International Conference on Autonomous Agents and Multi Agent Systems. IFAAMS (2018)

27. Watkins, C.J.H.: Learning from Delayed Rewards. King's College, Cambridge (1989)

Skylines for Symbolic Energy Consumption Analysis

Markus Klinik[1]($\boxtimes$), Bernard van Gastel[1,2], Cynthia Kop[1],
and Marko van Eekelen[1,2]

[1] Radboud University, Nijmegen, The Netherlands
{M.Klinik,B.vanGastel,C.Kop,Marko}@cs.ru.nl
[2] Open University, Heerlen, The Netherlands
{Bernard.vanGastel,Marko.vanEekelen}@ou.nl

Abstract. Energy consumption in embedded systems plays a large role as it has implications for the power supply and the batteries used. Programmers of these systems should consider how their programs control external devices, and where energy consumption hotspots lie. We present a static analysis to predict and visualize energy consumption of external devices controlled by programs written in a simple imperative programming language. Currently available energy consumption analysis techniques generate graphs over time, which makes it difficult to see from where in the source code the consumption originates. Our method generates graphs over source locations, called *skyline diagrams*, showing the maximum power draw for each line of source code.

Our method harnesses symbolic execution extended with support for controlling external devices. This gives accurate predictions and complete code path coverage, as far as the limits of computability allow. To make the diagrams easier to understand, we introduce a merge algorithm that condenses all skylines into a concise overview. We demonstrate the potential by analysing various example programs with our prototype implementation. We envision this approach being used to identify energy consumption hotspots of embedded systems during the design and development phase, in a less involved way than traditional approaches.

Keywords: Symbolic execution · Program analysis · Energy use

1 Introduction

Software that controls hardware is found in many places, such as washing machines, smartphones, or self-driving cars. The software running in such devices is in charge of orchestrating the hardware components, like sensors, motors, displays, or radios. Formal analysis of such devices is hard, because hardware and software have to be analysed together. In order to optimize energy consumption of such devices, especially when they are battery-powered, it is useful for programmers to have a prediction of energy-behaviour of all the components when

© Springer Nature Switzerland AG 2020
M. H. ter Beek and D. Ničković (Eds.): FMICS 2020, LNCS 12327, pp. 93–112, 2020.
https://doi.org/10.1007/978-3-030-58298-2_3

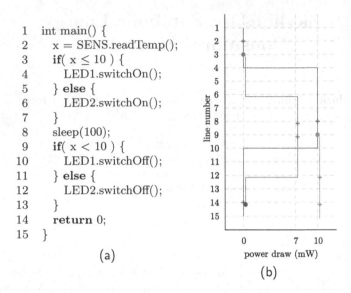

```
1   int main() {
2       x = SENS.readTemp();
3       if( x ≤ 10 ) {
4           LED1.switchOn();
5       } else {
6           LED2.switchOn();
7       }
8       sleep(100);
9       if( x < 10 ) {
10          LED1.switchOff();
11      } else {
12          LED2.switchOff();
13      }
14      return 0;
15  }
```

(a)

(b)

Fig. 1. (a) Sensor input controls a lamp. (b) All possible runs of the program. One run does not end at power draw zero, which indicates a bug.

running their program. Simulation or actual measurement of running devices can give some insight, but only for one specific scenario and hardware configuration.

We develop a static analysis based on symbolic execution that can visualize the energy behaviour of all possible executions of a program at once. This allows programmers to quickly assess the energy impact of a change, already during development. Our method is parametrized with hardware models, so that programmers can swap components and explore different hardware configurations.

In the domain of embedded systems and control software, the energy use of the processor is sometimes negligible. We therefore limit our scope to the energy use of the hardware components controlled by the software. If desired, programmers can bypass this restriction by modelling the processor as a hardware component and switching between its power states explicitly with corresponding component calls. Modelling processors as a hardware components is possible, because they often have approximately constant energy consumption. For example the popular ATmega328P, used on the Arduino UNO, has an amperage of 0.2 mA in Active Mode, 0.75 μA in Power-save Mode, and 0.1 μA in Power-down Mode [21].

We illustrate our approach with an example. The program in Fig. 1a reads a sensor value, and switches on either LED1 or LED2. It has a bug in line 9, where < is used instead of ≤. There are three possible executions, one of which does not end with a power draw of zero, as there exists a sensor value where LED1 is not switched off. The skyline diagram in Fig. 1b shows a merged view of the three executions. The horizontal axis shows power draw, and the vertical axis line numbers. Skylines that would be drawn on top of each other are shifted by a small offset. In this view, programmers can see that some component still consumes energy at the end of the function, and can start investigating the issue.

This paper brings together two distinct lines of earlier work: the energy consumption analysis by van Gastel et al. [10] and the skyline diagrams by Klinik et al. [20]. Our contribution is threefold. First, we introduce a symbolic execution engine that tracks hardware state and works with the programming language SECA (Symbolic Energy Consumption Analysis). Second, we define visualization rules for the results of the symbolic execution as diagrams of power draw over points in the source code. Third, we define an algorithm to reduce the number of plotted graphs, hiding redundant information, to make the diagrams more concise. Our proof-of-concept implementation is available online [3].

Remark. Our goal is to explore the idea of drawing energy skylines over source lines; not (yet) to make an industry-ready tool. To focus on this goal, our method considers a C-like language that lacks the complexity of C itself. Likewise, the well-known problem of exponential state-space explosion, and reduction techniques that may be used to manage this problem, is not included in our scope. Thus, we do not currently consider programs with thousands of lines.

2   Methodology

Given a program in the SECA language (Sect. 3), our system performs symbolic execution to examine all possible execution paths. For each path, the symbolic execution engine tracks the power draw of all components that the program controls, resulting in a graph that relates program points to energy consumption (Sect. 4). We call such graphs *skylines*. The result of symbolic execution is a set of skylines for every function, considering all calls to a function, across all execution paths. Our system then condenses these skylines into a summary of the energy behaviour of the program by *merging* common segments, to emphasize where skylines differ (Sect. 5). The merged skylines are rendered as *skyline diagrams*, with line numbers on the vertical axis and power draw on the horizontal axis. The paper ends with an analysis of a real-world example (Sect. 6), a discussion of related work (Sect. 7) and ideas for future work (Sect. 8).

Control Software. Our domain is control software, whose main purpose is to control hardware components like sensors or motors. It runs on embedded systems using low powered microprocessors, which have a negligible energy use compared to the software-controlled hardware. Control software has two key characteristics. First, it has low algorithmic complexity. We aim to analyse programs that, for example, regulate a central heating installation, not those that calculate square roots. Second, it contains statements that interact with hardware components. These component calls are the focus of our system, as we seek to find how their invocation influences the energy behaviour of the program. If programs have parts with high algorithmic complexity, which would overextend the capabilities of symbolic execution, such parts could be hidden in library calls and left out of the analysis.

SECA represents the behaviour of hardware components in a model similar to the one in [10]; essentially a labelled transition system where every state has a power draw, and state changes can only be initiated by the code.

Energy Consumption. Resources other than power draw can also be modelled, as long as they can be summed up. The analysis does not care; it sees resource consumption as a unitless number. We assume that components have rectangular power profiles, which means there is no ramp-up when switching them on.

Symbolic Execution. Symbolic execution [18] is a program semantics that traces all possible program execution paths. Whenever a program asks for input, for example from a sensor or terminal, a symbolic input variable any_i is created. When conditionals are encountered, execution splits into two paths: one for evaluating the condition to true, one to false. Each path is coupled with the constraint on the symbolic inputs that must hold for this path to be followed.

To illustrate the idea, consider the program: x = TEMP.readInt(); if (x <5) {y=7;} else {y=2*x+1;}. Symbolic execution results in two paths, one through the then- and one through the else-branch. The first one terminates with global state $[x \mapsto any_0, y \mapsto 7]$ and path constraint $any_0 < 5$. The second one terminates with $[x \mapsto any_0, y \mapsto 2any_0+1]$ and path constraint $\neg(any_0 < 5)$.

Path constraints can be given to an SMT (satisfiability modulo theories) solver, to prune infeasible paths, and calculate example values for the *any*s.

Symbolic execution does not terminate if there is a path that loops indefinitely. To bypass this problem, our system exits loops after a pre-defined number of iterations, and generates a warning. In such situations there could be paths whose energy usage is not reported, and hence the analysis is unsound. However, due to the nature of symbolic execution, all possible energy behaviours of a loop will often be discovered in less iterations than what is needed for the behaviours to occur in concrete execution. We expect situations with missed energy behaviours to be uncommon in typical programs.

Program Points. In previous work [20] we analysed resource consumption over time. This has several advantages, but does not clearly show which parts of the program contribute to which parts of a skyline. Here, we give up the time aspect and instead relate resource use directly to lines in the source code. This requires certain coding conventions; for example, there may be only one non-trivial expression or statement per line, and closing braces must be on their own line. The results are diagrams with a natural control flow from top to bottom with occasional jumps, which clearly relate parts of the program to their energy consumption. Consider for example the program in Fig. 2a. Symbolic execution results in the two skylines in Fig. 2b, which show the hotspots in lines 5 and 8.

Merging. Symbolic execution results in a set of skylines, one for every execution path. These skylines often have identical parts, only differing after or up to a certain point. Sometimes a skyline is equal to a second one for a few lines and then becomes equal to a third. This effect is common in loops, where a piece

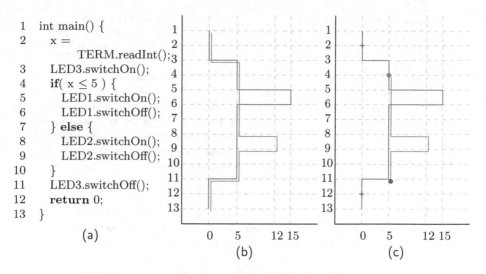

```
1   int main() {
2     x =
          TERM.readInt();
3     LED3.switchOn();
4     if( x ≤ 5 ) {
5       LED1.switchOn();
6       LED1.switchOff();
7     } else {
8       LED2.switchOn();
9       LED2.switchOff();
10    }
11    LED3.switchOff();
12    return 0;
13  }
```

(a)   (b)   (c)

Fig. 2. (a) A program with two execution paths (b) Its skylines (c) Its merged skylines

of code is executed repeatedly. The program in Fig. 2a has two execution paths that only differ during the execution of the conditional (lines 4–10). Figure 2c shows its skylines after merging. Until line 4 they are drawn as a single skyline. At line 4 is a *split point*, after which they are drawn separately. At line 11 they come together again, and continue so until the end of the function.

Our system aims to give programmers an idea of the energy behaviour of their programs, so that they gain insight where the hotspots lie. We argue that for this goal it is not required that skyline diagrams convey all information about all runs. Instead, we condense information such that unexpected spikes can be clearly identified. This comes at the cost of information loss about the exact number of runs, and losing the ability to fully trace individual runs.

3   The SECA Language

SECA (Symbolic Energy Consumption Analysis) is a small imperative programming language. We designed SECA to look like a simple form of C, without features like raw memory access and pointer arithmetic. Such features complicate the analysis and are not the focus of this paper. We believe that with some engineering effort, the analysis can be extended to support the style of C programs common in embedded and safety-critical systems. SECA is a variant of ECA [11], which is itself a variant of Nielson's **While** [22]. SECA programs can control external hardware through *component calls*. For example, the component call LED1.switchOn() invokes the switchOn functionality of the component LED1. Component calls can perform I/O and have return values, but no arguments. While it would be simple to allow arguments to the component calls for

$$e ::= \textsf{true} \mid \textsf{false} \mid i \mid x \mid e \; op \; e$$
$$\mid un \; e \mid id(\overline{e}) \mid id.id()$$
$$op ::= \textsf{\&\&} \mid || \mid \leq \mid < \mid + \mid - \mid *$$
$$un ::= - \mid \; !$$
$$s ::= \textsf{if}(e) \{ \overline{s} \} \textsf{ else } \{ \overline{s} \}$$
$$\mid \textsf{while}(e) \{ \overline{s} \} \; i$$
$$\mid x = e \mid \textsf{return } e \mid e$$
$$funcDef ::= id(\overline{x}) \{ \overline{s} \}$$

Fig. 3. Abstract syntax of SECA

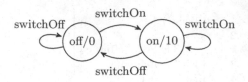

Fig. 4. Hardware component model for an LED. In state *on* it has a power draw of 10, in state *off* a power draw of 0. The transitions correspond to component functions.

the *concrete* component models, it would require signifcant changes to the *symbolic* component models. This would complicate the symbolic execution. For this paper we decided to keep this can of worms closed.

Assumptions. We provide no typing rules, but do require that programs are well-typed in the usual sense. We assume that all code paths of a function end in a return statement of the correct type, no references to undefined variables occur, and programs run on devices with all occurring hardware components. Void functions are allowed to end without return statements. In this case, the execution engine inserts an implicit return statement.

3.1 Syntax

A program is a list of function- and global variable declarations. There must be one function main. The abstract syntax of SECA is shown in Fig. 3. Overlined symbols stand for lists of that symbol; for example $\overline{s}$ is a list of statements.

Expressions are Boolean or integer constants, program variables, applications of binary or unary operators, function calls, and component calls. Operators are the usual Boolean connectives, comparisons and arithmetic. Function calls have a list of expressions, the parameters. Component calls have the form *name.function*() and invoke the specified function of the specified component. Statements are conditionals, while loops, assignments, returns, or expressions.

While loops are annotated with a loop counter i, which the semantics uses to limit loop iterations, and to draw skylines differently in the first loop iteration. This is further discussed in Sect. 3.2. The loop counter is not part of the concrete syntax, the programmer cannot access it, and it is initialised with zero. Assignments have a variable on the left hand side and an expression on the right hand side. Return statements end the current function call, and yield the given expression as the function's return value.

3.2 Semantics

SECA comes with four semantics, for different purposes. The *standard semantics* defines how programs are executed. The *energy-aware semantics* additionally traces the energy consumption during program execution in a skyline. The *symbolic execution semantics* executes all possible paths through a program. The *energy-aware symbolic execution semantics* traces all possible skylines a program can produce. The focus of this paper is the last one; the others are formally defined in a technical report [19]. Below, we will informally discuss the energy-aware semantics, as it is a useful foundation to understand the energy-aware symbolic execution semantics.

Components. To start, we must define the semantics of component calls. In order to analyse the energy consumption of programs, we need an estimation of how much energy their hardware components consume. Such an estimation is called a *hardware component model*, or *component model* for short.

Component models are labelled transition systems, not necessarily finite, where each state has a power draw. Transitions are labelled with *component functions* (e.g. switchOn). Formally, a *hardware component model* $\langle S, L, \delta, o \rangle$ consists of a set of states S, a finite set of labels L, a transition function $\delta : L \times S \to IO(\mathbb{Z} \times S)$ and a power draw function $o : S \to \mathbb{N}$. A *configuration* of a model is an element of S: the current state. Every component has a start state. We borrow Haskell's notation $IO(\mathbb{Z} \times S)$ to indicate that to produce the return value $\mathbb{Z} \times S$, the function may perform arbitrary I/O. Input-producing hardware like sensors or terminals use the return value $\mathbb{Z}$ to return the input. Actuators like motors should return 0. The power draw function o specifies how much power the component consumes in each state.

Let us consider an example. A component model of an LED is shown in Fig. 4. LEDs have two states, *on* and *off*, and transitions *switchOn* and *switchOff* between them. In the *on* state an LED has a power draw of 10, in the *off* state it has a power draw of 0. The component functions do not return values.

SECA programs always run in contexts where a number of component models are present. Such contexts are called *component states*, or *CStates* for short. A CState is a partial mapping from names to configurations. If the CState contains an LED, say under the name of LED1, programs in this context can contain the component calls LED1.switchOn() and LED1.switchOff().

Skylines. The energy-aware semantics generates *skylines*. A skyline is a list of *segments*. A segment is either a start point $S(l, p)$ at line l and power draw p, a forwards line $F(l)$, a backwards jump $J(l)$, or an edge $E(p)$. Every skyline has exactly one start point, which must be its first segment. Other segments are interpreted relative to their predecessors.

The y-axis of a skyline refers to line numbers. Using line numbers to identify program points requires the source code to be formatted so that every skyline-producing program point is on its own line, to avoid segments being drawn over each other. This concerns the left-hand side of assignments, **if** keywords, **while** keywords, the closing brace of the body of while loops, **return** keywords, and the closing parentheses of function- and component calls. Expressions that contain function- or component calls as subexpressions should be split over multiple lines. Even with these restrictions, segments may end up on top of each other when the same lines of code are executed more than once.

The Energy-Aware Standard Semantics. We explain by example how the semantics executes a program and constructs its skyline on the way. The program in Fig. 5 switches LED1 on five times in a loop, and then switches it off. The skyline fragments generated during execution are shown in Fig. 6.

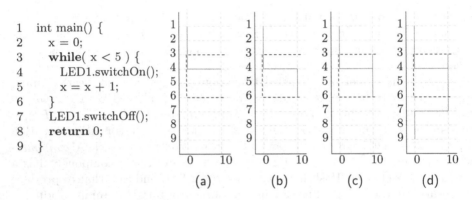

```
1   int main() {
2       x = 0;
3       while( x < 5 ) {
4           LED1.switchOn();
5           x = x + 1;
6       }
7       LED1.switchOff();
8       return 0;
9   }
```

Fig. 5. Stepwise construction of a skyline (a) After switching on LED1 (b) After the first loop iteration (c) After the second iteration (d) The final skyline

Execution of this program starts in a CState where LED1 is in state *off.* Figure 5a shows the skyline just after executing line 4, where the LED has been switched on. Lines 2 and 3 do not change the power draw, which yields two forward segments from line 1 to 2 and from line 2 to 3. LED1 is switched on in line 4, which extends the skyline with a forward segment from 3 to 4, followed by a rising edge to power draw 10.

$$[S(1,0), F(2), F(3), F(4), E(10), \quad (a)$$
$$F(5), F(6), J(3), \quad (b)$$
$$F(4), E(10), F(5), F(6), J(3), \quad (c)$$
$$F(4), E(10), F(5), F(6), J(3),$$
$$F(4), E(10), F(5), F(6), J(3),$$
$$F(4), E(10), F(5), F(6), J(3),$$
$$F(7), E(0), F(8), F(9)] \quad (d)$$

Fig. 6. Skyline fragments for Fig. 5.

Figure 5b shows the skyline after one loop iteration, when the loop condition in line 3 has been executed a second time. Line 5 has caused a forward segment from 4 to 5. Execution of line 3 has caused a forward segment from the last statement of the loop in line 5 to the closing brace of the loop in line 6, followed by a backwards jump to line 3, which is not visible in the diagram.

Figure 5c shows the skyline after two iterations. The second iteration starts at line 3 with power draw 10, and gives of three forward segments 3 to 4, 4 to 5, and 5 to 6. None of them change the power draw, as the LED is already on. These segments overlap with the segments of the previous iteration, and are drawn on top of each other. All subsequent iterations also generate identical segments.

After five loop iterations, the program exits the loop, with the skyline shown in Fig. 5d. Switching off the LED generates a falling edge to power draw 0 in line 7. The return statement finally generates two forward segments, one for itself from 7 to 8 and one for exiting the function from 8 to 9.

4 Energy-Aware Symbolic Execution

The energy-aware symbolic execution semantics tracks path constraints and energy skylines for each execution path. The result is a set of skylines for each function together with their path constraints.

In the symbolic semantics it is undesirable for component calls to perform I/O, because exploring all execution paths causes component calls to be executed multiple times. The symbolic semantics therefore uses component models where component calls return *symbolic values* with constraints. Symbolic values SVal are syntax trees whose leaves are constants or *symbolic inputs* any_i (variables that stand for an arbitrary integer). SVal is given by the grammar:

$$sv ::= \text{true} \mid \text{false} \mid i \mid any_i \mid sv \; op \; sv \mid un \; sv$$

A *symbolic component model* $\langle S, L, \delta, o \rangle$ consists of a set of states S, a finite set of labels L, a transition function $\delta : L \times S \to \text{SVal} \times \text{SVal} \times S$, and a power draw function $o : S \to \mathbb{N}$. As opposed to the concrete models in Sect. 3.2, δ can not perform I/O. The first returned SVal of δ is typically a constant or symbolic input, and the second is a constraint on that input. For example, where the concrete model of TERM.readInt() asks for input and returns the user's answer, the symbolic model returns a fresh symbolic input any_j, with the constraint true, as this input can be any integer. A temperature sensor in a cold room can return a fresh any_j, together with a constraint $13 \le any_j \wedge any_j \le 17$. A symbolic LED returns constant 0, with the constraint true.

4.1 The Energy-Aware Symbolic Execution Semantics

We now study the algorithm that computes all possible executions of SECA programs, together with their corresponding skylines. The algorithm records skylines of each function separately. This results in one skyline for each function call, for each execution path on which the call lies. The algorithm is defined by case distinction on the abstract syntax. We present the whole algorithm in Figs. 7 and 8, but provide a detailed description only for a few clauses. A complete description of the algorithm, as well as a formal definition of the semantics in the style common in programming language research, can be found in the technical report [19]. An implementation is available online [3].

$E : \textbf{Expr} \times \Sigma \to \mathcal{P}(\textbf{Val} \times \Sigma)$

$E[\![x]\!](\sigma) = \{ \langle lookup(x, \sigma), \sigma \rangle \}$ (1)

$E[\![e_1 \; op \; e_2]\!](\sigma) = \{ \langle v_1 \; op \; v_2, \sigma'' \rangle$ (2)
$| \langle v_1, \sigma' \rangle \in E[\![e_1]\!](\sigma)$
$, \langle v_2, \sigma'' \rangle \in E[\![e_2]\!](\sigma') \}$

$E[\![un \; e]\!](\sigma) = \{ \langle un \; v, \sigma' \rangle$ (3)
$| \langle v, \sigma' \rangle \in E[\![e]\!](\sigma) \}$

$E[\![f(\bar{e})]\!](\sigma) =$ (4)
$\{ \langle lookup(\#return, \sigma'''), \sigma'''[pc \mapsto \sigma.pc] \rangle$
$| \langle \bar{v}, \sigma' \rangle \in \overline{E[\![\bar{e}]\!]}(\sigma)$
$, \sigma'' = call[\![f(\bar{v})]\!](\sigma'[pc \mapsto []])$
$, \sigma''' \in X(\sigma'') \}$

$E[\![c.f()]\!](\sigma) = \{ \langle v, \sigma' \rangle \}$ (5)
where
$\sigma' = \sigma[cstate \mapsto cstate', sky \mapsto sky'$
$, \varphi \mapsto \varphi']$
$\langle v, \psi, s_c' \rangle = \delta_c(f, s_c)$
$cstate' = \sigma.cstate[c \mapsto s_c']$
$s_c = \sigma.cstate[c]$
$p = powerDraw(cstate')$
$l = lineOfCompCall$
$sky' = \sigma.sky ++ [F(l), E(p)]$
$\varphi' = \sigma.\varphi \land \psi$

$call : \textbf{Expr} \times \Sigma \to \Sigma$
$call[\![f(\bar{v})]\!](\sigma) = \sigma'$ (6)
where
$\sigma' = \sigma[env \mapsto env', sky \mapsto sky', pc \mapsto \bar{s}$
$, stack \mapsto stack']$
$env' = [\bar{x} \mapsto \bar{v}]$
$p = powerDraw(\sigma.cstate)$
$l = lineOfOpeningBrace$
$sky' = [S(l, p)]$
$\bar{s} = functionBody[\![f]\!]$
$stack' = push(\sigma, stack)$

$X : \Sigma \to \mathcal{P}(\Sigma)$

$$X(\sigma) = \begin{cases} \{\sigma\} & \text{if } \sigma.pc = [] \\[4pt] \bigcup \{ X(\sigma') \\ \quad | \; \sigma' \in S[\![s]\!](\sigma[pc \mapsto rest]) \} \\ \quad \text{if } \sigma.pc = [s] ++ rest \end{cases}$$

Fig. 7. The function E for expressions and X to execute whole programs

$S : \textbf{Stmt} \times \Sigma \to \mathcal{P}(\Sigma)$

$S[\![x = e]\!](\sigma) = \{ assign(x, v, \sigma')$ (1)
$| \langle v, \sigma' \rangle \in E[\![e]\!](\sigma[sky \mapsto \sigma.sky ++ [F(l)]])$
where $l = lineNumberOfAssignment \}$

$S[\![\textbf{if}(e) \{ \bar{s}_1 \} \textbf{else} \{ \bar{s}_2 \}]\!](\sigma) = \bigcup \{$ (2)
$\{ \sigma'[pc \mapsto pc_1, \varphi \mapsto \varphi_1]$
$, \sigma'[pc \mapsto pc_2, \varphi \mapsto \varphi_2] \}$
$| \langle v, \sigma' \rangle \in E[\![e]\!](\sigma[sky \mapsto \sigma.sky ++ [F(l)]])$
where
$l = lineOfIfKeyword$
$\varphi_1 = \sigma'.\varphi \land v$
$\varphi_2 = \sigma'.\varphi \land \neg v$
$pc_1 = \bar{s}_1 ++ \sigma'.pc$
$pc_2 = \bar{s}_2 ++ \sigma'.pc \}$

$S[\![\textbf{while}(e) \{ \bar{s} \} i]\!](\sigma) = \bigcup \{$ (3)
$\{ \sigma'[pc \mapsto loop, \varphi \mapsto \varphi_1], \sigma'[\varphi \mapsto \varphi_2] \}$
$| \langle v, \sigma' \rangle \in E[\![e]\!](\sigma[sky \mapsto sky'])$
where
$\varphi_1 = \sigma'.\varphi \land v$
$\varphi_2 = \sigma'.\varphi \land \neg v$
$$sky' = \begin{cases} \sigma.sky ++ [F(l)] & \text{if } i = 0 \\ \sigma.sky ++ [F(m), J(l)] & \text{otherwise} \end{cases}$$
$loop = \bar{s} ++ [\textbf{while}(e)\{\bar{s}\}(i+1)] ++ \sigma'.pc$
$l = lineOfWhileKeyword$
$m = lineOfClosingBrace \}$

$S[\![\textbf{return} \; e]\!](\sigma) =$ (4)
$\{ registerSkyline(f, sky'', \sigma'')$
$| \langle v, \sigma' \rangle \in E[\![e]\!](\sigma[sky \mapsto sky'])$
where
$sky' = \sigma.sky ++ [F(l)]$
$sky'' = \sigma'.sky ++ [F(m)]$
$sky_c' = \sigma_c.sky ++ [F(n), E(p)]$
$\langle \sigma_c, stack_c \rangle = pop(\sigma.stack)$
$\sigma'' = \sigma'[env \mapsto \sigma_c.env[\#return \mapsto v]$
$, pc \mapsto \sigma_c.pc, sky \mapsto sky_c', stack \mapsto stack_c]$
$l = lineOfReturnKeyword$
$m = lineOfClosingBrace$
$n = lineOfCallSite$
$p = powerDraw(\sigma') \}$

$S[\![e]\!](\sigma) = \{ \sigma' | \langle v, \sigma' \rangle \in E[\![e]\!](\sigma) \}$ (5)

Fig. 8. The function S for statements

Figures 7 and 8 show pseudocode for the functions E and S that compute symbolic skylines for expressions and statements respectively. We elaborate on some of the clauses below. Application of a function to syntactic arguments is denoted with double brackets $[\![-]\!]$, which have no further special meaning. A program state $\sigma \in \Sigma$ is a record with all information needed to execute a statement. It contains the values of local program variables env and global program variables $genv$, the current skyline sky, the current path constraint φ, the program counter pc (a list of statements to be executed after the current statement), the function call stack $stack$, and the CState $cstate$. The helper functions $lookup$ and $assign$ (not shown here) ensure that the scoping rules are respected, which means they prefer variables in env over $genv$.

Each clause of the semantics specifies how a single statement or expression together with a given program state produces the set of all possible immediate successor program states. Hence, a statement can be seen as a state transformer $\Sigma \rightarrow \mathcal{P}(\Sigma)$. To compose two functions of this type, we need glue code that applies the second function to every result of the first function. This is implemented by the function X in Fig. 7, which executes whole programs.

4.2 Evaluation of Expressions

The evaluation function E (Fig. 7) takes an expression e and a program state and returns the set of all possible values that e can evaluate to, together with the updated program states. Clauses **(1)** and **(3)** are not explained here.

Clause **(2):** To evaluate a binary operator, all possible values v_1 for e_1, and all possible values for e_2 are calculated. The evaluation of e_2 happens in the result state of the evaluation of e_1. The result is the set of the symbolic values $v_1\,op\,v_2$ for all combinations (v_1, v_2). These values are subject to constant folding (e.g. $1 + 2$ becomes 3), which is not shown here.

Clause **(4):** To evaluate a function call, first all arguments are evaluated. This is done by the sequential extension $\overline{E}$, which chains the state through the evaluation of the argument vector $\overline{e}$ and results in the set of all possible value vectors $\overline{v}$. For each vector $\overline{v}$, the helper function $call$, described below, prepares the function call, and X executes it. This execution will eventually end with a return statement. The return statement restores the program state so that σ''' can be used as the result state at the call site. The resulting value of the function call is the value of the #return register in σ'''.

Clause **(5):** To evaluate a component call, first the transition function δ_c of the component c is invoked, with the function name f and the component's current state s_c as arguments. This yields a return value v, a constraint ψ on v, and a new component state s'_c. The total power draw p after the call is computed. The skyline is extended with a forward segment $F(l)$ to the location l of the call site, followed by an edge $E(p)$ to the new power draw. The result of evaluating $c.f()$ is the return value v of δ_c, together with the updated program state.

Clause **(6):** The helper function $call$ prepares the program state for execution of the function. It first initializes the environment env' for the function body with the actual arguments. It then starts a new skyline for the call to f with the current power draw p at the location l of the opening brace of the function definition of f. It uses the function body $\overline{s}$ as program counter, and creates a new stack frame for the function call.

4.3   Execution of Statements

The function X (Fig. 7) recursively executes all statements of the program counter $\sigma.pc$, and collects the results. Execution of a SECA program starts in a program state that contains the body of the main function as program counter.

The function S (Fig. 8) executes a single statement in a given program state, and returns all possible successor program states.

Clause **(1)**: Assignments are executed by first extending the current skyline to the line of the assignment. Then e is evaluated to all its possible values, and the final results are all successor states where x has value v. Expressions can have side effects, so the successor states may have different skylines.

Clause **(2)**: Execution of conditionals starts with extending the current skyline with a forward segment $F(l)$ to the line l of the *if* keyword. Then, all possible values v of the condition e are computed. This results in paths into both branches, for each v. The path constraint for the *then* branch is extended with v, for the *else* branch with $\neg v$. The program counter pc_1 specifies that first the statements $\overline{s}_1$ of the *then* branch are executed, and after that the original continuation $\sigma'.pc$. Similarly for the *else* branch. If the SMT solver sees that φ_1 or φ_2 is unsatisfiable, their states are pruned (not shown here).

Clause **(3)**: For the first iteration of while loops, we need to generate a different skyline than for subsequent iterations. The first loop iteration can be recognized by the loop counter i being 0. If this is the case, the current skyline comes from outside the loop body, and we extend it with a forward segment $F(l)$ to the line of the *while* keyword. Otherwise, the current skyline comes from inside the loop body, and is extended with a forward segment $F(m)$ to the line m of the closing brace, followed by a backwards jump $J(l)$ to the beginning of the loop. In both cases, the condition e is evaluated to all possible values v. For every v, we generate two continuations: one for entering the loop with path constraint $\sigma'.\varphi \wedge v$ and one for exiting the loop with constraint $\sigma'.\varphi \wedge \neg v$. The program counter *loop* for entering the loop consists of the loop body $\overline{s}$, followed by the loop itself with incremented loop counter, then by what comes after the loop $\sigma'.pc$. The program counter for exiting needs no change, as $\sigma'.pc$ already contains the instructions following the loop. Our implementation uses the loop counter to bound the number of iterations. This is not shown here.

Clause **(4)**: The clause for return statements is more complicated than the others, as it has to deal with two different skylines: the one from the function that is about to return, and the one from the caller. Let f be the name of the current function. To execute a return statement, the current skyline is first extended with $F(l)$ to the location l of the return keyword. Then, the returned expression is evaluated. Next the skyline is extended with $F(m)$, to the location m of the closing brace of the function body. Then, the program state from before the function call is restored, but updated with all the changes made by f. For this, the topmost element σ_c of the call stack is removed; this is the program state of the caller. A new state σ'' is constructed, which the caller should use to resume execution; σ'' has the caller's original env, but with the #return register holding the return value. The program counter and call stack are restored to the ones from before the call. The caller's skyline $\sigma_c.sky$ is extended with a forward line $F(n)$ to the call site, and an edge $E(p)$ to the power draw p. Finally, the skyline of the function call is recorded in the list of all skylines of f. This is done with the function *registerSkyline*, which stores the given skyline in the given state, and returns the thus updated state.

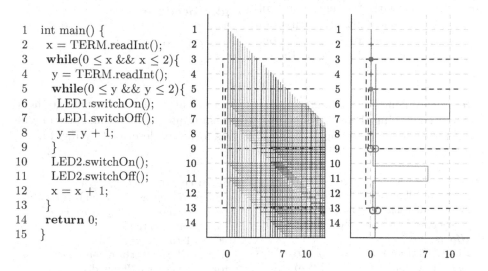

```
1    int main() {
2      x = TERM.readInt();
3      while(0 ≤ x && x ≤ 2){
4        y = TERM.readInt();
5        while(0 ≤ y && y ≤ 2){
6          LED1.switchOn();
7          LED1.switchOff();
8          y = y + 1;
9        }
10       LED2.switchOn();
11       LED2.switchOff();
12       x = x + 1;
13     }
14     return 0;
15   }
```

Fig. 9. A program with many execution paths, and its unmerged and merged skylines.

5   Merging Skylines

The skylines of a program often have many identical parts. Take for example the program in Fig. 9. Most of its execution paths have identical energy behaviour. To merge skylines, we use a three-phase algorithm: *preparation, merging* and *finalization*. It is executed independently for every function.

Preparation. First all skylines are split into *fragments* and stored in an array, giving each a unique index. Fragments represent single horizontal or vertical lines with explicit start and end points. Every fragment has a set of continuations: indexes of the fragments that follow it. Merging deletes explicit jumps $J(l)$: they are kept implicitly as fragments whose start point does not coincide with the end point of their predecessor. Initially each fragment has at most one continuation, but more may be added later. Preparation is shown in Fig. 11.

```
procedure COLOURIZE(frags)
  for i ← 1 to Nfrags do
    if (i > 1) ∧ (i ∈ frags[i−1].conts) ∧
    (frags[i − 1].end = frags[i].start)
  then
      colour[i] ← colour[i − 1]
    else
      colour[i] ← a fresh colour
    end if
  end for
end procedure
```

Fig. 10. Assigning colours

Merging. Whenever two fragments indexed i and j are equal, we can merge them by first combining their continuations, and then replacing all occurrences of j in continuations of other fragments by i. This is formally described by Fig. 12.

```
procedure PREPARE(skies(f))
  // input: all skylines of function f
  // output: frags, an array of fragments,
  // each with at most one continuation
  Nfrags ← 0
  for all Skyline sky ∈ skies(f) do
    // all skylines begin with S(l,p)
    let ⟨l, p⟩ be such that sky[1] = S(l, p)
    for i ← 2 to length(sky) do
      sky[i] is either F(l') or J(l') or E(p')
      in the first two cases, let p' = p
      in the last case, let l' = l
      if sky[i] is F(l') or E(p') then
        Nfrags ← Nfrags + 1
        frags[Nfrags].start ← ⟨l, p⟩
        frags[Nfrags].end ← ⟨l', p'⟩
        frags[Nfrags − 1].conts ← { Nfrags }
      end if
      ⟨l, p⟩ ← ⟨l', p'⟩
    end for
    // last fragment has no continuation
    frags[Nfrags].conts ← ∅
  end for
end procedure
```

Fig. 11. Initializing the *frags* array

```
procedure MERGE(frags, Nfrags)
  // frags, Nfrags as produced by prepare
  // output: modified frags with equal
  // fragments merged
  for i ← 1 to Nfrags − 1 do
    if frags[i] = null then continue
    for j ← i + 1 to Nfrags do
      if frags[j] = null
      or frags[i].start ≠ frags[j].start
      or frags[i].end ≠ frags[j].end
      then continue
      frags[i].conts ←
        frags[i].conts ∪ frags[j].conts
      frags[j] ← null
      for k ← 1 to Nfrags do
        if frags[k] ≠ null ∧
          j ∈ frags[k].conts then
          frags[k].conts ←
            (frags[k].conts \ { j }) ∪ { i }
        end if
      end for
    end for
  end for
end procedure
```

Fig. 12. Merging fragments

Visualization. Finally, fragments are grouped into skylines, by assigning the same colour to directly connected fragments. Figure 10 implements this. It then assigns a small diagonal offset to each colour group (not shown here), to avoid drawing lines on top of each other.

Statement Markers. Between two consecutive horizontal lines, a + indicates that a statement was executed at that point. Continuations are drawn as coloured bullets or circles: if $j \in frags[i].conts$ and $colour[i] \neq colour[j]$, then if $frags[i].end = frags[j].start$ then a bullet in $colour[j]$ is drawn at the end of fragment i. Otherwise, the continuation is a jump backwards; this is indicated by drawing an open circle in $colour[j]$ at the end of fragment i. Dotted lines in the diagram indicate the beginning and end points of loops.

6   A Real-World Example: Line-Following Robot

In this section we demonstrate how to apply our analysis to an existing real-world example, written in C. The program is simple enough that there is no potential for energy consumption optimization, but nonetheless our analysis gives insight into the program's energy behaviour.

We chose a random "simple line follower" project from the Arduino project database [1]. This robot has two motors and two sensors, and uses them to follow a line on the floor. It works as follows. The sensors are positioned to the left and right of the line. If only the left sensor sees the line, the robot turns left. Symmetrically for the right sensor. If neither sensor sees the line, the robot moves forward. If both sensors see the line, the robot stops. The code has potential for refactoring, as it contains unnecessary repetition. However our goal was not to find the most elegant line follower robot, but to apply our method to a real-world example.

The original source code, written in C, is almost valid SECA. We made two changes to the code for our parser to accept it. First, we defined the constants LOW and HIGH, and the function delay, which for our purpose is empty. Second, we replaced the statements that write to output pins and read from input pins with component calls. Figure 13 shows an excerpt of the code after these adjustments.

We then created the component models for motors and sensors in the source code of our analysis engine. The simulated motors have three states, *forward*, *backward*, and *stop*, and corresponding component calls. In the forward and backward states, motors have a power draw of 750 mW. The sensors have no power draw, and their read component call returns a symbolic value in $\{0, 1\}$.

Analysis Results. Figure 14 shows skyline diagrams for the functions *loop* (top) and *MoveForward* (bottom). The diagram for *MoveForward* illustrates that the function has two behaviours. One where the power draw increases in two steps from 0 to 1500 mW, and one where the power draw stays constant at 1500 mW. The functions *TurnLeft* and *TurnRight*, not shown here, look similar. The function *Stop*, also not shown, has the opposite behaviour: the power draw decreases

```
1   int main() {
2     while( true ) {
3       loop();
4     }
5     return 0;
6   }
7   void loop(){
8     if((SensorLeft.read()==LOW) &&
9       (SensorRight.read()==LOW)) {
10      MoveForward();
11    }
12    if((SensorLeft.read()==HIGH) &&
13      (SensorRight.read()==HIGH)) {
14      Stop();
15    }
16    if((SensorLeft.read()==LOW) &&
17      (SensorRight.read()==HIGH)) {
18      TurnLeft();
19    }
20    if((SensorLeft.read()==HIGH) &&
21      (SensorRight.read()==LOW)) {
22      TurnRight();
23    }
24  }
25  void MoveForward() {
26    MotorLeft.Forward();
27    MotorRight.Forward();
28    delay(20);
29  }
```

Fig. 13. Excerpt of line follower program

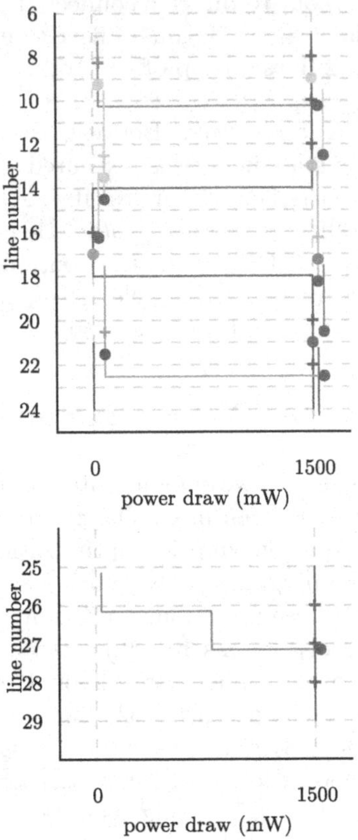

Fig. 14. Diagrams for *loop* (top) and *MoveForward* (bottom)

in two steps. The function *loop* has many behaviours, depending on the executed conditional. There are the cases where the power draw stays 0 or 1500 mW, or it can increase in lines 10, 18, or 22, or it can decrease in line 14.

Discussion. The function *loop* has high complexity for symbolic execution. We had to set the iteration limit to 2 for the analysis to terminate within 20 s on a ten year old laptop. The merged diagram would not change with more iterations. The high complexity occurs because firstly the four conditionals can be entered independently, and secondly the sensors are read in each condition, making the conditionals not mutually exclusive. This results in 16 possible executions of the function. Refactoring the program either by reading the sensors once at the start of loop() or by nesting the conditionals, reduces the number of possible executions to 4, making the analysis terminate in 2.4 s with iteration limit 2. An improved version of the robot program together with its skyline diagrams can be found on the project website [2].

7   Related Work

Directly related are the second author's previous works [11, 16] describing static energy analyses for the language ECA. The first derives energy bounds for a specific input scenario; the second is a symbolic analysis that over-approximates all possible paths. These works do not use skylines. They do use hardware models that also support incidental one-time energy costs. This incidental energy cost can be useful for approximating energy consumption that varies over time. Also closely related is the first author's previous work [20], which introduces skylines but also an overapproximation since it estimates resource use over time.

Most publications on energy efficiency of software approach the problem on a high level, defining programming and design patterns for writing energy-efficient code; see, e.g., [4, 24, 26]. In [9] and [25], a program is divided into *phases* describing similar behaviour. Based on the behaviour of the software, design-level optimizations are proposed to achieve lower energy consumption. Petri-net-based energy modelling techniques for embedded systems are proposed in [14, 23].

A general analysis for resource consumption is described in [17]. There are generic resource consumption analyses, built on techniques such as solving recurrence relations [5], amortized analysis [12], separation logic [7], and a Vienna Development Method style program logic [6]. Contrary to these approaches, our method has an explicit hardware model and a context in the form of component states. This enables the inclusion of state-dependent energy consumption.

In [13] and [15] energy consumption of the processor running embedded software is analysed for specific architectures (SimpleScalar in [13], and XMOS ISA-level models in [15]), while our approach is hardware-parametric and focuses on external hardware. Several tools perform a static analysis of the energy consumption of the CPU based on per-instruction measurements, such as in [8, 27].

8   Discussion and Future Work

This article proposes a new approach for visualizing the energy consumption of a system with external hardware without actually running the software or having a real test setup. The result is presented as skyline diagrams with a direct link to the source code, using line numbers. This visualization is generated by symbolic execution, followed by a merging algorithm to deal with the explosion of possible execution paths. There are few restrictions on the models of hardware components, allowing a user to model a wide variety of hardware components.

We have implemented all techniques of this article in Haskell as a proof of concept, using the Z3 SMT library to prune infeasible paths. Every skyline diagram in this paper and on the project website [2] was computed by this tool in a few seconds on a ten year old laptop. However, since symbolic execution has exponential complexity, it would only take a couple of nested loops containing component calls for the analysis to no longer be computed in feasible time.

The focus of this paper is on a minimal implementation, to explore the idea of drawing graphs over source lines. A larger case study using the implementation could result in useful feedback on how the process can be applied in practice. This case study should evaluate if programmers get feedback they can use, and if there is a practical need to use another technique instead of, or alongside, bounded symbolic execution. In particular, our visualization should lend itself well to abstract interpretation, which can be an alternative to symbolic execution. This would require incorporating parts of the merging algorithm into the abstract interpretation. A combination of symbolic execution and abstract interpretation would be more complex, but could provide powerful tooling.

Editor integration can improve usability, for instance by annotating or overlaying the source code with diagrams. It may also be useful to offer an interactive visualization that allows developers to explore skylines and recover information about individual execution paths, highlighting the relevant code.

Finally, our approach could track other resources. A similar methodology could be used to visualize memory usage, or even time. *Incidental*, one time, energy consumption of hardware component calls could also be relevant to show.

Acknowledgements. We would like to thank Rinus Plasmeijer, Olha Shkaravska, Tim Steenvoorden, and Nico Naus for many hours of fruitful discussion. Special thanks goes to Ralf Hinze, who created an exam question, the grading of which eventually led to the idea of resource skylines. Thanks also to Pieter Koopman who provided funding for this project.

References

1. Arduino project hub. https://create.arduino.cc/projecthub. Accessed 01 May 2020
2. SECA project wiki. https://gitlab.science.ru.nl/mklinik/eca-symbolic-execution/-/wikis/home. Accessed 06 Feb 2020
3. SECA source code repository. https://gitlab.science.ru.nl/mklinik/eca-symbolic-execution. Accessed 29 Jan 2020
4. Albers, S.: Energy-efficient algorithms. Commun. ACM **53**(5), 86–96 (2010)
5. Albert, E., Arenas, P., Genaim, S., Puebla, G., Zanardini, D.: COSTA: Design and implementation of a cost and termination analyzer for Java bytecode. In: de Boer, F.S., Bonsangue, M.M., Graf, S., de Roever, W.-P. (eds.) FMCO 2007. LNCS, vol. 5382, pp. 113–132. Springer, Heidelberg (2008). https://doi.org/10.1007/978-3-540-92188-2_5
6. Aspinall, D., Beringer, L., Hofmann, M., Loidl, H.W., Momigliano, A.: A program logic for resources. Theor. Comput. Sci. **389**(3), 411–445 (2007). https://doi.org/10.1016/j.tcs.2007.09.003
7. Atkey, R.: Amortised resource analysis with separation logic. In: Gordon, A.D. (ed.) ESOP 2010. LNCS, vol. 6012, pp. 85–103. Springer, Heidelberg (2010). https://doi.org/10.1007/978-3-642-11957-6_6
8. Brooks, D., Tiwari, V., Martonosi, M.: Wattch: a framework for architectural-level power analysis and optimizations. SIGARCH Comput. Arch. News **28**(2), 83–94 (2000)
9. Cohen, M., Zhu, H.S., Senem, E.E., Liu, Y.D.: Energy types. SIGPLAN Not. **47**(10), 831–850 (2012)
10. van Gastel, B.: Assessing sustainability of software - analysing correctness, memory and energy consumption. Ph.D. thesis, Open University (2016)

11. van Gastel, B., Kersten, R., van Eekelen, M.: Using dependent types to define energy augmented semantics of programs. In: van Eekelen, M., Dal Lago, U. (eds.) FOPARA 2015. LNCS, vol. 9964, pp. 20–39. Springer, Cham (2016). https://doi.org/10.1007/978-3-319-46559-3_2

12. Hoffmann, J., Aehlig, K., Hofmann, M.: Multivariate amortized resource analysis. In: Ball, T., Sagiv, M. (eds.) POPL 2011, pp. 357–370. ACM (2011)

13. Jayaseelan, R., Mitra, T., Li, X.: Estimating the worst-case energy consumption of embedded software. In: Proceedings of RTAS 2006, pp. 81–90. IEEE (2006). https://doi.org/10.1109/RTAS.2006.17

14. Junior, M.N.O., et al.: Analyzing software performance and energy consumption of embedded systems by probabilistic modeling: an approach based on coloured petri nets. In: Donatelli, S., Thiagarajan, P.S. (eds.) ICATPN 2006. LNCS, vol. 4024, pp. 261–281. Springer, Heidelberg (2006). https://doi.org/10.1007/11767589_15

15. Liqat, U., Kerrison, S., Serrano, A., Georgiou, K., Lopez-Garcia, P., Grech, N., Hermenegildo, M.V., Eder, K.: Energy consumption analysis of programs based on XMOS ISA-level models. In: Gupta, G., Peña, R. (eds.) LOPSTR 2013. LNCS, vol. 8901, pp. 72–90. Springer, Cham (2014). https://doi.org/10.1007/978-3-319-14125-1_5

16. Kersten, R., Toldin, P.P., van Gastel, B., van Eekelen, M.: A hoare logic for energy consumption analysis. In: Dal Lago, U., Peña, R. (eds.) FOPARA 2013. LNCS, vol. 8552, pp. 93–109. Springer, Cham (2014). https://doi.org/10.1007/978-3-319-12466-7_6

17. Kersten, R., Shkaravska, O., van Gastel, B., Montenegro, M., Eekelenvan Eekelen, M.: Making resource analysis practical for real-time Java. In: Proceedings of JTRES 2012, pp. 135–144. ACM (2012). https://doi.org/10.1145/2388936.2388959

18. King, J.C.: Symbolic execution and program testing. Commun. ACM **19**(7), 385–394 (1976)

19. Klinik, M., van Gastel, B., Kop, C., Eekelenvan Eekelen, M.: Skylines for symbolic energy consumption analysis - technical report. Technical report, Radboud University (2020). https://gitlab.science.ru.nl/mklinik/eca-symbolic-execution/blob/master/paper/techreport.pdf

20. Klinik, M., Jansen, J.M., Plasmeijer, R.: The sky is the limit: analysing resource consumption over time using skylines. In: Proceedings of the 29th Symposium on Implementation and Application of Functional Programming Languages, IFL 2017. ACM (2017)

21. Microchip Technology Inc.: ATmega48A/PA/88A/PA/168A/PA/328/P Data Sheet (2018)

22. Nielson, H.R., Nielson, F.: Semantics With Applications: A Formal Introduction. Wiley, Hoboken (1992)

23. Nogueira, B., Maciel, P., Tavares, E., Andrade, E., Massa, R., Callou, G., Ferraz, R.: A formal model for performance and energy evaluation of embedded systems. EURASIP J. Embed. Syst. **2011**(1), 1–12 (2011). https://doi.org/10.1155/2011/316510

24. Ranganathan, P.: Recipe for efficiency: principles of power-aware computing. Commun. ACM **53**(4), 60–67 (2010)

25. Sampson, A., Dietl, W., Fortuna, E., Gnanapragasam, D., Ceze, L., Grossman, D.: EnerJ: approximate data types for safe and general low-power computation. SIGPLAN Not. **46**(6), 164–174 (2011)
26. Saxe, E.: Power-efficient software. Commun. ACM **53**(2), 44–48 (2010). https://doi.org/10.1145/1646353.1646370
27. Sinha, A., Chandrakasan, A.P.: JouleTrack: a web based tool for software energy profiling. In: Proceedings of DAC 2001, pp. 220–225. ACM (2001)

Formally Verified Timing Computation for Non-deterministic Horizontal Turns During Aircraft Collision Avoidance Maneuvers

Yanni Kouskoulas[1]([envelope]), T. J. Machado[1,2], and Daniel Genin[1]

[1] The Johns Hopkins University Applied Physics Laboratory, Laurel, MD, USA
{yanni.kouskoulas,daniel.genin}@jhuapl.edu
[2] Department of Mathematics, New Mexico State University, Las Cruces, NM, USA
tjm@nmsu.edu

Abstract. We develop a library of proofs to support rigorous mathematical reasoning about horizontal aircraft turning maneuvers, and apply it to formally verify a timing computation for use during mixed horizontal and vertical aircraft collision avoidance maneuvers. We consider turns that follow non-deterministic circular turn-to-bearing horizontal motion, formalizing path-length and timing properties. These kinematics are the building blocks for Dubins trajectories, and can be used to formalize a variety of techniques, including those that contain non-determinism. The timing computation establishes, for intersecting trajectories, the exact bounds of time intervals when the horizontal position of the aircraft might coincide, and during which they must be at different altitudes to avoid collision.

1 Introduction

Autonomous and semi-autonomous systems that control ground vehicles, boats, and aircraft all need to reason about horizontal turns in order to create plans for future motion that meet system objectives.

We are motivated by aircraft collision avoidance maneuvers that combine vertical and horizontal advice to ensure multi-aircraft encounters are safely separated. These maneuvers advise aircraft to turn at the same time they change vertical velocity – the objective being to keep the aircraft separated in altitude during periods when their positions might coincide horizontally. This requires correctly computing the time interval that describes when in the future both aircraft might come into horizontal conflict.

This paper develops a formalization of *non-deterministic* turn-to-bearing motion, where a vehicle turns following a circular arc until reaching a certain bearing, and then follows a straight path thereafter. Turn-to-bearing motion is the building block for Dubins trajectories used in many different techniques in the literature (see Sect. 2), but here we consider that the parameters that

---

The original version of this chapter was revised: Equations 29 and 30 have been corrected. The correction to this chapter is available at
https://doi.org/10.1007/978-3-030-58298-2_13

M. H. ter Beek and D. Ničković (Eds.): FMICS 2020, LNCS 12327, pp. 113–129, 2020.
https://doi.org/10.1007/978-3-030-58298-2_4

describe our future path are non-deterministic and uncertain. The formalization is embodied in a library of proofs that are detailed descriptions of these kinematics, and are machine-checked to guarantee correctness. Each theorem in the text corresponds to proofs in the formalization.[1] We believe that the library can serve as a foundation for formal reasoning about horizontal turns in the Coq proof assistant, supporting the development of insight and correct reasoning for a wide variety of path planning and collision avoidance algorithms. Further, we hope that it helps guarantee a high level of correctness and robustness for robotic systems' horizontal motion, and that it provides the basis for certification artifacts (proofs) that can be used to establish system algorithm and software correctness.

Most importantly, we created these proofs because we wanted to formally verify a collision avoidance algorithm and were unable to find the necessary lemmas in the Coq standard library. We apply these lemmas to a pointwise computation for horizontal conflict intervals, appropriate for use with [8], which can handle analysis of aircraft collision avoidance advice that requires turning horizontally while simultaneously accelerating towards a target vertical velocity.

The contributions of this paper are: the development of a Coq library for reasoning about non-deterministic Dubins-style paths; an additional Coq library defining a variety of two-argument arctangent functions with different branch cuts that are each sensitive to the quadrant and sign of their arguments; a new expression for computing the appropriate angle necessary for connecting Dubins paths to a destination waypoint[2]; insight into the timing characteristics of horizontal turns following circular arc segments; and a simple, efficient, piecewise approach to calculating collision timing of horizontal conflict intervals based on this insight.

1.1   Non-deterministic Turn-to-Bearing Kinematics

We define *non-deterministic one-turn-to-bearing* motion as a set of trajectories representing a range of future motion possibilities that might be followed by the vehicle. We characterize this motion with a tuple that represents the set future trajectories that are possible $(x_0, y_0, \theta_0, r_\alpha, r_\beta, \theta_\alpha, \theta_\beta, s_\alpha, s_\beta)$ where: (x_0, y_0) and θ_0 are initial position and orientation of the vehicle; r_α, r_β, θ_α, θ_β are bounds on the turn radius and change in orientation after completing the turn, respectively; and s_α, s_β are bounds on the speed throughout the encounter, which unlike the other parameters, is assumed to vary continuously as a function of time. We adopt the convention of using positive radii and bearing offsets to represent counterclockwise (left) turns, and negative radii and bearing offsets to represent clockwise (right) turns. Left turns are represented by $0 < r_\alpha \leq r_\beta$ and $0 < \theta_\alpha < \theta_\beta < 2\pi$, while right turns by $r_\alpha \leq r_\beta < 0$ and $-2\pi < \theta_\alpha < \theta_\beta < 0$. In all cases, we assume $0 < s_\alpha \leq s_\beta$.

---

[1] Coq proofs are at https://bitbucket.org/ykouskoulas/ottb-foundation-proofs.

[2] There exist alternate expressions for this angle, but to our knowledge, the formulation in this paper is new.

Realization of a specific future trajectory requires drawing from this sample space. Each possibility in the set has parameters $r, \theta_c, s(t)$ satisfying the constraint predicate $\chi(r, \theta_c, s) = \theta_c \in [\theta_\alpha, \theta_\beta] \wedge r \in [r_\alpha, r_\beta] \wedge (\forall u, s(u) \in [s_\alpha, s_\beta])$ which represents a path with initial turn that we model using a circular arc of radius r, followed by a linear path tangent to the turn whose bearing is offset by θ_c from θ_0. The path is traversed with continuously varying speed $s(t)$. Figure 1 plots a visualization of turn-to-bearing envelopes and paths for $(x_0, y_0, \theta_0, r_\alpha, r_\beta, \theta_\alpha, \theta_\beta, s_\alpha, s_\beta) = (0, 0, 0, 3.22, 6.89, 2.41, 3.62, 1, 2)$.

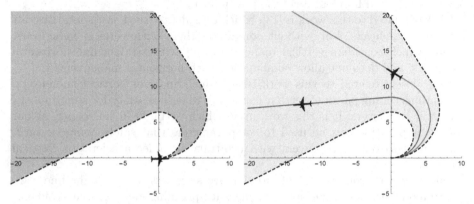

(a) Shaded area is reachable in the future.   (b) Paths show two possible trajectories.

Fig. 1. Vizualizing turn-to-bearing motion.

Components of the vehicle's trajectory for these kinematics are given by

$$J_x(t) = \begin{cases} r \sin\left(\frac{d(t)}{r} + \theta_0\right) - r \sin(\theta_0) + x_0 & d(t) \leq r\theta_c \\ (d(t) - r\theta_c)\cos(\theta_c + \theta_0) + r\sin(\theta_c + \theta_0) - r\sin(\theta_0) + x_0 & d(t) > r\theta_c \end{cases}$$
(1)

$$J_y(t) = \begin{cases} -r\cos\left(\frac{d(t)}{r} + \theta_0\right) + r\cos(\theta_0) + y_0 & d(t) \leq r\theta_c \\ (d(t) - r\theta_c)\sin(\theta_c + \theta_0) - r\cos(\theta_c + \theta_0) + r\cos(\theta_0) + y_0 & d(t) > r\theta_c \end{cases}$$
(2)

for overall trajectory $J(t) = J_x(t)\hat{x} + J_y(t)\hat{y}$. The distance traveled on the path is related to speed during the trajectory in the usual way, $d(t) = \int_0^t s(\gamma)d\gamma$.

2 Literature Review

A number of efforts have gone on to formalize horizontal motion and prove properties about it, but all have characteristics that distinguish them from the present work. For instance [7] develops an approach for maneuvering and coordinating vehicles following Dubins paths utilizing Kripke models which is verified via a model checker. They don't incorporate non-determinism in their turning models, and don't deal with timing characteristics of the turns. In [2], they use differential dynamic logic with KeYmaera X to model collision avoidance in automobiles with skidding, but unlike the present work they are concerned mainly with geometric properties of paths and do not consider timing. The work in [11] is an excellent treatment of collision avoidance in a wide variety of uncertain turning scenarios for ground robots. It assumes obstacles characterized by maximum velocity bounds, is not focused on timing analysis, and is not tailored for use in mixed vertical and horizontal collision avoidance.

Closely related to this work is [13], which considers curved, horizontal aircraft avoidance manuevers, but without combining them with vertical maneuvers; and [6], which considers vertical maneuvers, but with straight-line horizontal kinematics, and does not allow combination with horizontal maneuvers.

Also closely related to this work is [8], which analyzes vertical maneuvers, but contains timing parameters that can be set to ensure safety for simultaneous horizontal manuevers. It is this work upon which we build in this paper, as our timing computation can be used to set parameters that safely compose turn-to-bearing horizontal maneuvers with arbitrary bounded-acceleration vertical maneuvers.

Dubins paths, constructed of circular arc segments and straight lines, are used to model horizontal motion in many path planning and collision avoidance algorithms, such as [4, 5, 9, 10, 14, 15]. These examples are not formally verified, and although some are created with aircraft in mind, not designed for timing analysis nor the adversarial collision avoidance assumptions in our work.

Many years of work have gone into the tools and libraries that we used for our development, including the Coq proof assistant [1] and the Coquelicot extensions for its real library [3]. Our libraries are intended to contribute to this toolbox.

We develop a new expression for calculating allowable tangents to a turn; an alternate solution to this problem is reported in [12].

3   Reasoning Foundations for Turn-to-Bearing Maneuvers

The following sections describe the development of a library for reasoning about turn-to-bearing trajectories, and the application of this library to compute timing characteristics for safe maneuvering of simultaneously turning aircraft.

We first had to develop some definitions and trigonometric properties that were not available in our environment. We were then able to create a library for reasoning about turn-to-bearing paths.

3.1   Library Interface

The library we have developed is organized around the representation of a path in $\mathbb{R}^2$ and a predicate

$$\text{path\_segment}(D, f_x(d), f_y(d), (x_0, y_0), (x_1, y_1)) \tag{3}$$

which when true asserts: that $f_x(d)$ and $f_y(d)$ are parameterized functions describing the x and y positions of the path in the coordinate plane; that the resulting path is continuous and integrable; and that $f_x(d)$ and $f_y(d)$ are parameterized by the path distance, i.e. $\int_0^d \sqrt{(f_x'(\alpha))^2 + (f_y'(\alpha))^2}\, d\alpha = d$; that $(f_x(0), f_y(0)) = (x_0, y_0)$; and that $(f_x(D), f_y(D)) = (x_1, y_1)$. Parameterizing our path representation by path distance creates a canonical representation of the geometry for each path, isolating it from timing considerations associated with variations in speed during the maneuver, and allowing us to analyze each aspect separately and combine them in the end.

Note that although the turn-to-bearing paths in the library have a starting and ending point separated by distance D, the paths continue indefinitely.

The library also contains piecewise functions parameterizing the x and y positions for turn-to-bearing paths $H_x(r, \theta_0, x_0, \theta_c, rtp, d)$ and $H_y(r, \theta_0, y_0, \theta_c, rtp, d)$, meant to be used with the path_segment predicate. The functions are equivalent to Eqs. 1 and 2, differing only in that they are parameterized by distance d instead of time t. The functions are curried before being used in path_segment, instantiated with starting point (x_0, y_0), initial orientation θ_0, the turn radius r, and the angular offset for the final bearing θ_c. They also require an argument named rtp, which must be a proof object showing that $0 < r\theta_c < 2\pi|r|$, ensuring the signs of r and θ_c to be identical, and enforcing an upper bound on θ_c. The files *ttyp.v* and *tdyn.v* define the path_segment predicate, the parameterized turn-to-bearing paths, and prove lemmas about path continuity, differentiability, and path-length parameterization of H_x and H_y so they can be used with the path_segment predicate. Along with the parameterization, the library contains predicates straight and turning which indicate whether the parameters describing a path reach the final destination point while traveling in a straight line, or turning on a circular arc, respectively.

The rest of the library has: trigonometric definitions and identities that are missing from the Coq standard library (*atan2.v*, *strt.v* and *strt2.v*); lemmas that help the user introduce turn-to-bearing path_segment predicates into the context (*tlens.v*); lemmas that help derive consequences and mathematical relationships from turn-to-bearing path_segment assumptions (*tlens.v*); lemmas about timing intervals (*ttim.v*); and theorems about the computation of timing properties based on pathlength (*dtlen.v*). The size of the development is significant, around 40k lines of proof scripts.

Because Coq allows expression in a higher order logic, it permits quantification over any variable. This means we can hold the starting and ending points of the path fixed and quantify over the other parameters to reason about waypoints; or fix ranges of parameters and quantify over the radii and angles to reason about ranges of non-deterministic possibilities in turn radius and final bearing.

In this paper, for clarity, we present lemmas from the library in a standard position and orientation such that $(x_0, y_0) = (0, 0)$, $\theta_0 = 0$, and $(x_1, y_1) = (x, y)$. To analyze intersecting paths that are oriented and positioned arbitrarily with respect to one another, the more general form can be recovered by assuming that

$$x = (x_1 - x_0)\cos(\theta_0) + (y_1 - y_0)\sin(\theta_0) \tag{4}$$
$$y = -(x_1 - x_0)\sin(\theta_0) + (y_1 - y_0)\cos(\theta_0) \tag{5}$$

The library itself contains the translations and rotations to allow full generality when working with more than one path.

3.2   Trigonometric Properties

Geometric intuition which might seem simple does not always translate naturally to formal analysis in a proving environment.

First we needed to encode in our proving environment a basic understanding of the way circular turns may be combined with straight paths that exit the turns on a tangent. There are two tangent lines to a circle that arrive at any particular point outside the circle (see Fig. 2). One of the tangents is not useful because

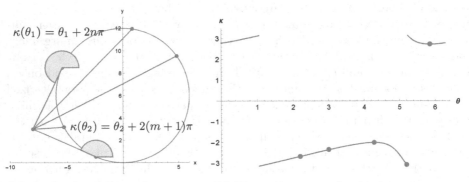

(a) Angle of each line segment is κ (b) Discontinuous κ_2; $\kappa' = 0$ points are tangent

Fig. 2. If we parameterize positions on a circular path using the angle associated with the tangent at each point, $\kappa(\theta)$ – not necessarily a tangent itself – is the angle of the line connecting the point on the circle to a point (x, y) outside the circle.

for counter-clockwise turns, it always results in a path with a discontinuous derivative. This is geometrically obvious to a human by inspection, but somewhat challenging to formalize in Coq.

Using a chord lemma from geometry we can infer that a vehicle approaching (x, y) from a circular turn will do so at an angle of $\theta_m = 2\operatorname{atan2}(y, x)$ and that the radius required to reach it will be $r_m = (x^2 + y^2)/(2y)$. We find that decreasing the radius of the turn decreases the angle, while increasing it makes (x, y) unreachable via a tangent line. Thus θ_m defines an upper bound on the approach angle. From inspection, we can see that the angle of the second tangent exceeds this boundary.

In order to formalize this geometric intuition, we define a function which given the orientation θ of the vehicle on a turning path of radius r would return the angle from the vehicle to the point (x, y).

$$\kappa(\theta) = \operatorname{atan}\left(\frac{y - r(1 - \cos(\theta))}{x - r\sin(\theta)}\right) \tag{6}$$

Both by construction, and by the periodicity of sin and cos, we note that κ is periodic with period 2π. For the remainder of this section we will restrict the domain of κ to $(0, 2\pi)$ for $r > 0$, and $(-2\pi, 0)$ for $r < 0$. As illustrated in Fig. 2b, the function κ is not continuous for all values of the destination point (x, y).

We define a series of functions based on a two-argument arctangent and different branch cuts, which have distinct, overlapping, and complementary domains upon which (x, y) yields a continuous function.

$$\kappa_2(\theta) = \operatorname{atan}_2\left(y - r(1 - \cos(\theta)), x - r\sin(\theta)\right) \tag{7}$$
$$\kappa_3(\theta) = \operatorname{atan}_2\left(-(y - r(1 - \cos(\theta))), -(x - r\sin(\theta))\right) + \pi \tag{8}$$
$$\kappa_4(\theta) = \operatorname{atan}_2\left(-(x - r\sin(\theta)), y - r(1 - \cos(\theta))\right) + \pi/2 \tag{9}$$

Henceforth, when we refer to properties of κ, we are choosing a variant with the branch cut oriented so that there is no discontinuity for the given destination point (x, y).

When κ is continuous, we show that the unique maximum and minimum values $\kappa(\theta_1)$ and $\kappa(\theta_2)$ correspond to the angles of the correct and incorrect tangent lines respectively (for $r > 0$, if $r < 0$ the maxima and minima are reversed). We prove that $\kappa(\theta) = \frac{\theta_m}{2}$ implies that $\theta = 0$ or $\theta = \theta_m$. Since $\frac{\theta_m}{2}$ is a value that κ takes on, it must be that $\kappa(\theta_1) \geq \frac{\theta_m}{2} \geq \kappa(\theta_2)$.

Our choice of domain ensures that 0 is not between θ_1 and θ_2, so we can use the Intermediate Value Theorem to show that θ_m is in-between θ_1 and θ_2 in the domain. Because θ_m is a limiting value of the approach angle, we can eliminate θ_2, which is always outside of the allowable range, leaving θ_1 as the angle of approach that ensures path continuity.

We calculate extremal values of κ, θ_1 and θ_2, by setting the derivative of κ to zero, and solving for the argument. Fortunately, each variant of the κ function for which the destination point (x, y) yields a continuous function has the same derivative

$$\kappa'(\theta) = \frac{r((2r - y)(\tan(\theta/2))^2 - 2x\tan(\theta/2) + y)}{(2(1 - \cos(\theta))/(\sin(\theta))^2) \cdot ((y - r(1 - \cos(\theta)))^2 + (x - r\sin(\theta))^2)} \tag{10}$$

for $\theta \notin \{0, \pi\}$. The sign of the denominator is always positive, and so the sign of κ' is directly related to the sign of the quadratic function in the numerator; the task of calculating the maximum and minimum is reduced to the problem of solving a quadratic in $\tan(\theta/2)$. The solution associated with the maximum value of κ is given in Eq. 14.

Reasoning about the continuity of the κ variants, handling their derivatives as the angle crosses the branch cut, and ordering of roots and angles to establish what "in-between" means in an angular domain that is a clock system is contained within the file *strt.v* and its corresponding documentation.

3.3   Turn-to-Bearing Path Properties

Parameters for turn-to-bearing trajectories must be selected in a way that the radius and angle of departure from the turn lead from the starting point to the ending point, and so that the distance is consistent with the path. In this section we state basic results about paths, and select a few proofs about which we provide some details in order to give a flavor of the reasoning in the library.

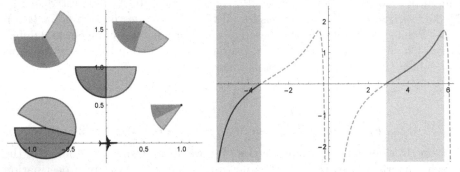

(a) Approaches for different points.   **(b)** r vs. θ for a single point $(-.8, .2)$.

Fig. 3. Relationship between allowable angle of approach and required radius to achieve that angle. Choosing angular ranges of approach also entails a turn direction; left turns are marked with violet and right turns marked with green. (Color figure online)

We can construct a turn-to-bearing trajectory by choosing an angle of approach θ for a point (x, y), and computing the turn radius required to arrive there with that orientation. The angle of approach is constrained because of the initial position and angle of the aircraft and the required kinematics, as in Fig. 3.

Theorem 1 (Turn-to-bearing dependent radius). *A vehicle following a turn-to-bearing trajectory can approach point (x, y) with a chosen angle θ when*

$$
\begin{aligned}
&(0 < \theta_m \wedge (\theta_m/2 < \theta \le \theta_m \vee -2\pi < \theta < \theta_m/2 - 2\pi)) \vee \\
&(\theta_m < 0 \wedge (\theta_m \le \theta < \theta_m/2 \vee \theta_m/2 + 2\pi < \theta < 2\pi))
\end{aligned}
\tag{11}
$$

using radius

$$
R(x, y, \theta) = \frac{x \sin(\theta) - y \cos(\theta)}{1 - \cos(\theta)}
\tag{12}
$$

We can also construct a turn-to-bearing trajectory by choosing a turn radius r, and computing the angle of approach that the radius entails when we arrive at (x, y). The choice of radius is constrained if the target point is on the same side as the direction of the turn, because the turn must be rapid enough to orient the aircraft in the direction of the target point before it has passed it.

Theorem 2 (Turn-to-bearing dependent approach angle). *A vehicle following a turn-to-bearing trajectory can approach point* (x, y) *using a turn with chosen radius* r *when*

$$\left(0 < y \wedge r \le \frac{x^2 + y^2}{2y}\right) \vee (y = 0 \wedge x < 0) \vee \left(y < 0 \wedge \frac{x^2 + y^2}{2y} \le r\right) \quad (13)$$

and the angle of approach is

$$\Theta(x, y, r) = \begin{cases} 2 \operatorname{atan}\left(\frac{x - \sqrt{x^2 - (2r - y)y}}{(2r - y)}\right) + P(x, y, r) & 2r - y \ne 0 \\ 2 \operatorname{atan}\left(\frac{y}{2x}\right) & 2r - y = 0 \wedge x > 0 \\ \pi \operatorname{sign}(r) & 2r - y = 0 \wedge x \le 0 \end{cases} \quad (14)$$

where P *is a phase correction given by*

$$P(x, y, r) = \begin{cases} 0 & (0 < r \wedge ((0 < x \wedge 0 < y) \vee x \le 0 \wedge 2r < y)) \\ & \vee (r < 0 \wedge ((x < 0 \wedge y < 0) \vee y < 2r)) \\ 2\pi & 0 < r \wedge (0 \le x \wedge y < 0 \vee x < 0 \wedge y < 2r)) \\ -2\pi & r < 0 \wedge (0 \le x \wedge 0 < y \vee x < 0 \wedge 2r < y). \end{cases} \quad (15)$$

It is not unexpected that for fixed (x, y), the first piece of $\Theta(x, y, r)$ is not differentiable or even always defined at $r = r_m$. What is surprising is that even if we define the endpoint to ensure the value of the function is finite, its rate of change is unbounded at the end of the interval. This is illustrated in Fig. 4, and made formalizing the relationship between the length of circular arc path segments and the rest of the turn-to-bearing kinematics interesting.

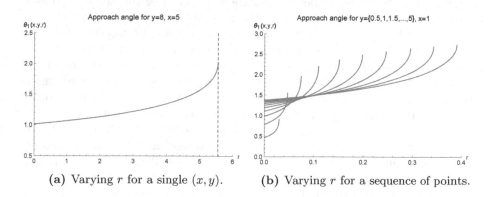

(a) Varying r for a single (x, y).   (b) Varying r for a sequence of points.

Fig. 4. Plot of the first piece of $\Theta(x, y, r)$ from Eq. 14

This geometry appears in a variety of contexts, including [12] at the bottom of p. 19:15, which has another expression that may be used to solve for the angle. We leave it to the interested reader to show the equivalence between the result we have proved, and alternate formulations. We also find a simplification for the tangent path length:

Theorem 3 (Straight path segment expression). *For a turn-to-bearing trajectory given by* $(r, \Theta(x, y, r))$, *that starts at the origin with* $\theta_0 = 0$ *and passes through* (x, y), *the square of the distance traveled on a straight line before we arrive at* (x, y) *is given by*

$$(x - r\sin(\Theta(x, y, r)))^2 + (y - r(1 - \cos(\Theta(x, y, r))))^2 = x^2 - (2r - y)y \quad (16)$$

4   Reasoning About the Timing of Intersecting Turns

This section describes our approach to analyzing the future safety of two vehicles following non-deterministic turn-to-bearing horizontal kinematics. The problem can be divided into computing the intersection of reachable envelopes where collisions might occur (geometry), and when they might occur (timing).

The geometry of the reachable envelope for a turn, such as the one pictured in Fig. 1a, is bounded by edges that are combinations of circular arcs and straight lines; the intersection of these areas may be computed in a straightforward manner. The rest of our discussion is focused on evaluating the timing of potential collisions at different points in space where the turns intersect.

4.1   Pointwise Collision Timing

We define the reachable envelope

$$E = \{p \,|\, \exists\, \theta_c, r, s, u \text{ s.t. } \chi(r, \theta_c, s) \wedge u > 0 \wedge J(u) = p\} \quad (17)$$

for a vehicle to be the set of points that are reachable over the range of possible future trajectories. For any point in the reachable envelope $p \in E$, there is a set of trajectories $\mathcal{T}(p) = \{J(t) \,|\, \exists\, \theta_c, r, s, u \text{ s.t. } \chi(r, \theta_c, s) \wedge u > 0 \wedge J(u) = p\}$ that can reach that point. Each trajectory $J \in \mathcal{T}(p)$ corresponds with a different choice of radius and final bearing (which determine the path), and future ground speed $s(t)$. Figures 5a and b illustrate two different points in the reachable envelope of the ownship from Fig. 1 and a set of paths followed by trajectories taken from the family of possibilities that would reach each point.

There is a corresponding set of arrival times $I(p) = \{t_a \,|\, J \in \mathcal{T}(p) \wedge J(t_a) = p\}$ during which that vehicle can arrive at p. The earliest and latest arrival time at point p for a single vehicle are given by $t_e(p) = \inf I(p)$ and $t_l(p) = \sup I(p)$, where $J(t)$ is the position of the aircraft following trajectory J at time t.

To analyze relative timing between two aircraft and determine whether collision is possible, we can look pointwise at the earliest and latest arrival times for each. We first define four logical predicates that express whether the earliest and latest arrival time at point p in the reachable area occur when the other vehicle may also be located at that point. Each time variable t in the subsequent equations has a subscript indicating whether the time is earliest possible $(_e)$ or latest possible $(_l)$ time of arrival, and a superscript indicating which aircraft timing is referenced, ^{i} for intruder or ^{o} for ownship.

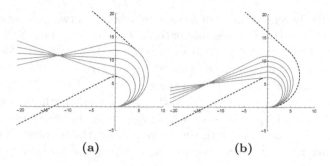

(a)   (b)

Fig. 5. Paths from the set of possible turn-to-bearing trajectories that reach two example points in space. The reachable envelope is shown as a set of dashed lines for a non-deterministic left turn; any point in the reachable envelope is reachable via these kinematics.

$$W_e^i(p) = t_e^o(p) \leq t_e^i(p) \leq t_l^o(p) \tag{18}$$

$$W_l^i(p) = t_e^o(p) \leq t_l^i(p) \leq t_l^o(p) \tag{19}$$

$$W_e^o(p) = t_e^i(p) \leq t_e^o(p) \leq t_l^i(p) \tag{20}$$

$$W_l^o(p) = t_e^i(p) \leq t_l^o(p) \leq t_l^i(p) \tag{21}$$

We combine these to define two predicates to evaluate safety, one using the earliest arrival time, and the other using the latest arrival time,

$$W_e(p) = W_e^i(p) \lor W_e^o(p) \tag{22}$$

$$W_l(p) = W_l^i(p) \lor W_l^o(p) \tag{23}$$

For two aircraft we define a conflict area $C = E^o \cap E^i$ to reflect the geometry of the intersection of future paths without timing considerations. We prove

Theorem 4 (Leading Lagging Equivalence). *For all points* $p \in C$, *predicates* $W_e(p) = W_l(p)$, *so we can drop the subscript.*

Theorem 5 (Pointwise Safety). $W(p)$ *correctly establishes safety at point* p: *when it is true, there exist circumstances that lead to collision at* p, *and when it is not there are no circumstances that lead to collision at* p.

Theorem 6 (Collision Timing). *For all points* $p \in C \land W(p)$, *a collision may only occur in the time interval* $[\max(t_e^i(p), t_e^o(p)), \min(t_l^i(p), t_l^o(p))]$, *and under the assumptions, no collision may occur outside this time interval.*

Consequently the earliest and latest collision times in an area C are given by

$$t_e = \inf_{p \in C \land W(p)} \max(t_e^i(p), t_e^o(p)) \tag{24}$$

$$t_l = \sup_{p \in C \land W(p)} \min(t_l^i(p), t_l^o(p)) \tag{25}$$

We can directly relate timing of a trajectory between two points to the range of path lengths for different possible paths connecting the points. The earliest arrival time to reach a point p, $t_e(p)$ is achieved by the trajectory following the shortest path and the highest ground speed, i.e. $\inf I(p) = \frac{d_{\min}(p)}{s_\beta}$, where $d_{\min}(p)$ is the length of the shortest path from the starting point to p. The latest arrival time is achieved by the trajectory following the longest path with the slowest ground speed, i.e. $\sup I(p) = \frac{d_{\max}(p)}{s_\alpha}$, where $d_{\max}(p)$ is the length of longest path from the starting point to p. In this way, we convert the problem of computing collision timing into a problem computing the range of possible path lengths between two points.

4.2   Path Length Properties

We can define a function that computes the distance of the path for a deterministic, left-turning turn-to-bearing trajectory starting from the origin with orientation $\theta_0 = 0$, passing through (x, y) with orientation θ, using a turn of radius r:

$$L(x, y, \theta, r) = r\theta + \|(x, y) - r(\sin\theta, 1 - \cos\theta)\| \tag{26}$$

Turn-to-bearing kinematics constrain the parameters for L, i.e. its arguments cannot all be chosen independently. Assume we fix the point we wish to reach, (x, y). We can independently choose the angle we approach our final point with, θ, and that determines the turn radius of the maneuver. Alternatively, we can choose the radius of our turn, and compute the angle of approach to the second point.

A central insight here is that for paths with the same starting and ending points, the path with a larger angle of approach will have a larger radius; and the path with a larger radius will be longer. More precisely:

Theorem 7 (Approach angle orders turn-to-bearing path radii). *Given two turn-to-bearing paths, (r_1, θ_1) and (r_2, θ_2) that pass through the same point (x, y), if $\theta_1 > \theta_2 > 0$, then the radius of the first path r_1 is longer than the radius of the second path r_2, i.e. $r_1 > r_2$:*

$$\theta_1 > \theta_2 > 0 \rightarrow R(x, y, \theta_1) > R(x, y, \theta_2) \tag{27}$$

Theorem 8 (Radius orders turn-to-bearing path lengths). *Given two turn-to-bearing paths, (r_1, θ_1) and (r_2, θ_2) that pass through the same point (x, y), if $r_1 > r_2 > 0$, then the first path length L_1 is greater than the second path length L_2, i.e. $L_1 > L_2$:*

$$r_1 > r_2 > 0 \rightarrow L(x, y, \Theta(x, y, r_1), r_1) > L(x, y, \Theta(x, y, r_2), r_2) \tag{28}$$

Maximum and Minimum Path Lengths. At each point in the reachable area, we can use the ordering of path lengths implied by Theorems 7 and 8 to find the minimum and maximum length path possible for uncertain turn-to-bearing motion constrained by non-deterministic bounds.

Theorem 9 (Minimum bearing-constrained path length). *For turn-to-bearing kinematics, given interval constraints on final bearing* $[\theta_\alpha, \theta_\beta]$ *and turn radius* $[r_\alpha, r_\beta]$ *where* $0 < r_\alpha$ *and* $0 < \theta_\alpha$, *and a reachable point* (x, y), *the minimum path length is given by*

$$d_{min}(x, y) = \begin{cases} L(x, y, \theta_m, r_m) & r_\alpha \leq r_m \leq r_\beta \wedge \theta_m \leq \max(\theta_\alpha, \Theta(x, y, r_\alpha)) \\ L(x, y, \Theta(x, y, r_\alpha), r_\alpha) & \theta_\alpha \leq \Theta(x, y, r_\alpha) \leq \theta_\beta \\ L(x, y, \theta_\alpha, R(x, y, \theta_\alpha)) & otherwise \end{cases}$$

(29)

Theorem 10 (Maximum bearing-constrained path length). *For turn-to-bearing kinematics, given interval constraints on final bearing* $[\theta_\alpha, \theta_\beta]$ *and turn radius* $[r_\alpha, r_\beta]$ *where* $0 < r_\alpha$ *and* $0 < \theta_\alpha$, *and a reachable point* (x, y), *the maximum path length is given by*

$$d_{max}(x, y) = \begin{cases} L(x, y, \theta_m, r_m) & r_\alpha \leq r_m \leq r_\beta \wedge \theta_m \leq \theta_\beta \\ L(x, y, \Theta(x, y, r_\beta), r_\beta) & x^2 + y^2 > 2r_\beta y \wedge \Theta(x, y, r_\beta) \leq \theta_\beta \\ L(x, y, \theta_\beta, R(x, y, \theta_\beta)) & otherwise \end{cases}$$ (30)

Right and Uncertain Turns. So far we have looked only at left turns, where the circle that defines our turn radius is positioned to the left of the vehicle, and the change in bearing is a relative angle in radians, positive according to the usual counter-clockwise convention. For non-deterministic left turns, $0 < r_\alpha \leq r_\beta$ and $0 \leq \theta_\alpha \leq \theta_\beta$.

We can handle other types of turns via symmetry. For right turns, we choose the convention of identifying turning trajectories using radii with negative numbers, and giving relative bearing with negative numbers as well. We describe non-deterministic right turns using parameters such that $r_\alpha \leq r_\beta < 0$ and $\theta_\alpha \leq \theta_\beta < 0$. For this convention, the path length for right turns is given by:

$$L^{right}(x, y, \theta, r) = L(x, -y, -\theta, -r)$$

(31)

The function that determines the maximum and minimum distance for right turns is related to that for left turns in the following way:

$$d^{right}(x, y, \theta_\alpha, \theta_\beta, r_\alpha, r_\beta) = d(x, -y, -\theta_\beta, -\theta_\alpha, -r_\beta, -r_\alpha)$$

(32)

for both minimum and maximum distance.

We can compute the distances associated with non-deterministic forward motion that might include either a left or a right turn, by requiring $r_\beta < 0 < r_\alpha$

and $\theta_\alpha \leq 0 \leq \theta_\beta$. The distance function then relates to the left and right distance functions:

$$
d^{\text{either}}(x,y,\theta_\alpha,\theta_\beta,r_\alpha,r_\beta) = \begin{cases} d(x,y,0,\theta_\beta,r_\alpha,\infty) & y > 0 \\ d^{\text{right}}(x,y,\theta_\alpha,0,-\infty,r_\beta) & y < 0 \\ x & y = 0 \end{cases} \tag{33}
$$

4.3 Exact Timing Wavefront

The observations in Theorems 9–10 allow us to subdivide the reachable envelope into different areas, using a piecewise function to describe its timing. Figures 6 and 7 illustrate, for a single vehicle and a particular choice of parameters, the different strategies that maximize and minimize path length, and the areas associated with each strategy. The bounding areas that enclose uniform strategies are shown with dashed lines that illustrates the limits where each strategy is appropriate for finding minimum and maximum length. For turns with different parameters, these shapes would change accordingly.

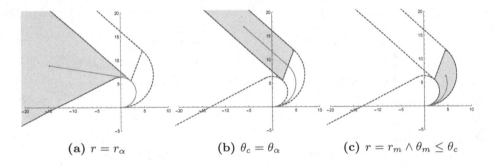

(a) $r = r_\alpha$ (b) $\theta_c = \theta_\alpha$ (c) $r = r_m \wedge \theta_m \leq \theta_c$

Fig. 6. Strategies described by Eq. 29 for minimum distance turn-to-bearing trajectories from the origin for each of three possible regions. Example trajectories illustrate the strategy for a single point in each region.

This means that if we want to find the longest and shortest paths to a point, we first consider paths with the greatest and smallest radii, r_α and r_β. Figures 6(a) and 7(a) illustrate individual trajectories that have minimum and maximum length for our example maneuver, constructed by using the minimum and maximum radii allowed. For some points, the most extreme turns could not produce trajectories that arrive at p, because the final bearings required by such trajectories are outside the parameters we have set for our motion, or because the points are inside the turning circle. Figures 6(b) and 7(b) illustrate individual trajectories that have minimum and maximum length for our example maneuver in this case. These are constructed by choosing radii that lead to most extreme values of bearing, so that the trajectory both reaches p, and does so

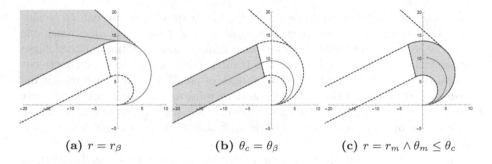

(a) $r = r_\beta$ **(b)** $\theta_c = \theta_\beta$ **(c)** $r = r_m \wedge \theta_m \leq \theta_c$

Fig. 7. Strategies described by Eq. 30 for maximum distance turn-to-bearing trajectories from the origin for each of three possible regions. Example trajectories illustrate the strategy for a single point in each region.

with an orientation that is allowed by the parameters of our turn. Finally, there are points in the reachable envelope that are reachable as part of the initial turn. For these points, this initial turn is the maximum-length path. If the bearing at point p is outside the allowable range, then this is also the minimum-length path. Figures 6(c) and 7(c) illustrate individual trajectories that have maximum and minimum length for our example maneuver, that must be constructed as circular arcs.

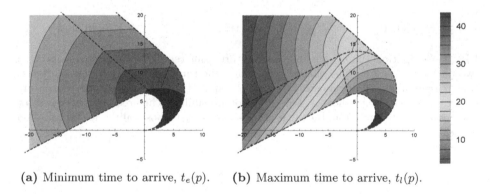

(a) Minimum time to arrive, $t_e(p)$.   **(b)** Maximum time to arrive, $t_l(p)$.

Fig. 8. Contour plot describing timing for a left turn with parameters used in Fig. 1. Each (x, y) position in the Cartesian plane is associated with a time to arrive at that position starting from $(0, 0)$ with orientation $\theta_0 = 0$, following turn-to bearing kinematics.

In Fig. 8 we use the parameters of our example maneuver in Fig. 1, combining all of the results from Theorems 9–10 together into a single contour plot of the earliest and latest times to reach each point in the reachable area. The contour lines plotted in Fig. 8a and b can be thought of as the outer and inner boundaries (respectively) of the irregular annulus at the instant corresponding to the value of the contour. As time progresses, this annulus expands, so we can treat this like a propagating wave that expresses location over time within the reachable area. The contours of equal timing for the minimum and maximum arrival times represent the shape of the leading and trailing edge of this wave, respectively. In addition to modeling and analyzing ranges of possibilities for turn-to-bearing kinematics, we will find that adding non-determinism also allows us to evaluate timing safety for small perturbations of turn-to-bearing – types of motion whose combination of trajectory and speed is sufficiently close, but not exactly the same.

Figure 9 shows how the timing computation can be used to analyze timing safety during a two-aircraft encounter. We analyze three different horizontal maneuvers for the aircraft at the origin, assuming a non-deterministic range of possibilities for forward motion of the other aircraft.

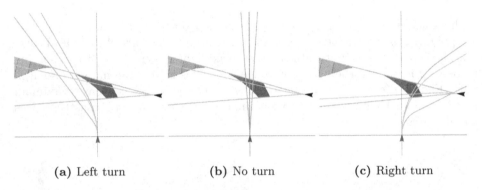

(a) Left turn   (b) No turn   (c) Right turn

Fig. 9. Computing timing possibilities for three different pilot maneuvers during a two-aircraft encounter. The shaded area shows the timing of collision possibilities at each horizontal position, indicating the timing required for vertical separation to ensure safety; darker shading indicates earlier collision possibility. The green trajectories show one possible realization from the range of non-deterministic possibilities for each motion model.

5   Conclusion

In this work, we have created a library that describes turn-to-bearing kinematics and allows us to reason about them without approximation. The representation allows non-determinism in all turn parameters by quantifying over state variables.

We have applied the library to compute timing intervals during which intersecting turns might collide, so they can be used to determine when aircraft must be vertically separated. We compute time intervals without approximation, for a given point where the turns intersect that account for arbitrary, non-deterministic bounds for speed during the horizontal maneuvers for each aircraft.

These computations are useful for correctly analyzing the safety of simultaneous horizontal and vertical maneuvers for collision avoidance.

References

1. The coq proof assistant. https://coq.inria.fr. Accessed 24 May 2020
2. Abhishek, A., Sood, H., Jeannin, J.-B.: Formal verification of braking while swerving in automobiles. In: Proceedings of the 23rd International Conference on Hybrid Systems: Computation and Control, HSCC 2020. Association for Computing Machinery, New York (2020)
3. Boldo, S., Lelay, C., Melquiond, G.: Coquelicot: a user-friendly library of real analysis for Coq. Math. Comput. Sci. **9**(1), 41–62 (2015). https://doi.org/10.1007/s11786-014-0181-1
4. Cons, M.S., Shima, T., Domshlak, C.: Integrating task and motion planning for unmanned aerial vehicles. Unmanned Syst. **02**(01), 19–38 (2014)
5. Isaiah, P., Shima, T.. A task and motion planning algorithm for the Dubins travelling salesperson problem. IFAC Proc. Vol. **47**(3), 9816–9821 (2014). 19th IFAC World Congress
6. Jeannin, J.-B., et al.: A formally verified hybrid system for safe advisories in the next-generation airborne collision avoidance system. STTT **19**(6), 717–741 (2017)
7. Jeyaraman, S., Tsourdos, A., żbikowski, R., White, B.A.: Formal techniques for the modelling and validation of a co-operating UAV team that uses Dubins set for path planning. In: Proceedings of the 2005, American Control Conference, 2005, vol. 7, pp. 4690–4695 (2005)
8. Kouskoulas, Y., Genin, D., Schmidt, A., Jeannin, J.-B.: Formally verified safe vertical maneuvers for non-deterministic, accelerating aircraft dynamics. In: Ayala-Rincón, M., Muñoz, C.A. (eds.) ITP 2017. LNCS, vol. 10499, pp. 336–353. Springer, Cham (2017). https://doi.org/10.1007/978-3-319-66107-0_22
9. Ma, X., Castanon, D.A.: Receding horizon planning for Dubins traveling salesman problems. In: Proceedings of the 45th IEEE Conference on Decision and Control, pp. 5453–5458, December 2006
10. McGee, T.G., Hedrick, J.K.: Path planning and control for multiple point surveillance by an unmanned aircraft in wind. In: 2006 American Control Conference, p. 6, June 2006
11. Mitsch, S., Ghorbal, K., Vogelbacher, D., Platzer, A.: Formal verification of obstacle avoidance and navigation of ground robots. Int. J. Robot. Res. **36**(12), 1312–1340 (2017)
12. Platzer, A.: Differential hybrid games. ACM Trans. Comput. Log. **18**(3), 19:1–19:44 (2017)
13. Platzer, A., Clarke, E.M.: Formal verification of curved flight collision avoidance maneuvers: a case study. In: Cavalcanti, A., Dams, D.R. (eds.) FM 2009. LNCS, vol. 5850, pp. 547–562. Springer, Heidelberg (2009). https://doi.org/10.1007/978-3-642-05089-3_35
14. Song, X., Hu., S.: 2D path planning with Dubins-path-based A⋆ algorithm for a fixed-wing UAV. In: 3rd IEEE International Conference on Control Science and Systems Engineering (ICCSSE), Beijing, China, pp. 69–73 (2017)
15. Zhao, Z., Yang, J., Niu, Y., Zhang, Y., Shen, L.: A hierarchical cooperative mission planning mechanism for multiple unmanned aerial vehicles. Electronics **8**, 443 (2019)

An Actor-Based Approach for Security Analysis of Cyber-Physical Systems

Fereidoun Moradi[1]($\boxtimes$), Sara Abbaspour Asadollah[1], Ali Sedaghatbaf[1], Aida Čaušević[1], Marjan Sirjani[1], and Carolyn Talcott[2]

[1] School of Innovation, Design and Engineering,
Mälardalen University, Västerås, Sweden
{fereidoun.moradi,sara.abbaspour,ali.sedaghatbaf,aida.causevic,
marjan.sirjani}@mdh.se
[2] SRI International, Menlo Park, CA, USA
clt@csl.sri.com

Abstract. In this work, we present an actor-based approach for security analysis of Cyber-Physical Systems at the design phase. We use Timed Rebeca, an actor-based modeling language, to model the behavior of components and potential attacks, and verify the security properties using Rebeca model checking tool. We employ STRIDE model as a reference for classifying the attacks. To demonstrate the applicability of our approach, we use a Secure Water Treatment (SWaT) system as a case study. We analyze the architecture of the SWaT system using three different attack schemes in which various parts of the system network and physical devices are compromised. In the end, we identify single and combined attack scenarios that violate security properties.

Keywords: Cyber-Physical Systems (CPS) · Cyber security · Attack scenarios · Rebeca · Secure Water Treatment (SWaT) · Attack detection

1 Introduction

Cyber-Physical Systems (CPS) refer to a system in which physical, computational and communication components are integrated to achieve a larger goal [1]. Generally, a CPS includes three kinds of components i.e. sensors, controllers and actuators. Sensors are responsible to gather data about the state of a physical process and submit them to the controllers. By analyzing the data, if the controllers detect a need for some changes in the process, they apply those changes by sending appropriate commands to the actuators [2]. Despite the advantages of combining cyber and physical spaces, connection to the Internet makes CPS exposed to several attacks, which may lead to undesirable changes in the physical process [3].

To tackle CPS attacks, it is required to consider security of CPS beyond the IT systems standard information security [4,5]. Several researchers have proposed formal or simulation methods to analyse the security of CPS [6–8].

© Springer Nature Switzerland AG 2020
M. H. ter Beek and D. Ničković (Eds.): FMICS 2020, LNCS 12327, pp. 130–147, 2020.
https://doi.org/10.1007/978-3-030-58298-2_5

The work presented in this paper is a step towards an actor-based approach for assessing the security aspects of CPS. We use Timed Rebeca as an actor-based modeling language [9–11] to model the behavior of CPS components and attack scenarios, and we utilize the STRIDE [12] model as a reference for classifying potential attacks on a CPS.

As an actor-based language, Rebeca [13,14] is well-suited for modeling complex behaviors in event-based asynchronous distributed systems [15]. Timed Rebeca is supported by a model checking tool suite Afra [16] and can be used for verifying CPS [17]. In this work, beside modeling a cyber-physical system, we propose a model for both kinds of attacks on communication and components. Using Timed Rebeca, an attacker is modeled as an actor to jeopardise the communication, and a compromised component is modeled as an actor with possible malfunction. In addition, we use the security threats category, STRIDE, to systematically map the reported CPS attacks in [18–20] to the STRIDE threat types and identify the attacks in our models. By model checking we analyze security of the CPS design to recognize where the potential attack scenarios can successfully cause a failure in the system. The output counter-example gives us the trace of events leading to a security failure which can then be used for developing mitigation plans.

We demonstrate the applicability of this method in practice using a case study on Secure Water Treatment (SWaT) system [21]. The natural mapping between the communicating entities in the problem domain and actors in Rebeca models makes the approach easy to understand and reuse [22].

The paper is organized as follows. In Sect. 2, we introduce Rebeca, and our approach for security analysis is introduced in Section 3. Section 4 shows how our attack models can be classified within the STRIDE model. In Sect. 5, we describe the case study and evaluate our experimental results. Section 6 discusses the related work and Sect. 7 concludes the paper and gives a summary of our future works.

2 An Actor-Based Modeling Language: Rebeca

Rebeca is an actor-based modeling language with formal foundation used for modeling concurrent and reactive systems with asynchronous message passing [13,23]. A Rebeca model consists of the definition of *reactive classes*, each describing the type of a certain number of *actors* (called *rebecs*, we use both terms rebec and actor interchangeably in the Rebeca context). Each reactive class declares the size of its message queue, a set of *state variables*, and the messages to which it can respond. Each rebec has a set of *known rebecs* to which it can send messages. The behavior of a rebec is determined by its *message servers*. Each rebec takes a message from its message queue and executes the corresponding message server. Taking a message from the queue to execute it can be seen as an event. Communication takes place by asynchronous message passing, which is non-blocking for both sender and receiver.

Rebeca comes with a formal semantics that makes it suitable for model checking purposes. Additionally, the language supports temporal logic to specify desired properties. Timed Rebeca [9,11] is an extension of Rebeca where computation time and network delay can be modeled. In Timed Rebeca, each rebec has its own local clock, but there is also a notion of global time based on synchronized distributed clocks of all rebecs. Messages that are sent to a rebec are put in its message bag together with their arrival time, and their deadline. Methods are executed atomically, but the passing of time during the execution of methods can be modeled. Timed Rebeca is used for modeling and analyzing of distributed systems in different ways. In [24], schedulability analysis of wireless sensor networks is performed, different design decisions and routing algorithms in Network on Chips are analyzed in [25], and faults are discovered and reported in the mobile ad-hoc network protocols in [26]. In [27], Sirjani, Lee and Khames-panah showed how Timed Rebeca can be used for formal verification of CPS, and in [28] it is shown how a CPS can be modeled using Timed Rebeca.

Afra tool [16] is an IDE with a dedicated model checker, Rebeca Model Checker (RMC), for verifying Rebeca family models. The tool provides development environment for models, property specification, model checking, and counter-example visualization.

3   Methodology

As depicted in Fig. 1, the proposed method for CPS security analysis includes the following steps: (1) the Rebeca model of the CPS is developed from the system design specifications, (2) the potential attack scenarios against the system are modeled, (3) the security properties are defined in terms of assertions or temporal logic, and (4) Afra is used to identify the events trace that leads to a security failure. The above steps are elaborated in the following subsections.

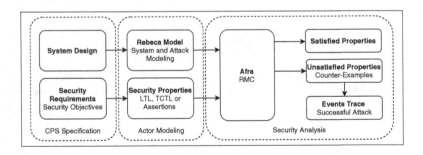

Fig. 1. The overview of the actor-based security analysis process.

3.1   Building the Rebeca Model of the Cyber-Physical System

We consider each CPS component and physical processes as an actor. We realise four types of actors in our Rebeca model, controllers, sensors, actuators and physical processes. Generally, the interaction scenarios between these actors follow a closed-loop feedback. Sensor observes the physical component's status, and sends the sensed data to the controller denoting the state of the physical component. Based on the received sensed data, the controller sends the control command to the actuator, and the actuator performs the actual physical change. The Rebeca model of a CPS includes reactive classes corresponding to the four categories of actors. In real cases, we may have different kinds of actors belonging to each category (e.g., temperature sensors, speed sensors, etc.), and each kind may be defined by a distinct reactive class.

Generally, the continuous behavior of physical components is expressed using differential equations like in Hybrid Automata [29]. Here, we abstract the continuous behavior and only model the discrete jump transitions among the states (states are called control modes in hybrid automata). We model the progress of time in each state using a delay statement in Timed Rebeca. In each actor representing a physical component, we use state variables to model different states. For example, different water levels of the low, medium, and high in a tank are modeled using state variables. Although increasing and decreasing the water level is a continuous behavior, we only model the change in the states after a certain amount of time using a delay statement. When a message for increasing or decreasing the water level is received from an actuator, the value of the state variable is set accordingly after a certain amount of time.

3.2   Attack Modeling

According to the malicious behaviour on communication channels and components three cases are considered as follows: (1) attacker targets the communication channel between two components through injecting malicious messages, (2) attacker manipulates the internal behavior of one or more components e.g. through malicious code injection, and (3) one or more attackers perform a coordinated attack to launch malicious behaviour on both the communication channels and the components. To illustrate these cases, we define three attack schemes.

Scheme-A: Attack on Communication indicates a situation in which an attacker injects malicious messages into the communication channels between the controller and its associated sensor or actuator. These messages may mislead the receiver and cause a system security failure. For example, as depicted in Fig. 2(a), attacker compromises the channel between the sensor and the controller, and injects a malicious data message that shows a state different from the real state of physical process. Note that the controller is not aware of the communication interruption, thus accepts the injected data and gives the faulty command to the actuator. Actuator performs the unintended action and may modify the physical process.

In the Rebeca model, a separate reactive class is defined to model the attacker's behavior in this scheme. This reactive class includes at least one message server to send malicious message(s), e.g. the sensed data message, to the target channel(s) at an appropriate time. To perform exhaustive security check, a set of Rebeca models is built that contains one or more attacker actors that target different channels at different injection times during CPS operation. These Rebeca models are inputs of executing CPS security analysis.

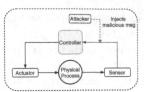 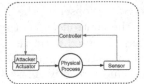 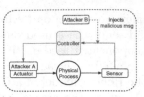

(a) *Scheme-A: Attack on Communication.* Example: Attacker injects malicious data into the communication channel between a sensor and the controller.

(b) *Scheme-B: Attack on Components.* Example: Attacker compromises an actuator.

(c) *Scheme-C: Combined Attack.* Example: Two attackers attack in a coordinated way.

Fig. 2. Three attack schemes in Rebeca model for security analysis of CPS.

Scheme-B: Attack on Components indicates a situation in which a number of components are compromised and do not function correctly. Attackers may have direct access to the components and perform physical attacks on them. They may damage some sensors/actuators or inject malicious code into the controllers. For example, as Fig. 2(b) shows, an attacker may compromise an actuator and perform an action over physical process different from the command issued by the controller. This action of the compromised actuator will effect the physical process state and sensor feedback report.

This scheme is modeled in the Rebeca model as an additional message server inside the reactive class corresponding to the target component. This message server models the incorrect functionality. In the above example, the Rebeca model includes the compromised actuator actor which has a message server sending the malicious message to the physical process actor once receiving a control command from the controller. Similar to Attack Scheme-A, all the possible Rebeca models including one or more compromised components are built and the models are analysed in the model checking step.

Scheme-C: Combined Attack is a combination of the previous two attack schemes in which both the system components and communication channels are compromised by attackers. Usually, this happens when more than one attacker try to attack the system in a coordinated way. Figure 2(c) illustrates a CPS with presence of two attackers in which attacker A compromises actuator to launch an alteration on the physical process, and attacker B injects a false data message into the channel from the sensor to the controller. This coordinated operation of attackers makes an unexpected change on the physical process without the controller awareness. Indeed, the injected data message is sent to the controller falsely showing that the expected action is performed rather than the malicious alteration. The modeling of this scheme would include various combinations of the defined attackers and compromised components as actors in a Rebeca model. We can choose many kinds of attack scenarios with assumption of compromised network or components in Rebeca model and check the attacks damage on the CPS system.

3.3 Model Checking and Security Analysis

The security objectives will be the basis for defining the security properties to be verified. Afra supports LTL, TCTL and assertions for property specification. The most important security objectives are *confidentiality*, *integrity* and *availability* [30] presented in Table 1 and referred to in Sect. 4.

We use RMC to automatically verify each of the specified security properties. If RMC detects that a property is not satisfied by the Rebeca model, it provides the modeler with a counter-example detailing the sequence of events that would lead to a security violation. The sequence of events determines a successful attack. Realising the possible successful attacks can be the basis for applying appropriate countermeasures. In some cases, it may be enough to change the security policies to protect the system against the attacks, and in some cases we may need a security component such as an intrusion detection system (IDS) to keep the system safe against intruders. As our future work, we would incorporate and check these solutions in the model.

The common problem in model checking is state-space explosion. In principle, a Timed Rebeca model of well-behaved reactive systems in general (including CPS), has a recurrent bounded behavior [11]. Although we model time, the model checking tool is able to distinguish when a newly generated state is already visited and the only difference is in the logical time stamps. If needed, while running the model checker we can use assertions to stop the process and look into the state space. In any case we can have a bound on the growing time stamps to stop the model checking at a certain time.

4   Attack Classification

STRIDE[1] is designed as a model for identifying different types of threats that a system may experience and the corresponding security objective which might be violated [12]. In Table 1, we classify the significant attacks on CPS (reported in [18–20]) based on the STRIDE categories. The cyber and physical attacks exploit emerging CPS-related vulnerabilities in the two aspects of *communication* and *component*, and are shown in Table 1 as *Scheme-A* and *Scheme-B*. *Scheme-A* consists of the attack scenarios which are secretly recording or modifying the data transmitted over the channels (e.g., eavesdropping, MITM and injection attack). *Scheme-B* includes the attacks that inject malicious code into the software components or perform a malicious alteration on a physical component (e.g., malware and physical attack). We can model each of the attacks using our methodology. In Sect. 5.1, we explain how some of these attacks can occur on communication and components of the SWaT system.

---

[1] The acronym STRIDE stands for **S**poofing, **T**ampering, **R**eputation, **I**nformation Disclosure, **D**enial of Service, and **E**levation of Privilege.

Table 1. Attack classification using STRIDE model.

Threat type (security objective)	Cyber and physical attack	Scheme-A	Scheme-B
Spoofing (authentication)	Masquerade attack		[19]
	Packet spoofing attack	[20]	
Tampering (integrity)	Man-in-the-middle (MITM)	[19]	
	Injection attack	[20]	[20]
	Replay attack	[19]	
	Malware (Virus or Worms)		[20]
	Physical attack	[20]	[18]
Reputation (non-repudiation)	On-Off attack		[18]
Information disclosure (confidentiality)	Eavesdropping	[19]	
	Malware (Spyware)		[20]
	Side-channel attack		[20]
	Physical attack	[20]	[18]
Denial of service (availability)	Resource exhaustion attack	[19]	[20]
	Interruption attack	[19]	
	Malware (Ransomware)		[20]
	Physical attack	[20]	[18]
Elevation of privilege (authorization)	Malware (Rootkit)		[20]

5   The SWaT Case Study and Evaluation

In this section, we discuss an experimental study on the SWaT testbed [21]. We first present the SWaT architecture and its security objectives. Then, we provide details on the Rebeca model, and finally, we discuss the security analysis results. The SWaT testbed is a scaled-down version of an industrial water treatment system. This testbed is used for several research and training purposes in the iTrust research center [21].

The water treatment process in the SWaT system consists of three stages. These stages include supplying raw water into the system, Ultra-Filtration (UF) and Reverse Osmosis (RO). In each stage, there is a PLC responsible for controlling a water tank. The PLC is directly connected to some actuators (i.e., valves or pumps) through a local network. A simple password-based authentication is the only mechanism employed to control access to the network, which makes the SWaT system vulnerable to eavesdropping or packet injection attacks [6].

At any stage during the execution of the water treatment process, each pump can be in *On* or *Off* state, and respectively each valve can be in one of the two states *Open* or *Close*. Also, three states are considered for the big tanks (i.e., $Tank_1$ and $Tank_2$): Low(l), Medium(m), and High(h), and two states for the small tank ($Tank_3$): Low(l) and High(h). During the system operation, whenever the water level of a tank changes to h, the associated sensor reports the change to the responsible PLC. That PLC will close the valve or turn off the pump that is pouring water into the tank. Also, the PLC may open a valve, turn a pump on, or send *open/on* requests to other PLCs when the water level in the tank is either l or m. The PLC_1, PLC_2 and PLC_3 are configured to interact with each other to manage the SWaT system.

A dataset collected from the SWaT system operation is available in the iTrust homepage for research purposes [31]. The dataset includes data about network traffic and sensor and actuator status during normal operation of the system. The dataset indicates that one millimeter increase or decrease in water level of $Tank_1$ and $Tank_2$ takes approximately two seconds. The sensors of $Tank_1$ or $Tank_2$ report the water level in millimeters. The capacity of $Tank_3$ is half capacity of $Tank_1$ and $Tank_2$, and its sensor reports only low and high levels of water to the corresponding PLC.

5.1 Security Objectives and Threats

We assume that malicious attackers have the ability of injecting arbitrary packets into the communication channels between PLCs and sensors/actuators, and also they are able to alter the functionality of sensors/actuators. Here we use the STRIDE terminology to explain the possible attack scenarios. An attacker may break through the network authentication, disguise herself as an actual system component (*spoofing threat*) and inject a packet into the channel between sensor and PLC (*tampering threat*). The *integrity* objective of the system is jeopardized when an attacker wants to mislead the PLC (*reputation threat*) by sending a packet that contains a value different from the real value of the water tank status. Another attack scenario is possible when an attacker wants to jeopardize the *availability* of the system by sending the same message to a communication channel several times. This repetition causes the channel to be overwhelmed with several packets (*denial of service threat*). It is even possible that the attacker changes the state of an actuator through bypassing the actual commands coming from the PLC.

In this experiment we focus on the *integrity* of SWaT system following the STRIDE model. In fact, we use model checking to detect the undesirable events that might happen while attackers tamper the channels (e.g., by injecting packets) and compromise sensors/actuators by altering their functionality (e.g., physical attack).

5.2 SWaT Actor Model

The actor model of the SWaT system is depicted in Fig. 3. In this model, each shape represents an actor which corresponds to a component in the SWaT abstract architecture. Each arrow models a message passed between two components. In the model, the messages that may be the targets of attackers are distinguished from the secure ones. The red points with numbers from one to six indicate the possible compromised channels where the attackers may inject messages. The compromised channels are due to the lack of strong authentication and tamper-resistant mechanisms.

The PLCs communicate with each other through a separate protected network. For example, the *open_Req/close_Req* or the *on_Req* message passed in the secured channel between the PLCs may not be the target of any attacker. However, the messages (l, m, and h) which are transmitted from the sensors to the PLCs may be tampered by an attacker to affect the decisions made by the PLCs. The blue points represent the components that may behave maliciously. Typically, the malicious behaviour of the component leads to a faulty data transmission. For instance, whenever a pump is compromised, it may transmit message *waterIncrease* to the connected tank once it receives the command *Turn Off* from the corresponding PLC.

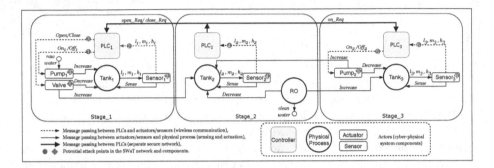

Fig. 3. SWaT actor model.

In the SWaT actor model, we assume that the water level in each tank is low in the initial state. Also, the water treatment process begins by pumping raw water to $Tank_1$ and it ends when the cleaned water flows out of $Tank_3$. During the process execution, each sensor sends water level information to the corresponding PLC periodically. In addition, based on the iTrust dataset (see Sect. 5) in the SWaT system the sensing period is 1 s, and the water level is changed every 1000 s. We use these values for setting the value of parameters (i.e., *sensing_interval* and *operationTimeTank*) in the Rebeca model.

5.3   The Rebeca Model of the SWaT System

Here, we provide a detailed explanation of the Rebeca model developed for the SWaT system. The complete model is available in [32]. Listing 1 shows an abstract view of the SWaT Rebeca model. The main block includes the declarations of all rebecs defined in the SWaT actor model (see Fig. 3) together with an attacker rebec (see Listing 1, lines 73–88). In each declaration, the first parameter list includes the known rebecs, those which the declared rebec communicates with. For example, the known rebecs of PLC_1 are $Pump_1$, Valve and $Sensor_1$. The second parameter list includes the parameters to be passed to the constructor of the rebec.

```
1    env boolean p1Compromised = false;  env int p1Compromised_time = 0;
2    ... // environment variables
3    env int chl = 1;  env int malMsg = 0;  env int attackTime = 0;
4    env int sensing_interval = 1;  env int operationTimeTank = 1000;
5    reactiveclass PLC1(5){
6        knownrebecs{ Pump1 pump1; Valve valve; sensorTank1 sensor1;}
7        statevars{ boolean openReqPlc2, pump1On, valveOpen; int waterLevelTank1;}
8        PLC1(){ openReqPlc2 = false; waterLevelTank1 = 0; pump1On = false; valveOpen = false;}
9        msgsrv processSensorData(int waterLevel){
10           if (waterLevel == 1){
11               if (waterLevelTank1 != waterLevel){ pump1.on(); pump1On = true;}
12           } else if (waterLevel == 2 && openReqPlc2 == true && pump1On == true && valveOpen == false){
13               if (waterLevelTank1 != waterLevel){ openReqPlc2 = false; valve.open(); valveOpen = true;}
14           } else {...}
15           waterLevelTank1 = waterLevel;}
16       msgsrv openReq(){ openReqPlc2 = true;}
17       msgsrv closeReq(){ valve.close();}
18   }
19   reactiveclass PLC2(5){...} reactiveclass PLC3(5){...}
20   reactiveclass Tank1(10){
21       knownrebecs{ sensorTank1 sensor;}
22       statevars{ boolean underFlow,low,medium,high,overFlow; int status;}
23       Tank1(){ underFlow = false; overFlow = false; low = true; medium = false; high = false;}
24       msgsrv status(){
25           if (underFlow){sensor.reportStatus(0);
26           } else if (low){sensor.reportStatus(1);
27           } else {...}}
28       msgsrv waterIncrease(){
29           delay(operationTimeTank);
30           ... //changes water level status
31           if (low == true) { medium = true; low = false; high = false;
32           } else if (medium == true) { high = true; low = false; medium = false;
33           } else if (high == true) { overFlow = true; low = false; medium = false; high = false;}}
34       msgsrv waterDecrease(){...}
35   }
36   reactiveclass Tank2(10){...} reactiveclass Tank3(10){...}
37   reactiveclass Pump1(10){
38       knownrebecs{ Tank1 tank1;}
39       statevars{ boolean On, maliciousAction;}
40       Pump1(boolean compromised, int compTime){
41           on = false; maliciousAction = false;
42           if (compromised == true) { self.maliciousAct() after(compTime);}}
43       msgsrv on(){
44           if(maliciousAction == true) { on = false; maliciousAction = false;
45           } else if (on == true) { //do nothing
46           } else { on = true; tank1.waterIncrease();
47               self.KeepOnpumping() after(operationTimeTank);}}
48       msgsrv KeepOnpumping(){
49           if (on == true) {
50               tank1.waterIncrease(); self.KeepOnpumping() after(operationTimeTank);}}
51       msgsrv off(){
52           if(maliciousAction == true) { on = true; tank1.waterIncrease();
53               self.KeepOnpumping() after(operationTimeTank); maliciousAction = false;
54           } else {on = false;}}
55       msgsrv maliciousAct(){ maliciousAction = true;}
56   }
57   reactiveclass Pump2(10){...} reactiveclass Valve(10){...}
58   reactiveclass SensorTank1(10){...} reactiveclass SensorTank2(10){...}
59   reactiveclass SensorTank3(10){...} reactiveclass reverseOsmosisUnit(5){...}
60   reactiveclass Attacker(3){
61       knownrebecs{ PLC1 plc1; PLC2 plc2; PLC3 plc3; Pump1 pump1; Pump2 pump2; Valve valve;}
62       Attacker(int chl, int maliciousMsg, int attackTime){
63           if (chl == 1) { self.channelPlc1P1(maliciousMsg, attackTime);
64           } else if (chl == 2) {self.channelPlc1S(maliciousMsg, attackTime);
65           } else {...}}
66       msgsrv channelPlc1Pi(int msg, int attackTime){
67           if(msg == 1) { pump1.on() after(attackTime);
68           } else if(msg == 0) { pump1.off() after(attackTime);}}
69       msgsrv channelPlc1S(int msg, int attackTime){
70           plc1.processSensorData(msg) after(attackTime);}
71       ... //message servers
72   }
73   main{
74       PLC1 plc1(pump1,valve,sensor1):();
75       PLC2 plc2(plc1,plc3,sensor2):();
76       PLC3 plc3(pump2,tank3,sensor3):();
77       Tank1 tank1(sensor1):();
78       Tank2 tank2(sensor2,unit):();
79       Tank3 tank3(sensor3,tank2):();
80       sensorTank1 sensor1(tank1,plc1):(s1Compromised,s1Compromised_time);
81       sensorTank2 sensor2(tank2,plc2):(s2Compromised,s2Compromised_time);
82       sensorTank3 sensor3(tank3,plc3):(s3Compromised,s3Compromised_time);
83       Pump1 pump1(tank1):(p1Compromised,p1Compromised_time);
84       Pump2 pump2(tank2,tank3):(p2Compromised,p2Compromised_time);
85       Valve valve(tank1,tank2):(vCompromised,vCompromised_time);
86       reverseOsmosisUnit unit(tank2,tank3):();
87       Attacker attacker(plc1,plc2,plc3,pump1,pump2,valve):(chl,malMsg,attackTime);
88   }
```

Listing 1: An abstract version of the SWaT system Rebeca model.

In addition to the main block, the Rebeca model includes the reactive classes defining the behavior of the SWaT actors. For example, the PLC_1 reactive class has three known rebecs which are instances of reactive classes $Pump_1$, Valve and $Sensor_1$ (see Listing 1, lines 5–18). The PLC_1 reactive class includes a Boolean state variable *openReqPlc2* whose value indicates whether a water request is received from PLC_2 or not. This variable is initialized to *false* in the constructor of PLC_1.

Two Boolean state variables *pump1On* and *valveOpen* indicate the current status of $Pump_1$ and Valve respectively. The definition of PLC_1 includes three message servers i.e., *processSensorData*, *openReq* and *closeReq*. The message server *processSensorData* processes the sensor data and issues commands *on* or *off* to $Pump_1$ and *open* or *close* to Valve accordingly. The message servers *openReq* and *closeReq* are activated once a message is received from PLC_2.

The reactive class $Pump_1$ includes four message servers *on*, *off*, *KeepOnpumping* and *maliciousAct* (see Listing 1, lines 37–56). The message servers *on* and *off* update the value of the state variable *On* based on the commands received from PLC_1. The message server *KeepOnpumping* calls *waterIncrease* which takes *operationTimeTank* units of time and increases the level of water for one level in the tank. This continues until the message server *off* receives the turn off message. Due to space limitations, we exclude the explanation of other reactive classes from this paper. Interested readers may refer to [32] for more details.

5.4   Attack Models in Rebeca

In the Rebeca model, we model compromised actors (Scheme-B Attacks) using two parameters that are passed to all the actors that can be compromised (see Listing 1). The first parameter sets the status of the actor, and the second parameter sets the time of the attack. For example, the reactive class of $Pump_1$ includes a variable *maliciousAction* that can be set to change the status of the component to be compromised or not compromised. If this variable is set to be compromised then although the pump receives a message to turn its status to *on*, it turns it to *off*. For changing the variable *maliciousAction* at different times in each run of the model, a message is sent to $Pump_1$ at a certain model time. This model time can be configured and is passed to the pump as a parameter. Similar to the compromised mode of $Pump_1$, whenever the value of the input parameter *compromised* is true for Valve, then both message servers *open* and *close* behave maliciously (for example the message server *open* changes the value of state variable *Open* to *false*). The message server *maliciousAct* corresponding to each sensor activates compromised mode for the sensor, which causes the sensor to report invalid water level to the corresponding PLC.

In addition to the reactive classes that define the normal and compromised behavior of SWaT components, the Rebeca model includes a reactive class named *Attacker* (see Listing 1, lines 60–72) that models the behaviour of potential attackers targeting channels to inject messages (Scheme-A Attacks).

As we assume that attackers may target the communication channels between any two components in the SWaT system, the *knownrebecs* section of reactive class *Attacker* includes all the other rebecs defined in the Rebeca model. The constructor of this class has three arguments representing the target channel, malicious message content, and attack time. Since there are six channels in the system, the value of the first argument would be a number between 1 and 6. Based on the value passed to this argument, the message server responsible for sending malicious messages to the corresponding channel is invoked by the constructor. Message content is another numeric argument whose value indicates either the water level in a tank, an *on/off* command for Pump, or an *open/close* command for Valve. Finally, the third argument represents the time during the system operation that the malicious message is sent to a channel.

5.5   Model Checking and Security Analysis

The goal of attacks on the SWaT system is to cause an overflow or underflow in one of the tanks. An overflow may harm some of the critical units such as the UF or RO and cause flow out unclean water. Also, an underflow may damage a valve or a pump. Accordingly, we consider *overflow* and *underflow* for each tank to be verified on the Rebeca model of the SWaT system.

Figure 4 represents an abstract view of the state transition diagram of the SWaT system during a normal operation. The diagram is derived manually from the state space generated automatically by Afra. Each state shows the water level in the three tanks and the status of the pumps and the valve. Each transition between two states indicates an increase or/and decrease of the water level of some tank(s). Whenever a *waterIncrease* or *waterDecrease* occurs in a tank, then the attached sensor informs the corresponding PLC to update the status of the pumps and the valve based on the sensed data. Each state in Fig. 4 represents a set of states and transitions in the state space generated by model checking. In each of these abstract states the total amount of progress of time in the including

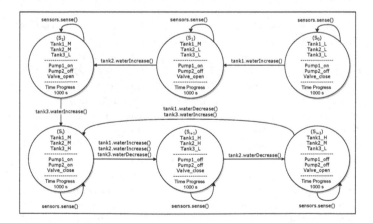

Fig. 4. The abstracted state transition of the SWaT system.

transitions is shown. The state space generated through model checking by Afra includes 42k states and 53k transitions.

In order to analyze the security properties of the SWaT system using the developed Rebeca model, we follow three attack schemes presented in Sect. 3.2. The outcome of the analysis includes the attack scenarios which lead the system to security violation. To cover all possible attack scenarios by model checking, we need to generate all combinations of different values for the input parameters of the attacker and the compromised components, and verify the model for each combination. A Python script is developed to automate input value generation and accumulation of the verification results. This approach is similar in its nature to the automated verification technique using symbolic modeling and constraint solving in [33]. Here we use an algorithmic approach to enumerate all the possible attack scenarios. In total we modeled 105 communication attacks and 84 attacks on components, and also the combination of these attacks (resulting in 8820 attack scenarios). Each attack scenario takes approximately twenty seconds to be verified by model checking, thus the total verification time for all attack scenarios (attacks on communication and components) is around one hour. Verification of each combined attack scenario takes around thirty seconds to complete, and the total verification time for all possible combinations is 72 hours. Totally, out of all above possible attack scenarios 29 cases successfully violate the system security which we report in Tables 2, 3 and 4.

Table 2 presents the outcomes of the analysis process for *Attack on Communication (Scheme-A)*. The results indicate at which system state the injected message has caused security violation. For example, assume that the system is in state S_0 (see the state transition diagram in Figure 4), and the attacker injects a malicious message into the channel between $Sensor_1$ and PLC_1 (see channels in Figure 3). This message wrongly reports the level of water in $Tank_1$ as being

Table 2. Model checking results in attack on communication (Scheme-A).

#	Tank	Property	Injected message	Communication channel	System state
1	$Tank_1$	Overflow	Water level in $Tank_1$ is low	$Sensor_1$ to PLC_1	S_{i+1}
2	$Tank_1$	Overflow	Turn on $Pump_1$	PLC_1 to $Pump_1$	S_{i+1}
3	$Tank_1$	Overflow	Water level in $Tank_1$ is low	$Sensor_1$ to PLC_1	S_{i+2}
4	$Tank_1$	Overflow	Turn on $Pump_1$	PLC_1 to $Pump_1$	S_{i+2}
5	$Tank_1$	Underflow	Water level in $Tank_1$ is high	$Sensor_1$ to PLC_1	S_0
6	$Tank_2$	Overflow	Water level in $Tank_2$ is medium	$Sensor_2$ to PLC_2	S_{i+1}
7	$Tank_2$	Overflow	Open Valve	PLC_1 to Valve	S_{i+1}
8	$Tank_3$	Overflow	Water level in $Tank_3$ is high	$Sensor_3$ to PLC_3	S_i
9	$Tank_3$	Overflow	Open Valve	PLC_1 to Valve	S_i
10	$Tank_3$	Underflow	Turn on $Pump_2$	PLC_3 to $Pump_2$	S_0
11	$Tank_3$	Underflow	Turn on $Pump_2$	PLC_3 to $Pump_2$	S_1
12	$Tank_3$	Underflow	Water level in $Tank_3$ is high	$Sensor_3$ to PLC_3	S_2
13	$Tank_3$	Underflow	Turn on $Pump_2$	PLC_3 to $Pump_2$	S_2
14	$Tank_3$	Underflow	Water level in $Tank_3$ is high	$Sensor_3$ to PLC_3	S_{i+2}
15	$Tank_3$	Underflow	Turn on $Pump_2$	PLC_3 to $Pump_2$	S_{i+2}

High. $Tank_1$ will underflow afterwards, because *Turn off Pump1* and *Open Valve* are issued by PLC_1 after receiving the message (line 5 in Table 2).

Table 3. Model checking results in Attack on Components (Scheme-B).

#	Tank	Property	Compromised component	Malicious behaviour	System state
1	$Tank_1$	Overflow	$Sensor_1$	Water level in $Tank_1$ is low	S_{i+1}
2	$Tank_1$	Overflow	$Pump_1$	Turn on	S_{i+1}
3	$Tank_1$	Overflow	$Sensor_1$	Water level in $Tank_1$ is low	S_{i+2}
4	$Tank_1$	Underflow	$Sensor_1$	Water level in $Tank_1$ is high	S_0
5	$Tank_2$	Overflow	$Sensor_2$	Water level in $Tank_2$ is medium	S_{i+1}
6	$Tank_3$	Overflow	$Sensor_2$	Water level in $Tank_2$ is low	S_i
7	$Tank_3$	Overflow	Valve	Open	S_i
8	$Tank_3$	Underflow	$Pump_2$	Turn on	S_1
9	$Tank_3$	Underflow	$Sensor_3$	Water level in $Tank_3$ is high	S_2
10	$Tank_3$	Underflow	$Pump_2$	Turn on	S_{i+1}
11	$Tank_3$	Underflow	$Sensor_3$	Water level in $Tank_3$ is high	S_{i+2}

Table 3 shows the results of model checking on the Rebeca model for *Attack on Components (Scheme-B)*. These results indicate at which system state the compromised component causes security violation. For example, assume that the system is in state S_{i+1} and $Sensor_2$ is compromised. This sensor sends a wrong report about the water level of $Tank_2$ to PLC_2. This report indicates the level of water as being Medium, whereas the real level is High. Upon receiving this report, PLC_2 opens Valve and causes $Tank_2$ to overflow (line 5 in Table 3).

The analysis results in Table 4 indicate that by using the modeling method presented in *Combined Attack (Scheme-C)*, such collaborative attack can be easily detected. For example assume that the system is in state S_0 and an attacker injects message *Open Valve* into the communication link between PLC_1 and Valve, and at the same time another attacker compromises $Pump_1$ to be turned off, then $Tank_1$ will underflow (line 1 in Table 4). As another example, if the system is in state S_1, $Sensor_2$ is compromised and a malicious message of high water level for $Tank_3$ is injected into the channel between $Sensor_3$ and PLC_3, then $Tank_3$ will underflow (line 3 in Table 4).

Note that the scenarios presented in Table 4 are those in which the single attacks (message injection or the compromised component) do not cause a security failure separately, but the combination leads to the security violation. If we assume that the system is robust against the scenarios in Table 2 and Table 3, the system may still be vulnerable against the collaborative attacks in Table 4.

Table 4. Model checking results in combined attack (Scheme-C).

#	Tank	Property	Injected message (communication channel)	Compromised component (malicious behaviour)	System state
1	$Tank_1$	Underflow	Open Valve (PLC_1 to Valve)	$Pump_1$ (Turn Off)	S_0
2	$Tank_3$	Underflow	Water level in $Tank_2$ is medium ($Sensor_2$ to PLC_2)	$Sensor_3$ (Water level in $Tank_3$ is high)	S_0
3	$Tank_3$	Underflow	Water level in $Tank_3$ is high ($Sensor_3$ to PLC_3)	$Sensor_2$ (Water level in $Tank_2$ is medium)	S_1

6 Related Work

Several modeling and simulation methods have been proposed for analyzing the security of CPS. In this section, we review the ones most related to the method presented in this paper. There are interesting works based on simulation. Wasicek et al. [34] propose an aspect-oriented technique to model attacks against CPS. They illustrate how Ptolemy [35] can be used to simulate the behavior of system components and detect anomalies. Taormina et al. [7] propose another simulation-based approach that is implemented in a MATLAB toolbox to analyze the risk of cyber-physical attacks on water distribution systems. In [1,8], the authors rely on simulation to perform their analyses. They propose a new metric to quantify the impact of attacks on components of the target CPS. This metric can be used to perform cost-benefit analysis on security investments.

Furthermore, there are several formal methods that examine CPS security. In [6], Kang et al. use Alloy to model SWaT behavior and potential attackers. They can discover the undetected attacks which cause safety failure (e.g., water tank overflow). The study is considered as run-time monitoring, which compares actual invariant of the SWaT system and output state in the Alloy model checker during system operation. Important attack scenarios are identified using this approach, and each run of the analysis considers only one point of the system to attack. In our approach we are able to detect scenarios with several attackers exploiting the communication and components vulnerabilities. Rocchetto and Tippenhauer [36] present another formal method for discovering feasible attack scenarios on SWaT. ASLan++ is the formal language used for modeling the physical layer interactions and CL-AtSe is a tool used to analyze the state space of the model and discover the potential attack scenarios. As the result, they succeed to find eight attack scenarios. They provide support for modeling different attacker profiles and only one profile can be active at each moment. Fritz and Zhang [37] consider CPS as discrete-event systems and model them using a variant of Petri nets. They propose a method based on permutation matrices to detect deception attacks. In particular, they can detect attacks by changing the input and output behavior of the system and analyzing its effect on the system behavior. Covert attacks and replay attacks are two kinds of attacks modeled and analyzed in this study. The combinations of attacks are not considered.

7 Conclusion and Future Work

In this paper, we present an approach to model and analyze the security properties of CPS using formal methods. We define three attack schemes targeting communication channels, components, and the combination of each, and then verify if the attacks could compromise the system security. In this approach, we use an actor-based modeling language Rebeca. The language facilitates modeling and analysis of the normal system behavior as well as the malicious behavior of potential attackers. We present a case study on a Secure Water Treatment (SWaT) System. This case study shows how each component in a Cyber-Physical System can be directly mapped to an actor in a Rebeca model. We demonstrate how the Afra model checking tool makes it possible to discover various potential attack scenarios. The presented approach enables the evaluation of the attack scenarios in a practical case study where some of the scenarios were not easily manually analyzable.

As future work, we intend to extend the application of our method to security analysis during run-time system operation and also analyze mitigation strategies together with attack scenarios. Moreover, we plan to use Hybrid Rebeca introduced in [38] where we are able to model physical actors with continuous behavior and also different network protocols.

Acknowledgment. This research is partly supported by Swedish Foundation for Strategic Research (SSF) via the Serendipity project, and KKS SACSys Synergy project (Safe and Secure Adaptive Collaborative Systems).

References

1. Lanotte, R., Merro, M., Muradore, R., Viganò, L.: A formal approach to cyber-physical attacks. In: IEEE 30th Computer Security Foundations Symposium (CSF), pp. 436–450. IEEE (2017)
2. Adepu, S., Mathur, A., Gunda, J., Djokic, S.: An agent-based framework for simulating and analysing attacks on cyber physical systems. In: Wang, G., Zomaya, A., Perez, G.M., Li, K. (eds.) ICA3PP 2015. LNCS, vol. 9530, pp. 785–798. Springer, Cham (2015). https://doi.org/10.1007/978-3-319-27137-8_57
3. The industrial control systems cyber emergency response team. https://www.us-cert.gov/ics. Accessed 23 Apr 2020
4. Stallings, W., Brown, L., Bauer, M.D., Bhattacharjee, A.K.: Computer Security: Principles and Practice. Pearson Education, London (2012)
5. Gollmann, D., Gurikov, P., Isakov, A., Krotofil, M., Larsen, J., Winnicki, A.: Cyber-physical systems security: experimental analysis of a vinyl acetate monomer plant. In: Proceedings of Cyber-Physical System Security, pp. 1–12. ACM (2015)

6. Kang, E., Adepu, S., Jackson, D., Mathur, A.P.: Model-based security analysis of a water treatment system. In: Proceedings of Software Engineering for Smart Cyber-Physical Systems, pp. 22–28. ACM (2016)

7. Taormina, R., Galelli, S., Tippenhauer, N.O., Salomons, E., Ostfeld, A.: Characterizing cyber-physical attacks on water distribution systems. J. Water Resour. Plann. Manage. **143**(5), 04017009 (2017)

8. Lanotte, R., Merro, M., Munteanu, A., Viganò, L.: A formal approach to physics-based attacks in cyber-physical systems. ACM Trans. Priv. Secur. (TOPS) **23**(1), 1–41 (2020)

9. Reynisson, A.H., et al.: Modelling and simulation of asynchronous real-time systems using timed Rebeca. Sci. Comput. Program. **89**, 41–68 (2014)

10. Sirjani, M., Khamespanah, E.: On time actors. In: Ábrahám, E., Bonsangue, M., Johnsen, E.B. (eds.) Theory and Practice of Formal Methods. LNCS, vol. 9660, pp. 373–392. Springer, Cham (2016). https://doi.org/10.1007/978-3-319-30734-3_25

11. Khamespanah, E., Sirjani, M., Sabahi-Kaviani, Z., Khosravi, R., Izadi, M.: Timed Rebeca schedulability and deadlock freedom analysis using bounded floating time transition system. Sci. Comput. Program. **98**, 184–204 (2015)

12. Shostack, A.: Threat Modeling: Designing for Security. Wiley, Hoboken (2014)

13. Sirjani, M., Movaghar, A., Shali, A., De Boer, F.S.: Modeling and verification of reactive systems using Rebeca. Fundamenta Informaticae **63**(4), 385–410 (2004)

14. Sirjani, M.: Rebeca: theory, applications, and tools. In: de Boer, F.S., Bonsangue, M.M., Graf, S., de Roever, W.-P. (eds.) FMCO 2006. LNCS, vol. 4709, pp. 102–126. Springer, Heidelberg (2007). https://doi.org/10.1007/978-3-540-74792-5_5

15. Sirjani, M., Jaghoori, M.M.: Ten years of analyzing actors: Rebeca experience. In: Formal Modeling: Actors, Open Systems, Biological Systems - Essays, pp. 20–56 (2011)

16. Afra: an integrated environment for modeling and verifying Rebeca family designs (2019). https://rebeca-lang.org/alltools/Afra. Accessed 09 Nov 2019

17. Sirjani, M., Khamespanah, E., Lee, E.: Model checking software in cyberphysical systems. In: COMPSAC 2020 (2020)

18. Giraldo, J., et al.: A survey of physics-based attack detection in cyber-physical systems. ACM Comput. Surv. (CSUR) **51**(4), 1–36 (2018)

19. Choi, S., Yun, J.-H., Kim, S.-K.: A comparison of ICS datasets for security research based on attack paths. In: Luiijf, E., Žutautaitė, I., Hämmerli, B.M. (eds.) CRITIS 2018. LNCS, vol. 11260, pp. 154–166. Springer, Cham (2019). https://doi.org/10.1007/978-3-030-05849-4_12

20. Flaus, J.-M.: Cybersecurity of Industrial Systems. Wiley, Hoboken (2019)

21. Mathur, A.P., Tippenhauer, N.O.: SWaT: a water treatment testbed for research and training on ICS security. In: Cyber-physical Systems for Smart Water Networks (CySWater), pp. 31–36. IEEE (2016)

22. Sirjani, M.: Power is overrated, go for friendliness! Expressiveness, faithfulness, and usability in modeling: the actor experience. In: Principles of Modeling - Essays Dedicated to Edward A. Lee, pp. 423–448 (2018)

23. Rebeca (2019). http://rebeca-lang.org/Rebeca. Accessed 03 June 2019

24. Khamespanah, E., Sirjani, M., Mechitov, K., Agha, G.: Modeling and analyzing real-time wireless sensor and actuator networks using actors and model checking. Int. J. Softw. Tools Technol. Transfer. **20**(5), 547–561 (2017). https://doi.org/10.1007/s10009-017-0480-3

25. Sharifi, M., Mosaffa, Z., Mohammadi, S., Sirjani, M.: Functional and performance analysis of network-on-chips using actor-based modeling and formal verification. In: ECEASST, vol. 66 (2013)

26. Yousefi, B., Ghassemi, F., Khosravi, R.: Modeling and efficient verification of wireless ad hoc networks. Formal Aspects Comput. **29**(6), 1051–1086 (2017). https://doi.org/10.1007/s00165-017-0429-z
27. Sirjani, M., Lee, E., Khamespanah, E.: Model checking cyberphysical systems. Mathematics **8**(7), 1067 (2020)
28. Sirjani, M., Provenzano, L., Asadollah, S.A., Moghadam, M.H.: From requirements to verifiable executable models using Rebeca. In: International Workshop on Automated and verifiable Software sYstem DEvelopment, November 2019
29. Henzinger, T.A.: The theory of hybrid automata. In: Proceedings, 11th Annual IEEE Symposium on Logic in Computer Science, New Brunswick, New Jersey, USA, 27–30 July 1996, pp. 278–292. IEEE Computer Society (1996)
30. Samonas, S., Coss, D.: The CIA strikes back: redefining confidentiality, integrity and availability in security. J. Inf. Syst. Secur. **10**(3), 21–45 (2014)
31. iTrust: Secure water treatment (SWaT) dataset (2019). https://itrust.sutd.edu.sg/itrust-labs_datasets/dataset_info/. Accessed 17 Sept 2019
32. Rebeca (2020). http://rebeca-lang.org/allprojects/CRYSTAL
33. Burch, J.R., Clarke, E.M., Long, D.E., McMillan, K.L., Dill, D.L.: Symbolic model checking for sequential circuit verification. IEEE Trans. Comput. Aided Des. Integr. Circuits Syst. **13**(4), 401–424 (1994)
34. Wasicek, A., Derler, P., Lee, E.A.: Aspect-oriented modeling of attacks in automotive cyber-physical systems. In: ACM/EDAC/IEEE Design Automation Conference (DAC) (2014)
35. Buck, J., Ha, S., Lee, E.A., Messerschmitt, D.G.: Ptolemy: a framework for simulating and prototyping heterogeneous systems. In: Readings in Hardware/software Co-Design, pp. 527–543 (2001)
36. Rocchetto, M., Tippenhauer, N.O.: Towards formal security analysis of industrial control systems. In: ACM Asia Conference on Computer and Communications Security, pp. 114–126. ACM (2017)
37. Fritz, R., Zhang, P.: Modeling and detection of cyber attacks on discrete event systems. IFAC-PapersOnLine **51**(7), 285–290 (2018)
38. Jahandideh, I., Ghassemi, F., Sirjani, M.: Hybrid Rebeca: modeling and analyzing of cyber-physical systems. In: Chamberlain, R., Taha, W., Törngren, M. (eds.) CyPhy/WESE - 2018. LNCS, vol. 11615, pp. 3–27. Springer, Cham (2019). https://doi.org/10.1007/978-3-030-23703-5_1

Formal Verification of Industrial Systems

Scalable Detection of Amplification Timing Anomalies for the Superscalar TriCore Architecture

Benjamin Binder[1(✉)], Mihail Asavoae[1], Florian Brandner[2],
Belgacem Ben Hedia[1], and Mathieu Jan[1]

[1] CEA, List, 91191 Gif-sur-Yvette, France
benjamin.binder@cea.fr
[2] LTCI, Télécom Paris, 19 Place Marguerite Perey, 91120 Palaiseau, France

Abstract. Real-time systems are subject to strong timing requirements, and thus rely on worst-case timing analyses to safely address them. Undesired timing phenomena, called timing anomalies, threaten the soundness of timing analyses. In this regard, we consider the following inauspicious partnership - a compositional timing analysis and amplification timing anomalies. Precisely, we investigate how the industrial, superscalar TriCore architecture is amenable for compositional timing analyses via a formal evaluation of amplification timing anomalies. We adapt and extend a specialized abstraction, called canonical pipeline model, to quantify the amplification effects in a model of a dual-pipelined TriCore, its asynchronous store buffer, data dependencies, and structural hazards. We use model checking to efficiently detect amplification timing anomalies and report the associated complexity results.

Keywords: Timing anomalies · TriCore architecture · Model checking

1 Introduction

Real-time systems need to satisfy strong timing requirements and consequently, relying on worst-case timing reasoning to provide the necessary timing guarantees. In this context, an important analysis is the Worst-Case Execution Time (WCET) analysis, which should compute safe and, desirably, tight bounds on the execution time. The complexity of the underlying architecture makes it necessary to perform the execution time analysis in a compositional way [8] by adding up the timing contributions of individual micro-architecture elements. A standard compositional timing analysis would consider separate timing analyses for caches and the pipeline and then combine their respective timing results.

Compositional timing analysis is not always possible due to undesired timing phenomena called timing anomalies [15]. A particular type - the amplification timing anomalies - manifests when a local timing variation leads to an increased global timing variation. In order to perform a sound compositional timing analysis, it becomes essential to bound this amplification effect. In this regard, it is

© Springer Nature Switzerland AG 2020
M. H. ter Beek and D. Ničković (Eds.): FMICS 2020, LNCS 12327, pp. 151–169, 2020.
https://doi.org/10.1007/978-3-030-58298-2_6

desirable to use formal modeling and verification in order to fully explore possible sources of amplifications. Recent work [11] proposed to use model checking along with a specialized abstraction to evaluate pipelined architectures with respect to amplification timing anomalies. However, this abstraction was only used to compare so-called *time-predictable* pipelines, which are rather simple.

In this work, we consider a processor mainly used in the automotive field - the TriCore architecture [10]. Briefly, this is a *superscalar* processor architecture and features two specialized pipelines, one for arithmetic operations and one for memory accesses. The two pipelines interact due to data dependencies and structural hazards, causing superscalar effects. The processor is connected to an external bus that may be accessed concurrently by the program memory interface (PMI) and the data memory interface (DMI). It also comes with an asynchronous *store buffer* to reduce the write pressure through the DMI. With this complex memory design, it appears likely that the TriCore suffers from amplification timing anomalies and in this context, the applicability of the aforementioned pipeline abstraction from [11] and their precise occurrences need to be investigated. *Can amplification timing anomalies be tracked efficiently for this pipeline? If so, how?* Our main contribution is that detecting these anomalies over a model, which fully represents possible dependencies between the TriCore pipelines, is possible – however, only with appropriate reductions. These reductions efficiently remove useless pipeline configurations, with respect to timing anomalies, from the state space that has to be explored by the model checker. We analyze complexity results for different evaluation settings, with both generic and TriCore specific reductions. Our formal TriCore model and its settings are available on a GitHub repository [3].

This paper is organized as follows. Section 2 introduces the amplification timing anomalies and a specialized abstraction to address them, called canonical pipeline model. Section 3 presents how to adapt this particular model to the TriCore architecture. The evaluation setting and results are reported in Sect. 4. Finally, Sect. 5 presents related work before concluding in Sect. 6.

2   Tracking Amplification Timing Anomalies

2.1   Amplification Timing Anomalies

An amplification timing anomaly, shown in Fig. 1, appears when a local timing variation Δ_L leads to a larger global timing variation Δ_G. These timing variations manifest at the level of *one execution path*, due to *different initial conditions*. Multiple reasons could cause Δ_L: variable instruction latency, variable memory access time (e.g., due to DRAM page conflicts or cache misses), delays due to contention of memory accesses (e.g., because of the bus arbitration).

Modern micro-architecture features like out-of-order pipelines, branch prediction or prefetching mechanisms could lead to anomalous timing behaviors. However, even simple, in-order processors may suffer from timing anomalies as presented in [6]. More precisely, when a (load/store) instruction A is about to perform a data memory access, another instruction B, further in the program and thus less advanced in the pipeline, can have already entered the pipeline for fetching. Instruction B could have generated a memory bus access, i.e., after an instruction cache miss. Two executions are possible, depending on whether the memory access of A is a data cache hit or miss. In case of a hit, instruction A proceeds without stalling the pipeline (and independent of state of the memory bus). In case of a miss, it should wait for more than one miss: the completion of the one of B and its own one. Figure 1 illustrates this case, where the local variation Δ_L is caused by the switch from a data cache hit to a cache miss for instruction A, while the global variation Δ_G is greater than Δ_L because of the instruction cache miss of instruction B.

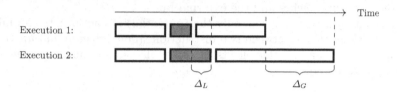

Fig. 1. Schematic of an amplification timing anomaly.

2.2 UCLID5 Modeling and Verification Tool

UCLID5 is a modeling, specification and verification language [17]. It offers abstractions to design computational system models and supports a range of techniques to formally verify properties on these models. In particular, LTL (Linear Temporal Logic) properties can be specified and then verified by *Bounded Model Checking* (BMC). In this case, model checking is performed up to a *specified* number of transitions that constitutes the *bound*. Models are composed of a set of typed variables, whose valuations define model states. A *next* block specifies the next value of each changed variable with parallel assignments, i.e., all changes are simultaneously applied at the end of the block, the prime operator referring to the new value of a variable. Each execution of the *next* block makes up a transition. The notion of time is not inherently present in UCLID5: in our models, each transition represents a clock cycle of the processor.

Non-specified initial values, in the *init* block, are arbitrarily set, in accordance with variable types. Moreover, *assumptions* can be formulated to control at any step the range of possible values for a variable, which might also introduce abstract non-determinism. These two points draw up the *state space* of the verification problem. When a property is violated, the model checker provides a (single) counter-example showing a detailed trace with the evolution of specified variables. A particular trace can be obtained through assumptions. Unfortunately, the verification tool does not provide any statistics (number of states/memory consumption).

2.3 Basic Canonical Pipeline Model

A canonical pipeline model, in [11], is designed to expose amplification timing anomalies in time-predictable processor pipelines. It uses UCLID5 to model and verify these pipelines using bounded model checking. This canonical model is used to verify the absence of such anomalies on PRET [12], Patmos [16], and SIC [6] pipelines or to identify execution scenarios that trigger such anomalies on the K1 [4] pipeline. These models address the *timing behavior* of the considered processors only, consequently:

- Instruction variants are not distinguished individually, only classes such as, for instance, load/store or arithmetic/logic operations.
- Computations, i.e., arithmetic, are not modeled, only the pipeline logic that may impact how instructions advance through pipeline stages as well as the interactions with caches and the external bus.
- Cache content is not modeled, only the (potential) impact of hits and misses.
- Only the interactions between two instructions (*downstream* and *upstream*) are modeled explicitly, side-effects of other instructions in the pipeline are over-approximated.

The *downstream* instruction precedes (not necessarily directly) the *upstream* instruction in the flow of instructions. Therefore the downstream instruction (older) is more advanced in the pipeline, i.e., in later stages of the pipeline, compared to the upstream instruction (younger). Each instruction is characterized at a given instant by a tuple:

$$\langle class, bl, stage, latency, delay, stalled, progress \rangle,$$

where *class* denotes the instruction class, *bl* the vector of baseline latencies for each pipeline stage, *stage* the current pipeline stage, *latency* the remaining amount of cycles to complete the baseline latency for the current pipeline stage, and *delay* the accumulated delay in cycles due to stalling so far. The last two fields are Booleans related to the pipeline logic, where *stalled* indicates that the instruction suffers a pipeline stall caused by another instruction, whereas *progress* indicates whether the instruction may proceed to the next stage. The progression of an instruction through the pipeline is illustrated in Fig. 2. Each attribute of both instructions is represented by UCLID5 variables.

Progression and Stalling Logic. When an instruction enters a pipeline stage, its *latency* is initialized with the corresponding value in *bl*. Then, every transition (UCLID5 *next* block) keeping the instruction one more cycle in the stage while it is not impacted by the decision of the stalling logic makes its *latency* decrease. Baseline latencies in *bl* are *minimal* latencies, as some conditions may require stalling and thus delay instructions, making them spend more time in a stage than they require themselves. The result (*progress*) from the advancement logic is based both on the remaining cycles (*latency*) and on the conditions that may induce stalling (*stalled*). In addition to the processor's actual pipeline stages, the models contain two special stages, *pre* and *post*, where instructions reside before entering the actual pipeline and after completion respectively.

From a structural point of view, the downstream instruction can progress in the pipeline, provided the memory bus is not busy if the instruction has to

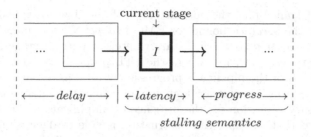

Fig. 2. Canonical pipeline model from [11]: the advancement of (upstream or down-stream) instruction I in the pipeline is allowed by the *progress* attribute, which depends on the *latency* in its current stage and on the stalling semantics. The *delay* attribute enumerates the number of cycles when I was stalled so far because of the other (downstream or upstream) instruction.

access main memory. Hence, although the downstream instruction precedes in the instruction flow, it can be delayed because of a shared resource, i.e., the bus, prompting a structural hazard. This is actually a source of amplification timing anomalies. The upstream instruction, besides being also potentially blocked by the bus being busy, can be impeded in its progression by the next stage being still occupied by the downstream instruction. Beyond these structural aspects, architectures may implement stalling strategies that stop the pipeline progression to enforce a more regular behavior. Such additional stalling logics have been modeled in [11] using this canonical pipeline model. In particular, in the *whole* progression logic, on which this work is based, the entire pipeline is stalled as soon as an instruction induces a miss.

Verification Procedure. The basis of the verification procedure consists in initializing the bounded model checking in UCLID5 with the downstream instruction placed anywhere in the pipeline (*stage* attribute) and the upstream instruction at *pre*, i.e., about to be issued. Actually, that means choosing successively all the different possible current stages for the downstream instructions when the upstream instruction enters the pipeline. In this way, all possible distances between instructions in the pipelines are evaluated. All classes of instructions and all possible baseline latencies are exhaustively explored by model checking. *The state space is built at the initialization step* (*init* block), through assumptions (see Sect. 2.2) that let *choices in values* (non-determinism) for the variables representing the downstream initial pipeline stage, the classes of both instructions and the fields of baseline latencies for the stages that may access memory (i.e., local timing variation).

A relevant bound of model checking has to be specified. For the purpose of studying the effects of local variations for the downstream instruction, the model checker should perform transitions, i.e., advance the instructions through the pipeline, up to the completion of the downstream instruction. That means that this instruction has reached *post* stage, which is specified by an LTL property: $G(step = depth \implies stage_{down} = post)$ where the variable *step* counts the number of transitions, the current stage of the downstream instruction is $stage_{down}$ and the *specified* bound for BMC is *depth*. The minimal exploration depth (bound) required to reach a state where the current stage of the downstream instruction is *post*, i.e., where the LTL property is verified, in all progression scenarios of the pipeline is progressively established in a binary-search fashion, starting from an arbitrary high enough value that satisfies this property.

The necessary condition for the presence of amplification timing anomalies from [11] states that the upstream instruction is able to delay the downstream instruction. Whenever a downstream instruction is stalled, its *delay* variable is incremented. If an increase of variable *delay* is found by the model checker, there can be an amplification timing anomaly. The generated counter-example, in particular the initial state of both the upstream and the downstream instructions, can be analyzed. This property indicates that the total execution time of a sequence may not be compositional, i.e., some hardware reasons prevent from considering instructions independently and thus the combination of their timing effects. It is a necessary but not sufficient condition, as strictly positive delay values do not imply amplification timing anomalies (i.e., false positives). The negation of this condition, a sufficient condition for the absence of amplification anomalies, is formulated using the LTL property: $G(delay_{down} = 0)$.

3   Canonical Pipeline Model for the TriCore Architecture

The TriCore architecture is composed of two principal pipelines - an Integer (I) and a Load/Store (LS) pipeline, and a third, specialized one for hardware loops. The three pipelines form the execution unit, as described in detail in [10, p. 218]. In the following, we focus our investigation of amplification timing anomalies on a compact TriCore architecture consisting of the two principal pipelines, as shown in Fig. 3. Structurally, the two pipelines are quite similar, however they provide different functionality. The I-pipeline mainly handles arithmetic instructions, whereas the LS-pipeline manipulates memory addresses and all related instructions, i.e., load and store instructions.

The *Instruction Fetch* (IF) stages of the two pipelines operate either in-sync on so-called *fetch bundles* (i.e., pairs of I- and LS-instructions) or on a single I- or-LS instruction (meanwhile a bubble is inserted in the other pipeline). Both IF stages are connected to the *Program Memory Interface* (PMI). The PMI is comprised of an instruction cache and a scratchpad and is in-turn connected to

Table 1. Possible baseline latencies for memory operations.

Cache hit/local PMI scratchpad	1	Cache hit (1 line)/DMI scratchpad	1
Flash access & PPB hit	4	Cache hit (2 lines)	2
Flash access & PPB miss	8	Flash memory access (cache miss)	10
DMI scratchpad (via SRI bus)	5	PMI scratchpad (via SRI bus)	5
(a) Program Memory Interface		(b) Data Memory Interface	

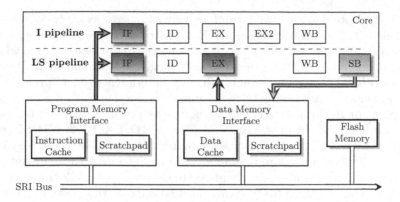

Fig. 3. The TriCore architecture: the principal pipelines and the memory system with input (in blue) and output (in red) buses. (Color figure online)

the *Shared Resource Interconnect Bus* (SRI). The SRI allows to fetch instructions from a Flash Memory in case of an instruction cache miss, and may cause the pipeline to stall. Memory accesses to data are performed exclusively in the LS-pipeline. Load instructions read data in the EX stage, while store instructions place their data in an asynchronously operating store buffer. Loads and stores access the SRI through the *Data Memory Interface* (DMI) and thus too may cause stalling. Loads, the store buffer, and the PMI contend for the shared SRI bus and may thus interfere with each other. Notably, any of the three components may delay an access of any of the other three components. Generally speaking, however, the store buffer has the lowest priority [10, p. 228].

The remaining pipeline stages cannot cause stalling and complete in a single cycle. Note that only a few multi-cycle instructions (fused multiply-accumulate) make use of the EX2 stage in the I-pipeline. However, the two pipelines may interact with each other – even for instructions that do not belong to the same fetch bundle. Data dependencies and structural hazards in the I-pipeline may stall the LS-pipeline for several cycles. Whereas stalls in the LS-pipeline also stall the I-pipeline for the same number of cycles [9]. Possible baseline latencies for instruction fetches (IF) and memory accesses (EX/store buffer) are reported in Table 1. Next, we present successive extensions of the canonical pipeline model (cf. Sect. 2), designed to identify amplification timing anomalies in the TriCore architecture. We detail structural modifications (due to a second pipeline) and functional extensions (to accommodate the stalling logic, store buffer, and data-dependencies).

3.1 Dual Pipeline and Stalling Logic

The original canonical pipeline model [11] features only a single pipeline. Consequently, the *upstream* and *downstream* instructions have to be *duplicated* in order to model the interactions between the I- and LS-pipelines of the TriCore. We thus consider four instructions, called *dw.p* and *up.q*, where $p, q \in \{I, LS\}$

respectively. Note that the two *dw* and *up* instructions respectively do not necessarily belong to the same fetch bundle. Each instruction is associated with three additional Boolean attributes, *pbus*, *dbus*, and *conflict*, which indicate whether the instruction needs to access the SRI bus through the PMI and/or DMI respectively and whether the instruction is subject to interference due to priority rules. *pbus* and *dbus* are set whenever the required instruction/data does not reside in the cache or the local scratchpad memory. The pipeline structure is modeled as a totally ordered set of stages: $\mathcal{S} = \{pre, \mathrm{IF}, \mathrm{ID}, \mathrm{EX}, \mathrm{EX2}, \mathrm{WB}, \mathrm{SB}, post\}$, where the stages EX2 and SB (for store buffer) are optional – as in Fig. 3.

The verification procedure is adapted likewise. The *up.LS* instruction serves as the reference point and is initially placed in the *pre* stage, while the three other instructions can be placed freely in any pipeline stage by the model checker. The only limitation is that the instruction *dw.p* has to succeed *up.p*, $p \in \{I, LS\}$, in the respective pipeline according to the total order $\mathcal{S}$.

Formula 1 specifies under which conditions an *up.p* instruction is allowed to advance to the next stage in our dual-pipeline model:

$$progress'_{up.p} := latency_{up.p} \leq 1 \wedge \neg stalled'_{up.p} \wedge \neg conflict_{up.p}$$
$$\wedge\ next_{up.p} \neq stage'_{dw.p} \tag{1}$$

The attribute *latency* (cf. Sect. 2.3) is used to check whether the *up* instruction has completed its work in the current stage (e.g., completed its *own* cache miss). The Boolean attribute *stalled* indicates stalling due to the pipeline logic, which might impede the instruction from advancing, e.g., due to another instruction experiencing a cache miss. The newly introduced *conflict* attribute is used to model interference on the SRI bus. Finally, the *up.p* instruction may only advance if the corresponding *downstream* instruction *dw.p* does not occupy the *next* stage. Note that the above formula reuses UCLID5's notation to describe state transitions (see Sect. 2.2), where names with a check mark ($progress'_{up.p}$) indicate values of the new/next state, while regular names refer to values of the current state.

Formula 1 depends on the stalling logic of the dual-pipeline, represented by the instruction attribute *stalled*. The following two formulas illustrate one variant of such a stalling logic, called *whole* [9,11], where both pipelines are stalled simultaneously whenever some instruction in the pipeline stalls. For now we ignore store instructions, they are handled in the next section introducing the modeling of the store buffer.

$$stalled'_{up.LS} := common_{dw}$$
$$\vee\ (stage_{up.I} = \mathrm{IF} \wedge pbus_{up.I} \wedge latency_{up.I} > 1) \tag{2}$$

$$stalled'_{up.I} := common_{dw}$$
$$\vee\ (stage_{up.LS} = \mathrm{IF} \wedge pbus_{up.LS} \wedge latency_{up.LS} > 1)$$
$$\vee\ (stage_{up.LS} = \mathrm{EX} \wedge dbus_{up.LS} \wedge latency_{up.LS} > 1) \tag{3}$$

$$common_{dw} := (\forall p \in \{I, LS\}: stage_{dw.p} = \mathrm{IF} \wedge pbus_{dw.p} \wedge latency_{dw.p} > 1)$$
$$\vee\ (stage_{dw.LS} = \mathrm{EX} \wedge dbus_{dw.LS} \wedge latency_{dw.LS} > 1) \tag{4}$$

Here, $common_{dw}$ denotes stalling of the *upstream* instructions in the I- and LS-pipelines due to the *downstream* instructions. Aside from this, the $up.LS$ instruction may only experience additional stalling when $up.I$ is in the IF stage (second line of Formula 2), while the $up.I$ instruction may in addition experience such stalling when $up.LS$ is in the EX stage (third line of Formula 3).

It now remains to model the interference of the shared SRI bus on the considered instructions. We model a fixed-priority scheme for the SRI bus, where data memory accesses are prioritized over instruction fetches (side-effects of the store buffer are modeled later):

$$conflict_{up.LS} := (stage_{up.LS} = pre \land pbus_{up.LS})$$
$$\land (stage_{down.LS} = ID \land dbus_{down.LS}) \tag{5}$$
$$conflict_{up.I} := (stage_{up.I} = pre \land pbus_{up.I})$$
$$\land ((stage_{down.LS} = ID \land dbus_{down.LS})$$
$$\lor (stage_{up.LS} = ID \land dbus_{up.LS})$$
$$\lor (stage_{down.LS} = pre \land pbus_{down.LS})) \tag{6}$$

Formula 5 indicates that memory loads may only experience interference on the SRI bus during instruction fetch and thus are stalled in the pre stage (first line). Similarly, the *downstream* instruction $dw.LS$ must be in the ID stage and about to enter the EX stage where it will access the SRI bus (second line). The $up.I$ instruction may also experience interference during instruction fetch from the $dw.LS$ and $up.LS$ instructions when either of them is about to enter the EX stage while accessing the SRI bus (lines 1 to 3 of Formula 6). The last line deals with the particular case where the $up.I$ and $dw.LS$ instructions are in the same fetch bundle, but span over two caches lines or scratchpad accesses.

The formulas for the *downstream* instructions are slightly simpler since certain cases, e.g., checking whether the next stage is available, can be excluded due to the ordering of the instructions. In particular, the priority rule about data memory accesses and instruction fetches prevent interference on the SRI bus from $up.LS$, i.e., the $conflict$ attribute of the $dw.LS$ instruction is always false:

$$conflict_{dw.LS} := \bot \tag{7}$$

3.2   Store Buffer

We model the asynchronously operating store buffer as a special pipeline stage, SB, placed at the end of the LS-pipeline between WB and $post$ (see Fig. 3). Asynchronous memory accesses of the buffer are modeled using the regular baseline latencies associated with the SB stage, similar to those of loads.

Fill Status. The store buffer of the TriCore architecture contains several entries. Multiple store instructions may thus place their data into the store buffer without stalling – as long as the store buffer has free entries. Consequently, and in contrast to regular stages, the *up.LS* and *dw.LS* instructions may *both* occupy an entry of the store buffer at the same time. However, we do not model the actual fill level (number of entries occupied). Instead, it suffices to introduce a new Boolean instruction attribute *prio_SB* that is associated with *up.LS* and *dw.LS* when they represent store instructions. Situations where the buffer is full when a store instruction performs its memory access are modeled by its *prio_SB* being set. The model checker consequently explores all possible scenarios where the buffer's fill status impacts the arbitration between SRI bus accesses.

Stalling. A store may only stall the pipeline when the buffer is full. When the *prio_SB* attribute of a store is not set, the instruction will stall in the WB stage. This new source of stalls needs to be considered in Formulas 2, 3, and 4 in order to model the *whole* pipeline logic accordingly. This requires two kinds of changes: (a) existing terms modeling stalls in the EX stage only apply to instructions with the *class* attribute being *load* and (b) new stall conditions for stores in the WB stage need to be added as additional terms. We will refine the stalling mechanism once more in Sect. 3.3 when data dependencies are introduced.

SRI Bus Conflicts. The store buffer may asynchronously access the SRI bus and thus may cause additional bus conflicts. It generally has the lowest priority and only starts a new transfer when the bus is idle. However, an ongoing transfer of the buffer may cause interferences even when the bus initially was idle. In addition, the store buffer is assigned the highest priority when it is full. These new forms of bus conflicts have to be added as disjunctions in Formulas 5 and 6. The existing terms modeling conflicts related to instructions in the ID stage only apply to loads – similar to the terms for stalling before. In addition, new conflicts arise from store instructions that are currently in the WB stage and about to enter SB when the *dbus* and *prio_SB* (the store buffer *is* full) attributes are set.

Finally, we also have to consider that the *dw.LS* instruction may experience conflicts itself when the store buffer is *not* full. This form of conflict as a disjunction with $\bot$ in Formula 7 actually leads to the following refined formula:

$$
\begin{aligned}
conflict_{dw.LS} := \ & (stage_{dw.LS} = WB \land class_{dw.LS} = store \land dbus_{dw.LS} \\
& \land \neg prio\_SB_{dw.LS}) \\
& \land ((stage_{up.I} = pre \land pbus_{up.I}) \\
& \quad \lor (stage_{up.LS} = pre \land pbus_{up.LS}) \\
& \quad \lor (stage_{dw.I} = pre \land pbus_{dw.I}) \\
& \quad \lor (stage_{up.LS} = ID \land class_{up.LS} = load \land dbus_{up.LS})) \quad (8)
\end{aligned}
$$

This states that a *dw.LS* store instruction in the WB stage (first two lines) may suffer interference from instruction fetches by both *upstream* instructions as well as *dw.I* (lines 3 to 5) as well as a memory load by *up.LS* (last line).

3.3 Store Buffer and Dependent Loads

On the TriCore architecture, a store followed by a dependent load that accesses the same memory address causes a *memory reference hazard*. The architecture then must ensure that the load obtains the correct most-up-to-date value by stalling the load until the store completes. Table 2 exemplifies this situation: case (a) shows the hazard that would occur, while case (b) shows the stalling introduced to resolve it.

In the pipeline model, this hazard may occur when $dw.LS$ is a store instruction in the WB or SB stage, and when $up.LS$ is a load that is about to access memory in the EX stage [9]. However, we need to distinguish whether both instructions refer to the same address. This is achieved by introducing a new global Boolean attribute *memdep* that indicates when it is set that $dw.LS$ and $up.LS$ are two dependent load/store instructions. The model checker again explores all possible assignments of this variable – while respecting consistency, e.g., the two instructions have to be in the right instruction classes, et cetera. Moreover, as the data cache has a write-allocate policy [10], the dependent load will always experience a cache hit, i.e., $dbus_{up.LS}$ is not set. Finally, since the dependent load stalls the pipeline, the access of the store buffer to the SRI bus is prioritized – similar to the case when the store buffer is full. Consequently, the $prio\_SB_{dw.LS}$ attribute is set.

Now it remains to model the impact of these stalls by extending the pipeline logic. Two cases have to be considered: (a) the side-effect of the stalled load on other instructions, according to the *whole* stalling logic, and (b) the stalling of the load itself. The former case concerns both *downstream* instructions and $up.I$ (illustrated through Formula 3), for which an additional disjunction is required as follows:

$$\ldots \vee (stage_{up.LS} = EX \wedge memdep \wedge stage'_{dw.LS} \neq post) \tag{9}$$

In the latter case, the same disjunction has to be added to Formula 1, as a new term of stalling that does not refer to stalling due to *another* instruction. In addition, we have to modify the handling of the baseline latency of the EX stage. The dependent load only performs the cache access *after* the store buffer has actually written the store's data to the memory. Consequently, the baseline latency may only *progress* once the store completed. This is important, for instance, to model unaligned memory accesses touching two cache lines (see Table 1b).

Table 2. A memory reference hazard between a store and a dependent load.

	t_{-1}	t_0	t_1	t_2	t_3	t_4		t_{-1}	t_0	t_1	t_2	t_3	t_4	t_5	t_6
Store	IF	ID	EX	WB	SB	SB		IF	ID	EX	WB	SB	SB		
Load		IF	ID	EX	WB				IF	ID	EX	EX	EX	EX	WB

(a) The load depends on the store and there would be a memory reference hazard.   (b) Stall cycles are introduced to solve the hazard.

3.4   Write-after-Write Dependencies and Structural Hazards

Certain *Write-after-Write* (WAW) dependencies on registers may cause structural hazards on the TriCore. This occurs when two instructions try to write to the same register, which may only happen due to a WAW dependence between a load and multi-cycle instructions using the EX2 stage of the I-pipeline or a WAW dependence within a fetch bundle. Both situations are resolved by stalling of up to 2 cycles in the worst case. Table 3 shows an example using a fetch bundle consisting of a multiply-accumulate (A) and a load instruction (B) that both write to the same register [9]. Instruction A takes two cycles to execute, i.e., spends an extra cycle (in EX2). In order to enforce in-order completion, instruction B in the LS-pipeline has to stall for two cycles (Table 3b). As can be seen, these stalls (are intended to) alter the relative position between instructions and thus differ from the *whole* pipeline logic applied everywhere else.

Similarly to dependent loads, a set of new attributes is associated with the instructions of the LS-pipeline ($waw\_dw_{i.LS}$ and $waw\_up_{j.LS}$, $i, j \in \{up, dw\}$), which indicate a WAW dependence between an *upstream* or *downstream* load to either $dw.I$ or $up.I$ respectively. As usual the model checker explores all possible assignments of these attributes, while ensuring consistency (e.g., stores cannot cause WAW dependencies).

The stalling logic of instructions in the LS-pipeline is then extended to encode the various scenarios by adding a disjunction to Formula 2 for $up.LS$ (and its equivalent for $dw.LS$):

$$\ldots \vee (stage_{up.LS} = ID \wedge$$
$$((waw\_dw_{up.LS} \wedge (stage_{dw.I} = ID \vee stage_{dw.I} = EX)) \vee$$
$$(waw\_up_{up.LS} \wedge (stage_{up.I} = ID \vee stage_{up.I} = EX)))) \qquad (10)$$

This formula states that the $up.LS$ instruction in ID (first line) may suffer stalling when it depends either on the $dw.I$ (second line) or the $up.I$ instruction (third line). The number of total stall cycles is iteratively determined by the current stage (ID or EX) of the related instruction, which may progress meanwhile.

Table 3. Write-after-Write dependencies and structural hazards may alter the relative distance between instructions.

Cycle	Instr.	t_0	t_1	t_2	t_3	t_4
I pipeline	A	IF	ID	EX	EX2	WB
LS pipeline	B	IF	ID	EX	WB	

Cycle	Instr.	t_0	t_1	t_2	t_3	t_4	t_5
I pipeline	A	IF	ID	EX	EX2	WB	
LS pipeline	B	IF	ID	ID	ID	EX	WB

(a) Both instructions are issued in parallel and there would be a WAW hazard.

(b) Two stall cycles are introduced to solve the WAW hazard.

4   Evaluations

In this section, we conduct experiments on our model for the TriCore architecture. Aside from expanding the results of the comparative study from [11], with a more complex architecture, the current investigation also aims to assess the scalability of the canonical model for tracking amplification anomalies. Then, we evaluate possible refinements when data dependencies are considered, we analyze a counter-example showing an amplification timing anomaly and finally, we address a code-specific extension. Table 4 reports the results, in terms of minimal depth for the downstream instructions to reach *post* stage (see Sect. 2.3) and of verification runtimes, for various configurations of the TriCore model (Tx) reflecting the aforementioned features and detailed thereafter. It also mentions for comparison representative results from the basic in-order model [11].

Table 4. Evaluations of various configurations of the TriCore model (TRx), compared to the basic in-order model with the *whole* stalling logic [11] (INx).

Core model	Inter. reduc.	Store Buffer	Gen. reduc.	Mem. dep.	WAW	WAW reduc.	Code-specif.	Min. depth	Runtime (h:min:s)
Basic In-order (IN1)								33	0:00:29
Basic In-order (IN2)		✓						33	0:00:15
TriCore, single pipeline (TR1)	✓	✓						38	0:06:42
TriCore, single pipeline (TR2)	✓	✓	✓					38	0:05:14
TriCore, single pipeline (TR3)	✓	✓	✓	✓				38	0:05:23
TriCore, dual pipeline (TR4)		✓	✓	✓				53	8:23:04
TriCore, dual pipeline (TR5)	✓	✓	✓	✓	✓			>53	>7:23:53
TriCore, dual pipeline (TR6)	✓	✓	✓	✓	✓	✓		53	6:52:15
TriCore, dual pipeline (TR7)	✓	✓	✓	✓	✓	✓	✓	42	0:28:49

4.1   Basic TriCore Model

Firstly, we evaluate the TriCore model without data dependencies.

TriCore Adaptation. On this condition, instructions within the isolated I-pipeline do not interfere with the LS-pipeline. The single I-stage that may affect the whole execution is IF. Since stalling entails the same stall cycles in the LS-pipeline, modeling instruction progressions in the I-pipeline is not relevant with respect to timing anomalies. Their initial *stage* is thus set to *post*. This feature is referred to as *Inter(ference) reduc(tion)* in Table 4. The model becomes quite similar to those from [11]. Table 4 provides the result for the whole-logic basic in-order pipeline from [11], with the same verification infrastructure (IN1). The significant relative difference in runtimes - from seconds (IN1) to minutes (TR1) - is due to the state space of the TriCore model being extended by the multiple possible baseline latencies for the additional stage SB.

General Reductions. While the low complexity of the case studies in [11] did not enhance systematic state space reductions, refinements of the verification procedure are desirable for the Tricore. First, varying the values of baseline latencies (*bl*) of stages that will never be reached by an instruction, because its initial stage is greater in the pipeline order, is vain for the verification procedure. These values are thus systematically enforced to one at the initial step:

$$\forall i \in \{up, dw\}, \ \forall p \in \{I, LS\}, \ \forall s \in \mathcal{S}, \ s < stage_{i.p} \implies bl_{i.p}.s = 1 \qquad (11)$$

This kind of reductions is implemented in UCLID5 as *assumptions* (see Sect. 2.2).

Furthermore, all values in the range defined by the maximal value of the possible baseline latencies of the *initial* stage must be preserved. Indeed, an instruction may have already completed partially its latency for its current stage before the *up.LS* instruction is about to enter the pipeline (*pre*). Nevertheless, the state space can be reduced by retaining only concrete baseline latencies for non-initial stages.

Evaluations (TR2) and (IN2) in Table 4 restart respectively (TR1) and (IN1) with these *Gen(eral) reduc(tions)* added. Though the absolute differences are not substantial, the relative (20 % and 48 %) gains on execution times are significant. The preserved partial baseline latencies for SB are responsible for the lower global decline as to the TriCore model.

4.2 Data Dependencies

The specific refinements of the TriCore model are evaluated hereafter. A key point here is to carefully handle the state space explosion.

Memory References. Evaluation (TR3) shows that the additional verification time when adding data memory references to the TriCore model (by relaxing the value of the *memdep* attribute now possibly set) is only of 9 s. Actually, as explained in Sect. 3.3, the single situation allowing this kind of dependencies is a load following a store, with the baseline latency for the load in EX excluding cache misses by design.

Dual Pipeline. Dealing with WAW dependencies requires the second pipeline in the model, marked in Table 4 by 2nd *pipeline*. Evaluation (TR4) shows a state space explosion and a significantly higher runtime, even in the absence of WAW dependencies. Though modeling the I-pipeline without WAWs does not impact amplification anomalies, this evaluation exposes the associated state space explosion. On the one hand this setting generates multiple cases with different baseline latencies for fetching in the I-pipeline, and on the other hand it causes more stalling cases of both pipelines.

WAW Dependencies. Some reductions are thus necessary before modeling WAW dependencies. The I-pipeline may interfere with the LS-pipeline when actual WAWs are explored. In that case, the following Boolean attributes may be set and the *Interference reduction* needs to be refined:

$$(\neg waw\_up_{up.LS} \wedge \neg waw\_up_{dw.LS}) \iff stage_{up.I} = post$$

$$(\neg waw\_dw_{up.LS} \wedge \neg waw\_dw_{dw.LS}) \iff stage_{dw.I} = post \qquad (12)$$

The reduction holds only when an instruction in the I-pipeline does not interfere with the LS-pipeline, namely it does not cause dependencies for any LS-instructions. However, the previous depth of 53 is not enough to verify the property. Indeed, hazards cause more stall cycles and more transitions to complete. (TR5) already takes more than 7 h, despite the *Interference Reduction*. Besides, WAW hazards can only happen in ID and EX. Hence, in the same line as the *General reductions*, there is no need to explore the (no-effect) occurrences of data dependencies if these stages are outreached. At the initial step, we thus assume the so-called WAW *reduction*:

$$stage_{dw.LS} > ID \implies (\neg waw\_up_{dw.LS} \wedge \neg waw\_dw_{dw.LS})$$

$$stage_{up.I} > EX \implies (\neg waw\_up_{up.LS} \wedge \neg waw\_up_{dw.LS})$$

$$stage_{dw.I} > EX \implies (\neg waw\_dw_{up.LS} \wedge \neg waw\_dw_{dw.LS}) \qquad (13)$$

The first implication means that the LS-instruction non-fixed in *pre* is always considered independent from both I-instructions. The last two implications mean that I-instructions after EX stage do not cause dependencies for any LS-instructions. Note that these last two implications are stronger than the first one when combined with Formulas 12, since they transitively boil down to replacing all the targeted stages by *post*, i.e., applying the *Interference reduction* at best. With the WAW *reduction* (TR6), the verification with possible WAW hazards still requires the former bound of 53 and a sensible verification runtime.

4.3   Analysis of a Provided Counter-Example

Table 5 reproduces graphically a counter-example showing a timing anomaly, provided by the verification procedure when executing evaluation (TR6). The example is based on two multiply-accumulate instructions (*up.I* and *dw.I*) and a load following a store (*up.LS* and *dw.LS*), with the store buffer not full. The load does not dependent on the store but has a WAW dependence with *up.I*. The data writing in SB (*dw.LS*) and the data reading in EX (*up.LS*) have both baseline latencies of 5 cycles, representing scratchpad accesses through the SRI bus (see Table 1b).

To confirm the presence of the timing anomaly, another execution scenario with the same instruction classes, same order, same dependencies, and same initial stages but without delays must be deduced from the counter-example (see end of Sect. 2.3). Table 5 shows such a scenario (*), whose I-pipeline flow is unchanged but in which the load no longer accesses the SRI bus since data is accessible after a cache hit. Due to the store buffer and its conflict rule, this scenario entails a global timing variation $\Delta_G = t_{14} - t_9 = 5$ (see Fig. 1) larger than the local variation $\Delta_L = 5 - 1 = 4$ relative to the data operation of the load (see Table 1b).

Note that similar counter-examples without data dependencies can be generated by the model checker, under the specified assumptions. Unlike the SB, data dependencies do not introduce new kinds of anomalies. The delays introduced by the related stalls are indeed not the primary sources of timing anomalies, since they are not due to *unknown* hardware configurations (e.g., a switch from a cache hit to a bus access) while executing the code but inherent to it. However, our model accurately represents the occurrence of data dependencies and the timing behavior of the counter-example of Table 5.

Table 5. A counter-example provided by the verification procedure on TriCore (TR6) and a deduced counterpart (*) without timing anomalies.

pipeline	instr.	class	t_0	t_1	t_2	t_3	t_4	t_5	t_6	t_7	t_8	t_9	t_{10}	t_{11}	t_{12}	t_{13}	t_{14}
I	dw	mac	ID	EX	EX2	WB	post										
	up	mac	IF	ID	EX	EX2	WB										
LS	dw	store	IF	ID	EX	WB	WB	WB	WB	WB	WB	SB	SB	SB	SB	SB	post
	up	load	pre	IF	ID	ID	EX	EX	EX	EX	EX	WB	post	post	post	post	post
LS	dw	store	IF	ID	EX	WB	SB	SB	SB	SB	SB	post					
*	up	load	pre	IF	ID	ID	EX	WB	post	post	post	post					

4.4   Code-Specific Verification

The aforementioned verification setting generates *generic* counter-examples. In the presence of an application code, more *specific* counter-examples are generated or even the absence of amplification timing anomalies could be proved in the code. A first step towards generating specific counter-examples requires to fix the types of the four instructions and their code order, through UCLID5 assumptions. For example, (TR7) restarts evaluation (TR6) after restricting both I-instructions to be of class multiply-accumulate and both LS-instructions to be loads. The total order imposed on the four instructions is the following: $stage_{up.LS} \leq stage_{up.I} \leq stage_{dw.LS} \leq stage_{dw.I}$. As expected, the set of counter-examples does not include the store buffer and the case of Table 5. Also, the execution time is 30% less than for (TR6), making the case for a code-specific timing anomalies detection.

5   Related Work

The notion of timing anomaly, and implicitly its first (semi-formal) definition, is introduced in the context of the WCET analysis in [13]. It is further refined (and accompanied by a simple detection criterion), in [20] and it is formally defined in [15]. Several approaches are proposed towards formally reasoning about timing anomalies in pipelined systems [1,5], but mainly for counter-intuitive timing anomalies. [7] provides an example of amplification timing anomalies over a Cortex-M4 processor due to shared-bus blocking. Different approaches are then proposed to overcome amplification timing anomalies, in particular one based on a adapted stalling logic [6]. In [11], we propose a canonical pipeline model and bounded model checking to focus on amplification timing anomalies.

The work in [14] proposes a formalization of the TriCore architecture which is then explored, using model checking, towards identification of memory inferences. From a formalization point of view, our model differs from that of [14] in one important aspect. We consider a finer timing granularity as we propose a core-level micro-architecture modeling, as opposed to an inter-cores model. Our formal investigation of amplification timing anomalies is a prerequisite to the analysis in [14]. Another compositional timing analysis is presented in [21], sharing the same TriCore pipeline timing granularity as ours. However to implement a symbolic pipeline analysis modeling the fetch and decode stages is sufficient [21], while tracking amplification timing anomalies requires a modeling of the temporal behavior of all pipeline stages.

A variant of the TriCore dual-pipeline is used in the time-predictable multicore platform, named Merasa [19]. It is designed to be time-predictable in the sense of the measurement-based timing analysis. To the best of our knowledge, the predictability aspects of a Merasa core (or pipeline) are not formally investigated using static methods. Finally, the TriCore architecture is considered in [18] with respect to its integration into a WCET analyzer called Otawa [2]. The analyzer provides an architecture description language which allows custom architecture designs to be plugged into the timing analysis engine of Otawa. The work in [18] describes the TriCore architecture (i.e., I- LS- and loop pipeline) in the architecture description language, providing accurate timing information. Likewise, our TriCore model considers similar timing parameters and is also integrated, however into a formal specification and verification framework.

6   Conclusion and Future Work

In this paper we proposed a formal and executable model of the TriCore architecture, which is used in the automotive industry. Our model is specialized to evaluate real-time systems with respect to a type of undesired timing phenomena, called amplification timing anomalies. We extended an existing abstraction called canonical pipeline model by considering both structural and functional elements of the TriCore architecture: stalling logic, store buffer, data dependencies. Each of these elements are encoded and evaluated with the UCLID5 formal verification framework. We showed how to achieve a scalable detection of amplification timing anomalies by integrating appropriate reductions in the aforementioned new functionalities introduced by the TriCore architecture.

As future work, we pursue a similar formal investigation of the TriCore architecture for counter-intuitive timing anomalies. This direction should imply further extensions to the current TriCore model, notably at the level of execution units and accurate formal ISA semantics. Complementary, we are currently evaluating how to integrate such formal pipeline models into a WCET analyzer.

References

1. Asavoae, M., Hedia, B.B., Jan, M.: Formal executable models for automatic detection of timing anomalies. In: 18th International Workshop on Worst-Case Execution Time Analysis (WCET), Barcelona, Spain, pp. 2:1–2:13 (2018)
2. Ballabriga, C., Cassé, H., Rochange, C., Sainrat, P.: OTAWA: an open toolbox for adaptive WCET analysis. In: Min, S.L., Pettit, R., Puschner, P., Ungerer, T. (eds.) SEUS 2010. LNCS, vol. 6399, pp. 35–46. Springer, Heidelberg (2010). https://doi.org/10.1007/978-3-642-16256-5_6
3. Binder, B., Jan, M.: UCLID5 model for tricore (2020). https://github.com/t-crest/patmos-sail/tree/master/uclid/tricore
4. de Dinechin, B.D., van Amstel, D., Poulhiès, M., Lager, G.: Time-critical computing on a single-chip massively parallel processor. In: Proceedings of the Conference on Design, Automation & Test in Europe (DATE 2014), pp. 97:1–97:6 (2014)
5. Eisinger, J., Polian, I., Becker, B., Metzner, A., Thesing, S., Wilhelm, R.: Automatic identification of timing anomalies for cycle-accurate worst-case execution time analysis. In: Proceedings of the Workshop on Design & Diagnostics of Electronic Circuits & Systems (DDECS), Prague, Czech Republic, pp. 15–20, April 2006
6. Hahn, S., Reineke, J.: Design and analysis of SIC: a provably timing-predictable pipelined processor core. In: 2018 IEEE Real-Time Systems Symposium (RTSS), pp. 469–481, December 2018
7. Hahn, S., Jacobs, M., Reineke, J.: Enabling compositionality for multicore timing analysis. In: Plantec, A., Singhoff, F., Faucou, S., Pinho, L.M. (eds.) Proceedings of the 24th International Conference on Real-Time Networks and Systems, RTNS 2016, Brest, France, 19–21 October 2016, pp. 299–308. ACM (2016)
8. Hahn, S., Reineke, J., Wilhelm, R.: Towards compositionality in execution time analysis: definition and challenges. SIGBED Rev. **12**(1), 28–36 (2015)
9. Infineon Technologies AG: TriCore 1 Pipeline Behaviour and Instruction Execution Timing, June 2004
10. Infineon Technologies AG: AURIX TC21x/TC22x/TC23x Family 32-Bit Single-Chip Microcontroller User's Manual, December 2014
11. Jan, M., Asavoae, M., Schoeberl, M., Lee, E.: Formal semantics of predictable pipelines: a comparative study. In: Proceedings of the 25th Asia and South Pacific Design Automation Conference, United States. IEEE (2020)
12. Liu, I., Reineke, J., Lee, E.A.: A PRET architecture supporting concurrent programs with composable timing properties. In: 44th Asilomar Conference on Signals, Systems, and Computers, November 2010
13. Lundqvist, T., Stenstrom, P.: Timing anomalies in dynamically scheduled microprocessors, pp. 12–21, December 1999
14. Nguyen, V.A., Jenn, E., Serwe, W., Lang, F., Mateescu, R.: Using model checking to identify timing interferences on multicore processors. In: ERTS 2020–10th European Congress on Embedded Real Time Software and Systems, Toulouse, France, pp. 1–10 (2020)
15. Reineke, J., et al.: A definition and classification of timing anomalies. In: 6th International Workshop on Worst-Case Execution Time (WCET) Analysis, Dresden, Germany, July 2006
16. Schoeberl, M., et al.: T-CREST: time-predictable multi-core architecture for embedded systems. J. Syst. Arch. Embed. Syst. Des. **61**(9), 449–471 (2015)

17. Seshia, S., Subramanyan, P.: UCLID 5: integrating modeling, verification, synthesis and learning, pp. 1–10, December 2018
18. Sun, W.T., Jenn, E., Cassé, H.: Build your own static WCET analyser: the case of the automotive processor AURIX TC275. In: 10th European Congress on Embedded Real Time Software and Systems (ERTS 2020), January 2020
19. Ungerer, T., et al.: Merasa: multicore execution of hard real-time applications supporting analyzability. IEEE Micro **30**(5), 66–75 (2010)
20. Wenzel, I., Kirner, R., Puschner, P.P., Rieder, B.: Principles of timing anomalies in superscalar processors. In: International Conference on Quality Software (QSIC 2005), Melbourne, Australia, pp. 295–306, September 2005
21. Wilhelm, S., Wachter, B.: Towards symbolic state traversal for efficient WCET analysis of abstract pipeline and cache models. In: 7th International Workshop on Worst-Case Execution Time (WCET) Analysis, Pisa, Italy, 3 July 2007 (2007)

A Formally Verified Plasma Vertical Position Control Algorithm

May Wu[1,2], Jessie Rosenberg[2], and Nathan Fulton[2(✉)]

[1] Massachusetts Institute of Technology, Cambridge, USA
[2] MIT-IBM Watson AI Lab, IBM Research, Cambridge, USA
nathan@ibm.com

Abstract. Tokamak fusion reactors generate energy by using a magnetic control system to confine hot plasma in a toroidal chamber. In large reactors, incorrect implementation of plasma stabilization algorithms can result in significant physical damage to the reactor. This paper explains how a combination of formal verification and numerical simulation can be used to analyze the safety of a vertical stabilization algorithm of a tokamak fusion reactor.

1 Introduction

Fusion reactors generate energy by capturing energy released when two atomic nuclei fuse together [1]. Fusion of atomic nuclei occurs when the nuclear force pulling the nuclei together exceeds the electrostatic force pushing them apart. Because the nuclear force only exceeds the electrostatic force over very short distances, fusion reactors must first strip away the electron clouds surrounding the nuclei. This is achieved by heating the fuel atoms to extremely high temperatures, resulting in a super hot and electrically charged ion cloud. To generate net positive energy, fusion reactors must first generate a plasma and then confine the plasma inside a reaction chamber. Confining the plasma requires careful control of its position, shape, and movement.

Tokamak reactors achieve this control objective by exploiting the charged nature of the plasma column. The charged plasma field is enclosed in a toroidal chamber, and magnetic coils are wrapped around the exterior of the chamber [8]. The plasma column in tokamak reactors is typically elongated vertically to increase fusion efficiency, but this results in a destabilizing force on the plasma. Vertical stabilization algorithms ensure that the plasma does not touch the top or bottom of the reaction chamber by controlling the vertical position of the elongated plasma. Vertical stabilization is one of the simplest but most important control problems in tokamak reactors.

The push for fusion reactors that produce more energy than they consume motivates the ongoing construction of very large tokamak reactors [39]. As tokamak reactors grow larger, safety interlocks for magnetic control algorithms become more important. Large reactors are extremely expensive, and improperly controlled plasma could permanently damage the reactor. Therefore, deploying

© Springer Nature Switzerland AG 2020
M. H. ter Beek and D. Ničković (Eds.): FMICS 2020, LNCS 12327, pp. 170–188, 2020.
https://doi.org/10.1007/978-3-030-58298-2_7

an experimental control algorithm on a very large reactor requires extensive pre-validation. This need for extensive pre-validation slows down the deployment of novel control algorithms, and poses a significant challenge when considering the use of control algorithms with black box machine learning components.

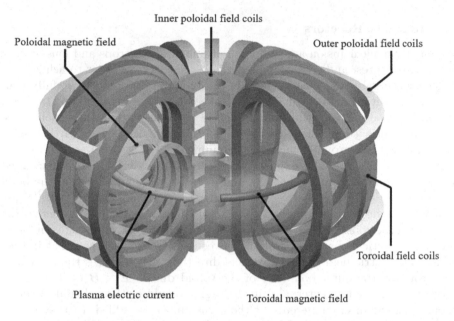

Fig. 1. A diagram of a Tokamak reactor with key features of the magnetic control system labeled, rendered by SolidWorks and based on a similar diagram in [8].

This paper considers the possibility of constructing software safety interlocks for the magnetic control systems of tokamak reactors. To illustrate the role the formal verification could play in supporting fusion research, we show how a hybrid systems theorem prover can be used to verify a vertical stabilization algorithm for an existing tokamak device. Because we are interested in enabling safe experimentation (e.g., via parameter tuning), we decompose the verification procedure into two phases: a first phase that reduces a parametric hybrid systems model to a non-parametric model, and a second phase in which a numerical ODE solver is used to check individual parameter choices for correctness.

The rest of this paper is organized as follows. Section 2 explains how tokamak fusion reactors work, precisely characterizes the vertical stabilization problem, and introduces the logic we use to specify and verify the vertical stabilization algorithm. Section 3 describes the T-15 vertical stabilization control algorithm that we verify. Section 4 presents our formalization of an established model for vertical plasma stabilization Section 5 discusses the details of our formal proof. Section 6 discusses related work, and Sect. 7 closes with a discussion of possible future work on formal methods for fusion reactors.

2   Background

This section introduces the vertical stabilization problem for tokamak reactors, assuming very little background in fusion or plasma control. We then introduce the logic and tool we use to prove the correctness of vertical stabilization.

2.1   Tokamak Reactors

Plasmas for nuclear fusion are composed of unbound electrons and ions at very high temperatures, and correspondingly high velocities. In order to achieve net fusion energy gain, the plasma must be confined and its shape carefully controlled. Magnetic confinement systems take advantage of the Lorentz force, wherein charged particles will spiral in helical paths around magnetic field lines. In the magnetic confinement design called a tokamak [32], shown in Fig. 1, toroidal coils wrap around the smaller circumference of a toroid and generate a magnetic field oriented along the larger circumference. This causes the charged particles to gyrate around that field, and induces confinement within the body of the toroid.

However, the magnetic field B from toroidal coils is nonuniform across the diameter of the coils. Along with the curvature of the toroid, this results in forces to create a vertical charge separation between electrons and ions. That in turn induces an electric field E in the vertical direction, which causes the plasma to move towards the outer boundary of the toroid due to $E \times B$ drift. In order to compensate for this external drift, a magnetic field in the poloidal direction (around the small circumference of the torus) must be added, to reshape the circumferential magnetic field lines into helices. The degree of helicity, or the ratio of the number of toroidal circuits to poloidal circuits, gives the tokamak safety factor q, a measure of the stability of the tokamak design. In tokamaks the poloidal magnetic field is generated by a current driven through the plasma itself.

This basic tokamak design, which generates a plasma with a circular cross-section, suffices for theoretical confinement of the plasma. However, in order to improve performance, it is necessary to vertically elongate the plasma cross-section. There are several reasons for this. A vertically elongated plasma results in a higher safety factor q, enabling stable operation with a higher plasma current for a given tokamak geometry and toroidal magnetic field strength. Additionally, a vertically elongated plasma allows the placement of a divertor [21], which increases efficiency by removing impurities and fusion byproducts from the plasma while the reactor is operating. Moreover, tokamaks with particular elongated plasma shapes can operate in a high-confinement regime, with confinement times that can be 2 to 3 times longer than the standard low-confinement regime [22].

Plasma shaping is performed using an additional set of poloidal magnetic field coils placed outside of the toroidal coils, as shown in Fig. 1. If the plasma is vertically centered between the outer poloidal coils, then its vertical position is at equilibrium when the currents on the upper and lower coil are the same.

However, if the plasma is displaced vertically, this creates an instability, and the plasma is rapidly accelerated toward the upper or lower wall of the chamber. Therefore, an active feedback loop and vertical stabilization is necessary to maintain confinement and the desired plasma shape [3,8].

2.2 Vertical Stabilization

The vertical stabilization methodology we consider is that used in the T-15 Tokamak [24]. In this design, a pair of outer poloidal field coils are positioned between the toroidal coil and the vacuum vessel of the plasma. Operating as part of a feedback control system, these coils generate a magnetic field distribution that can compensate for the plasma's vertical instability and bring the system back to equilibrium.

We follow the stabilization model of Mitrishkin et al. [28], which utilizes a multiphase thyristor rectifier, a type of high power switching device, as the actuator. The controller is based on a linear combination of physically measurable elements: the plasma vertical displacement, and the current and voltage of the outer poloidal coils. An unstable linear model is used for the plasma, as the position displacements are assumed to be small relative to the major or minor radii of the tokamak, and we use a linear rectifier model as well.

Relatively simple models have been chosen to illustrate the fundamental dynamics of the system, as a starting point for future work on more complex models. In using a linear model for the plasma, we make the assumption that the displacement of the plasma's position from equilibrium is relatively small in comparison to the plasma's major and minor radii. This model holds in the case in which the plasma starts near the equilibrium position, as calculated by numerical simulation for example, and that the plasma position remains in closed-loop control. As stated in Mitrishkin et al. [28], this is a common simplification for plasma control systems models in order to make the dynamics models tractable. We justify this assumption by noting that one condition of successful closed-loop operation is that the plasma must not deviate far enough from equilibrium to escape the small-signal regime. Such simplified models have been used successfully in operational plasma control systems for many years [28]. Mitrishkin et al. reference such models in use for the tokamaks T-11 and Globus-M, in operation for more than 10 years [28]. They also reference background work leading to the selection of the linear first-order rectifier model from a Russian study [5] and communications with the ASDEX Upgrade tokamak team [9].

The system of three equations used to model the stabilization system in the T-15 tokamak are: the plasma model,

$$\tau_{plasma} \frac{\partial Z}{\partial t} - Z_{ref} = K_{plasma} I,$$

the model for the outer poloidal field coils,

$$L \frac{\partial I}{\partial t} + RI = U,$$

and the multiphase thyristor rectifier model,

$$\tau_{rectifier}\frac{\partial U}{\partial t} + U = K_{rectifier}V.$$

Here, τ_{plasma} and K_{plasma} are the time constant and gain of the plasma model, $\tau_{rectifier}$ and $K_{rectifier}$ are the time constant and gain of the rectifier model, I and U are the current and voltage of the outer poloidal field coils, and Z is the plasma vertical position. R is the resistance of the control coil, and L is its inductance. The controller output V is specified by the state feedback synthesis method [44], determined by controller gains K_0, K_1, K_2, and K_3. By applying gains to each of the state variables and the reference plasma vertical position (Z_{ref}), the controller output voltage is determined:

$$V \doteq K_0 Z_{ref} - K_1 Z - K_2 I - K_3 U.$$

2.3 Differential Dynamic Logic

This paper uses differential dynamic logic (d$\mathcal{L}$) to formally specify and verify the correctness of a vertical stabilization algorithm. Differential dynamic logic is a logic for specifying and verifying properties about hybrid time dynamical systems [33,35] and has been previously used to verify properties about adaptive cruise control [27], aircraft collision avoidance [18], and SCUBA dive computers [4]. The terms of d$\mathcal{L}$ are those of real arithmetic:

$$\theta ::= x \mid r \mid \theta \cdot \theta \mid \theta + \theta \mid \theta - \theta \mid \frac{\theta}{\theta}$$

where $x \in \text{Vars}$ is a variable, $r \in \mathbb{R}$ is a real number, and $\frac{\theta}{\theta}$ defined whenever the denominator is not equal to zero.

Differential dynamic logic is used to reason about reachability properties of hybrid programs. Hybrid programs are generated by the grammar following:

$$\alpha, \beta ::= x := \theta \mid \alpha; \beta \mid \alpha \cup \beta \mid ?\varphi \mid \alpha^* \mid \mathbf{x}' = \theta \& \varphi$$

where x is a variable, θ is a term, and φ is a formula (the grammar and meaning of d$\mathcal{L}$ formulas is reviewed below). The meaning of hybrid programs is defined over mappings from variables to real values (these mappings are called states):

- The assignment program $x := \theta$ assigns to the variable x the value θ, leaving all other variables in the state unchanged.
- The nondeterministic choice program $\alpha \cup \beta$ transitions from an initial starting state s_0 to any new state that can be reached by executing either α or β from s_0.
- The sequential composition program $\alpha; \beta$ first runs the program α and then, from the resulting states, runs the program β.
- The test/assert program $?\varphi$ terminates if φ is false, or continues executing without any change to the state if φ is true.

- The loop program α^* transitions from a state s_0 to any state that can be reached by executing α zero or more times. Looping is equivalent to a non-deterministic choice over a countable number of options:
$\alpha^* \equiv \{\text{NO\_OP} \cup \alpha \cup \alpha; \alpha \cup \alpha; \alpha; \alpha \cup \alpha \cup \dots \}$
- The continuous evolution program $\mathbf{x}' = f \& \varphi$ follows the system of differential equations $\mathbf{x}' = f$ forward for any amount of time so long as φ remains true throughout.

The formulas of d$\mathcal{L}$ form a first order logic for specifying reachability properties about hybrid programs. The grammar of d$\mathcal{L}$ formulas follows:

$$\varphi, \psi ::= \varphi \wedge \psi \mid \neg \varphi \mid \forall x, \varphi \mid \exists x, \varphi \mid [\alpha]\varphi$$

where the meaning of $[\alpha]\varphi$ is that after every execution of α, φ is true.

Differential dynamic logic is implemented by the KeYmaera X theorem prover [13]. This paper uses KeYmaera X and, in particular, implements custom proof search scripts using the Bellerophon tactical programming language [12].

2.4   Example: Ball Suspended in Cylinder

We now use a highly simplified version of the plasma vertical stabilization problem to illustrate how d$\mathcal{L}$ and hybrid programs are used to specify properties about dynamical systems. Consider a sphere suspended at the center of a cylinder. The cylinder's height is equal to its diameter, and the sphere's position may change. The controller must choose, at each control step, whether the first derivative of the sphere's position should increase or decrease. The controller's objective is to ensure that the ball does not touch the sides of the cylinder. This problem is illustrated in the diagram following (Fig. 2):

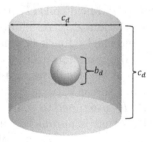

Fig. 2. Ball suspended in cylinder.

Denote by c_d the diameter and height of the cylinder, by c_r the radius of the cylinder, by $b_r = \frac{b_d}{2}$ the radius of the sphere, by b_p the offset of the ball's position from the midpoint of the cylinder, and by b_v the vertical velocity of the sphere. We will assume the ball is contained within the cylinder, so b_r is significantly smaller than c_r. The control program must choose, at each control step, a value of $\frac{\partial b_p}{\partial t}$ that prevents the ball from touching the sides of the cylinder. The fact that that sphere never touches the cylinder's boundaries is expressible using the d$\mathcal{L}$ formula:

$$A > 0 \wedge B > 0 \wedge T > 0 \wedge b_p < c_r - b_r \rightarrow [\text{model}]b_p < c_r - b_r$$

where:

$$\text{model} \equiv \{\text{ctrl}; t := 0; \text{plant}\}^*$$
$$\text{ctrl} \equiv \text{ctrl}_A \cup b_v := 0 \cup \text{ctrl}_B$$
$$\text{ctrl}_A \equiv ?b_p + AT < c_r - b_r; b_v := A$$
$$\text{ctrl}_B \equiv ?b_p - BT < c_r - b_r; b_v := -B$$
$$\text{plant} \equiv \{b_p' = b_v, t' = 1 \wedge t \leq T\}$$

This simple example demonstrates how the dynamics of a moving object can be modeled in d$\mathcal{L}$ by referring to its offset from a fixed reference point (in this case, the center of the cylinder).

3   The T-15 Vertical Stabilization Controller

This section reviews the controller model for vertical stabilization of the T-15 tokamak via a multiphase thyristor rectifier. The model is substantially similar to the model presented in Mitrishkin et al. [28]. The system consists of four main components: the controller, the rectifier, the coil system, and the plasma of the tokamak. Figure 3 illustrates the control scheme, wherein each component is represented as an individual control block.

The Controller block represents a feedback controller with four inputs and one output. The four inputs consist of the measured voltage output from the rectifier (U), the current in the outer poloidal field coils (I), the plasma vertical position (Z), and a vertical reference position Z_{ref}. As shown in Fig. 3, the controller amplifies the input signal Z_{ref} and the feedback signals U, I, and Z by controller gains $K0, \ldots, K3$. At the summing junction inside the controller, the resulting amplified Z_{ref} signal is added and the resulting amplified feedback signals are subtracted to produce the output signal V.

The controller gains $K_0, \ldots, K_3$ are tuned to achieve the desired performance. This paper considers an analysis that is parametric in one of these gains (K_0). Our analysis applies for an entire range of possible values of K_0 instead of, e.g., numerically checking each possible value. The goal of this partially parametric analysis is to lay the groundwork for a fully parametric analysis.

The control signal V is sent to the multiphase thyristor rectifier system of the tokamak, which is represented by the Rectifier block in Fig. 3. The multiphase thyristor rectifier system functions as the actuator for the vertical position control system. By regulating phases of thyristor bridges and utilizing a pulse-phase control circuit, the multiphase thyristor rectifier system outputs a regulated voltage (U) to control the tokamak's outer poloidal field coil [28]. In our model, we

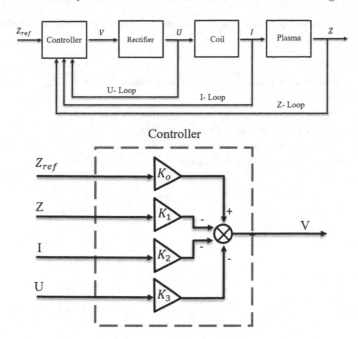

Fig. 3. System block diagrams for the vertical stabilization controller. (a) The tokamak is represented by a system block diagram. The overall system consists of a feedback controller, a multiphase thyristor rectifier, a control coil system, and tokamak plasma. These are represented, respectively, by the Controller, Rectifier, Coil, and Plasma system blocks. V is the output from the controller, U is the voltage measures at the output of the rectifier, I is the current measured from the output control coil system, and Z is the measure plasma vertical position. (b) The controller stabilizes the vertical plasma position by amplifying the input signal Z_{ref} and the feedback signals U, I, and Z by their respective gains $K0$ through $K3$. The resulting amplified Z_{ref} signal is added and the resulting amplified feedback signals are subtracted to produce the output signal V at the summing junction.

generalized the behavior of the multiphase thyristor rectifier as a single system, instead of modeling the thyristor bridges separately. As discussed in Sect. 2.2, this assumption holds in the case of small deviations from equilibrium, where the system is assumed to be under closed-loop control. We use the rectifier time constant, $\tau_{rectifier}$ and the rectifier gain, $K_{rectifier}$ to describe the multiphase thyristor rectifier.

The voltage U is the drive signal for the outer poloidal field coil, which is represented by the Coil system block in the overall system block diagram. This voltage induces a current in the coils, modulated by its properties and environment. The output of the Coil system block is a current (I) regulated between an upper and lower operational limit.

Next we model the impact of the Coil system on the plasma itself. In addition to the outer poloidal field coil, a tokamak contains inner poloidal field coils,

Table 1. Meanings and physical constraints on variables occurring in the plasma vertical stabilization model.

Variable	Meaning	Constraints
Z_{ref}	Desired plasma position (externally specified)	$0 < Z_{min} < Z_{ref} < Z_{max}$
V	Controller output	
K_0	Controller gain constant for desired plasma position	>0
K_1	Controller gain constant for plasma position	>0
K_2	Controller gain constant for current	>0
K_3	Controller gain constant for voltage	>0
Z	Plasma position	$0 < Z_{min} < Z < Z_{max}$
U	Rectifier voltage	$0 < U_{min} < U < U_{max}$
I	Coil current	$0 < I_{min} < I < I_{max}$
τ_{plasma}	Plasma time constant	>0
$\tau_{rectifier}$	Rectifier time constant	>0
K_{plasma}	Plasma constant	>0
$K_{rectifier}$	Rectifier constant	>0
R	Resistance of coil	device-specific
L	Inductance of coil	device-specific

toroidal field coils, a primary transformer, ohmic heating coils, and other control coils depending on the tokamak design, as shown in Fig. 1. For the "Plasma" block in our KeYmaera X model, we abstract the response of the plasma and the feedback of these other control systems into one differential equation that describes the relationship between the plasma parameters and the final plasma vertical position, represented by the plasma time constant τ_{plasma} and the plasma gain K_{plasma}. This abstraction again holds in the stem remains in the small-signal regime near equilibrium and does not experience large deviations, in which case the complexities of the individual components would become apparent. For the T-15 tokamak, τ_{plasma} and K_{plasma} were estimated using a DINA plasma model [23, 28]. The output of the Plasma block arises from a sensor system that measures the plasma vertical position Z.

Table 1 presents a summary of the model variables, as well as their operational constraints. In addition to the variables already discussed, there are several constants that are used in our model. The resistance R and the inductance L of the outer poloidal control coil vary across different tokamak designs. For the T-15 tokamak that we study in this work, Mitrishkin et al. calculated the resistance and inductance of T-15 tokamak to be $0.09\,\Omega$ and $0.0042\,0042\,H$ respectively.

4   The Model

This paper contributes a partially verified controller for T-15 vertical stabilization. The primary task is to verify that, for a particular choice of controller gains, the plasma's position will not exceed a maximum threshold. The maximum thresholds represent the boundaries of model validity (in particular, the boundaries of model validity will be smaller than the boundaries of the tokamak chamber, so remaining within these bounds ensures that the plasma remains within the tokamak's chamber).

Table 1 reviews the variables used in our model. The goal of the control algorithm is to drive the plasma's position Z to the desired set = point Z_{ref}. The safety constraint proven in this paper is that the plasma's position Z stays below a maximum safe value Z_{max}.

```
1   ∃ K₀, K₁, K₂, K₃ .
2   τ_plasma = .0208 ∧ τ_rectifier = 0.0033 ∧ R = 0.09
3   ∧L = 0.0042 ∧ K_rectifier = 2000
4   ∧0 = Z_min < z < Z_max < 0 ∧ z = i = u = 0
5   ∧ 0 ≤ U_min < U_max ∧ 0 ≤ I_min < I_max
6   →
7   [
8       Z_ref := *; ? Z_min ≤ Z_ref ∧ Z_ref < Z_max;
9       ? Z = Z_ref → z = (-K_plasma)/I ∧ I = U/R ∧ U = K_rectifier/(K₀Z_ref − K₁Z − K₂I − K₃U) ;
10      {
11          Z' = Z/τ_plasma + (K_plasma I)/τ_plasma ,
12          I' = U/L − RI/L ,
13          U' = (-U)/τ_rectifier + (K_rectifier(K₀Z_ref − K₁Z − K₂I − K₃U))/τ_rectifier
14      }
15  ] ( zMin<z<zMax )
```

The model verified in this paper is listed above. The first nine lines state constraints on the physically realizable values for various parameters.

Line 1 existentially quantifies over the choice of gain $K_0, \ldots, K_3$. The constraint is eventually provided as input by the user and its correctness is checked using numerical simulation. The rest of the preconditions for the model, on Lines 2–4, express straight-forward constraints on the minimum and maximum value parameters and additionally set the values of constants to values appropriate for the T-15 reactor.

Line 8 models the choice of a new reference vertical position for the plasma. We assume that the reference position is provided as input from an external control module. In our model, we simply assert that the external module provides a reference value that is within the safety envelope.

Line 9 specifies the values that Z, I, and U should have when the plasma's vertical position is at the reference point. The condition presented is a conjunction formed by two simplified z and U equations and is derived via Ohm's Law letting $z = z_{ref}$ and $I = U/R$. The entire program terminates when the condition in Line 9 is false. This is a condition on the valid choices of $K_0, \ldots, K_3$; i.e., this line should be understood as constraining the choice of gains for the controller, not the dynamics of the rest of the system.

Line 11 to Line 13 displays the model equations from Sect. 2.2 rewritten with the derivative term on the left hand side. Line 15 models the condition we want to ensure, which is to maintain z between z_{Min} and Z_{Max}.

5 The Analysis

Our model and corresponding analysis decompose the plasma's dynamics into two phases: an initialization phase and a steady-state phase. The graphs on page 12 visualize these two phases for the Z, I, and U variables.

Our proof is formalized in the KeYmaera X theorem prover. This section provides an intuition for how the geometry of the system relates to our formal derivations. We also comment on how the geometric intuitions underlying our informal description of the formal proof are encoded in the proof assistant. Before discussing our proofs, we recall a few inference rules from the proof calculus of d$\mathcal{L}$.

5.1 The Proof Calculus of Differential Dynamic Logic

The primary proof techniques used for this construction are *differential cuts*, *differential induction*, and *differential weakening*. We briefly recall these proof techniques; our treatment is not exact, but contains enough formality that the reader will understand our proof. A full development of the proof calculus is presented in [36].

Differential cuts are similar to cuts in propositional logic [34]. Unlike propositional logic, d$\mathcal{L}$ does not admit cut elimination; i.e., differential cuts strictly increase the deductive power of the logic. To prove that φ is an invariant of an ODE c restricted to the domain F, it suffices to find some G such that G is an invariant and, additionally, φ in an invariant of c restricted to the domain $F \wedge G$. As an inference rule,

$$\frac{\Gamma \vdash [c\&F]G \qquad \Gamma \vdash [c\&F \wedge G]\varphi}{\Gamma \vdash [c\&F]\varphi} DC$$

Differential induction proves invariants about differential equations by reasoning about the Lie derivatives of formulas. Geometrically, differential induction proves that a property φ is true throughout the flow of an ODE $\mathbf{x}' = \theta$ by establishing that, at every point in the vector field, derivatives point into the set φ. As an inference rule,

$$\frac{\Gamma, F \vdash \varphi \qquad \vdash F \to [\mathbf{x}' := \theta](\varphi')}{\Gamma \vdash [\mathbf{x}' = \theta \& F]\varphi} DI$$

Finally, differential weakening simply states that the domain constraint on an ODE is itself an invariant of the ODE. Stated as an inference rule (Fig. 4),

$$\frac{\Gamma \vdash \varphi \qquad \Gamma_{\text{const}} \vdash F \to \varphi}{\Gamma \vdash [\mathbf{x}' = \theta \& F]\varphi} DW$$

where Γ_{const} is the subset of formulas in Γ that do not mention any of the variables occurring primed in $\mathbf{x'} = \theta$.[1]

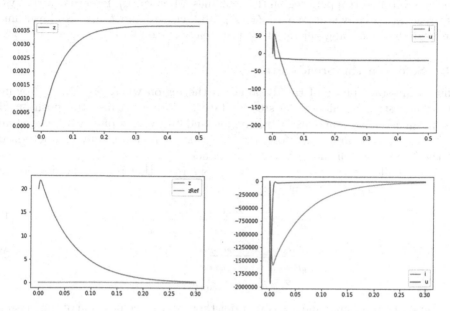

Fig. 4. Above: the dynamics of Z, I, and U as Z approaches Z_{ref} for parameter values $L = 0.0042$, $R = 0.09$, $Z_{ref} = 0.002$, $\tau_{plasma} = 0.0208$, $\tau_{rectifier} = 0.0033$, $K_{plasma} = 0.0000178$, $K_{rectifier} = 2000$, $V = 0.1$, and $\mathbf{K} = [100.0, 243.3287, 0.0032, 0.0013]$. These are the parameters that were used in Matriskin et al. [28]. Below: similar simulation but with $Z_{ref} < Z$. The data for these figures were generated using the SciPy scipy.integrate.odeint function [42] and the figures were rendered by the matplotlib library [20]. Notice that the graph of Z is scaled differently from the graphs of I and U so that its magnitude is large enough to see.

In addition to these inference rules that allow reasoning about reachability properties about differential equations, we will denote by $\mathbb{R}$ the inference rule which proves φ whenever φ is in the modality-free fragment of d$\mathcal{L}$. This fragment of d$\mathcal{L}$ is the first-order logic over real-closed fields and it is decidable via quantifier elimination; the decidability result is due to Tarski [41] and its effective algorithm to Collins [7].

5.2 Proof Structure

The vertical stabilization process, subject to appropriate control, has two phases: an *initialization phase* and a *steady state* phase. Our formal proof decomposes

---

[1] There are also conditions on the occurrences of these variables in φ; however, in our case, those conditions are irrelevant because φ is simply a formula of first-order logic over real arithmetic and there are therefore no conditions. Platzer's uniform substitution calculus provides a full discussion of the static semantics of d$\mathcal{L}$ [35].

into these two phases. During the initialization phase, Z approaches Z_{ref} monotonically. Proving safety within this phase requires establishing that the system operates within a trapping region that confines Z below Z_{ref}. Eventually, the system reaches a steady state where $Z = Z_{ref}$ and where I and U are also invariant. We begin by describing our proof for the steady state phase.

5.3   Safety in the Steady State

The steady-state phase of the dynamics is the region where $Z = Z_{ref}$. Proving that the system is safe at the steady state is simple because the position of the plasma is invariant within this region and the values of the other system variables are constant. Therefore, the steady-state phase is fully characterized by the intersection of the z, i, and u nullclines.

The z nullcline where $z = Z_{ref}$ gives a constraint that relates the position of the plasma to the coil current (I):

$$\frac{\partial z}{\partial t} = 0 = \frac{Z_{ref}}{\tau_{plasma}} + \frac{K_{plasma}I}{\tau_{plasma}} \tag{1}$$

$$\frac{Z_{ref}}{\tau_{plasma}} = \frac{-K_{plasma}I}{\tau_{plasma}} \tag{2}$$

$$Z_{ref} = -K_{plasma}I \tag{3}$$

Similarly, the I nullcline is a constraint that relates the position of the plasma to the rectifier voltage:

$$\frac{\partial I}{\partial t} = 0 = \frac{U}{L} - \frac{RI}{L} \tag{4}$$

$$\frac{U}{L} = \frac{RI}{L} \tag{5}$$

$$I = \frac{U}{R} \tag{6}$$

Finally, the U nullcline constrains the choice of controller gains in terms of the current state of the system:

$$\frac{\partial U}{\partial t} = \frac{-U}{\tau_{rectifier}} + \frac{K_{rectifier}V}{\tau_{rectifier}} \tag{7}$$

$$U = \frac{1}{1 + K_3 K_{rectifier}}V \tag{8}$$

Notice that the control branch corresponding to this steady state asserts that each of these equations hold; we abbreviate the conjunctions of Eqs. (3), (6), and, (8) as SSA:

$$\text{SSA} \equiv U = \frac{1}{1 + K_3 K_{rectifier}}V$$

$$\wedge I = \frac{U}{R}$$

$$\wedge Z_{ref} = -K_{plasma}I$$

Composing these nullclines gives a fixedpoint where $Z = Z_{ref}$. We introduce a new soundness-critical proof rule to KeYmaera X which allows us to reason about this fixed-point:

$$\frac{\Gamma, y = y_0 \vdash [\mathbf{x}' = \mathbf{f}(\mathbf{x}) \wedge y = y_0]P, \Delta \qquad \Gamma \vdash (\mathbf{x} = 0)'}{\Gamma, y = y_0 \vdash [\mathbf{x}' = \mathbf{f}(\mathbf{x})]P, \Delta} DFP$$

where $\mathbf{x}$ and $\mathbf{f}$ are vectors. I.e., if $y = y_0$ initially and the derivative of each primed variable is 0 initially, then $y = y_0$ after any flow. Given this extension, we can then easily prove that the system is safe whenever it enters the fixed-point in a safe configuration:

$$\frac{\dfrac{\ast}{\Gamma_{const}, Z_{min} < z_0 < Z_{max} \vdash x = x_0 \rightarrow Z_{min} < Z < Z_{max}} \mathbb{R}}{\dfrac{\Gamma, Z_{min} < z_0 < Z_{max}, \mathsf{SSA} \vdash [\text{plant} \wedge x = x_0]Z_{min} < Z < Z_{max}}{\Gamma, Z_{min} < z_0 < Z_{max}, \mathsf{SSA} \vdash [\text{plant}]Z_{min} < Z < Z_{max}} DW} DFP$$

where Γ_{const} are the formulas in Γ that only mention variables that do not occur primed in the ODEs plant. In this case, that includes the assumption from our controller's assertion that $Z_{ref} < Z_{max}$. The result of the proof involves proving Δ_1, which is $\Gamma, \mathsf{SSA} \vdash [\text{plant}]Z < Z_{ref}$.

5.4 Proving the System Remains Safe While Approaching the Reference Value

The remainder of the proof involves showing that the controller induces a trapping region that keeps Z above (or below) Z_{ref}, and furthermore that this trapping region is sufficient to ensure that $Z_{min} < Z < Z_{max}$.

Instead of establishing this property globally for an infinite set of possible controller gains, we instead observe that each variable at this point in the proof will have a specific value chosen by an experiment designer. The existential quantifiers on Line 1 will have already been instantiated with values known to satisfy Line 9. Therefore, any trusted numerical integrator can be used to simulate the full system dynamics out to the fixed point, at which point global reachability is established using the technique described in the previous section.

6 Related Work in Formal Methods

To the best of the authors' knowledge, formal methods tools have not been previously applied to the verification of plasma control algorithms in tokamak devices. Therefore, our related work discussion focuses on:

1. applications of formal methods in powerplant control systems,
2. other hybrid systems verification tools also capable of proving properties about control systems for fusion reactors.

6.1   Applications of Formal Methods in Power Plants and Similar Control Systems

The Cyber-Physical Systems and Formal Methods research communities have developed many approaches toward verifying industrial control systems. A thorough survey of the past half century of research in this area is hardly possible, so we focus instead on formal methods for industrial control systems that might be relevant to future work in formal methods for plasma control systems.

Formal methods have been used extensively for verification and validation of nuclear fission power plants. Wassyng and Lawford report on a large-scale verification project at the Darlington nuclear power plant [43] and Németh et al. applied coloured petri nets to the verification of a primary-to-secondary leaking safety procedure [30]. Lahtinen's thesis provides a through survey of these and other formal methods efforts in the nuclear domain [26].

Most of the work on nuclear safety verification focuses on ensuring the safety of an already mature system. Therefore, much of the effort in these projects goes into modeling and verifying the dynamics of large-scale control systems such as programmable logic controllers. This paper focuses on the verification of controller design rather tha the verification of concrete implementations; therefore, work on verifying programmable logic controllers, such as the toolkits of Garcia et al. [17] and Pakonen et al. [31], are highly complementary to the work in this paper.

In addition to the obvious focus on nuclear fusion, another fundamental difference between our work and prior work on formal verification of control systems is the intended mode of use. Most applications of formal methods focus on mature domains where the fundamental design principles are well-understood and the primary problem is ensuring the correct implementation of a closed-loop system. Fusion, on the other hand, remains an unsolved problem. Perhaps the primary contribution of this paper is the simple suggestion that domain-specific and light-weight formal methods tools could be very useful to fusion researchers.

6.2   Hybrid Systems Case Studies and Tools

Although no other papers consider verification of fusion reactors, the dynamical system studied in this paper is mathematically similar to systems studied in other tools.

Reachability analysis tools for continuous and hybrid systems are capable of analyzing the linear system studied in this paper. For example, Althoff et al. introduce an approach toward reachability analysis of linear systems with uncertain parameters using matrix zonotopes and interval matrices [2]. The Flow* tool uses Taylor models for reachability analysis of nonlinear systems [6]. The dReal [16] and dReach [25] tools provide more automated analyses by framing hybrid systems reachability in terms of δ-decision procedures, and tools such as PHAver [10] and SpaceEx [11] are also well-suited to verification of hybrid systems. Automated analysis of both linear and nonlinear systems is also possible within KeYmaera X. The Pegasus tool introduced a set of nonlinear control benchmark problems, some of which exhibit dynamics similar to those studied in this paper [40].

Although our work used the KeYmaera X tool, fusion control systems might pose interesting verification challenges for other hybrid systems tools. Our use of KeYmaera X was motivated by two considerations. First, the authors' familiarity with this tool's implementation details enabled us to rapidly make the changes to the tool required to enable our analysis technique. Second, our plan for future work includes modeling more complex aspects of the fusion reactor's control systems and synthesizing safety interlocks that enable the use of reinforcement learning for these systems. KeYmaera X provides a method for composing verification results [29]. Because data-driven methodologies can play an important role in plasma design [37,38], KeYmaera X's support for incorporating safety interlocks into learning systems [14] – especially in cases where some aspects of the control system are not captured by a first-principles model [15] or represented in explicitly modeled quantities [19] – provides another motivation for its use as a platform for this work.

7 Conclusion

Net positive fusion energy is an unsolved problem, and control design is a fundamental component of any fusion reactor. Experimenting with new controller designs is risky on large reactors where failures can cause millions of dollars in damage and even set back progress in the field. Our hope is that the formal methods community can contribute a set of robust safety interlocks of modern fusion reactors. This paper makes a first small step toward that vision by demonstrating that safety properties about vertical stabilization algorithms are possible to state and analyze using a combination of theorem proving and numerical integration.

Acknowledgments. We thank Cristina Rea, Darren Garnier, and other members of the MIT Plasma Science and Fusion Center for their helpful conversations. We also thank the anonymous reviewers for their helpful feedback.

References

1. Peeters, A.G.: The Physics of Fusion Power (2008)
2. Althoff, M., Krogh, B.H., Stursberg, O.: Analyzing Reachability of Linear Dynamic Systems with Parametric Uncertainties. In: Rauh, A., Auer, E. (eds.) Modeling, Design, and Simulation of Systems with Uncertainties. Mathematical Engineering, vol. 3, pp. 69–94. Springer, Heidelberg (2011). https://doi.org/10.1007/978-3-642-15956-5_4
3. Ambrosino, G., Albanese, R.: Magnetic control of plasma current, position, and shape in tokamaks: a survey or modeling and control approaches. IEEE Control Syst. Mag. **25**(5), 76–92 (2005)

4. Bajaj, V., Elmaaroufi, K., Fulton, N., Platzer, A.: Verifiably safe scuba diving using commodity sensors: work-in-progress. In Proceedings of the International Conference on Embedded Software Companion, EMSOFT 2019, New York, NY, USA (2019). Association for Computing Machinery
5. Bulgakov, A.A.: A new theory of controlled rectifiers (1970). (in Russian)
6. Chen, X., Sankaranarayanan, S.: Decomposed reachability analysis for nonlinear systems. In: 2016 IEEE Real-Time Systems Symposium (RTSS), pp. 13–24 (2016)
7. Collins, G.E., Hong, H.: Partial cylindrical algebraic decomposition for quantifier elimination. J. Symb. Comput. **12**(3), 299–328 (1991)
8. De Tommasi, G.: Plasma magnetic control in tokamak devices. J. Fusion Energy **38**(3), 406–436 (2019)
9. A. Kallenbach for the ASDEX Upgrade Team and the EUROfusion MST1 Team: Overview of ASDEX upgrade results. Nucl. Fusion **57** (2017)
10. Frehse, G.: PHAVer: algorithmic verification of hybrid systems past HyTech. STTT **10**(3), 263–279 (2008)
11. Frehse, G., et al.: SpaceEx: scalable verification of hybrid systems. In: Gopalakrishnan, G., Qadeer, S. (eds.) CAV 2011. LNCS, vol. 6806, pp. 379–395. Springer, Heidelberg (2011). https://doi.org/10.1007/978-3-642-22110-1_30
12. Fulton, N., Mitsch, S., Bohrer, B., Platzer, A.: Bellerophon: tactical theorem proving for hybrid systems. In: Ayala-Rincón, M., Muñoz, C.A. (eds.) ITP 2017. LNCS, vol. 10499, pp. 207–224. Springer, Cham (2017). https://doi.org/10.1007/978-3-319-66107-0_14
13. Fulton, N., Mitsch, S., Quesel, J.-D., Völp, M., Platzer, A.: KeYmaera X: an axiomatic tactical theorem prover for hybrid systems. In: Felty, A.P., Middeldorp, A. (eds.) CADE 2015. LNCS (LNAI), vol. 9195, pp. 527–538. Springer, Cham (2015). https://doi.org/10.1007/978-3-319-21401-6_36
14. Fulton, N., Platzer, A.: Safe reinforcement learning via formal methods: toward safe control through proof and learning. In: McIlraith, S., Weinberger, K. (eds.) Proceedings of the Thirty-Second AAAI Conference on Artificial Intelligence (AAAI 2018), pp. 6485–6492. AAAI Press (2018)
15. Fulton, N., Platzer, A.: Verifiably safe off-model reinforcement learning. In: Vojnar, T., Zhang, L. (eds.) TACAS 2019, Part I. LNCS, vol. 11427, pp. 413–430. Springer, Cham (2019). https://doi.org/10.1007/978-3-030-17462-0_28
16. Gao, S., Kong, S., Clarke, E.M.: dReal: an SMT solver for nonlinear theories over the reals. In: Bonacina, M.P. (ed.) CADE 2013. LNCS (LNAI), vol. 7898, pp. 208–214. Springer, Heidelberg (2013). https://doi.org/10.1007/978-3-642-38574-2_14
17. Garcia, L., Mitsch, S., Platzer, A.: HyPLC: hybrid programmable logic controller program translation for verification. In: Bushnell, L., Pajic, M. (eds.) ICCPS, pp. 47–56 (2019)
18. Ghorbal, K., Jeannin, J.-B., Zawadzki, E., Platzer, A., Gordon, G.J., Capell, P.: Hybrid theorem proving of aerospace systems: applications and challenges. J. Aerospace Inf. Sys. **11**(10), 702–713 (2014)
19. Hunt, N., Fulton, N., Magliacane, S., Hoang, N., Das, S., Solar-Lezama, A.: Verifiably safe exploration for end-to-end reinforcement learning. arXiv preprint arXiv:2007.01223 (2020)
20. Hunter, J.D.: Matplotlib: a 2D graphics environment. Comput. Sci. Eng. **9**(3), 90–95 (2007)
21. Janeschitz, G., et al.: The ITER divertor concept. J. Nucl. Mater. **220–222**, 73–88 (1995). Plasma-Surface Interactions in Controlled Fusion Devices
22. Keilhacker, M.: H-mode confinement in tokamaks. Plasma Phys. Control. Fusion **29**(10A), 1401–1413 (1987)

23. Khayrutdinov, R.R., Lukash, V.E.: Studies of plasma equilibrium and transport in a tokamak fusion device with the inverse-variable technique. J. Comput. Phys. **109**(2), 193–201 (1993)
24. Kirnev, G.S., et al.: Superconducting tokamak T-15 upgrade. In FT/P7-3, Proceedings of the 21st IAEA Fusion Energy Conference (2006)
25. Kong, S., Gao, S., Chen, W., Clarke, E.: dReach: δ-reachability analysis for hybrid systems. In: Baier, C., Tinelli, C. (eds.) TACAS 2015. LNCS, vol. 9035, pp. 200–205. Springer, Heidelberg (2015). https://doi.org/10.1007/978-3-662-46681-0_15
26. Lahtinen, J.: Model checking large nuclear power plant safety system designs: dissertation. Ph.D. thesis, Aalto University, Finland, 2016. BA1606 SDA: SHP: SASUNE Nuclear Project code: 108550 165 p. + app. 75
27. Loos, S.M., Platzer, A., Nistor, L.: Adaptive cruise control: hybrid, distributed, and now formally verified. In: Butler, M., Schulte, W. (eds.) FM 2011. LNCS, vol. 6664, pp. 42–56. Springer, Heidelberg (2011). https://doi.org/10.1007/978-3-642-21437-0_6
28. Mitrishkin, Y.V., Pavlova, E.A., Kuznetsov, E.A., Gaydamaka, K.I.: Continuous, saturation, and discontinuous tokamak plasma vertical position control systems. Fusion Eng. Des. **108**, 35–47 (2016)
29. Müller, A., Mitsch, S., Retschitzegger, W., Schwinger, W., Platzer, A.: Tactical contract composition for hybrid system component verification. STTT **20**(6), 615–643 (2018). Special issue for selected papers from FASE'17
30. Németh, E., Bartha, T., Fazekas, Cs., Hangos, K.M.: Verification of a primary-to-secondary leaking safety procedure in a nuclear power plant using coloured Petri nets. Reliab. Eng. Syst. Saf. **94**(5), 942–953 (2009)
31. Pakonen, A. , Mätäsniemi, T., Lahtinen, J., Karhela, T.: A toolset for model checking of plc software. In: 2013 IEEE 18th Conference on Emerging Technologies Factory Automation (ETFA), pp. 1–6 (2013)
32. Pironti, A., Walker, M.: Fusion, tokamaks, and plasma control: an introduction and tutorial. IEEE Control Syst. Mag. **25**(5), 30–43 (2005)
33. Platzer, A.: Differential dynamic logic for hybrid systems. J. Autom. Reas. **41**(2), 143–189 (2008)
34. Platzer, A.: The complete proof theory of hybrid systems. In: LICS, pp. 541–550. IEEE (2012)
35. Platzer, A.: A uniform substitution calculus for differential dynamic logic. In: Felty, A.P., Middeldorp, A. (eds.) CADE 2015. LNCS (LNAI), vol. 9195, pp. 467–481. Springer, Cham (2015). https://doi.org/10.1007/978-3-319-21401-6_32
36. Platzer, A.: Logical Foundations of Cyber-Physical Systems. Springer, Cham (2018). https://doi.org/10.1007/978-3-319-63588-0
37. Rea, C., et al.: Disruption prediction investigations using machine learning tools on DIII-D and Alcator C-Mod. Plasma Phys. Control. Fusion **60**(8), 084004 (2018)
38. Cristina, R., Granetz, R.S.: Exploratory machine learning studies for disruption prediction using large databases on DIII-D. Fusion Sci. Technol. **74**(1–2), 89–100 (2018)
39. Shimomura, Y., Aymar, R., Chuyanov, V., Huguet, M., Parker, R., et al.: ITER overview. Nucl. Fusion **39**(9Y), 1295 (1999)
40. Sogokon, A., Mitsch, S., Tan, Y.K., Cordwell, K., Platzer, A.: Pegasus: a framework for sound continuous invariant generation. In: ter Beek, M.H., McIver, A., Oliveira, J.N. (eds.) FM 2019. LNCS, vol. 11800, pp. 138–157. Springer, Cham (2019). https://doi.org/10.1007/978-3-030-30942-8_10
41. Tarski, A.: A decision method for elementary algebra and geometry (1948)

42. Virtanen, P., et al.: SciPy 1.0: fundamental algorithms for scientific computing in Python. Nat. Methods **17**, 261–272 (2020)
43. Wassyng, A., Lawford, M.: Lessons learned from a successful implementation of formal methods in an industrial project. In: Araki, K., Gnesi, S., Mandrioli, D. (eds.) FME 2003. LNCS, vol. 2805, pp. 133–153. Springer, Heidelberg (2003). https://doi.org/10.1007/978-3-540-45236-2_9
44. Williams, R.L., Lawrence, D.A., et al.: Linear State-Space Control Systems. Wiley, Hoboken (2007)

The First Twenty-Five Years of Industrial Use of the B-Method

Michael Butler[2] , Philipp Körner[1]([⊠]) , Sebastian Krings[1] ,
Thierry Lecomte[3], Michael Leuschel[1]([⊠]) , Luis-Fernando Mejia[3],
and Laurent Voisin[4]

[1] Institut für Informatik, Universität Düsseldorf,
Universitätsstr. 1, 40225 Düsseldorf, Germany
{p.koerner,sebastian.krings,leuschel}@hhu.de
[2] University of Southampton University Road, Southampton SO17 1BJ, UK
mjb@ecs.soton.ac.uk
[3] CLEARSY, 320 avenue Archimède, 13100 Aix-en-Provence, France
{thierry.lecomte,fernando.mejia}@clearsy.com
[4] Systerel, 1090 rue René Descartes, 13100 Aix-en-Provence, France
laurent.voisin@systerel.fr

Abstract. The B-Method has an interesting history, where language and tools have evolved over the years. This not only led to considerable research and progress in the area of formal methods, but also to numerous industrial applications, in particular in the railway domain. We present a survey of the industrial usage of the B-Method since the first toolset in 1993 and the inauguration of the driverless metro line 14 in Paris in 1999. We discuss the various areas of applications, from software development to data validation and on to systems modelling. The evolution of the tooling landscape is also analysed, and we present an assessment of the current situation, lessons learned and possible new directions.

1 Introduction

The B-Method [4] for software and systems development and its successor Event-B [6] has a rich history. B has originally been developed as a successor to Z [10] by Jean-Raymond Abrial in the 1990s, focusing on two key concepts: refinement to gradually develop models and tool support, in particular proof and code generation.

More concretely, B is based on first-order-logic and set theory and follows the correct-by-construction approach. A formal B model consists of a collection of B machines. Each B machine may contain constants with properties and variables with invariants. The state of a B machine can be modified by operations, which may have preconditions associated with them. The invariants are a crucial concept of B, stipulating properties which hold initially and which must be preserved by every operation. B machines can be refined, whereby, e.g., datatypes can be replaced by more concrete ones or non-determinism can be reduced or removed. A refinement machine is linked to an abstract machine via a gluing invariant,

© Springer Nature Switzerland AG 2020
M. H. ter Beek and D. Ničković (Eds.): FMICS 2020, LNCS 12327, pp. 189–209, 2020.
https://doi.org/10.1007/978-3-030-58298-2_8

which stipulates how its states correspond to states in the abstract machine. An implementation machine is a refinement machine written in the B0 subset of the language. The B-Method also describes how to derive proof obligations to ensure that the invariants always hold and that every refinement machine correctly realises its abstraction. If all proof obligations are discharged, the implementation machines are "correct by construction": they correctly implement the initial abstract B specification.

As of today, the industrial applications of B can be classified into three categories:

- the original B for software development (classical B) [4]: refine specifications until a low-level subset of B (B0) is reached where code generation is applied.
- B for system modelling (Event-B) [6]: model an entire system, not just a particular software component and then verify critical properties and understand why a system is correct.
- B for data validation: express properties in B and check data and configuration parameters in a certified manner.

In this article, we discuss these three classes of applications in turn (Sects. 2, 3 and 4), focussing on railway applications where B had its most significant impact. We then discuss applications in other areas in Sect. 5, the tools behind the industrial applications in Sect. 6 and finally conclude with lessons learnt over the years in the final Sect. 7.

2   B for Software: The Early Days and Industrial Uptake

In the 80s, RATP (Régie Autonome des Transports Parisiens, Paris railway transport operator and infrastructure manager) and the consortium[1] in charge of the development of SACEM, the train protection system deployed on the Parisian RER Line A, faced the validation of the first control/command software of a safety critical railway signalling system ever operated in France. Without a real background in that domain they started using a tool based on Hoare Logic to verify assertions included in the code. Then they consulted Jean-Raymond Abrial who proposed the formalisation and verification of a formal specification of the software with what can be considered as a sketch of the B-Method. His proposal was accepted, validation engineers were trained, a formal specification was written and verified. Eventually, in 1988, SACEM was put into operation to the satisfaction of all.

In the same year, Abrial presented "The B Tool" [2] with an unnamed syntax. Most of the further developments, both on the language and on advanced tooling, were initiated during industrial projects in Paris.

After the SACEM experience, RATP, guided by Claude Hennebert, requested the use of the B-Method for the development of the safety critical software of

---

[1] Consisting of Alsthom (today Alstom), Compagnie des Signaux (today Hitachi), and Matra Transport (today Siemens Transportation, France).

the train protection system of the driverless Paris Métro Line 14. Alstom, with this project in mind, but also for their own developments, decided to use the B-Method. These are the origins of the development and use of the B-Method, and of formal methods in general, in the French railway industry.

In 1989, Alstom, RATP and SNCF (Société Nationale des Chemins de fer Français), willing to industrialise the B-Method, launched a project whose purpose was threefold: firstly, to train engineers in the principles of the method, secondly, to develop tools to support it and, thirdly, to create methodological guides to use it. This project, funded partially by the French government and driven by Alstom, established a close collaboration with J.-R. Abrial and the team of Ib Sørensen at British Petroleum then at B-Core. Additionally, Abrial was still in contact with a research group in Oxford and certainly was influenced in technical details.

After some training sessions given by J.-R. Abrial, an Alstom team started the development of railway applications with the first version of the B language and tools provided by J.-R. Abrial and his colleagues. The fundamental syntactic and semantic concepts of the language (VARIABLES, INVARIANT, INITIALISATION, OPERATIONS) were already present in this version, but in 1991 it turned out that evolutions of the language and tools were necessary to structure, analyse and prove software of industrial size and complexity. This is the reason why structuring (INCLUDES, IMPORTES, PROMOTES, EXTENDS), sharing (SEES, DEFINITIONS) and configuration (CONSTANTS, PROPERTIES, VALUES) clauses were introduced in the language. With the support of J.-R. Abrial, Alstom decided to develop its own set of tools for the new language. After two years of development, in 1993, the first version of what was called the B-Toolset was delivered internally, including a type checker, a proof obligation generator and a theorem prover able to manage software of industrial size and complexity. By that time, J.-R. Abrial proposed to Alstom that the Digilog company (then Steria, today CLEARSY) should industrialise these tools and make them available to RATP and to Matra Transport, the supplier that won the Paris Métro Line 14 contract (cf. Sect. 2.2). The work by Digilog on B started in 1995[2], the contract related to L14 between RATP, SNCF and INRETS was signed in 1996. Alstom accepted and Digilog developed ATELIER B based on Alstom's B-Toolset.

The development of the language and of supporting tools was a very important aspect of the industrialisation of the B-Method. No less important was the definition of an effective and efficient development process and methodology for the new technology, while training engineers to use it.

2.1   Early Adoption

The introduction of the B-Method in an existing conventional software development environment necessarily induced the modification of the development process known and accepted by the development, verification and validation teams, the clients and the safety assessors. Doubts were numerous considering that the

---

[2] Which is the justification for the title of this article.

new process should comply with applicable railway standards, that it should be close to the existing process in order to reuse its infrastructure as much as possible, and consequently, that the activities related with the B-Method must be included within the phases of this process. Some questions were:

- Where should the definition of B abstract machines be included? In the software specification phase or in the software design phase?
- How should B components and formal proofs be documented?
- How should B components and formal proofs be verified, when and by whom?
- How should verification efforts be documented?
- How should module testing, integration and validation testing phases be modified in order to take advantage of the formal proof of B components?
- How should the development of the part of the software that does *not* need to be formally developed interact with the development of the part of the software that needs to be formally developed?

The companies that introduced the B-Method in their software development process reacted according to their own practices and experience. When it was decided to introduce it for the development of safety critical software of railway systems, the B-Method was neither taught nor used anywhere. Its first users were trained by J.-R. Abrial himself, who followed also the first developments. The methodology for using the B-Method and good practices were defined during these first developments. They address the following questions:

- How to create the architecture of a large B model?
- How to write the operations of abstract machines?
- How to refine abstract data with concrete data?
- How to refine operations?
- How to write loops?

User guides were written and some rules were automated with tools. Once the tools and good practices were developed and defined, training courses in the B-Method were given to all staff in the organisation dealing with software engineering: software development engineers, verifiers, validators, safety assurance engineers and their managers. The sustainability of the B-Method in industry has been made possible by the creation of an eco-system including RATP, the operator that requested the application of the method, CLEARSY, the company that maintains the tools supporting B in the long term, the engineering schools and universities that train engineers, conduct research and provide tools, and finally, the companies that provide B expertise and technical assistance. The existence of international conferences on formal methods and, particularly, on the B-Method and the participation of the industrial companies in these events contributes to the dissemination and sustainability of the method.

2.2 Driverless Metro Software: Météor and Its Successors

Paris Line 14. The most well-known success story of B is the Parisian Métro Line 14. The main goal was to reduce the time interval between trains, yet ensuring the correctness and safety of the system. For this, the train control was automated and the trains are able to travel without a human driver. All safety critical components, i.e., the train control and the controllers for the automatic doors dividing the passengers from the tracks, have been formally developed using B. Since October 1998, the metro works flawlessly and not a single issue was caused by software. The same holds for the shuttle train at the Roissy Airport that drives since 2007.

The B models for the Line 14 and the Roissy Shuttle have 115 000 and 183 000 lines of code, 27 800 and 43 610 proofs and a manual proof percentage of 8.1% and 3.3%, respectively. More information concerning both metros and their full development statistics can be found in [5] and Sect. 4.2 of [62].

In neither case, unit testing was performed. Instead, formal development and proof gave enough confidence in the correctness of the generated Ada code which was used without change. The only tests performed were tests concerning the integration with non-critical software parts and global validation tests.

Early projects, such as the Line 14, pushed tool development. One example is semi-automatic refinement [22], which by now is included as BART in ATE-LIER B. Going through (data) refinement steps manually is tedious. Often, this work can be automated though: such a tool can drastically improve development speed, in particular if code generation from B0 is required.

Canarsie CBTC. Siemens has evolved the product for Line 14 and installed it on many metro lines world-wide, notably on the Canarsie Line [31] in New York. 53 trains operate without interruption on 17 km of track consisting of 24 stations. In contrast to the Parisian Line 14, two different types of trains are mixed on the track: more modern trains are equipped with CBTC (computer- or communications-based train control) systems, whereas older trains are not. This results in a system that is far more complex than its counterpart in Paris.

Again, the software components of the system are split into parts that are safety-critical, and those that are non-critical for safety. All safety-critical parts have been developed in B; the only exceptions are components that cannot be expressed in a B model, including low-level communications, sensor, motors, breaks and file input/output.

The Canarsie Line was one of the first industrial applications that included the use of automatic refinement tools. Even though more proof obligations had to be discharged, these tools proved to speed up the process considerably. One of the key sentences concerning the usage of formal methods can be found in the description of the project:

> *"Beyond the technological challenge of using such a complex formal method in an industrial context, it is now clear for us that building software using B is not more expensive than using conventional methods. Better, due to our experience in using this method, we can assert that using B is cheaper when considering the whole development process (from specification to validation and sometimes certification)."* [31]

Safety-Critical Train Software at Alstom. Alstom has been a long time proponent of using the B-Method for safety critical software. Most Alstom trains now include some software which was produced from a B specification. Table 1 gives an overview of the important railway products where software was developed with the B-Method. The URBALIS 400 product, with its over 100 installations worldwide, represents currently the most widespread use of the B-Method for software in the world.

Table 1. Overview of Alstom Projects

Product	Size (kloc)	First commissioning
Train speed controller for Calcutta Metro	Small (<10)	1992
KVB, train protection system for French mainlines (no high-speed trains) trains	Medium (10..50)	1995
SACEM extension for Paris RER Line A	Small (<0)	1996
Train speed controller for Cairo Metro	Small (<10)	1997
Speed controller for Lyon Metro	Small (<10)	1998
Lineside Electronic Unit (LEU) for mainlines in Australia, China, France, Greece, Italy, Spain, The Netherlands	Small (<10)	2000
URBALIS 200, train protection system for metro lines in Chile, China, Egypt, India, South Korea, Spain	Medium (10..50)	2003
URBALIS 400, CBTC system for metro lines in Australia, Brazil, Chile, China, Dubai, France, Italy, Mexico, Panama, Qatar, Saudi Arabia, Singapore, Spain, The Netherlands, Vietnam	Large (50..250)	2008

2.3　Code Generation for Hardware

There were a few research projects on using B for hardware, e.g., at the Atomic Weapons Establishment (AWE) [32] or within the PUSSEE research project [60], with applications for SmartCards (see Sect. 5 below). Only recently has B been used to develop hardware for railway applications, which we describe below.

Platform Screen Doors Controllers. CLEARSY has developed several safety systems controlling the opening and closing of the Platform Screen Doors (PSD) installed in Metro stations in order to ensure passengers protection. These systems are independent of the train signalling and automatic operating systems; they can be installed in a Metro which is already in service. Due to the expansion of the urban population in most big cities in the world, PSD are a first step towards full automation of a non-automatic, already existing metro line. The PSD controllers developed by CLEARSY are specified and programmed with B.

First controllers used a dedicated translator from B to Ladder Logic [45], more recent ones use the CLEARSY Safety Platform. Paris lines 1 and 13, São Paulo lines 2 and 3, and Stockholm Citybanan metros have been equipped with such PSD controllers, certified SIL3 or SIL4.

The CLEARSY Safety Platform. The CLEARSY Safety Platform [40] is both a hardware and software platform, aimed at easing the development and the deployment of safety critical applications, up to SIL4. It relies on the integration of the B-Method for programming (including mathematical proof), redundant code generation (to guard against hardware bugs or hardware failure) and compilation, and a hardware platform that ensures a safe execution of the software. Safety principles are built-in in the hardware and the safety library. The associated IDE is based on ATELIER B and the B language supported [43] has been specialised to address the specific hardware, to better ensure safety, and to minimise the proof effort. As of today, the CLEARSY Safety Platform has been certified 3 times with different certification bodies, for international railways applications.

3   B for System Modelling

From Software to Systems: Event-B for System Modelling. The success of the Parisian Métro Line 14 showed that, given a set of software requirements, one could develop formally a program that fulfils it and prove it correct. But the software requirements used as input make some assumption on the environment in which the software is to be operated: logical interfaces to other pieces of software as well as electronic and physical devices such as motors.

Therefore, if the software requirements are wrong or do not fit the operational environment, the resulting system as a whole would malfunction. It was thus felt necessary to move the application of formal methods to an earlier phase in the system development process, namely in the system design phase. System design is performed by very capable engineers, but addresses very complex systems with a lot of moving parts and is difficult to reason about informally.

It was thus felt necessary to extend the B-Method to system design activities [3,9] and another notation was gradually derived from the B language, finally crystallising into Event-B, aiming for proven system studies where computation is distributed. In four EU projects concerning the development and industrialisation of Event-B, numerous industrial partners were involved, including Siemens, Bosch, SAP, Space Systems Finland, Alstom, CLEARSY, Gemplus, Leonardo and Critical Software Technologies.

New York Flushing Line. CLEARSY used Event-B, supported by the ATELIER B tool, on two major industrial rail projects for New York City Transit (NYCT) to support safety assurance [57]. In the first project for the New York Flushing line, formal models of a CBTC were developed and key safety properties were specified and proved at the system level. The main safety properties addressed were avoidance of train collisions, avoidance of trains traversing unlocked switches (causing derailment) and avoidance of over-speeding. The second project for NYCT involved an implementation of interlocking different from the first. Because the system level models were abstracted from details of the implementation, it was possible to reuse models from the first project in the second project, considerably reducing safety analysis effort in the second project. A key benefit of the system level formal analysis of [57] was the way precise properties required of the various sub-systems were identified in the design and the assumptions made in one sub-system about other sub-systems. Since different sub-systems were provided by different companies, this ensured that these assumptions were clearly communicated to relevant stakeholders at early stages of the development, avoiding problems later during the systems' integration phase.

Octys. In [28], CLEARSY outline how they used Event-B supported by Atelier B to perform safety analysis of an existing CBTC system called Octys for RATP. Some key insights into the benefits of formalisation are described. For each safety property to be verified, the approach was to describe the property informally and an informal argument was developed to explain why the property held. This helped to frame the subsequent formal modelling and reasoning. It was found that it was very difficult to achieve a high level of rigour through the informal reasoning and that the formal reasoning filled in gaps in the reasoning, providing more complete arguments for safety. The formal reasoning also allowed the isolation of a minimal set of assumptions required to prove the desired property. This allowed for identification of gaps in the assumptions, whereby the informal safety requirements were improved.

URBALIS 400 Zone Controller. In 2018 [29] the software for the Zone Controller of the Alstom URBALIS 400 CBTC developed using classical B (see Sect. 2.2 above) underwent a rigorous systems analysis. While the classical B method ensured that the implementation is correct wrt. the software specification, it does not guarantee that the algorithms themselves are correct wrt. system level requirements. The analysis was formalised with an Event-B model which links environment variables (the real position of the trains) with software variables (protection envelopes). Atelier B and ProB were used to analyse the system and extract key properties that ensure the correct and safe functioning. These properties are of crucial importance when tuning or extending the algorithms of the zone controller.

RailGround. As part of the EU H2020 Enable-S3 project, Thales Austria GmbH and the University of Southampton applied Event-B and UML-B to the *Rail-Ground* interlocking system [25]. The project used UML-B, which allows editing Event-B models using a UML-like graphical representation.

As well as demonstrating the feasibility of modelling a complex interlocking system in UML-B, the project also demonstrated benefits of using the UML diagrammatic notation. The diagrammatic models were found to be easier to communicate to domain experts than the textual models.

ETCS Hybrid Level 3. HL3 is a novel train control concept that aims at increasing the throughput of trains without additional rails. Thales Deutschland GmbH and Universität Düsseldorf used the B-Method to develop a reference model for a new approach to railway interlocking, Hybrid ERTMS/ETCS Level 3 (HL3), as part of a field demonstration of the feasibility of the HL3 principles [35]. The focus of the project was on the use of the model-checking and execution capabilities of PROB both for validation of the model *and* for use of the model as a reference implementation of the HL3 principles during the field demonstration. A graphical visualisation of the railway environment made it easy for the domain experts to provide feedback on the formal model, leading to improvements of the specification. A lot of the complexity of HL3 concerns degraded modes and corner cases, and the formalisation and validation approach allowed these to be addressed comprehensively. Execution of the B model on PROB was used to conduct field tests with real trains in realtime.

EULYNX. Founded in 2014, EULYNX is a joint European project by several railway infrastructure providers aiming at a standardisation of interfaces and signaling systems. One of EULYNX members, the infrastructure division of the German railway company Deutsche Bahn, uses model-based systems engineering for their interlocking systems. Using SysML has led to improved specifications and thus increased the quality of the interlocking system. However, SysML is merely a semi-formal language. In consequence, within the European Shift2Rail project, an approach based on UML-B has been used to introduce an Event-B representation into the development process [17,55]. This effectively enables formal verification of interlocking systems specified in SysML.

4   B for Data Validation

In the last decade, the B language gained a new application area: aside from proving software correct, it can be used to ensure that *assumptions* about configuration data hold (often dubbed *data validation*). Indeed, a safety critical system often contains many data parameters which are instantiated differently for each particular deployment of the system. These parameters underlie restrictions to ensure the proper functioning of the system. When a system is incorrectly configured, this can lead to disaster. It turned out that the B language was very convenient to express properties for correct configuration.

This intuition gave rise to the development of the OVADO [1] tool for RATP, which took place in parallel of the early development of the RODIN platform. Prior to adopting such a tool, RATP used to have dedicated tools developed in order to check the correctness of configuration data for systems received from their suppliers. But these dedicated tools were expensive to develop and quite inflexible. Any change in the requirements made it necessary to change the software of the tool. In contrast, with a generic tool like OVADO, one just needs to modify the B expression of the property to reflect the change and run the OVADO tool again.

In some cases, when the software was developed from a B specification, these properties were already expressed in B and used during the formal safety proof. This was, e.g., the case for the Paris Line 1 and 14 metro systems and other installations of the same system in Barcelona or São Paulo. This was one of the first industrial uses of data validation using PROB by Siemens [33,49,50], independently[3] conducted in 2008–2009 within the EU Deploy project. Before 2009, Siemens was using ATELIER B with custom proof rules and tactics, dedicated to deal with larger data values [19,20]. This, however, did not scale to many larger properties or data values, meaning that manual validation was required that was cost intensive and error prone. Indeed, the use of PROB did uncover at least one issue that was missed by the manual validation.

In order to better address industrial needs, tools developed dialects of the B language and domain specific data validation languages on top of B [44]. In the context of data validation string manipulations are important; hence PROB now allows usage of B's sequence operators on strings (e.g., for concatenation). Additionally, support for reading and writing XML was added to PROB during a case study in cooperation with Thales [36].

Data validation with B has now been applied to many railway systems worldwide, some of which are:

- Line 1 Paris, the second CDGVAL line LISA at the CDG airport in Paris, São Paulo line 4, ALGER line 1, Barcelona line 9, all by Siemens using a tool called RDV built-on top of PROB [33,49,50],
- more metro lines in Paris managed by RATP using OVADO, which includes a tool developed by CLEARSY called predicateB as first chain, and PROB as secondary tool chain [1,12].
- by Alstom for their URBALIS 400 CBTC system in 2014 using a tool based on PROB called DTVT developed by CLEARSY for various lines, e.g., in Mexico, Toronto, São Paulo and Panama [44].
- Alstom and SNCF also applied data validation for ETCS-Level 1 software in 2018 using another tool developed by CLEARSY using PROB.
- Together with Systerel, Alstom conducted data validation of the Octys CBTC for RATP in 2017 using the OVADO tool.
- by Thales using a tool based on PROB called Rubin for checking engineering rules of their ETCS Radio Block Centre (some aspects of Rubin are discussed in [36]).
- Other tools based on PROB were developed by CLEARSY such as Dave for General Electric or the latest generation tool called Caval.

An important aspect of these applications is the certification of the tools according to EN50128. Indeed, this norm stipulates that a data validation tool is of class T2, namely a tool that "*supports the test or verification of the design*

---

[3] Initially the PROB team was unaware of the development of OVADO.

or executable code, where errors in the tool can fail to reveal but cannot directly create errors in the executable software" [26]. The tools mentioned above satisfy the T2 requirements, e.g., by using a rigorous specification of the tool's purpose and a rigorous testing process (see, e.g., [14]). The Caval tool obtained a T2 certificate in November 2019. The tools DTVT and OVADO even use a double chain: a primary tool that conducts the verification and a secondary tool that re-checks the result of the first tool.

5   Projects Outside the Railway Domain

Only few projects outside the railway industry are known to use B. Below, we present two additional areas of application.

Modelling Vehicles. In the early 2000s, several projects were initiated to model vehicles, e.g., to improve the failure diagnostic of the first full-electronic multi-plexed Peugeots as well as to ease the integration of the sub-systems of a one-time built military vehicle.

Due to the existence of the vehicles and the complexity of the design, the modelling adopted was a flat (no refinement) Event-B specification of the functional specification sided with a dictionary model providing additional semantics and natural language translation elements. A tool, Composys, was developed to automate validation and test functional architectures. It contained a static checking tool for B machines, a component-based consistency checking tool, and a natural language technical documentation generator.

Smart Cards. When it comes to smart cards, the use of formal methods is mandatory for certification, if a high EAL security level is required. In this case, the functional specification of the software library is proved to comply with the security policy, both formalised with Event-B. Hence, application developers are assured that whatever the API calls, the smart card security is enforced i.e., no secret is disclosed. Several certifications have been obtained at the highest levels, in France and in Germany.

B was also used for embedded software development [39] while Event-B was used for hardware development [16]. The former used the default ATELIER B C code generator while the latter was based on a dedicated translator from Event-B to synthesisable VHDL.

6   B-Method Tools Throughout the Years

In this section, we will discuss tools for the B-Method that were developed throughout the years. As expected, not all of them survived. While some have been replaced by successors, others were only of academic interest. Given that most of the tools, including their features and peculiarities, are documented by various research papers and journal articles we keep things brief and reference the publications below.

B-Toolkit. One of the first tools for use with the B-Method is the B-Toolkit [46,56] by B-Core. The B-Toolkit already was reasonably complete, offering editing, type checking, animation, proof obligation generation and discharge, documentation generation, and a first code generator targeting C. B-Toolkit is no longer supported. Its source code has been released under a BSD license at https://github.com/edwardcrichton/BToolkit.

Click'n Prove. Click'n Prove [8] was an experimental user interface meant to explore new ways to interact with a prover (by clicking rather than command-line) and served as a basis for the RODIN interactive prover interface. Click'n Prove was built on top of XEmacs. Internally, it was using the ATELIER B tools for proving.

ATELIER B. As mentioned above, the success of B in the railway domain drove the implementation and improvement of B-Method tools, such as ATELIER B, initially to be used for software validation [2,27].

In order to be useful for the safety-critical applications mentioned, ATELIER B needed to be verified and validated itself. To do so, several tasks were performed under the overall responsibility of RATP [41]:

- the theorem prover was subject to external expertise,
- a dedicated tableau-based prover was built to validate most of the theorem prover's mathematical rules,
- a committee was set up to demonstrate unprocessed rules by hand,
- a small automated prover was developed to verify the correctness of the dedicated tableau-based prover.

When it was created in 2001, CLEARSY gathered ATELIER B property rights from Alstom and RATP. ATELIER B is currently used by more than 30% CBTC-based automatic metros worldwide, for embedded and track-side safety software. This IDE is under continued development with new peripheral functions, e.g.:

- an automatic refiner tool, BART [42], similar to the one used by Siemens for the Canarsie line,
- a framework to automatically prove and review added mathematical proof rules, that generates a report for the safety case,
- a generic new proof obligation generator,
- integration of the ProB model checker, SMT solvers and the Why3 platform in the interactive prover,
- an improved C code generator targeting PIC32 microcontrollers,
- a compiler from B0 models to binary files for the CLEARSY Safety Platform.

While initially only supporting classical B, current versions of ATELIER B support Event-B machines as well. These Event-B machines are described using an adapted textual representation, with additional keywords (such as `ref`) and more liberal refinement which is dealt with by the proof obligation generator. This renders ATELIER B one of the two major IDEs for Event-B, the other one being RODIN.

Rodin. RODIN [7] has been developed during the RODIN, Deploy and Advance projects. As a complete IDE, RODIN features the Event-B modelling database/storage, a type checker for Event-B and a proof engine [59] as well as different editors. Central parts of RODIN have been formally specified and proved using Click'n Prove [7].

As the team developing RODIN knew how much implementation effort went into building ATELIER B from the ground up, they were looking into ways to build RODIN on top of an existing framework and finally settled for Eclipse, from which RODIN inherits its main UI, the handling of workspaces and many internals. Just like Eclipse, RODIN is based on plugins and could (at least in theory) be extended to formalisms other than Event-B.

RODIN itself does not include a prover for Event-B. Instead, it just maintains proof trees in sequent calculus and allows reasoners and tactics to be added by plugins. In particular, ATELIER B's provers can be added to RODIN alongside others, e.g., SMT solvers. Influenced by the interactive control of provers implemented in Click'n Prove, RODIN provides a user interface for interactive proof, in which the different reasoners can be applied, proof tactics can be performed and the proof tree can be explored graphically. By doing so, provers can be used collaboratively inside a single proof.

Several code generators are available for RODIN, as are other extensions via the plugin mechanism. Among the most prominent ones are extensions for the composition and decomposition of models [23] and the theory plugin, which permits extending the mathematical core of Event-B by custom theories [51,52].

PROB. PROB [47,48] is an animator, constraint solver and model checker for the B-Method. Its development started in 2001 with a first alpha release made in October 2003. It filled a gap in the B tooling landscape at the time, supporting the interactive and automatic validation of high-level specifications. Indeed, following classical B's correct-by-construction approach it is vital that the high-level specifications correctly capture the high-level requirements and functionality.

By then, only the B-Toolkit animator provided some very limited form of validation, and required the user to provide values for parameters and existentially quantified variables, the validity of which was checked by the BToolkit prover. This approach was justified by the undecidability of the B language, but was tedious for the user and prevented automated validation. In contrast, PROB allows fully automatic animation of specifications, i.e., values for constants, parameters are computed by PROB's constraint solver rather than explicitly given by users. Unknown to the PROB team at the time (around 2000), another team pursued similar ideas leading to the CLP-S solver [21] and the BZTT tool [11] based on it. This work also gave rise to a company (Lerios), which concentrated on model-based test-case generation and later ported the technology to an imperative programming language. Unfortunately, the development of BZTT and CLP-S has stopped; the tool is no longer available.

Using a variety of explicit-state and symbolic model checking approaches, PROB can be used to systematically check a specification for invariant violations [48]. Furthermore, PROB supports LTL model checking, and distributed explicit state model checking. Model checking aside, the constraint-solving capabilities of PROB can also be used for model finding, symbolic model checking and deadlock checking as well as test-case generation and drive several of the animation, visualisation and data validation tools that will be discussed below.

Animation and Visualisation Tools. For the industrial applicability of formal methods, visualisation and graphical model animation allow formal method experts to communicate with domain experts and enable them to identify errors. This may go as far as having a "management view", that is easy to understand and hides all technical details [41]. Many visualisation and animation tools have been developed for B and Event-B. Among the first ones are BRAMA [58], which uses Flash to graphically visualise models. AnimB [54], a plugin for RODIN, also provides graphical visualisations based on Flash. Several tools were developed building on top of PROB: starting from an early prototype using Flash [15], BMotionStudio has been developed for editing and displaying visualisations [37]. Later on, BMotionStudio was superseded by BMotionWeb [38], an animation engine based on common web technologies, and the simpler VisB [61] based on SVG graphics. Another web-based animator was JEB [63], which was independently developed in JavaScript.

7 Discussion and Conclusions

Development of the B language and tools has been driven by industrial needs, which probably explains part of its success. A recent survey in the railway domain [13] cites mature tooling as the most important reasons to use a specific formal method. Mainly ATELIER B and PROB have been developed for a long time and have proven themselves in industry projects. They both are mature tools that also are actively maintained and further features are developed. The reader may also wish to consult older surveys on industrial use of formal methods in general such as [18,34,53,62].

Current Situation of B. Here is our assessment of the current situation concerning the use of B in industry:

- B is arguably among the formal methods of greatest industrial impact, albeit mainly in the railway sector.
- There is still little industrial use of B in production outside of railways. B seems like a DSL for the railways: topologies can be well expressed using B relations, integer arithmetic is sufficient in many applications. In railways, we have clearly defined operating environments which enable exhaustive formal modelling and inductive reasoning.
- The flagship products of Alstom's U400 and the successors of Météor are still operating and being installed on new lines. URBALIS 400 is running on over 100 lines and has 25% of the worldwide market in CBTC systems.[4]

---

[4] See the site (accessed 25/5/2020): https://www.alstom.com/our-solutions/signalling/urbalis-cbtc-range-future-signalling-systems.

- Code generation for B has now moved to hardware level but the use of classical B for software (outside of hardware) is not increasing. It has not caught on in Siemens to other products and is not being applied to new products at Alstom anymore. One reason may be the need for experienced people. Moving from formal modelling to code generation requires a lot of extra resources. New tools like automatic refinement (BART) help to some extent, but one still spends a lot of time discharging proof obligations of little practical value (and it takes time to identify the really crucial proof obligations that pose essential problems).
- RODIN has had a lot of academic impact, but real industrial use for production systems is still somewhat disappointing. Several aspects of RODIN were stimulating academic research and experimentation, but were possibly detrimental for industrial use, e.g.: the use of Eclipse with its extension mechanism, the core language without sequences and machine inclusions, models being stored in an extensible database rather than a textual format. For example, the extension mechanism enabled experimentation, but it is confusing for industrialists to know which extensions are stable and are suitable for industrial use. The absence of a textual format was detrimental for team collaboration and versioning. Also, the tight link to Eclipse makes it more difficult to use RODIN as a stand-alone headless tool, in case a company's development practice is not centred around Eclipse.
  An exception here is UML-B [30] and Coda [24], where the tight integration with Eclipse enabled graphical modelling and industrial applications (cf. Sect. 3). Also, machine inclusion and textual format are now supported by the new CamilleX plug-in.[5]
- B for data validation has caught on and is being used for a wide range of railway products.
- There is an increased interest and activity by a wider range of industrial players for systems modelling with B. This is one area were we foresee considerable growth in the coming years, and where B could maybe move to more widespread use outside the railway domain.

What Made B Successful in the Beginning. The ability to specify programs rigorously and to demonstrate the compliance of their implementation with their specification was a major concern for RATP and Alstom in the beginning. The B-Method answered that need. The following factors also played a major role to enable B's initial breakthrough:

- the availability of tools to validate and verify the B formal notation,
- the more tractable proof obligations, thanks to the B machine structuring clauses and the use of successive refinement,
- the availability of code generators for B0, providing tangible benefits in terms of testing and certification efforts.

---

[5] See https://wiki.event-b.org/index.php/CamilleX.

Common Success and Fail Factors in Industrial Uses. We can identify the following common success factors for the industrial applications of the B-Method:

- *Tooling.* Formal methods can be of value without tool support, just as a technique to aid and focus human reasoning on complex systems. However, tooling provides many additional benefits and the availability of tools played a major role in most of B's successful industrial use cases.
- *Effectiveness of the method.* Thanks to the B-Method it was actually possible to specify, develop and prove formally programs and avoid a lot of tests.
- *Regulatory constraints.* The requirement (or at least strong steer) from the guiding authorities, e.g., RATP, for the suppliers to use formal methods is definitely a success factor in several of the case studies.
- *Expertise.* Formal method eduction is not widespread among programmers and engineers. Hence, the availability of B experts to provide support to a project team is crucial for success.
- *Documentation.* The availability of a methodological guide explaining how to model common artefacts in B (e.g., state machines, iterators) is important. This allows the spread of good practice among project teams and avoid each individual reinventing the wheel.

The following fail factors appeared multiple times.

- *Functional requirements.* Even formally developed programs may not fit the functional user needs. In other words, using the B-Method does not prevent developing the wrong program.
  This threat can be countered by early uses of animation on the high-level formal specification along with involvement of domain experts.
- *Investment.* Human investment is high and it is difficult to retain employees skilled with the B-Method. Some managers are convinced that formal modelling and proving is no fit for their "low-grade engineers".
- *Predictability.* Proof is not full automatic, therefore, it is difficult to predict costs and delays of software development.
- *Scalability.* As far as Event-B is concerned, missing decomposition features and collaboration support in RODIN prevented modelling some more complex systems by larger teams.
- *Disruption.* The B-Method for software has a disruptive impact on existing software development practices; it basically requires to replace the existing software development cycle with a new one.
- *Business plans.* The development of bug-free software is often not an important objective of software companies, and may even be opposite to their business plans based on consulting and paid upgrades.

Challenges. We see the following challenges which lie ahead to a successful broader adoption of the B methodology.

- *Proof and refinement.* More automation in proof is needed, for example by combining provers and constraint solvers, thereby reducing the need for costly interactive proof. Better feedback for failed proof attempts and assistance in finding inductive invariants would lower barriers for users. The automation of refinement should be dramatically improved in order to reduce manual work.

- *Manage complex systems and models.* In particular, one challenge is to help users understand bigger formal models, e.g., by new visualisation techniques or extraction of knowledge guided by machine learning techniques. Automated correction and suggestions, especially helping non-formal methods experts.
- *Increase expressivity.* Guided by the work in data validation, it would be beneficial, e.g., to enable more convenient use of n-ary relations and associated projections, as the standard projections functions *prj1* and *prj2* on nested pairs are very cumbersome to use. Another challenge is to be able to express possibly recursive, higher-order functions so that proof, constraint solving, animation and execution are possible. Finally, a principled solution to replace the brittle DEFINITIONS of classical B should be sought.
- *Increase value of B formal modelling by making formal models executable.* Execution makes formal models accessible to domain experts and enables formal models to be used as cost-effective prototypes. Formal models can also play the role of interactive requirement or specification documents.
- *Marketing.* Efficient packaging of B tools such as the CLEARSY Safety Platform to both attract students and industry for practical applications.
- *Alternate approaches for B software development.* With the progress of model checking techniques, it will be maybe worth to develop conventionally and then verify formally, leading to less disruption of existing development practices.
- *Combine systems modelling with implementation.* Bridge the gap between Event-B systems modelling and classical B software development, providing a seamless process and along with supporting tools for combined systems modelling and implementation.

Acknowledgements. We would like to show our gratitude to Jean-Raymond Abrial, who provided us with sources, discussions, insider information and knowledge from his personal experiences developing B and Event-B. We also thank the reviewers of FMICS for their extensive feedback and suggestions.

References

1. Abo, R., Voisin, L.: Formal implementation of data validation for railway safety-related systems with OVADO. In: Counsell, S., Núñez, M. (eds.) SEFM 2013. LNCS, vol. 8368, pp. 221–236. Springer, Cham (2014). https://doi.org/10.1007/978-3-319-05032-4_17
2. Abrial, J.R.: The B tool (abstract). In: Bloomfield, R.E., Marshall, L.S., Jones, R.B. (eds.) VDM 1988. LNCS, vol. 328, pp. 86–87. Springer, Heidelberg (1988). https://doi.org/10.1007/3-540-50214-9_8
3. Abrial, J.-R.: Extending B without changing it. In: Proceedings B, pp. 169–190 (1996). ISBN 2-906082-25-2
4. Abrial, J.-R.: The B-Book. Cambridge University Press, Cambridge (1996)

5. Abrial, J.-R.: Formal methods: theory becoming practice. J. Univ. Comput. Sci. **13**(5), 619–628 (2007)
6. Abrial, J.-R.: Modeling in Event-B: System and Software Engineering. Cambridge University Press, Cambridge (2010)
7. Abrial, J.-R., Butler, M., Hallerstede, S., Voisin, L.: An open extensible tool environment for Event-B. In: Liu, Z., He, J. (eds.) ICFEM 2006. LNCS, vol. 4260, pp. 588–605. Springer, Heidelberg (2006). https://doi.org/10.1007/11901433_32
8. Abrial, J.-R., Cansell, D.: Click'n prove: interactive proofs within set theory. In: Basin, D., Wolff, B. (eds.) TPHOLs 2003. LNCS, vol. 2758, pp. 1–24. Springer, Heidelberg (2003). https://doi.org/10.1007/10930755_1
9. Abrial, J.-R., Mussat, L.: Introducing dynamic constraints in B. In: Bert, D. (ed.) B 1998. LNCS, vol. 1393, pp. 83–128. Springer, Heidelberg (1998). https://doi.org/10.1007/BFb0053357
10. Abrial, J.-R., Schuman, S., Meyer, B.: Specification language. In: On the Construction of Programs: An Advanced Course. Cambridge University Press (1980)
11. Ambert, F., et al.: BZ-testing-tools: a tool-set for test generation from Z and B using constraint logic programming. In: Proceedings FATES, pp. 105–120 (2002). Technical report, INRIA
12. Badeau, F., Doche-Petit, M.: Formal data validation with Event-B. In: Proceedings of DS-Event-B 2012, Kyoto, CoRR, abs/1210.7039 (2012)
13. Basile, D., et al.: On the industrial uptake of formal methods in the railway domain. In: Furia, C.A., Winter, K. (eds.) IFM 2018. LNCS, vol. 11023, pp. 20–29. Springer, Cham (2018). https://doi.org/10.1007/978-3-319-98938-9_2
14. Bendisposto, J., Krings, S., Leuschel, M.: Who watches the watchers: validating the ProB validation tool. In: Proceedings F-IDE, EPTCS, vol. 149 (2014)
15. Jaffuel, E.: Using B machines for model-based testing of smartcard software. In: Julliand, J., Kouchnarenko, O. (eds.) B 2007. LNCS, vol. 4355, pp. 2–2. Springer, Heidelberg (2006). https://doi.org/10.1007/11955757_2
16. Benveniste, M.: On using B in the design of secure micro-controllers: an experience report. ENTCS **280**, 3–22 (2011)
17. Berglehner, R., Cherif, I., Rasheeq, A.: An approach to improve SysML railway specification using UML-B and EVENT-B. Poster presented at RSSRail 2019 (2019)
18. Bicarregui, J.C., Fitzgerald, J.S., Larsen, P.G., Woodcock, J.C.P.: Industrial practice in formal methods: a review. In: Cavalcanti, A., Dams, D.R. (eds.) FM 2009. LNCS, vol. 5850, pp. 810–813. Springer, Heidelberg (2009). https://doi.org/10.1007/978-3-642-05089-3_52
19. Boite, O.: Méthode B et Validation des Invariants Ferroviaires. Master's thesis, Université Denis Diderot (2000). Mémoire de DEA de logique et fondements de l'informatique
20. Boite, O.: Automatiser les preuves d'un sous-langage de la méthode B. Technique et Science Informatiques **21**(8), 1099–1120 (2002)
21. Bouquet, F., Legeard, B., Peureux, F.: CLPS-B—a constraint solver for B. In: Katoen, J.-P., Stevens, P. (eds.) TACAS 2002. LNCS, vol. 2280, pp. 188–204. Springer, Heidelberg (2002). https://doi.org/10.1007/3-540-46002-0_14
22. Burdy, L., Meynadier, J.-M.: Automatic refinement. In: Proceedings BUGM at FM 1999 (1999). https://www.clearsy.com/wp-content/uploads/sites/7/dl/lilian_burdy/ug020003.pdf
23. Butler, M.: Decomposition structures for Event-B. In: Leuschel, M., Wehrheim, H. (eds.) IFM 2009. LNCS, vol. 5423, pp. 20–38. Springer, Heidelberg (2009). https://doi.org/10.1007/978-3-642-00255-7_2

24. Butler, M.J., et al.: Modelling and refinement in CODA. In: Proceedings Refine, EPTCS, vol. 115, pp. 36–51 (2013)
25. Butler, M.J., et al.: formal modelling techniques for efficient development of railway control products. In: Fantechi, A., Lecomte, T., Romanovsky, A. (eds.) Reliability, Safety, and Security of Railway Systems. Modelling, Analysis, Verification, and Certification. LNCS, vol. 10598, pp. 71–86. Springer, Cham (2017). https://doi.org/10.1007/978-3-319-68499-4_5
26. CENELEC: Railway Applications: Communications, Signalling and Processing Systems. Software for Railway Control and Protection Systems. EN50128: 2001 (2001)
27. ClearSy: Atelier B, User and Reference Manuals. Aix-en-Provence, France (2009). http://www.atelierb.eu/
28. Comptier, M., Déharbe, D., Perez, J.M., Mussat, L., Thibaut, P., Sabatier, D.: Safety analysis of a CBTC system: a rigorous approach with Event-B. In: Fantechi, A., Lecomte, T., Romanovsky, A. (eds.) RailReliability, Safety, and Security of Railway Systems. Modelling, Analysis, Verification, and Certification. LNCS, vol. 10598, pp. 148–159. Springer, Cham (2017). https://doi.org/10.1007/978-3-319-68499-4_10
29. Comptier, M., Leuschel, M., Mejia, L.-F., Perez, J.M., Mutz, M.: Property-based modelling and validation of a CBTC zone controller in Event-B. In: Collart-Dutilleul, S., Lecomte, T., Romanovsky, A. (eds.) RSSRail 2019. LNCS, vol. 11495, pp. 202–212. Springer, Cham (2019). https://doi.org/10.1007/978-3-030-18744-6_13
30. Dghaym, D., Dalvandi, M., Poppleton, M., Snook, C.F.: Formalising the hybrid ERTMS Level 3 specification in iUML-B and Event-B. Int. J. Softw. Tools Technol. Transf. 22(3), 297–313 (2020)
31. Essamé, D., Dollé, D.: B in large-scale projects: the Canarsie line CBTC experience. In: Julliand, J., Kouchnarenko, O. (eds.) B 2007. LNCS, vol. 4355, pp. 252–254. Springer, Heidelberg (2006). https://doi.org/10.1007/11955757_21
32. Evans, N., Ifill, W.: Hardware verification and beyond: using B at AWE. In: Julliand, J., Kouchnarenko, O. (eds.) B 2007. LNCS, vol. 4355, pp. 260–261. Springer, Heidelberg (2006). https://doi.org/10.1007/11955757_24
33. Falampin, J., Le-Dang, H., Leuschel, M., Mokrani, M., Plagge, D.: Improving railway data validation with ProB. In: Romanovsky, A., Thomas, M. (eds.) Industrial Deployment of System Engineering Methods, pp. 27–43. Springer, Heidelberg (2013). https://doi.org/10.1007/978-3-642-33170-1_4
34. Fitzgerald, J.S., Bicarregui, J., Larsen, P.G., Woodcock, J.: Industrial deployment of formal methods: trends and challenges. In: Romanovsky, A., Thomas, M. (eds.) Industrial Deployment of System Engineering Methods, pp. 123–143. Springer, Heidelberg (2013). https://doi.org/10.1007/978-3-642-33170-1_10
35. Hansen, D., et al.: Using a formal B model at runtime in a demonstration of the ETCS hybrid level 3 concept with real trains. In: Butler, M., Raschke, A., Hoang, T.S., Reichl, K. (eds.) ABZ 2018. LNCS, vol. 10817, pp. 292–306. Springer, Cham (2018). https://doi.org/10.1007/978-3-319-91271-4_20
36. Hansen, D., Schneider, D., Leuschel, M.: Using B and ProB for data validation projects. In: Butler, M., Schewe, K.-D., Mashkoor, A., Biro, M. (eds.) ABZ 2016. LNCS, vol. 9675, pp. 167–182. Springer, Cham (2016). https://doi.org/10.1007/978-3-319-33600-8_10

37. Ladenberger, L., Bendisposto, J., Leuschel, M.: Visualising Event-B models with B-motion studio. In: Alpuente, M., Cook, B., Joubert, C. (eds.) FMICS 2009. LNCS, vol. 5825, pp. 202–204. Springer, Heidelberg (2009). https://doi.org/10.1007/978-3-642-04570-7_17

38. Ladenberger, L., Leuschel, M.: BMotionWeb: a tool for rapid creation of formal prototypes. In: De Nicola, R., Kühn, E. (eds.) SEFM 2016. LNCS, vol. 9763, pp. 403–417. Springer, Cham (2016). https://doi.org/10.1007/978-3-319-41591-8_27

39. Lanet., J.-L.: The use of B for Smart Card. In: Proceedings FDL, vol. 2 (2002)

40. Lecomte, T.: The CLEARSY Safety Platform. https://www.clearsy.com/en/our-tools/clearsy-safety-platform/. Accessed 21 Jan 2020

41. Lecomte, T.: Applying a formal method in industry: a 15-year trajectory. In: Alpuente, M., Cook, B., Joubert, C. (eds.) FMICS 2009. LNCS, vol. 5825, pp. 26–34. Springer, Heidelberg (2009). https://doi.org/10.1007/978-3-642-04570-7_3

42. Lecomte, T.: Return of experience on automating refinement in B. In: Proceedings SETS (2014)

43. Lecomte, T.: Developing Safety Critical Applications. CLEARSY Systems Engineering (2019). Accessed 21 Jan 2020

44. Lecomte, T., Burdy, L., Leuschel, M.: Formally checking large data sets in the railways. In: Proceedings of DS-Event-B, CoRR, abs/1210.6815 (2012)

45. Lecomte, T., Servat, T., Pouzancre, G., et al.: Formal methods in safety-critical railway systems. In: Proceedings SBMF, pp. 29–31 (2007)

46. Lee, M., Sørensen, I.H.: B-tool. In: Prehn, S., Toetenel, W.J. (eds.) VDM 1991. LNCS, vol. 551, pp. 695–696. Springer, Heidelberg (1991). https://doi.org/10.1007/3-540-54834-3_53

47. Leuschel, M., Bendisposto, J., Dobrikov, I., Krings, S., Plagge, D.: From animation to data validation: the ProB constraint solver 10 years on. In: Formal Methods Applied to Complex Systems: Implementation of the B Method, ISTE, chapter 14, pp. 427–446. Wiley (2014)

48. Leuschel, M., Butler, M.J.: ProB: an automated analysis toolset for the B method. STTT 10(2), 185–203 (2008)

49. Leuschel, M., Falampin, J., Fritz, F., Plagge, D.: Automated property verification for large scale B models. In: Cavalcanti, A., Dams, D.R. (eds.) FM 2009. LNCS, vol. 5850, pp. 708–723. Springer, Heidelberg (2009). https://doi.org/10.1007/978-3-642-05089-3_45

50. Leuschel, M., Falampin, J., Fritz, F., Plagge, D.: Automated property verification for large scale B models with ProB. Formal Asp. Comput. 23(6), 683–709 (2011)

51. Maamria , I., Butler, M.:. Rewriting and well-definedness within a proof system. In: Proceedings PAR, vol. 43. EPTCS (2010)

52. Maamria, I., Butler, M., Edmunds, A., Rezazadeh, A.: On an extensible rule-based prover for Event-B. In: Frappier, M., Glässer, U., Khurshid, S., Laleau, R., Reeves, S. (eds.) ABZ 2010. LNCS, vol. 5977, pp. 407–407. Springer, Heidelberg (2010). https://doi.org/10.1007/978-3-642-11811-1_40

53. Mashkoor, A., Kossak, F., Egyed, A.: Evaluating the suitability of state-based formal methods for industrial deployment. Softw. Pract. Exp. 48(12), 2350–2379 (2018)

54. Metayer, C.: AnimB website. http://www.animb.org/

55. Rasheeq, A.: An approach to improve SysML railway specification using UML-B and Event-B. Master's thesis, Frankfurt University of Applied Sciences (2019)

56. Robinson, K.: The B method and the B toolkit. In: Johnson, M. (ed.) AMAST 1997. LNCS, vol. 1349, pp. 576–580. Springer, Heidelberg (1997). https://doi.org/10.1007/BFb0000503

57. Sabatier, D.: Using formal proof and B method at system level for industrial projects. In: Lecomte, T., Pinger, R., Romanovsky, A. (eds.) RSSRail 2016. LNCS, vol. 9707, pp. 20–31. Springer, Cham (2016). https://doi.org/10.1007/978-3-319-33951-1_2

58. Servat, T.: BRAMA: a new graphic animation tool for B models. In: Julliand, J., Kouchnarenko, O. (eds.) B 2007. LNCS, vol. 4355, pp. 274–276. Springer, Heidelberg (2006). https://doi.org/10.1007/11955757_28

59. Voisin, L., Abrial, J.-R.: The Rodin Platform has turned ten. In: Ait Ameur, Y., Schewe, K.D. (eds.) Abstract State Machines, Alloy, B, TLA, VDM, and Z Proceedings ABZ. LNCS, vol. 8477, pp. 1–8. Springer, Heidelberg (2014). https://doi.org/10.1007/978-3-662-43652-3_1

60. Voros, N.S., Snook, C.F., Hallerstede, S., Masselos, K.: Embedded system design using formal model refinement: an approach based on the combined use of UML and the B language. Design Autom. Embed. Syst. 9(2), 67–99 (2004)

61. Werth, M., Leuschel, M.: VisB: a lightweight tool to visualize formal models with SVG graphics. In: Raschke, A., Méry, D., Houdek, F. (eds.) ABZ 2020. LNCS, vol. 12071, pp. 260–265. Springer, Cham (2020). https://doi.org/10.1007/978-3-030-48077-6_21

62. Woodcock, J., Larsen, P.G., Bicarregui, J., Fitzgerald, J.S.: Formal methods: practice and experience. ACM Comput. Surv. 41(4), 19:1–19:36 (2009)

63. Yang, F., Jacquot, J., Souquières, J.: JeB: safe simulation of Event-B models in JavaScript. In: Proceedings APSEC, vol. 1, pp. 571–576. IEEE (2013)

A Safety Flasher Developed with the CLEARSY Safety Platform

Thierry Lecomte[✉], Bruno Lavaud, Denis Sabatier, and Lilian Burdy

ClearSy, 320 Avenue Archimède, Aix en Provence, France
thierry.lecomte@clearsy.com

Abstract. The CLEARSY Safety Platform (CSSP) is both a hardware and software platform aimed at developing safety critical applications. A smart combination of hardware features (double processor) and formal method (B method and code generators) was used to produce a SIL4-ready platform where safety principles are built-in. A first version, SK0, was released for education purpose with a restricted application template. An industry-strength version, CS0, was then released, providing more degrees of freedom at the cost of a more tricky development and engineering process. This article presents the new CS0 modelling paradigm, lists the conditions to be verified by the system developed, and briefly introduces a first application, software only: a safety flasher.

Keywords: B method · Safety platform · Automated proof

1 Introduction

In several industrial standards (EN50128 for SIL3/SIL4, IEC61508 SIL3/SIL4, ISO 26262 for ASIL4), formal methods are highly recommended when developing safety critical software for the highest safety levels, for the specification, the development and/or the verification phases. However formal methods are highly recommended just like many other non-formal (combination of) techniques, as these recommendations are setup collectively and represent the industrial best practices. A generic, safe execution platform has been researched for years [5] [6], combining safety electronics and defect-free proven software[1]. The CSSP was initially an in-house development project before being funded by the R&D collaborative project *LCHIP* (Low Cost High Integrity Platform) [7] to obtain a generic version of the platform (i.e. not only aimed at railway systems).

This paper shows the evolution of the CSSP, based on a number of building blocks previously used on in-house applications, from a starter kit for education to a more versatile safety computer for industry. Both hardware (based on commercial standard products) and software (based on Atelier B CASE tool as well

---

[1] The software model is proved to be defect-free - complying with its formal specification and without programming errors. The code generators and the compilers are not defect-free. They are not required to be defect-free as the defects are detected with divergent behaviour during execution.

© Springer Nature Switzerland AG 2020
M. H. ter Beek and D. Ničković (Eds.): FMICS 2020, LNCS 12327, pp. 210–227, 2020.
https://doi.org/10.1007/978-3-030-58298-2_9

as standard products like gcc) aspects are presented, as well as the programming model, adapted to allow more freedom for the software developer.

This paper is structured in five parts. Section 2 introduces the Terminology. Section 3 briefly introduces the B method. Section 4 introduces the CSSP SK_0 and CS_0. Section 5 introduces some bits of a CS0 application of a safety flasher. Section 6 concludes on this first application of the CSSP.

2 Terminology

This section contains specific definitions, concepts, and abbreviations used throughout this paper.

Atelier B[2] is an Integrated development environment (IDE) supporting the B method [1] and the B language for software development, and Event-B [2] for system-level analysis. Atelier CSSP is Atelier B extended with redundant code generator tool-chain, boot loader, and a new project type (CSSP project).

B0 is a subset of the B language that must be used at implementation level. It contains deterministic substitutions and concrete types. B0 definition depends on the target hardware associated to a code generator.

CRC: cyclic redundancy check [8], is an error-detecting code commonly used in digital networks and storage devices to detect accidental changes to raw data.

HEX is a file format [9] that conveys binary information in ASCII text form. It is commonly used for programming microcontrollers, EPROMs, and other types of programmable logic devices.

PLC: programmable logic controller [10], is an industrial digital computer which has been ruggedized and adapted for the control of any activity that requires high reliability control and ease of programming and process fault diagnosis.

Safety computer usually refers to a computer controlling a system where the emission of an erroneous output could injure or kill people. Safety techniques (error detection, redundancy, etc.) have to be used to lower the probability of occurrence of such a failure below an acceptable level defined by standards.

SIL: Safety Integrity Level [11], is a relative level of risk-reduction provided by a safety function. Its range is usually between 0 and 4, SIL4 being the most dependable and used for situations where people could die.

Reliability is the ability of a system to continuously perform its required functions under stated conditions for a specified time.

Output states (memory vs physical). A controller computes new values for its outputs every cycle. These values (stored in memory) are used to change (with signal conversion components) the physical state of the outputs. Identity between values in memory and outputs physical state are checked regularly (with a monitor checking the signal conversion) to assess if the controller is still able to control. Depending on how the outputs are implemented (relays, transistors),

---

[2] https://www.atelierb.eu/en/.

changing state may take more or less time and identity check has to be delayed accordingly.

3   Introduction to the B Method

B [1] is a method for specifying, designing, and coding software systems. It covers central aspects of the software life cycle (Fig. 1): the writing of the technical specification, the design by successive refinement steps and model decomposition (layered architecture), and the source code generation.

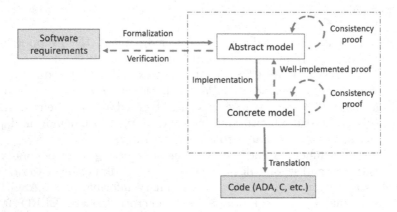

Fig. 1. A typical B development cycle, from requirements to code.

B is also a modelling language that is used for both specification, refinement (Fig. 2), and implementation (Fig. 3). It relies on substitution calculus, first order logic and set theory. All modelling activities are covered by mathematical proof that finally ensures that the software system is correct.

B is structured with modules and refinements. A module is used to break down a large software into smaller parts. A module has a specification (called a machine) where both a static and a dynamic description of the requirements are formalised. It defines a mathematical model of the subsystem composed of:

– an abstract description of its state space and possible initial states,
– an abstract description of operations to query or modify the state.

This model establishes the external interface for that module: every implementation will conform to this specification. Conformance is assured by proof during the formal development process. A module specification is refined. It is re-expressed with more information: adding some requirements, refining abstract notions with more concrete notions, getting to implementable code level. Data refinement introduces new variables to represent the state variables for the refined component, with their linking invariant. Algorithmic refinement transforms the operations of the refined component. A refinement may also be refined.

The final refinement of a refinement sequence is called the implementation, it contains only B0-compliant models. In a component (machine, refinement, or implementation), sets, constants, and variables define the state space while the invariants define the static properties for its state variables. The initialisation phase (for the state variables) and the operations (for querying or modifying the state) define the way variables are modified. From these, proof obligations are computed such as: the static properties are consistent, they are established by the initialisation, and they are preserved by all the operations. Atelier B contains a model editor merging model and proof (Fig. 4) by displaying the number of proof obligations associated to any line of a B model, its current proof status (fully proved or not) and the body of the related proof obligations.

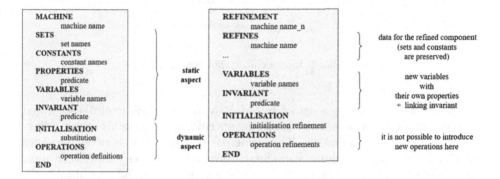

Fig. 2. Structure of MACHINE and REFINEMENT components.

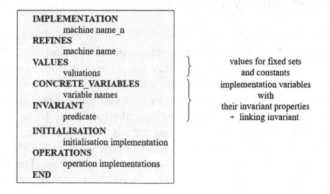

Fig. 3. Structure of IMPLEMENTATION component.

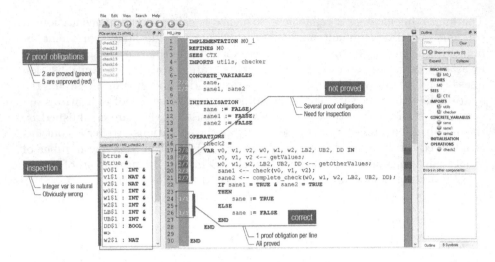

Fig. 4. Atelier B model editor showing proof status.

Finally a B project is a set of linked B modules. Each module is formed of components: an abstract machine (its specification), possibly some refinements and an implementation. The principal dependencies between modules are IMPORTS links (forming a modular decomposition tree) and SEES links (read only transversal visibility). Sub-projects may be grouped into libraries. A software developed in B may integrate or may be integrated with traditionally developed code.

4   CLEARSY Safety Platform

The CLEARSY Safety Platform is a generic PLC able to perform command and control over inputs and outputs. For safety critical applications, the PLC has to be able to determine whether it is fully functional or not. In case of failure, the PLC should move to restrictive mode where all the outputs are deactivated. The stronger the risk of harming people in case of failure, the higher the Safety Integrity Level. For SIL3 and SIL4, the computations have to be performed by a minimum of two processors and checked with a voting system.

The CLEARSY Safety Platform is made of two parts: an IDE to develop the software and an electronic board to execute this software. The IDE is based on Atelier B and extended with dedicated tool-chains to generate and check bare-metal applications (no underlying operating system). The electronic board embeds two microcontrollers PIC32 able to deliver around 50 DMIPS. From the standards, their failure rate is considered as 10^{-5}/h.

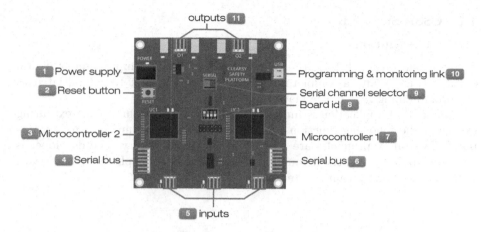

Fig. 5. The CSSP starter kit SK_0 board, with its two microcontrollers μC_1 and μC_2. It embeds 3 digital inputs and 2 digital outputs. To increase the number of usable I/O, boards can be connected through the serial bus: inputs states are propagated through all boards, all boards executing the same complete logic taking into account all the inputs. The board is programmed and monitored from the Atelier CSSP IDE through a USB link.

The overall safety principles[3] are common to all instances of the CLEARSY Safety Platform (starter kits SK_0 and SK_1, Core CS_0):

- the vital part of the application is developed and proved with B, and produces two different binaries B_1 and B_2 (so-called REPLICATED) obtained by two diverse code generation and compilation chains. Both binaries are going to be executed sequentially and their (replicated) variables checked to be equal.
- the non-vital part NV is developed in C, including the top-level sequencer.
- the two identical microcontrollers PIC32 execute the same software, made of the B_1, B_2, and NV. Software is protected by CRC, and CRC verification is done at bootload (upload) and during execution. Memory (variables) is checked during execution. Messages are exchanged between the two microcontrollers to ensure liveness.
- permissive outputs (high state) require both microcontrollers to activate these outputs (provide energy). The failing of the two microcontrollers at the same time is neglected as common failures modes are avoided due to the hardware design, software tool chain, and verification performed.

The CSSP is available as a starter kit, mainly aimed at education, and as an industry-ready version, for safety critical applications.

---

[3] The safety case contains all the details leading to complete demonstration (SIL4) but is not disclosed here (the safety case is around 120 pages). The CSSP has already been certified 3 times.

4.1 CSSP Starter Kit

4.1.1 Description

Available since end of 2017, the board provides 3 digital inputs and 2 digital outputs (Fig. 5), and a complete development environment to get initiated to the programming in B of the platform.

The kind of application is limited to control and command while executing cyclically the following functions: read inputs, perform computation, set outputs[4]. The safety principles are built-in in the safety library. The developer is only able to fill the user_logic function (Fig. 6). Safety principles are out of reach of the developer who cannot alter them.

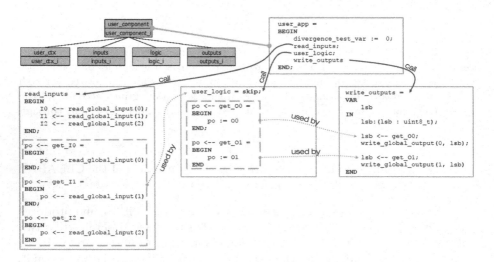

Fig. 6. Modelling the user_logic function. In the central component box, the substitution skip has to be replaced by a user-defined substitution involving inputs and outputs variables. This specification substitution is used to verify its implementation. As such, it has to be precise enough to enable meaningful proof.

4.1.2 Development Cycle

The SK_0 development cycle is as follows:

- specification model is written first from the natural language requirements (Function), then comes the implementation model, both using the same language (B).
- models are proved to be coherent and to be correct refinements. The proof is automatic if the complexity of the model is not too high for the Atelier B theorem prover. Frequent interactive demonstrations can be turned in proof tactics to be applied automatically,

---

[4] The top-level sequencer is hard-coded and cannot be modified.

– source code or binary is generated from implementation model:
  - Binary 1 (HEX file) is directly compiled from the implementation B model. The compiler has been developed in-house for supporting this technology.
  - Binary 2 (HEX file as well) is generated in two steps. First, Implementation models are translated to C, using the Atelier B C code generator. Then the C code is compiled with gcc (Fig. 7).

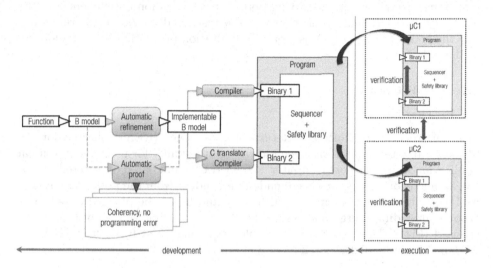

Fig. 7. CSSP application development and execution.

– The two binaries are linked to a top-level sequencer and a safety library, both software developed in B by the CSSP IDE development team once for all, to constitute the final software.
– This software is then loaded on the flash memory of the two microcontrollers (bootload mode).
– When the board enters the execution mode or is reset, the content of the flash memory is copied in RAM for both microcontrollers which start executing it.
– For each microcontroller, the top-level sequencer enters a never-ending loop and
  - calls in sequence Binary 1 then Binary 2 for one iteration
  - calls the safety library in charge of performing verification.
  - If the verification fails, the board enters panic mode, deactivates its outputs and enters an infinite loop doing nothing.

4.1.3 Return of Experience

The platform has been presented and experimented at the occasion of several hands-on sessions organised at university sites in Europe, North and South America. Teaching formal methods is eased as students are able to see their model running in and interacting with the physical world. It was the occasion to demonstrate how formal methods could be used with embedded systems and IoT. Less theoretic profiles may be introduced/educated to more abstract aspects of computation. Clock (synchronous modelling) and combinatorial (asynchronous modelling) exercises were a starting point for specification enrichment and the discovery of the formal proof. However the restricted development framework and the little number of I/Os is seen as a limitation preventing its real adoption in the industry.

4.2 CSSP Core

4.2.1 Description

In order to counterbalance the Return of Experience (REX) collected for the SK_0 and to obtain a hardware generic enough to qualify for most safety critical application fields, the core computer, so-called CS_0 and based on two redundant PIC32 microcontrollers, has been made independent from the power supply and its I/Os. The CS_0 has a smart card format and has to be plugged on a motherboard providing energy and connection to I/Os. A first version of this motherboard (Fig. 8) has been made available beginning of 2020, together with the CS_0, providing 32 digital inputs and 32 digital outputs.

Fig. 8. The CSSP Core CS_0 board plugged on its hosting motherboard.

4.2.2   Development Cycle

The development cycle is similar to the SK_0's one:

- B models are used to develop vital functions (so-called REPLICATED) that will be used to generate two different binaries with two different tool-chains.
- HEX files are obtained either via direct compilation from B0 models or via C code generation then C compilation.

However several differences offer far more degrees of freedom with the architecture/behaviour of the application:

- B models may represent both functions executed cyclically by the application sequencer and functions executed during interrupt. Several entry points may be used with the B project.
- The developer has to define its own sequencing - the way the functions are called in sequence.
- The developer is able to add any non-vital software and to link it with the rest of the application.
- Computation between μC_1 and μC_2 could be asymmetric, one microcontroller doing more/different things than the other one.

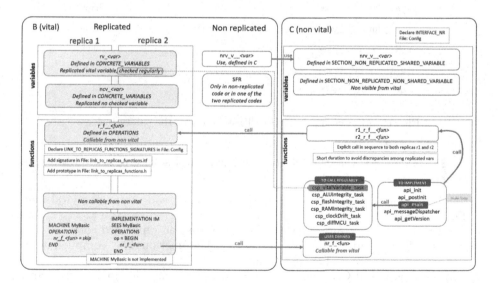

Fig. 9. Architecture of a CSSP application, made of C and B code.

Figure 9 shows that a CSSP application is composed of a vital part (left), replicated and modelled with B, and a non-vital part (right), developed in C. Five C functions have to be implemented, including the main loop *api_main* which has to call regularly the functions named *csp_*_task* in charge of the safety verification. For example the Clock drift task manages all the time drift related topics. As a general statement a task is always non-blocking and execute fast (less than 200 μs). The regularity of the calls have to comply with Fig. 10 where the minimum calling frequencies are defined. If not called often enough, the safety tasks will trigger a shutdown of the platform (which impacts the availability of the product but not its safety).

From the no vital C code, replicated code may be activated in sequence. This code may:

- use replicated vital variables - their contents is checked regularly to be equal among the two replicas.
- use replicated no checked variables - their contents is not checked, allowing to have different algorithms being executed on the two replicas.
- use special function registers (SFR) used for hardware configuration (to program pins to be input or output for example).
- access non replicated variables defined in the non vital C code.
- call non vital user defined function through a BASIC machine[5].

Task (name of function to call)	Minimum required calls per period	Period
csp_vitalVariable_task()	1	500ms
csp_ALUIntegrity_task()	1	30min
csp_flashIntegrity_task()	8196	30min
csp_RAMIntegrity_task()	400	30min
csp_clockDrift_task()	1	10sec
csp_diffMCU_task()	1	10sec

Fig. 10. Minimum expected call frequency of the safety tasks.

To enable the cohabitation of vital and non vital software, several software interfaces have been defined:

- identifiers allow to discriminate vital (replicated) code from non-vital one. For example:
  - nr_v__var1 represents the variable var1 from non-replicated code,
  - r1_f_Foo() and r2_f_Foo() represent the function Foo compiled with respectively the tool-chain1 1 and 2.
- Exposing non-vital C variable to the B model. During design you may need to forward non-vital data acquired by the non vital layer to the vital software implemented in B. The information can be transmitted to the vital software through two possible means: as a parameter of the replicated function or as a shared variable read by the two replicated functions.

---

[5] In B, a BASIC machine is a component with a formal specification (a B machine) but with a handwritten implementation. A BASIC machine allows to integrate third party software in a B project.

- several configuration files defining the nature of the variables, constants, functions, memory mapping, etc.

4.3   Services

The CLEARSY Safety Platform offers several vital services:

- Vital voter of memory payload: if you want to secure an array of memory. For instance if you want to emit a vital message on a network.
- Vital voter for register: if you want to apply a vital value into a register of the microcontroller.
- Minimum timing guarantee: if you want to ensure that a minimum duration elapsed since a given event occurs, before triggering an action.
- Deadline guarantee: if you want to ensure that a given permissive state is not maintained longer than a timeout or if you want to guarantee that a given action is executed more often that a timeout.

Similarly the CLEARSY Safety Platform offers a number of non-vital services:

- Utility functions for type and endianess conversion
- Communication layer between the two microcontrollers: if you want to exchange any kind of data (vital or non-vital) between the two processors.
- Utility functions for controlling the debug LEDs of the Safety Computer Board.
- Utility functions to retrieve the globally unique serial number: if you want to have a unique number in your design or if you need to send serial number to CLEARSY for troubleshooting.
- Utility functions to retrieve temperature from the built-in sensor
- Utility functions for reading or writing into the 1kB EEPROM provided by the Safety Computer Board.

4.4   Safety Case

The CSSP CS_0 is a generic safety computer. The following failure modes are covered by the CSSP built-in mechanisms and thus do not need to be taken into account in the safety case of the user application:

- Random transient upset in the duplicated variable (i.e. the one prefixed with r_v__ in the user vital software)
- Permanent or transient modification of specific registers (SFR, CP0)
- Modification of the flash memory content
- Damage on the Random Access Memory (RAM)
- Compilation error on the vital software (the one written in B0)
- Perturbation on the clock frequency and timing variable
- Correct software has been uploaded on the target
- Damage on the Arithmetic and Logic Unit

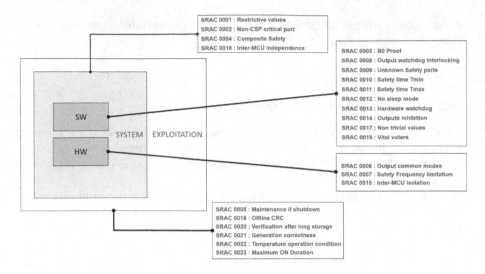

Fig. 11. Safety related application conditions.

However the CSSP CS_0 is not sufficient *per se* as it needs *a minima* I/O[6] and a power supply, to be provided by a hosting motherboard. The motherboard together with the CSSP CS_0 have to comply to a number of safety conditions, named Safety Related Applications Conditions (SRAC) in order to include the CSSP CS_0 certificate into its safety case.

4.5 Safety Related Application Conditions

The application developed with the CSSP CS_0 shall meet the 23 SRAC[7] in Fig. 11, either related to the software, hardware, system, or to the exploitation conditions. Otherwise the certificate of the CSSP is not valid and none of the properties offered by the CSSP can be considered as granted.

Each SRAC is structured as follows :

- Statement: official text of the SRAC
- Verification proposal: Example of how to check if the SRAC is fulfilled or not
- Associated risk: Explanation of the associated hazard if the SRAC is not fulfilled.

---

[6] I/O requirements are so diverse among the safety systems we have been involved into that we have decided to separate I/O from the safety computer.

[7] They are not detailed here, but may be found in the CSSP CS_0 User Manual.

The verification proposal is provided as example or suggestion. The end user and the application team is free of using any means and method to verify and validate that the SRAC are respected. The proposal is only provided for helping the end user to determine how the compliance to the SRACs can be claimed.

5   The Safety Flasher

The safety flasher is a simple application[8], making a bulb to flash - the bulb is alternatively switched on and off. It has been selected as a first example as it is simple to present and to specify, allowing to introduce the different elements of a CSSP development and how they relate, without diving at the same time into the complexity of the application. The chosen safety property is also trivial.

This application is very similar in its nature to the CSSP clock example [4], except that with the CS_0, the specification is not "the output is being updated" but rather, to be sure that the bulb is not on all the time. In other terms, before switching the bulb on, we need to be sure that the bulb has been continuously off during "enough time". In other terms:

Definition 1. *For any t0 before now where the bulb is on, there is t1 not too old (greater than periodMax+periodMin) such that on t1..t1+periodMin the bulb was off.*

The bulb with permanent switched-off aspect represents the safe default mode, either if the flasher is off or if a failure was detected, leading to a restrictive mode where outputs are deactivated.

In the top-level B component (csp_safetyFlasher), it translates (first refinement) in:

```
!t0.(t0 : C_safetyFlasher_periodMin..v_safetyFlasher_clock
   & t0 /: v_safetyFlasher_restrictive
   => #t1.(t1 : t0-C_safetyFlasher_periodMin-C_safetyFlasher_periodMax..t0 &
      t1..t1+C_safetyFlasher_periodMin <: v_safetyFlasher_restrictive
   )
)
```

The api_main function (Fig. 12) shows that inside the infinite loop, several functions (named as csp__task) are called based on elapsed time (but with different delays). These functions are in charge of performing the safety verifications of the board. The calling of these functions in due time is the responsibility of the developer[9]. If these functions (performing the verifications indicated by their name and in relation with the SRACs), are not called (often enough - Fig. 10), the board will enter a restrictive mode where outputs are deactivated.

---

[8] The complete safety flasher model and code are going to be available on [3].

[9] The situation is different from the SK_0 where these function calls were included once for all in the top-level sequencer, not modifiable by the developer.

```
105    void SECTION_NON_REPLICATED_NON_SHARED_FUNCTION api_main()
106    {
107        uint64_t l_timeMs = nr_f__getTimeMs();
108        uint64_t l_time = nr_f__getTime();
109        uint32_t l_lastTempTime = l_timeMs;
110        uint64_t l_timeVitalVariables = l_time;
111        uint64_t l_timeALU = l_timeMs;
112        uint32_t l_ioCounter = 0;
113        uint8_t lsb = 0;
114        uint8_t l_uid[16];
115        bool flagUID = false;
116
117        timerInit();
118
119        while(1) {
120            csp_commTask();
121            csp_tmpTask();
122            csp_eepromTask();
123            if(nr_f__getTimeMs() > MIN_RESTRICTIVE_STARTUP_TIME_IN_MS)
124            {
125                flasherTask();
126            }
127
128            l_timeMs = nr_f__getTimeMs();
129            l_time = nr_f__getTime();
130
131            if (l_time > l_timeVitalVariables + VITALVARIABLES_FREQUENCY) {
132                l_timeVitalVariables = l_time;
133                csp_vitalVariables_task();
134            }
```

Fig. 12. The beginning of the handwritten application, never ending, main loop. The first four tasks are called at each iteration. *csp_vitalVariables_task* is called when the target frequency is reached.

The B component contains four functions, one is called directly by the application, the three others are called by interrupt:

- *r_f__safetyFlasher_flash*: the main logic called cyclically (Fig. 13)
- *r_f__safetyFlasher_testOutput*: safety code called in the interrupt function to generate the safety frequency (20 kHZ on μC_1 or 12 kHZ on μC_2);
- *safetyFlasher_watchdogTimer*: called by the watchdog that check that the watchdog deadline for this function has not been reached.
- *r_f__safetyFlasher_getAddressAndValue*: used in the interrupt routine that generates the safety frequency to comply with the SRAC "Output watchdog interlocking", ensuring that if the safety watchdog dies, all outputs are restrictively blocked.

In the rest of the document, we ignore the low-level interrupt operations and focus on the cyclic operation *safetyFlasher_flash* (Fig. 14).

```
void SECTION_NON_REPLICATED_NON_SHARED_FUNCTION flasherTask()
{
    if(1_nextCmd != nr_v__safetyFlasher_command)
    {
        nr_v__safetyFlasher_command = 1_nextCmd;

        csp_commSendMessageToReplica(CSP_COMM_END_OF_RESERVED_TYPE+1,
            &nr_v__safetyFlasher_command,
            sizeof(nr_v__safetyFlasher_command));

        uint64_t 1_time = nr_f__getTime();
        r1__r_f__safetyFlasher_flash((uint32_t)(1_time >> 32),(uint32_t)(1_time & 0xffffffff));
        r2__r_f__safetyFlasher_flash((uint32_t)(1_time >> 32),(uint32_t)(1_time & 0xffffffff));
    }
}
```

Fig. 13. The handwritten flasherTask() function called cyclically by the application main loop. It calls in sequence the two replicas of the operation *safetyFlasher_flash*.

```
64      r_f__safetyFlasher_flash(p_clockH, p_clockL) =
65      VAR
66          li64H,
67          li64L,
68          lb
69      IN
70          li64H :(li64H : uint32_t);
71          li64L :(li64L : uint32_t);
72          lb :(lb : BOOL);
73
74          lb <-- vitalClock_checkAccuracy(p_clockH, p_clockL, C_safetyFlasher_clockAccuracy);
75          IF lb = TRUE
76          THEN
77              IF nr_v__safetyFlasher_command = 1
78              THEN
79                  IF rv_safetyFlasher_lastCommand = SFALSE
80                  THEN
81                      li64H, li64L <-- get_add_uint64(rv_safetyFlasher_lastCommandApproachedTimeH,
82                          rv_safetyFlasher_lastCommandApproachedTimeL,0,C_safetyFlasher_periodMin);
83                      lb <-- get_lt_uint64(li64H, li64L, p_clockH, p_clockL);
84                      IF lb = TRUE
85                      THEN
86                          rv_safetyFlasher_watchdogTimeoutH, rv_safetyFlasher_watchdogTimeoutL
87                          <-- get_add_uint64(p_clockH, p_clockL, 0, C_safetyFlasher_watchdogTimeoutPermissive) ;
88                          rv_safetyFlasher_lastCommand := STRUE ;
89                          rv_safetyFlasher_lastCommandApproachedTimeH, rv_safetyFlasher_lastCommandApproachedTimeL
90                          <-- get_add_uint64(p_clockH, p_clockL, 0, C_safetyFlasher_clockAccuracy)
91                      END
92                  END
93              ELSIF rv_safetyFlasher_lastCommand = STRUE
94              THEN
95                  rv_safetyFlasher_lastCommand := SFALSE ;
96                  rv_safetyFlasher_lastCommandApproachedTimeH, rv_safetyFlasher_lastCommandApproachedTimeL
97                  <-- get_add_uint64(p_clockH, p_clockL, 0, C_safetyFlasher_clockAccuracy)
98              END
99          END
100     END;
```

Fig. 14. The replicated function *safetyFlasher_flash*, as it is manually implemented in B. 3 local variables are declared with the clause VAR. Their type is then provided (unit32_t, BOOL). The first call to the operation *vitalClock_checkAccuracy* provides a value to the variable *lb*. Operation calls and tests are always performed in sequence, not at the same time. Operations *get_add_uint64* and *get_lt_uint64* are used for respectively performing addition and testing order of unsigned 64-bit integer values.

In order to retrieve the current value of the elapsed time since startup the software designer can call the function *nr_f_getTime()* (Fig. 13) which returns a *uint64_t* corresponding to a non-vital estimate of the time since startup expressed in 125 μs step. Before using this value in the B0-implemented vital software, the designer shall check the accuracy of the value provided by the non-vital layer.

This check has to be done by calling the function *vitalClock_checkAccuracy (clock, accuracy)* which returns true only if the clock from the non-vital software is equal to the actual time (now) at a given tolerance (accuracy parameter). The tolerance takes into account temperature, ageing and standard drift of quartz over the lifetime of the product. Predefined operations are used for 64-bit computation: *get_add_uint64* for the addition of two 64-bit integers, *get_lt_uint64* for their comparison ("lesser than"). As only *uint32_t* type is available, 64-bit integers are decomposed into two 32-bit (most-significant and less-significant) integers.

The B modelling contains a total of 6 machines, 3 intermediate refinements, and 4 implementations. The *csp_safetyFlasher_i* implementation contains less than 200 lines. The overall B project is proved automatically with the addition of 13 mathematical rules (UNION, modulo, sequence, intervals) and around 70 proof tactics. The safetyFlasher_main.c file contains 330 lines, 200 related to the application main loop.

6 Conclusion and Perspectives

The CSSP provides a consistent environment to seamlessly develop proven command and control applications. Its objective is to reduce the development and certification efforts by not requiring expert resources to complete and by simplifying the safety demonstration. It has evolved recently to provide a framework more versatile and usable for the development of safety critical applications. This framework makes precise the various verifications to complete on the final systems, including software and hardware ones. Many of these have to be completed manually (they are not covered by a formal model or a formal proof). Similarly, with the possibility to add your own non-vital code to the application, new risks appear to make a mistake and to perturb the behaviour of the device. It is needed to assess in the future how much effort/time is still saved when using it. An on-going project, RAIL-MAP[10], has started to use it for the demonstration of a Railway Modular Automatic Pilot.

Acknowledgements. The work and results described in this article were partly funded by:

– BPI-France (Banque Publique d'Investissement) and Métropole Aix-Marseille as part of the project LCHIP (Low Cost High Integrity Platform) selected for the call AAP-21.

– ADEME (Agence de l'Environnement et de la Maitrise de l'Energie) selected for the programme "Vehicle of the Future" of Investissements d'Avenir.

---

[10] https://www.ademe.fr/sites/default/files/assets/documents/rail-map.pdf.

References

1. Abrial, J.: The B-Book - Assigning Programs to Meanings. Cambridge University Press, Cambridge (2005)
2. Abrial, J.: Modeling in Event-B - System and Software Engineering. Cambridge University Press, Cambridge (2010)
3. CLEARSY: the clearsy safety platform programming handbook (2020). https://github.com/CLEARSY/CSSP-Programming-Handbook. Accessed 29 May 2020
4. CLEARSY: Github clearsy (2020). https://github.com/CLEARSY/. Accessed 29 May 2020
5. Lecomte, T.: Double cœur et preuve formelle pour automatismes sil4. 8E-Modèles formels/preuves formelles-sûreté du logiciel (2016)
6. Lecomte, T.: The bourgeois gentleman, engineering and formal methods. In: Symposium, AFFORD 2019, Porto, Portugal, 7–11 October 2019. Proceedings (2019)
7. Lecomte, T., et al.: Low cost high integrity platform. In: Symposium, ERTS 2020, Toulouse, France, 29–31 January 2020. Proceedings (2020)
8. Wikipedia contributors: cyclic redundancy check – Wikipedia, the free encyclopedia (2020). https://en.wikipedia.org/wiki/Cyclic_redundancy_check
9. Wikipedia contributors: Intel hex – Wikipedia, the free encyclopedia (2020). https://en.wikipedia.org/wiki/Intel_HEX. Accessed 08 May 2020
10. Wikipedia contributors: programmable logic controller – Wikipedia, the free encyclopedia (2020). https://en.wikipedia.org/wiki/Programmable_logic_controller. Accessed 08 May 2020
11. Wikipedia contributors: safety integrity level – Wikipedia, the free encyclopedia (2020). https://en.wikipedia.org/wiki/Safety_integrity_level. Accessed 08 May 2020

Temporal Logic and Model Checking

Formal Verification of OIL Component Specifications using mCRL2

Olav Bunte[1]([✉]), Louis C. M. van Gool[2], and Tim A. C. Willemse[1]

[1] Eindhoven University of Technology, Eindhoven, The Netherlands
o.bunte@tue.nl
[2] Canon Production Printing, Venlo, The Netherlands

Abstract. To aid in making software bug-free, several high-tech companies are moving from coding to modelling. In some cases model checking techniques are explored or have already been adopted to get more value from these models. This also holds for Canon Production Printing, where the language OIL was developed for modelling control-software components. In this paper we present OIL and give its semantics. We define a translation from OIL to mCRL2 to enable the use of model checking techniques. Moreover, we discuss informal validity requirements on OIL component specifications and show how these can be formalised and verified using model checking. To test the feasibility of these techniques, we apply them to two models of systems used in production.

1 Introduction

To better understand a software system, developers can create abstract models during the design phase. One such model is a behavioural model, which describes the executions of the system. To prove that this model meets the requirements the software should satisfy, one can use model checking, which enables checking of requirements for all executions of the model. While model checking holds great promise, industry so far seems reluctant to adopt the technique. One reason is that most model checking tools build on academic languages, not tailored to the needs of the average engineer.

One company that has shown an interest in using models in the development of control software is Canon Production Printing. To investigate the benefits of a *Model-Driven Engineering* approach to software engineering, a new language for modelling the behaviour of control software, called *Open Interaction Language* (OIL), was developed within the company.

While printing is the primary business domain of Canon Production Printing, OIL contains no logic or language constructs specifically tailored to this domain and can therefore also be used in other business domains. With the use of dedicated tooling one can automatically generate efficient executable code from such models. Moreover, OIL follows a philosophy of separation of concerns, which helps the engineer to cope with complex behaviour by enabling one to model separate aspects of the system separately in a concise way. This philosophy also allows for a

© Springer Nature Switzerland AG 2020
M. H. ter Beek and D. Ničković (Eds.): FMICS 2020, LNCS 12327, pp. 231–251, 2020.
https://doi.org/10.1007/978-3-030-58298-2_10

readable and unambiguous visual representation, which is often deemed an indispensable tool in discussions among engineers.

OIL was not specifically designed to allow for scalable formal analysis on models written in the language. It is therefore unclear to what extent it is feasible to analyse such models. In this paper, we set out to investigate exactly this question. Our contributions are as follows. We define a formal operational semantics for OIL and identify a number of validity requirements on OIL component specifications. These validity requirements ensure that code, generated from the OIL models, behaves reliably and predictably. To enable the use of model checking techniques, we have defined and implemented a translation from OIL component specifications to mCRL2 [17]. The latter is supported by a powerful toolset [10] offering model checking and equivalence checking facilities. Interestingly, the separation of concerns philosophy of OIL poses the biggest challenge in devising this translation. This is mainly due to the large semantical gap between OIL concepts and concepts typical to academic languages such as mCRL2. Our translation from OIL to mCRL2 is implemented in the Spoofax language workbench [36]. We have defined the validity requirements in terms of the μ-calculus so that they can be formally verified on OIL specifications. To test the feasibility of our methods, we have applied these techniques to some models of systems that are used in production at Canon Production Printing. Technical details can be found in [9]; in this paper we focus on the more salient aspects of the work.

Related Work. There is a large body of work reporting on the successful application of model checking to industrial cases. These works typically focus on specific business domains, such as for example railway management [2,3,5,7,26,27], automotive [23,24,32,34] and biomedical [21,30]. The modelling languages UML and SysML can be used to model systems of any business domain. A lot of research has gone into verification of models written in these languages, see for example [7,12,19,24,25,29,31,37] and the references therein.

Works on modelling control software close to ours are those on the FSM language used at CERN [20] and on the Dezyne language developed by the company Verum [6]. The FSM language used at CERN enforces a strict architecture that is tailored to the specific application domain; for general use, this architecture is often too rigid. Using the Dezyne language, a software engineer can model a software system and automatically verify that such a model adheres to the interfaces it uses or implements. Compared to Dezyne, OIL is primarily a modelling language, focussing on ease of use, flexibility and an unambiguous visualisation, whereas Dezyne was designed with verification as the primary focus.

Outline. In Sect. 2 we introduce OIL and its semantics informally by means of a small example and present the validity requirements. Using the same example, we show in Sect. 3 how OIL specifications are translated to mCRL2 and how to formally verify the validity requirements. In Sect. 4 we show the results of some experiments on OIL models of systems used in production. Lastly, we discuss our techniques and results in Sect. 5 and conclude in Sect. 6.

2   OIL

OIL (Open Interaction Language) was created by Van Gool within Canon Production Printing as a language to analyse and visualise the communication behaviour of software systems, partly based on [16]. Using dedicated tooling, one can visualise an OIL specification, analyse traces on it and generate executable code. Originally the syntax of OIL was based on XML. However, as XML is not very user friendly due its verbosity, a more compact syntax has been designed by Denkers [13]. Although OIL is a textual language, it was designed to have a readable yet unambiguous graphical representation. In the following section we will give an informal description of the core constructs of OIL by means of an example.

2.1   A Brief Introduction to OIL

Each OIL specification consists of a number of *global state variables*, *areas* and *transitions*. A *global state* assigns a value to each global state variable. Updating the global state is done by means of simultaneous assignment. Which updates are performed and when is determined by the areas and transitions.

Areas are organised in a tree structure, so an area is either a *root area* or has a *parent*. OIL distinguishes between three types of areas: *regions*, *states* and *scopes*. A region contains a collection of states and refers to a global state variable. A state in this region represents a value of the referred to global state variable, also called the *variable for this state*. A region is typically used to define an aspect of the behaviour of the system and the different states of that aspect. A scope contains a boolean expression that serves as an invariant. It is typically used to restrict possible behaviour.

Transitions have a *source* and *target* area and are labelled with an *event*. Optionally, a transition can have a guard, a collection of assignments and an assert. A transition between two states typically represents the update of a variable from the value of the source state to the value of the target state.

Example. Figure 1 depicts an example OIL component specification of a system with overheating issues, which will serve as a running example in this section. The example has three global state variables: `power`, `job` and `tmp`. The variable `power` models whether the system is switched off (`'off'`) or on (`'on'`), the variable `job` models whether the system is idle (`'idle'`) or busy handling a job (`'busy'`) and the integer variable `tmp` models the temperature of the system. The initial global state maps `power` to `'off'`, `job` to `'idle'` (as can be seen by a slight colouring of the corresponding states) and `tmp` to 20 (not shown in the figure). For brevity of notation, we will denote such a global state as $\langle$`'off'`, `'idle'`, 20$\rangle$. Global state variables are prepended with the keyword '`this`' to indicate that these belong to the scope of the modelled component.

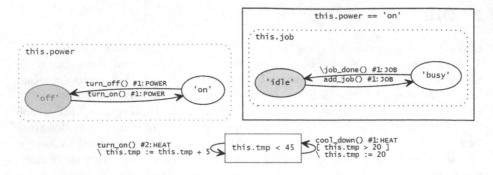

Fig. 1. The visualisation of an OIL specification of a system with overheating issues. (Colour figure online)

The example has eight areas: two regions, each containing two states, and two scopes. Regions are drawn as dotted boxes, states as ovals, scopes as solid boxes and transitions as arrows. Areas are directly contained in their parent area. The two regions refer to the variables **power** and **job** and contain states for each value of these variables. Each transition between two states updates a variable to its other value. The top right scope models that the system may only handle jobs when it is switched on. An alternative way of modelling this restriction would be to make the region that refers to **job** a child of state 'on'. The value of **tmp** can be updated by the assignments (the expressions preceded by a backslash) of the lower two transitions. The right transition of these two has a guard (the expression between square brackets) that requires the temperature to be more than 20. The scope these transitions have as source and target limit the temperature to be less than 45.

Each area is associated with a condition (the *area condition*) and an update (the *area update*). The area condition of a region is true iff it is a root area or the area condition of its parent area is true. For the area condition of a state we additionally require that the variable for this state has the value of this state, whereas for the area condition of a scope we additionally require that its invariant holds. We say that an area is *active* given a global state iff its area condition is true in this global state. The area update of a region or scope performs no assignments if it is a root area, else it equals the area update of its parent area. For a state the area update is extended with the assignment of the value of this state to the variable for this state.

Example. In the running example there are three active areas in the initial global state, coloured green. The region referring to **power** is active since it is a root area. The state with value 'off' is active since its parent is active and the initial global state maps **power** to 'off' (**power** = 'off'). The bottom scope is active since it is a root area and its invariant is true. An example of an area update is the one for state 'off', which is **power** := 'off'.

An update of the global state is triggered by the occurrence of an event. Whenever an event occurs, all transitions that are labelled with this event that can fire, do fire. A transition can fire if its *transition precondition* is true, that is when its source area is active and its guard is true in the current global state. When a transition fires, its *transition update* is applied, defined by the area update of its target area in combination with the transition's assignments. All updates of transitions that fire are applied simultaneously. If these updates try to change the same variable to two different values, we say that these updates are *incompatible*. This causes the event to fail, resulting in an inconsistent state. An event can also fail if after applying the transition updates the *transition postcondition* of one of its fired transitions is not met, that is if one of the fired transition's target area is inactive or assert is false.

Example. Suppose that in the initial global state of the running example the event `turn_on()` occurs. This event corresponds to two transitions, identified as `turn_on()` #1 and `turn_on()` #2. Both transitions can fire since their source areas are active. When they fire, `turn_on()` #1 updates `power` to `'on'` and `turn_on()` #2 updates `tmp` to `tmp + 5`, resulting in the global state ⟨`'on'`, `'idle'`, 25⟩. In this global state both target areas are active, since `power = 'on'` and `tmp < 45`, and therefore the event succeeds.

It is possible for an event to fail in the running example. When `turn_on()` occurs in the global state ⟨`'off'`, `'idle'`, 40⟩, both transitions fire and result in the global state ⟨`'on'`, `'idle'`, 45⟩. Since in this resulting global state it does not hold that `tmp < 45`, transition `turn_on()` #2 (and therefore the event `turn_on()`) fails. This failure models a crash of the system due to overheating. To make this restriction more explicit to the user of the system, a guard `[this.temp < 40]` can be added to `turn_on()` #2.

As mentioned in the introduction, OIL follows the *separation of concerns* philosophy. This philosophy enables one to model different aspects of the system separately, which helps keeping the OIL models of complex systems compact. The running example shows this philosophy well. There are three different parts of the specification that each model a different aspect of the system: the top left region models the power aspect, the top right region models the job aspect and the bottom part models the temperature aspect. The separation of concerns philosophy also allows one to easily change the specification if an aspect of the system changes. For instance, if more detailed job handling is required for the running example, the top right part of the OIL model that models the handling of jobs can be easily replaced with a more refined one.

Such separate parts of an OIL model can interact with each other by means of references to global state variables, such as `power` referred to by both the top left region and the top right scope. They can also interact with each other by synchronising on the same event. Synchronisation occurs whenever separate parts of an OIL model contain transitions of the same event. When these transitions can fire and the corresponding event occurs, the transitions fire simultaneously, making these separate parts proceed simultaneously.

We can force such synchronisation, that is make sure that separate parts only proceed with an event if all involved parts can proceed, by restricting the possible combinations of transitions of an event that can fire simultaneously. In OIL this is done by labelling transitions with one or more *concerns*. Typically, every separate part of an OIL model is associated with a unique concern. We say that an event is part of a concern if one of its transitions is labelled with that concern. Then an event may only occur if for each concern this event is part of, at least one of its transitions labelled with that concern can fire. We refer to this as the *concern condition*. If an event occurs and its concern condition is met, all transitions labelled with this event that can fire, do fire.

Example. In the running example there are three concerns defined, namely POWER, JOB and HEAT, shown after the event name on a transition. The two transitions of event turn_on() are both labelled with different concerns, namely POWER and HEAT, which makes event turn_on() only allowed if both transitions can fire. This forces synchronisation between the part modelling the power of the system with the part that models the temperature of the system, making it illegal to turn the system on when it is already on.

In OIL component specifications we distinguish between two types of events: *reactive* and *proactive* events. Reactive events are events that the component receives from the environment, whereas proactive events are events that the component produces itself, either internal or sent to the environment. This distinction determines in which way the code generated from an OIL specification is executed: when a component is running in an environment it uses a scheduler with run-to-completion semantics, which prioritises proactive events over reactive events. At the level of OIL's semantics, this effectively partitions the set of global states in a set of *quiescent* global states from which no proactive events are possible and a set of non-quiescent global states from which only (at least one) proactive events are possible. If there is a choice between multiple proactive events, the scheduler chooses arbitrarily.

Example. In the running example only event job_done() is proactive, which is indicated in the visualisation with a backslash preceding the event name. Whenever a component with this specification is in a global state where event job_done() can be produced, no other event is possible. Any other global state in this example is quiescent.

The formal semantics of OIL is defined by associating a Labelled Transition System (LTS) to each syntactically correct OIL model. The LTS for the example specification has a total of 16 reachable states and 28 reachable transitions. See Fig. 2 for a visualisation of this LTS.

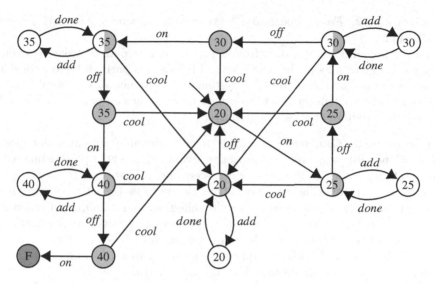

Fig. 2. The LTS that describes the semantics of the running example OIL specification of Fig. 1. The left half of a state is gray iff power = 'off', the right half of a state is gray iff job = 'idle' and the value of tmp is written in the state. The red state with label F indicates that an event has failed. Action label *on* refers to event turn_on(), *off* to turn_off(), *add* to add_job(), *done* to job_done() and *cool* to cool_down(). (Colour figure online)

2.2   Validity of OIL Component Specifications

The scheduler that is used to execute the code generated from an OIL model is required to run as efficiently as is possible. This means that the scheduler performs only the most basic checks to prevent system crashes. To guarantee error-free code execution, engineers have adopted informal rules to which OIL models should adhere, and that help prevent such situations. In the process of formalising the semantics of OIL, we have formalised these rules as four validity requirements. These validity requirements are expressed as constraints on the set of paths permitted in the LTS underlying an OIL model. Below we give only an informal explanation of these requirements and the rationale behind them.

Requirement 1. *Safe lookaheadlessness:* Reachable proactive events should not fail.

When the scheduler checks which proactive events are possible, it only checks the transition preconditions and concerns. It does not consider the postconditions as this is computationally expensive, since it would require to apply the updates that correspond to the event and then roll back for every proactive event. By posing this requirement, we prevent the scheduler from possibly producing failing events. We do allow reactive events to fail, as this is considered inappropriate usage of the component by the environment.

Requirement 2. *Finite proactivity:* All reachable sequences of proactive events must be finite.

If a component reaches a state from which an infinite path of proactive events is possible, such as a loop, the scheduler will follow this path and never consider a reactive event. In the scope of a system of components, this would result in a component that never reacts to events from other components, effectively blocking the progress of other components.

Requirement 3. *Confluent proactivity:* In all reachable non-quiescent global states, all possible sequences of proactive events that end up in a quiescent global state must end up in bisimilar quiescent global states.

When the scheduler has the choice between multiple proactive events, there are multiple routes of proactive events the scheduler can take until it reaches a quiescent state. Since the scheduler chooses between proactive events arbitrarily, the choice between these routes is non-deterministic. If some of these routes end up in behaviourally different quiescent global states, this non-determinism permeates the whole component, which is considered undesirable.

Requirement 4. *Predictable proactivity:* In all reachable non-quiescent global states, all possible sequences of proactive events that end up in a quiescent global state must consist of the same multi-set of events.

In case these routes of proactive behaviour consist of different events, it would mean that whether an event is produced or not is determined non-deterministically. This is undesired, as this event may be needed for other components to proceed. The scheduler is free to choose the order in which the events are produced however.

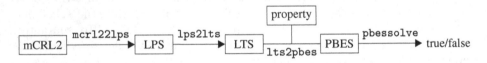

Fig. 3. One of the basic work flows in the mCRL2 toolset for generating an LTS and for checking a mu-calculus property. The edges are labelled with tool names.

3   Model Checking OIL Specifications with mCRL2

To enable the formal verification of OIL specifications we have formalised OIL's LTS semantics in the modelling language mCRL2 [17] by means of a translation. With the mCRL2 toolset [10] one can visualise and simulate an mCRL2 specification and apply model checking techniques to it, such as checking properties and equivalence. Properties can be stated in the modal μ-calculus extended with data [17]. See Fig. 3 for the workflow in the mCRL2 toolset that we use to analyse mCRL2 specifications.

In the following subsections we highlight the key parts of the translation from OIL to mCRL2 (Sect. 3.1), its implementation in Spoofax [36] (Sect. 3.2) and our formalisation of the four validity requirements (Sect. 3.3). We again use the OIL specification of Fig. 1 as running example.

3.1 Translation to mCRL2

To represent the global state we define a type GS_type, which is an object that contains all global state variables. To query or change the value of a variable in a global state we define getter and setter functions GET_v and SET_v for every global state variable v. For each area a, we define functions AC_a and AU_a for the area condition and area update respectively. To model that proactive events have priority over reactive events, we define the quiescence condition QC, which is true iff the current global state is quiescent. Reactive events are only allowed when the quiescence condition is true.

The process specification consists of two processes: the main recursive process P and a process FAIL that models event failure by means of a self-loop labelled with an action failure. Process P is a monolithic process with one parameter of type GS_type that represents the current global state and consists of a non-deterministic choice between so-called summands, each representing one event and its transitions. Each summand models what happens when that event occurs and is of the form:

$$PPC_e(s) \land CC_e(s) \rightarrow (POST_e(UPD_e(s)) \rightarrow e.P(UPD_e(s)) \diamond e.\text{FAIL})$$

where s is the global state parameter and e is the event this is the summand of. The operators $b \rightarrow p$ and $b \rightarrow p \diamond q$ are conditional process operators. For either operator, process p is executed iff condition b is true. For the latter operator, process q is executed iff b is false.

The proactive priority condition function $PPC_e(s)$ is true in case e is a proactive event, else it equals QC. The function $CC_e(s)$ is the concern condition, which can be easily encoded in mCRL2 using conjunctions and disjunctions over transition preconditions. The rest of the summand is more complex however. With $UPD_e(s)$ we update the current global state to a new one using the transition updates of the transitions of event e. The updates are applied in some fixed order by sequentially rewriting the global state for every update. A complication is that we need to use the original global state s and not the intermediate global state that is being updated for getting values of global state variables to correctly simulate the simultaneous update. Also, to only apply the updates of those transitions that fire, we need the transition preconditions. In mCRL2 we define this sequential update by nesting update functions.

The check whether transition updates are compatible poses another issue. We could check whether assignments to the same variable result in different values before updating the state. However, since we do not know beforehand what transitions of an event will fire, we need to check compatibility for every pair of transitions in the worst case, which can lead to a number of checks quadratic in the number of transitions. Instead, inspired by the C++ code generator from the original OIL tooling, we check compatibility after doing the update. This is done by creating a compatibility check $x == e$ for every assignment $x := e$. Now if two assignments are incompatible when updating the global state, the second assignment effectively overwrites the first, which will make the compatibility check of the first assignment false. These compatibility checks are performed in the function $POST_e(s)$, together with the transition postconditions of the transitions of event e. Similar to $UPD_e(s)$, the transition preconditions are used to only check the postconditions and compatibility checks of transitions that have fired.

Each summand models the following behaviour:

– If $PPC_e(s) \wedge CC_e(s) \wedge POST(UPD_e(s))$ holds, event e is enabled and after execution of e, recurse to P with the updated global state $UPD_e(s)$.
– If $PPC_e(s) \wedge CC_e(s) \wedge \neg POST(UPD_e(s))$ holds, event e is enabled and after execution of e, execute process FAIL.
– If $\neg(PPC_e(s) \wedge CC_e(s))$ holds, event e is not enabled.

For the purpose of testing the translation to mCRL2, a version of the translation was created that defined auxiliary variables in each summand, one for every transition precondition and one for the updated state. This was done to make the generated mCRL2 specification more readable. Somewhat to our surprise, experiments showed that this version required considerably more time for model checking because more rewriting effort was needed. The tool lpssumelm from the mCRL2 toolset can typically eliminate such auxiliary variables. Remarkably, it is not able to so on mCRL2 specifications generated by the translation from OIL.

Example. See Fig. 4 for part of the main process P of the running example, showing only the summand for the event turn_on() with auxiliary variables. Line 4 corresponds to $PPC_e(s)$. On line 5 we define auxiliary variables f1 and f2 which represent the transition preconditions of the transitions turn_on() #1 and turn_on() #2 respectively. This is done using the sum-operator to declare the variables, followed by conditions to fix their values. The concern condition $CC_e(s)$ is checked on line 6. On lines 7–8 we define the auxiliary variable uv_GS which represents the updated state $UPD_e(s)$. Note that the update functions here are nested to update the global state sequentially. The variables f1 and f2 are supplied to the update functions to only apply the updates of transitions that can fire. The postconditions $POST_e(s)$ are shown on lines 9–10. Note that the compatibility check GET_tmp(uv_GS) == GET_tmp(v_GS) + 5 is added due to the update SET_tmp(.., f2, GET_tmp(v_GS) + 5). On line 11 the action turn_on is done and then the process recurses with the updated global state, or it starts the failure process, depending on whether the postconditions were true.

```
1  proc
2    P(v_GS : GS_type) =
3      ...
4      QC(v_GS) ->
5      sum f1, f2 : Bool.(f1 == AC_off(v_GS) && f2 == AC_heat(v_GS)) ->
6      (f1 && f2) ->
7      sum uv_GS : GS_type.(uv_GS == AU_heat(SET_tmp(AU_on(v_GS,
8                                   f1), f2, GET_tmp(v_GS) + 5), f2)) ->
9      ((f1 => AC_on(uv_GS)) &&
10       (f2 => (AC_heat(uv_GS) && GET_tmp(uv_GS) == GET_tmp(v_GS) + 5)) ->
11      turn_on.P(uv_GS) <> (turn_on.FAIL) +
12      ...;
```

Fig. 4. Part of the main process P of the mCRL2 specification generated from the running example of Fig. 1, showing only the summand for the event **turn_on()** with auxiliary variables.

3.2   Implementation of the Translation

The translation from OIL to mCRL2 has been implemented in the Spoofax language workbench [36] using the model transformation language Stratego [8]. It makes use of the already available Spoofax implementations of OIL by Denkers [13] and mCRL2 by Van Antwerpen[1]. A total of 20 separate consecutive transformations are used to translate an OIL specification to an mCRL2 specification. See Fig. 5 for a visualisation of this pipeline. An OIL specification is first transformed to the normalised AST, which serves as a middle ground between OILXML and OILDSL. On this normalised AST a number of desugaring and explication transformations have been defined, which are required for the transformation to the desugared AST. This desugared AST is semantically equivalent to the normalised AST, reduced to basic constructs. To annotate variables with types, static analysis is applied on the desugared AST. Inspired by the work of Frenken [15] on a C++ code generator for OIL in Spoofax, an additional intermediate representation is generated before generating mCRL2, called OILSEM. This intermediate representation is close to the formal definition of the semantics of OIL. On this representation we add compatibility checks to the postconditions of transitions. Lastly, we transform the OILSEM representation to mCRL2.

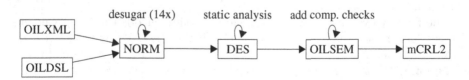

Fig. 5. The transformation pipeline implemented in Spoofax from OIL specification to mCRL2 specification. NORM refers to the normalised AST and DES refers to the desugared AST.

---

[1] https://github.com/MetaBorgCube/metaborg-mcrl2.

The transformations consist of about 1200 lines of code and 400 transformation rules. Most desugar transformations are fairly small with at most 40 lines of code and 10 transformation rules. The most complex transformation is the one from OILSEM to mCRL2 with 300 lines of code and 130 transformation rules.

During the development of the translation to mCRL2 we have relied on the mCRL2 toolset to check for regressions and correctness of the translation. Whenever a new aspect of OIL was added to the translation, an OIL specification illustrating this aspect was translated to mCRL2. Then the corresponding LTS was generated using the mCRL2 toolset to check whether the implementation of the new aspect resulted in expected behaviour. Also, we used equivalence checking to test whether a refactoring in the translation to mCRL2 did not change the behaviour of generated mCRL2 specifications, such as the one that adds auxiliary variables to summands. This was done by comparing the LTS before with the LTS after the refactoring, for a test set of OIL specifications. In a few occasions this has revealed subtle errors in refactorings that might have been overlooked otherwise. Equivalence checking was also applied to test whether mCRL2 specifications generated from the current translation and from one written in Python, developed in an exploratory phase of this project, have the same behaviour. This showed that there was a subtle mistake in the original Python translation that resulted in faulty behaviour in some generated mCRL2 specifications. In general, the use of formal methods during the development process has given us more confidence regarding the correctness of the translation implemented in Spoofax.

3.3   Formal Verification of Validity Requirements

The validity requirements posed in Sect. 2.2 are too complex to be checked on an OIL component specification directly, for instance by means of static analysis. This is mainly because these requirements are about patterns in the global behaviour of the component, which cannot be easily extracted from the structure of the OIL specification. To expose these patterns, we use the translation to mCRL2 and the mCRL2 toolset to generate the underlying LTS. To check the validity requirements on the LTS we define them in terms of the μ-calculus. In this subsection we cover the challenges faced when doing so and provide pattern-like formulae. We use E for the set of all events and E_P for the set of all proactive events in an OIL specification. Wherever possible, we use regular expressions as short-hands.

The first two validity requirements can be easily encoded in the μ-calculus. For safe lookaheadlessness we need to check whether there is any proactive event followed by the `failure` action, which can be encoded by a μ-calculus formula of the form $[E^*][E_P][\texttt{failure}]\mathit{false}$. With finite proactivity we want to enforce finiteness of proactive behaviour, which can be expressed by a least fixpoint operator as follows: $[E^*]\mu X.[E_P]X$. The remaining two Requirements 3 and 4, confluent proactivity and predictable proactivity, are not so easily encoded in the μ-calculus however.

For confluent proactivity we need to be able to check whether states are bisimilar. Since the μ-calculus is based on actions, this is not possible without augmenting the model. To be able to identify bisimilar quiescent states, we first reduce the LTS modulo bisimulation [35] and then add a self-loop to each quiescent state with the action $i(j)$, for some index j that is unique for each quiescent state. Then we can check the requirement with a μ-calculus formula of the form:

$$[E^*](\langle E_P \rangle true \Rightarrow \exists_{j:\texttt{Nat}} : [E_P^*]([E_P]false \Rightarrow \langle i(j) \rangle true))$$

For predictable proactivity we need to be able check whether sequences consist of the same multi-set of events. Since we use μ-calculus with data, we can build up and store the sequences of proactive events encountered by mapping each proactive event to some value. To check multi-set equality we need to define additional maps and corresponding equations in the data specification of the (generated) mCRL2 specification. Then we can check the requirement with a μ-calculus formula of the form:

$$[E^*](\langle E_P \rangle true \Rightarrow \exists_{w \in E_P^*} : \nu X(w' : E_P^* := \epsilon).$$
$$\bigwedge_{e \in E_P} [e]X(w' + e) \wedge ([E_P]false \Rightarrow w \approx w'))$$

where ϵ is the empty list and $\approx$ is multi-set equality.

The μ-calculus formulae for the last two requirements quantify over an infinite dataset: the set of natural numbers and the set of all sequences of proactive events are infinite. Therefore, checking these formulae does not terminate without augmenting the LTS further. For each non-quiescent state s, we first follow some sequence of proactive events w until we reach some quiescent state with index j. Then we add two self-loops to s: one with action $\texttt{ti}(j)$ (target index) and one with action $\texttt{tw}(w)$ (target word). See Fig. 6 for a visualisation of this extension. Note that these transformations do not truly modify the behaviour represented by the model. These actions can then be used in the μ-calculus formulae for Requirements 3 and 4 right after the existential quantifier to give the rewriter a fixed value for the enumeration. It is possible to encode these two requirements in μ-calculus formulae for which such extensions to the LTS are not necessary while guaranteeing termination. However, this exploits knowledge of how the tools currently check these properties, which is undesirable in general.

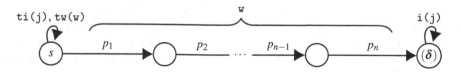

Fig. 6. A visualisation of how the LTS is extended with actions i, $\texttt{ti}$ and $\texttt{tw}$ to help check the mu-calculus formulae for confluent proactivity and predictable proactivity. The actions $p_1, \ldots, p_n$ correspond to proactive events. A (δ) within a state indicates that this state is quiescent.

Transformations have been defined in Spoofax to automatically generate the μ-calculus formulae of all four validity requirements from an OIL specification. These transformations have been defined on OILSEM to reuse the translation to mCRL2 as much as possible. To add the i(j), ti(j) and tw(w) self-loops, a dedicated graph transformation is applied after the LTS is generated and reduced modulo bisimulation.

4   Experiments

To test the feasibility of our techniques, we have used two OIL models representing systems used in production at Canon Production Printing. We refer to these two models as EPC and AGA. In the rest of this section we will give some results and experiences regarding experiments done on these models.

To obtain the size of the global state space, we generate the LTS from the generated mCRL2 specification. This LTS is then reduced modulo bisimulation to remove any superfluous behaviour. Afterwards we extend this LTS with additional information as explained in Sect. 3.3 and check the validity requirements on it. See Fig. 3 for the tools used to generate an LTS and to check a property.

The experiments are done on a laptop with Windows 10, an Intel Core i7-56500U 2.50 GHz processor and 16 GB of RAM. Although the mCRL2 toolset tends to run slower on Windows machines, it is the main operating system used within Canon Production Printing. This way we can test whether we can achieve acceptable performance within the default production environment. With regard to the time needed for the translations, we split the transformation pipeline in two: the translation from OIL specification to analysed desugared AST and from analysed desugared AST to mCRL2 or μ-calculus. This is done because the analysed desugared AST can easily be reused to do multiple translations. For all timings mentioned we have taken the average of at least five runs, except if the time is larger than half an hour, in which case it is only run once.

4.1   The EPC Case

The EPC model is an OIL specification with a total of 10 global state variables, 5 regions, 1 scope, 26 states, 29 transitions and 27 events. It starts with an initialisation phase, then enters a loop and from this loop it can return to the initial state via a termination phase. It models a system used in production, but the code generated from the model itself is not used in production. The analysed desugared AST of the EPC OIL specification is generated in 6.9 s. From this analysed model the mCRL2 specification is generated in 3.3 s. The LTS can be generated from the mCRL2 specification in 10 s. This LTS has 6466 states, 94 actions and 11491 transitions. After reduction modulo strong bisimulation, the LTS has 1178 states and 3207 transitions.

All four validity requirements are met on this model. The reduced LTS is extended with extra information needed for the last two validity requirements in 0.6 s. See Table 1 for the times needed to generate each requirement and check them on this LTS.

Table 1. The time needed to generate each requirement from the analysed desugared AST and the time needed check the requirement on the reduced LTS for both the EPC and the AGA case. The times shown are in seconds.

	Requirement 1		Requirement 2		Requirement 3		Requirement 4	
	Generate	Check	Generate	Check	Generate	Check	Generate	Check
EPC	0.06	0.7	0.06	0.4	0.1	0.9	57	1.3
AGA	1.9	35	1.8	22	2.1	129	76	125

4.2 The AGA Case

The AGA model is an OIL specification with a total of 55 global state variables, 18 regions, 2 scopes, 179 states, 220 transitions and 185 events. It starts with an initialisation phase and then enters a loop. It models a system used in production and, unlike the EPC model, it is used to generate the actual code for this system. The analysed desugared AST of the AGA OIL specification is generated in 26 s. From this analysed model the mCRL2 specification is generated in 130 s. To be able to generate the LTS for this model within a reasonable amount of time, some changes needed to be made to the OIL specification:

- We gave event parameters of reactive events with an infinite domain a fixed value. These parameters represent values received from the environment. In case such a parameter has an infinite domain, there would be an infinite number of transitions possible in the LTS, which causes the generation of the LTS to not terminate. Since the values of these parameters were only used to be passed on to other components, this change does not affect the control flow behaviour of the model.
- We removed the assignments of global state variables that are at most only used to pass information on to other components. This keeps these variables at their initial values, which avoids creating multiple branches in the LTS. Note that this effectively abstracts away some event parameters in proactive events, used to send information to the environment. This is no issue, since we are (for now) only concerned with the behaviour of a single component.
- We added assignments to reset global state variables to their initial value after their value becomes irrelevant. This makes the branches in the LTS that represent different values for this variable converge earlier.

After these changes, the LTS can be generated in 63 min[2]. The resulting LTS has 113844 states and 177156 transitions. After reduction modulo strong bisim-

---

[2] As mentioned earlier, the mCRL2 toolset tends to run slower on Windows machines. This is mostly because the compiling rewriter (passing option `-rjittyc` to `lps2lts`, the state space generation tool), which is typically much faster than the default rewriter, is not available on Windows machines. To experiment what improvement the compiling rewriter could bring we used a virtual machine running Ubuntu 20.04 and using half the laptop's memory. On this virtual machine the LTS can be generated in 6 min from the mCRL2 specification using the options `-bo` for `mcrl22lps` and the option `-rjittyc` for `lps2lts`.

ulation, the LTS has 23372 states and 40820 transitions. Some of this reduction is due to non-optimal placement of the resets. However, investigation shows that this is not the only reason for the observed reduction. For instance, we found that the value of a certain global state variable has no effect on the behaviour if another global state variable was set to false.

All validity requirements are met on this model. The reduced LTS is extended with extra information needed for the last two validity requirements in 28 s. See Table 1 for the times needed to generate each requirement and check them on this LTS.

These validity requirements are of course not the only properties we can check on these models. For instance, we can check deadlock freedom with the μ-calculus formula $[E^*]\langle E\rangle true$, which we can verify to be true on the AGA model. A more interesting property is whether it is always possible to go to the start of the loop in the AGA model. This requirement can be encoded with the μ-calculus formula $[E^*]\langle E^*.\texttt{start}\rangle true$, where $\texttt{start}$ represents the event at the beginning of the loop. Checking this formula on the AGA model results in false, which is due to events in the loop that are deliberately put in the model to fail. Removing these events from E and checking the formula again results in true. These formulae can be checked on the reduced LTS within a few seconds.

5   Discussion of Results

Our translation from OIL to mCRL2 and the subsequent verification of two OIL specifications show that it is possible to model check OIL specifications. The current implementation of this translation comprises a large number of smaller transformations to bridge the large semantical gap between OIL and mCRL2. While this is beneficial for the maintainability and reusability of (parts of) the translation, a monolithic translation would be more efficient. However, the experiments show that for increasingly large models the current translation time is rather insignificant compared to the time needed for model checking. The generation of the fourth validity requirement seems to be an exception to this, but investigation showed that the large generation time is caused by an issue in the pretty printer generated by Spoofax.

At the same time, it is clear that improvements are necessary before model checking can be made available to the average engineer. These improvements concern both automating some of the preprocessing of OIL models needed to scale the analysis and enhancements to the back-end verification methodology we currently use.

Process Structure. We have chosen to describe the semantics of OIL in mCRL2 by using a single monolithic process with a parameter that represents the global state. A drawback of having a monolithic approach over a compositional approach would be the inability to reuse processes whenever only a part of an OIL specification changes. In the monolithic approach, the whole process specification needs be generated anew. Also, the separate composable processes could be reduced before being combined which could speed up the state space generation of the whole model. Another typical benefit of a compositional approach is maintainability. OIL seems to be quite suitable for a compositional approach due to the separation of concerns. However, we think that a compositional approach for describing the semantics of OIL in mCRL2 would be more complex than the current monolithic approach, mainly for two reasons.

Firstly, processes defined in mCRL2 lack a notion of shared variables and can only exchange information via communication of actions. Since from every part in an OIL specification any global state variable can be read or assigned to, the global state would need to be synchronised between all processes frequently. A possible alternative would be to model the global state as a separate process, but such solutions typically scale poorly due to the overhead induced by the extra communications needed by the main process with this additional parallel process.

Secondly, it is complex to model the atomicity of simultaneously firing OIL transitions in mCRL2 in a compositional manner. Communications of actions in mCRL2 seem suitable to describe synchronisation on an event by means of concerns by creating a process for each concern. However, this synchronisation also requires updating the global state, if these updates are found to be compatible, and checking whether the event fails. To share results and prevent race conditions between processes when checking compatibility, updating the global state and checking the postconditions, additional communication would be needed.

Automating Preprocessing. As the AGA case clearly shows, the state space of an OIL specification has the potential to explode if it has many global state variables. To help the state space generator, we manually analysed the usage of these variables and adapted the OIL specification. This is both tedious and error-prone, and therefore a candidate for automation. We note that there is a wealth of literature on such static analysis; see for instance research in the fields of program slicing [33] and live variable analysis [14]. A more interesting challenge, however, is to investigate whether it is possible to implement such static analysis techniques at the meta-level in a language workbench such as Spoofax, so that such techniques become available to all languages defined in such a workbench.

We remark that the mCRL2 toolset already contains some tools that help reduce the state space by removing variables that have no effect on behaviour, such as lpsparelm, lpssumelm and lpsstategraph [28]. However, experiments have shown that these tools are not very effective on mCRL2 specifications generated from OIL specifications. This is due to our monolithic representation of the global state. To make these tools more effective, the structure of the generated mCRL2 will have to be redesigned or the tools have to be improved.

Enhanced Back-End. The μ-calculus is a good fit for encoding two out of the four validity requirements, namely safe lookaheadlessness and finite proactivity. For confluent proactivity and predictable proactivity however, changes needed to be made to the model. We do remark that this is the first time that we have come across a functional property that cannot be expressed in the first-order modal μ-calculus without adding non-trivial information to the model. It may be necessary to resort to an even more expressive logic, such as a higher-order fixed point logic [1] or some hybrid logic [22], to encode such properties without modifying the model. The downside of using such logics is that, as far as we are aware of, no toolset supports such logics. Alternatively, it may be possible to check these requirements more efficiently using other techniques, for instance by encoding these requirements directly in a parameterised Boolean equation system [18] (see Fig. 3), thereby sidestepping the limitations of the μ-calculus, or by building dedicated verifiers.

Another aspect that could be exploited is that specifications such as the AGA model have a number of global state variables set during the initialisation phase. These basically create configurations for the behaviour that is defined in the loop after the initialisation phase. This could be exploited by modelling them as features instead and apply techniques in the context of software product lines [11]. Some research has already been done regarding model checking software product lines in the context of mCRL2 [4].

6   Conclusion

We have discussed our formalisation of the semantics of OIL, a language for modelling system behaviour. Although OIL was not specifically designed for the efficient application of formal methods, we have been able to define and implement a translation from OIL component specifications to mCRL2 to enable formal verification of such OIL specifications. We have introduced four validity requirements and showed how these can be checked on an OIL specification using mCRL2 and the μ-calculus. Lastly, we have translated two OIL specifications that model systems used in production to mCRL2 and formally verified the four validity requirements on them, thereby positively answering the question whether OIL models can be verified. Scalability could become a concern, as the second case study illustrates. At the same time, the modifications we made to the second case to speed up the analysis show that standard static analyses techniques are likely to help in mitigating such concerns.

Future Work. As software systems typically consist of multiple components, research is needed regarding how to formalise their interaction. We expect this to give rise to more model checking challenges such as checking system wide properties.

OIL can also be used to define protocols, which model the communication behaviour between components. By translating protocol specifications to mCRL2, they can be used to check whether the interaction among components conforms to the protocol. What type of conformance relation would best fit OIL still needs to be investigated.

Due to its mathematical nature, the μ-calculus is not a suitable language for use by software engineers. Since OIL is aimed to be used in an industrial setting, we plan to investigate how engineers can easily define properties without losing precision.

OIL is also used to model existing components (as illustrated by our first case study). To check for regressions between these OIL specifications and the existing implementations, one can use model-based testing; preliminary work in this direction for OIL was carried out by Frenken [15].

Acknowledgements. We thank Canon Production Printing for funding the VOICE-B project, of which this work is part of. We thank Jasper Denkers for his help with understanding Spoofax and its languages and for his remarks on this paper. We thank the reviewers for their helpful comments.

References

1. Axelsson, R., Lange, M., Somla, R.: The complexity of model checking higher-order fixpoint logic. Logical Methods Comput. Sci. **3**(2), 7 (2007)
2. Basile, D., ter Beek, M.H., Ferrari, A., Legay, A.: Modelling and analysing ERTMS L3 moving block railway signalling with simulink and UPPAAL SMC. In: Larsen, K.G., Willemse, T. (eds.) FMICS 2019. LNCS, vol. 11687, pp. 1–21. Springer, Cham (2019). https://doi.org/10.1007/978-3-030-27008-7_1
3. ter Beek, M.H., et al.: Adopting formal methods in an industrial setting: the railways case. In: ter Beek, M.H., McIver, A., Oliveira, J.N. (eds.) FM 2019. LNCS, vol. 11800, pp. 762–772. Springer, Cham (2019). https://doi.org/10.1007/978-3-030-30942-8_46
4. ter Beek, M.H., de Vink, E.P., Willemse, T.A.C.: Family-based model checking with mCRL2. In: Huisman, M., Rubin, J. (eds.) FASE 2017. LNCS, vol. 10202, pp. 387–405. Springer, Heidelberg (2017). https://doi.org/10.1007/978-3-662-54494-5_23
5. Berger, U., James, P., Lawrence, A., Roggenbach, M., Seisenberger, M.: Verification of the European rail traffic management system in real-time Maude. Sci. Comput. Program. **154**, 61–88 (2018)
6. van Beusekom, R., et al.: Formalising the Dezyne modelling language in mCRL2. In: Petrucci, L., Seceleanu, C., Cavalcanti, A. (eds.) FMICS/AVoCS -2017. LNCS, vol. 10471, pp. 217–233. Springer, Cham (2017). https://doi.org/10.1007/978-3-319-67113-0_14
7. Bouwman, M., Janssen, B., Luttik, B.: Formal modelling and verification of an interlocking using mCRL2. In: Larsen, K.G., Willemse, T. (eds.) FMICS 2019. LNCS, vol. 11687, pp. 22–39. Springer, Cham (2019). https://doi.org/10.1007/978-3-030-27008-7_2
8. Bravenboer, M., Kalleberg, K.T., Vermaas, R., Visser, E.: Stratego/XT 0.17. A language and toolset for program transformation. Sci. Comput. Program. **72**(1–2), 52–70 (2008)
9. Bunte, O., van Gool, L.C.M., Willemse, T.A.C.: Semantics and model checking of OIL component specifications. Technical report, Eindhoven University of Technology (2020)
10. Bunte, O., et al.: The mCRL2 toolset for analysing concurrent systems. In: Vojnar, T., Zhang, L. (eds.) TACAS 2019. LNCS, vol. 11428, pp. 21–39. Springer, Cham (2019). https://doi.org/10.1007/978-3-030-17465-1_2

11. Cordy, M., et al.: A decade of featured transition systems. In: ter Beek, M.H., Fantechi, A., Semini, L. (eds.) From Software Engineering to Formal Methods and Tools, and Back. LNCS, vol. 11865, pp. 285–312. Springer, Cham (2019). https://doi.org/10.1007/978-3-030-30985-5_18

12. Csertán, G., Huszerl, G., Majzik, I., Pap, Z., Pataricza, A., Varró, D.: VIATRA - visual automated transformations for formal verification and validation of UML models. In: ASE, pp. 267–270. IEEE Computer Society (2002)

13. Denkers, J., van Gool, L., Visser, E.: Migrating custom DSL implementations to a language workbench (tool demo). In: SLE, pp. 205–209. ACM (2018)

14. Fernandez, J., Bozga, M., Ghirvu, L.: State space reduction based on live variables analysis. Sci. Comput. Program. **47**(2–3), 203–220 (2003)

15. Frenken, M.: Code generation and model-based testing in context of OIL. Master's thesis, Eindhoven University of Technology (2019)

16. van Gool, L.: Formalising interface specifications. Ph.D. thesis, Eindhoven University of Technology (2006)

17. Groote, J.F., Mousavi, M.R.: Modeling and Analysis of Communicating Systems. MIT Press, Cambridge (2014)

18. Groote, J.F., Willemse, T.A.C.: Parameterised boolean equation systems. Theor. Comput. Sci. **343**(3), 332–369 (2005)

19. Hansen, H.H., Ketema, J., Luttik, B., Mousavi, M.R., van de Pol, J.: Towards model checking executable UML specifications in mCRL2. Innovations Syst. Softw. Eng. **6**(1–2), 83–90 (2010). https://doi.org/10.1007/s11334-009-0116-1

20. Hwong, Y., Keiren, J.J.A., Kusters, V.J.J., Leemans, S.J.J., Willemse, T.A.C.: Formalising and analysing the control software of the compact muon solenoid experiment at the Large Hadron Collider. Sci. Comput. Program. **78**(12), 2435–2452 (2013)

21. Islam, M.A., Cleaveland, R., Fenton, F.H., Grosu, R., Jones, P.L., Smolka, S.A.: Probabilistic reachability for multi-parameter bifurcation analysis of cardiac alternans. Theor. Comput. Sci. **765**, 158–169 (2019)

22. Kernberger, D., Lange, M.: Model checking for hybrid branching-time logics. J. Logic. Algebraic Methods Program. **110**, 100427 (2020)

23. Kim, J.H., Larsen, K.G., Nielsen, B., Mikučionis, M., Olsen, P.: Formal analysis and testing of real-time automotive systems using UPPAAL tools. In: Núñez, M., Güdemann, M. (eds.) FMICS 2015. LNCS, vol. 9128, pp. 47–61. Springer, Cham (2015). https://doi.org/10.1007/978-3-319-19458-5_4

24. Kölbl, M., Leue, S.: Automated functional safety analysis of automated driving systems. In: Howar, F., Barnat, J. (eds.) FMICS 2018. LNCS, vol. 11119, pp. 35–51. Springer, Cham (2018). https://doi.org/10.1007/978-3-030-00244-2_3

25. Latella, D., Majzik, I., Massink, M.: Automatic verification of a behavioural subset of UML statechart diagrams using the SPIN model-checker. Formal Aspects Comput. **11**(6), 637–664 (1999). https://doi.org/10.1007/s001659970003

26. Limbrée, C., Cappart, Q., Pecheur, C., Tonetta, S.: Verification of railway interlocking - compositional approach with OCRA. In: Lecomte, T., Pinger, R., Romanovsky, A. (eds.) RSSRail 2016. LNCS, vol. 9707, pp. 134–149. Springer, Cham (2016). https://doi.org/10.1007/978-3-319-33951-1_10

27. Mitsch, S., Gario, M., Budnik, C.J., Golm, M., Platzer, A.: Formal verification of train control with air pressure brakes. In: Fantechi, A., Lecomte, T., Romanovsky, A. (eds.) Reliability, Safety, and Security of Railway Systems. Modelling, Analysis, Verification, and Certification. RSSRail 2017. Lecture Notes in Computer Science, vol. 10598, pp. 173–191. Springer, Cham (2017). https://doi.org/10.1007/978-3-319-68499-4_12

28. van de Pol, J., Timmer, M.: State space reduction of linear processes using control flow reconstruction. In: Liu, Z., Ravn, A.P. (eds.) ATVA 2009. LNCS, vol. 5799, pp. 54–68. Springer, Heidelberg (2009). https://doi.org/10.1007/978-3-642-04761-9_5

29. Remenska, D., et al.: From UML to process algebra and back: an automated approach to model-checking software design artifacts of concurrent systems. In: Brat, G., Rungta, N., Venet, A. (eds.) NFM 2013. LNCS, vol. 7871, pp. 244–260. Springer, Heidelberg (2013). https://doi.org/10.1007/978-3-642-38088-4_17

30. Sankaranarayanan, S., Kumar, S.A., Cameron, F., Bequette, B.W., Fainekos, G.E., Maahs, D.M.: Model-based falsification of an artificial pancreas control system. SIGBED Rev. **14**(2), 24–33 (2017)

31. Schäfer, T., Knapp, A., Merz, S.: Model checking UML state machines and collaborations. Electron. Notes Theor. Comput. Sci. **55**(3), 357–369 (2001)

32. Schrammel, P., Kroening, D., Brain, M., Martins, R., Teige, T., Bienmüller, T.: Successful use of incremental BMC in the automotive industry. In: Núñez, M., Güdemann, M. (eds.) FMICS 2015. LNCS, vol. 9128, pp. 62–77. Springer, Cham (2015). https://doi.org/10.1007/978-3-319-19458-5_5

33. Silva, J.: A vocabulary of program slicing-based techniques. ACM Comput. Surv. **44**(3), 12:1–12:41 (2012)

34. Toennemann, J., Rausch, A., Howar, F., Cool, B.: Checking consistency of real-time requirements on distributed automotive control software early in the development process using UPPAAL. In: Howar, F., Barnat, J. (eds.) FMICS 2018. LNCS, vol. 11119, pp. 67–82. Springer, Cham (2018). https://doi.org/10.1007/978-3-030-00244-2_5

35. Valmari, A.: Bisimilarity minimization in $O(m \log n)$ time. In: Franceschinis, G., Wolf, K. (eds.) PETRI NETS 2009. LNCS, vol. 5606, pp. 123–142. Springer, Heidelberg (2009). https://doi.org/10.1007/978-3-642-02424-5_9

36. Visser, E., et al.: A language designer's workbench: a one-stop-shop for implementation and verification of language designs. In: Onward!, pp. 95–111. ACM (2014)

37. Zhang, S.J., Liu, Y.: An automatic approach to model checking UML state machines. In: SSIRI (Companion), pp. 1–6. IEEE Computer Society (2010)

Temporal-Logic Query Checking over Finite Data Streams

Samuel Huang(iD) and Rance Cleaveland(✉)(iD)

Department of Computer Science, University of Maryland, College Park, MD, USA
{srhuang,rance}@cs.umd.edu

Abstract. This paper describes a technique for solving *temporal-logic queries* over finite sets of finite-length *data streams*. Such data streams arise in many domains, including server logs, program testing, and financial and marketing data; temporal-logic formulas that are satisfied by all data streams in a set can provide insight into the underlying dynamics of the system generating the streams. Our approach to finding such formulas involves *queries*, or formulas that include an unknown, given in a variant of Linear Temporal Logic (LTL). Solving such a query involves computing all propositional formulas that, when substituted for the unknown in the query, yield an LTL formula satisfied by all data streams in the set. We give an automaton-based approach to solving these queries and demonstrate a working implementation via a pilot study.

Keywords: Temporal logic · Query checking · Data streams · Automata

1 Introduction

A central problem in system analysis may be phrased as the *behavioral understanding problem*: given concrete observations of a system's behavior, infer high-level properties characterizing this behavior. Such properties can be used for a variety of purposes, including system specification, software understanding (when the system in question is software), and root-cause failure analysis. Several researchers have studied variants of this problem in a several contexts, from software engineering [1] to data mining [2] and artificial intelligence [18,19].

This paper considers the following variant of the behavioral understanding problem: given (1) a finite set of finite-length *data streams* encoding observations of system behavior, and (2) a temporal-logic *query* ("formula with a hole") interpreted over such streams, infer formulas that, when plugged into the "hole," yield a temporal-logic formula satisfied by all data streams in the given set. For example, if the query in question has form **G** var, where var is the "hole" and **G** is the "always operator," then a solution ϕ would be a formula that holds at

---

Research supported by US National Science Foundation Grant CNS-1446365 and US Office of Naval Research Grant N000141712622.

M. H. ter Beek and D. Ničković (Eds.): FMICS 2020, LNCS 12327, pp. 252–271, 2020.
https://doi.org/10.1007/978-3-030-58298-2_11

each time point across all data streams. Using our query-solving technology, an engineer can collect different system executions, which might be in the form of system logs or experimentally observed data, and then pose queries to develop insights into the dynamics of the underlying system.

Our query-checking methodology is automaton-based; given a temporal-logic query and a finite set of finite data streams, we construct finite-automata containing instances of the query's unknown and develop automata-based techniques to compute solutions for the unknown. To express queries we use a variant of linear-time temporal logic (LTL) [28], which we call Finite LTL, that is syntactically identical to LTL but it is interpreted with respect to finite, rather than infinite, data streams. As with LTL formulas, a Finite LTL formula may be converted into a finite automaton that accepts exactly the data streams that make the formula true; in the case of Finite LTL, traditional finite automata suffice [23], rather than the ω-automata needed by LTL. We then show how Finite LTL queries, which are Finite LTL formulas with propositional unknowns embedded in them, may be converted into semantically equivalent *finite query automata* (FQAs). We show how appropriately composing the FQA for the negation of a query with an individual data stream yields a new FQA satisfying the following: solutions to the original query problem for given data stream correspond to propositional formulas that, when plugged into the occurrences of the propositional unknown in the composite FQA, make the language of the resulting automaton empty. These insights form the basis for our approach.

The rest of this paper is structured as follows. The next section discusses related work in temporal logic and query checking and defines finite data streams formally. The section following then presents Finite LTL and formalizes the associated query-checking problem. We subsequently define finite query automata, show how to construct them from Finite LTL queries, and develop our automaton-based method for solving these queries with respect to finite sets of data streams. The paper concludes with a set of preliminary experimental results using a prototype implementation and a discussion of future research directions.

2   Background and Related Work

This section reviews relevant work in temporal logic and query checking and defines terminology for finite data streams.

2.1   Temporal Logic

Temporal logics are formalisms for reasoning about system behavior. First introduced to the computer-science community by Amir Pnueli [28], temporal logics have been extensively studied as the basis for formal specification and verification of many types of hardware [16] and software [21] systems. These logics extend traditional propositional/first-order logics with additional operators, or *modalities*, for describing the truth and falsity of different properties over time. When a system is finite-state, the task of checking whether or not it satisfies a given temporal property is typically decidable; *model checkers* [5, 12] are tools used for this purpose. Checking whether a temporal formula is *satisfiable* is also in general decidable; in this case the temporal logic is often termed decidable [31].

Linear Temporal Logic (LTL) and Finite Variants. Pnueli's original logic is called *Linear Temporal Logic*, or LTL, because formulas are interpreted with respect to infinite sequences of system states. These sequences can be thought of as non-terminating system executions; a system satisfies an LTL formula iff all its executions do. LTL extends propositional logic with modalities **X**, or "next," and **U**, or "until," from which other modalities such as **F** ("eventually") and **G** ("always") can be derived. Model checking and satisfiability are both decidable for LTL and typically rely on the use of automata-theoretic techniques [32].

In this paper we are concerned with LTL interpreted over *finite*, rather than infinite, sequences of states. Later we formally define our logic, Finite LTL [23]; here we describe other variants of LTL over finite sequences. De Giacomo and Vardi [14] define LTL_f and discuss how another logic, Linear Dynamic Logic over finite traces, LDL_f, is more expressive than LTL_f but still has a PSPACE-complete satisfiability problem. De Giacomo et al. [13] argue about how conversion from standard LTL over infinite sequences to finite sequences is often misused or misappropriated and present a variant of LTL_f. Roşu [29] gives a sound and complete proof system for his version of finite-sequence temporal logic. Fionda and Greco [17] restrict negation to only atomic formulas and consider a fragment LTL_f, $LTL_{f,s}$, that allows only a single atomic proposition to be true at each time instance. All of these logics require the sequences used to interpret formulas to be non-empty. In contrast, our Finite LTL allows empty sequences as models also. We also note that finite interpretations of LTL, typically involving three-valued logic, are used in runtime-monitoring applications [26, 29].

2.2 Query Checking

Temporal-logic query checking was first proposed by Chan in 2000 [9]. His formulation of the problem was as follows: given a Kripke structure [6] describing the operational behavior of a system, and a Computation-Tree Logic (CTL) [11] query, or formula containing placeholders for missing subformulas, compute propositional formulas that, when plugged into the placeholders, yield a formula satisfied by the Kripke structure. Chan also identified a fragment of CTL, which he called CTL^v, whose placeholders have unique strongest solutions, and presented an efficient algorithm for computing these. Subsequent work has extended the classes of CTL queries that can be solved [7] and explored its use in system understanding [20]. Others [10, 22] have also considered LTL as the basis for queries that are solved with respect to Kripke structures.

2.3 Data Streams

We now give formal definitions for data streams. $\mathbb{N}$ is the set of natural numbers.

Definition 1. *Let $\mathcal{AP}$ be a set of atomic propositions. Then a* finite data stream *over $\mathcal{AP}$ is a sequence $(t_0, A_0) \ldots (t_{n-1}, A_{n-1}) \in (\mathbb{N} \times 2^{\mathcal{AP}})^*$ such that $t_i \leq t_j$ holds for all $0 \leq i \leq j < n$. We sometimes refer to the (t_i, A_i) in a data stream as* observations *and the t_i as* time stamps*. We use $\Pi^{\mathcal{AP}}$ to represent the set of all data streams over $\mathcal{AP}$.*

Intuitively, atomic propositions are specific properties that can hold of a state in a system. Data stream $\pi = (t_0, A_0) \ldots (t_{n-1}, A_{n-1})$ can then be seen as the result of observing the system for a finite period of time, where at each observation (t_i, A_i) every atomic proposition $a \in A_i$ is true and $a \notin A_i$ is false at time t_i. Note that Definition 1 requires that timestamps increase monotonically throughout the data stream. We use ε to denote the empty data stream, $|\pi| = n$ for the length of data stream $\pi = (t_0, A_0) \ldots (t_{n-1}, A_{n-1})$, $\pi_i = (t_i, A_i)$ for the ith-indexed step in π, and $\pi(i) = (t_i, A_i) \ldots (t_{n-1}, A_{n-1})$ for the suffix of π obtained by removing the first i elements from π. Note that π_i is only defined when $i < |\pi|$, while $\pi(i)$ is defined when $i \leq |\pi|$, and that $\pi(0) = \pi$ and $\pi(|\pi|) = \varepsilon$. The rest of the paper focuses on so-called *normalized* data streams, which are defined as follows.

Definition 2. *Data stream π is* normalized *iff for all $i < |\pi|$, $\pi_i = (i, A_i)$.*

In a normalized data stream, the time stamps of the elements in the sequence begin at 0 and increase by 1 at every step. In such data streams we can omit the explicit time stamps and instead represent the stream as a finite sequence $A_0 \ldots A_{n-1}$. For normalized data stream $\pi = A_0 \ldots A_{n-1}$ we abuse notation and write $\pi(i)$ as follows: $\pi(i) = A_i \ldots A_{n-1}$. This definition makes $\pi(i)$ normalized.[1]

3   Finite LTL Query Checking

This section introduces the logic Finite LTL and its query-checking problem. LTL is interpreted with respect to infinite sequences of states; in contrast, our data streams are finite, reflecting the intuition that an observation of a system execution must end at some point. Accordingly, while Finite LTL has the same syntax as LTL, its semantics is different, as it is given in terms of finite normalized data streams. Fix a (nonempty) set $\mathcal{AP}$ of atomic propositions.

Syntax of Finite LTL. The set of Finite LTL formulas is defined by the following grammar, where $a \in \mathcal{AP}$: $\phi ::= a \mid \neg\phi \mid \phi_1 \wedge \phi_2 \mid \mathbf{X}\phi \mid \phi_1 \mathbf{U} \phi_2$. Finite LTL formulas may be constructed from atomic propositions using the traditional propositional operators $\neg$ ("not") and $\wedge$ ("and"), as well as the modalities of "next" ($\mathbf{X}$) and "until" ($\mathbf{U}$). We use $\Phi^{\mathcal{AP}}$ to refer to the set of all Finite LTL formulas, omitting $\mathcal{AP}$ if it is clear from context. We call formulas that do not involve any use of $\mathbf{X}$ or $\mathbf{U}$ *propositional*, and write $\Gamma^{\mathcal{AP}} \subsetneq \Phi^{\mathcal{AP}}$ for the set of all such propositional formulas. We also have the following standard derived notations: *false* $= a \wedge \neg a$; *true* $= \neg false$; $\phi_1 \vee \phi_2 = \neg((\neg\phi_1) \wedge (\neg\phi_2))$;

---

[1] This detail, while necessary to point out, is not important in what follows, since the properties we consider in this paper are insensitive to specific time-stamp values.

$\phi_1 \mathbf{R} \phi_2 = \neg((\neg\phi_1)\mathbf{U}(\neg\phi_2)); \overline{\mathbf{X}}\phi = \neg\mathbf{X}(\neg\phi); \mathbf{F}\phi = true \mathbf{U}\phi; \mathbf{G}\phi = \neg\mathbf{F}(\neg\phi).$
The operators $\wedge$ and $\vee$, and $\mathbf{U}$ and $\mathbf{R}$, are duals in the usual logical sense, with $\mathbf{R}$ often referred to as the "release" operator. We introduce $\overline{\mathbf{X}}$ ("weak next") as the dual for $\mathbf{X}$. The operators $\mathbf{F}$ and $\mathbf{G}$ capture notions of "eventually" and "always," respectively.

Semantics of Finite LTL. The semantics of Finite LTL is given as a relation $\pi \models \phi$ defining when normalized data stream π satisfies formula ϕ.

Definition 3. *Let ϕ be a Finite LTL formula, and let π be a normalized data stream. Then $\pi \models \phi$ is defined inductively on the structure of ϕ as follows.*

- $\pi \models a$ *iff* $|\pi| \geq 1$ *and* $a \in \pi_0$
- $\pi \models \neg\phi$ *iff* $\pi \not\models \phi$
- $\pi \models \phi_1 \wedge \phi_2$ *iff* $\pi \models \phi_1$ *and* $\pi \models \phi_2$
- $\pi \models \mathbf{X}\phi$ *iff* $|\pi| \geq 1$ *and* $\pi(1) \models \phi$
- $\pi \models \phi_1 \mathbf{U} \phi_2$ *iff* $\exists j: 0 \leq j \leq |\pi|: \pi(j) \models \phi_2$ *and* $\forall k: 0 \leq k < j: \pi(k) \models \phi_1$

We write $[\![\phi]\!]$ for the set $\{\pi \mid \pi \models \phi\}$ of data streams satisfying ϕ and call ϕ_1 and ϕ_2 logically equivalent, notation $\phi_1 \equiv \phi_2$, if $[\![\phi_1]\!] = [\![\phi_2]\!]$. We say that ϕ_1 is weaker than ϕ_2 (ϕ_2 is stronger than ϕ_1), notation $\phi_1 \leq \phi_2$, if $[\![\phi_2]\!] \subseteq [\![\phi_1]\!]$.

Intuitively, $\pi \models \phi$ is intended to hold if data stream π satisfies ϕ. Thus, π satisfies atomic proposition a iff $|\pi| \geq 1$ (so π_0, the "current state," is defined) and $a \in \pi_0$, while π satisfies $\neg\phi$ iff it fails to satisfy ϕ. Satisfying $\phi_1 \wedge \phi_2$ requires satisfying both ϕ_1 and ϕ_2. For π to satisfy $\mathbf{X}\phi$ it must be the case that $|\pi| \geq 1$ so that $\pi(1)$ exists; then π makes $\mathbf{X}\phi$ true provided that $\pi(1)$, the sequence beginning in the "next state" of π, satisfies ϕ. Finally, π satisfies $\phi_1 \mathbf{U} \phi_2$ iff there is some suffix of π making ϕ_2 true, with every larger suffix satisfying ϕ_1.

The meaning of the derived operators can be understood from their definitions, but we do wish to comment on $\mathbf{F}$, $\mathbf{G}$ and $\overline{\mathbf{X}}$. Note that $\pi \models \mathbf{F}\phi$ holds iff some suffix of π satisfies ϕ. Similarly, $\pi \models \mathbf{G}\phi$ holds iff ϕ is true for every suffix of π. As for $\overline{\mathbf{X}}\phi$, its semantics is nuanced: π can satisfy $\overline{\mathbf{X}}\phi$ if either $\pi = \varepsilon$ (because $\varepsilon \not\models \mathbf{X} \not\phi$ for any ϕ), or $|\pi| \geq 1$ and $\pi(1)$ satisfies ϕ. Thus, for π to satisfy $\overline{\mathbf{X}}\phi$ π can either be empty or satisfy $\mathbf{X}\phi$. This observation highlights a difference between LTL and Finite LTL: $\mathbf{X}$, which is its own dual in LTL, does not have this property in Finite LTL.

There are other subtleties in the semantics related to ε; for example, $\varepsilon \models \neg a$ for any atomic proposition a, and the meanings of $\mathbf{F}\phi$ and $\mathbf{G}\phi$ can be nonintuitive depending on whether or not $\varepsilon \models \phi$. The paper [23] discusses these issues in detail and shows how they may be addressed via simple encodings.

The Propositional Fragment of Finite LTL. This paper makes heavy use of $\Gamma^{\mathcal{AP}}$, the propositional fragment of Finite LTL, so we comment briefly on the properties of it here. First, it is easy to see that for any propositional formula $\gamma \in \Gamma^{\mathcal{AP}}$ and non-empty data streams π and π' such that $\pi_0 = \pi'_0$, $\pi \models \gamma$ iff $\pi' \models \gamma$. That is, only the first state in a non-empty data stream matters for determining if the stream satisfies γ. It is also shown in [23] that, despite the presence of ε in the semantics, formulas in $\Gamma^{\mathcal{AP}}$ enjoy the usual properties of propositional logic: deMorgan's Laws, etc. We also have the following.

Definition 4. *Let $\gamma \in \Gamma^{\mathcal{AP}}$. The equivalence class of γ with respect to $\equiv$ is $[\gamma]_\equiv = \{\gamma' \in \Gamma^{\mathcal{AP}} \mid \gamma' \equiv \gamma\}$. We write $C_{\Gamma^{\mathcal{AP}}} = \{[\gamma]_\equiv \mid \gamma \in \Gamma_{\mathcal{AP}}\}$ for the set of equivalence classes of $\Gamma_{\mathcal{AP}}$ and extend $\wedge$ and $\vee$ and $\leq$ to $C_{\Gamma^{\mathcal{AP}}}$ as follows: (1) $[\gamma_1]_\equiv \wedge [\gamma_2]_\equiv = [\gamma_1 \wedge \gamma_2]_\equiv$; (2) $[\gamma_1]_\equiv \vee [\gamma_2]_\equiv = [\gamma_1 \vee \gamma_2]_\equiv$; (3) $[\gamma_1]_\equiv \leq [\gamma_2]_\equiv$ iff $\gamma_1 \leq \gamma_2$. Finally, we define $[\gamma_1, \gamma_2] = \{\gamma' \in \Gamma^{\mathcal{AP}} \mid \gamma_1 \leq \gamma' \leq \gamma_2\}$ to be the* propositional interval *bounded below by γ_1 and above by γ_2, inclusive.*

If $\mathcal{AP}$ is finite then so is $C_{\Gamma^{\mathcal{AP}}}$, even though $\Gamma^{\mathcal{AP}}$ is not. It is well-known that $\leq$ induces a lattice on $C_{\Gamma^{\mathcal{AP}}}$, with $\wedge$ being the least upper bound (join) operator and $\vee$ being the greatest lower bound (meet) operator. Moreover, $[false]_\equiv$ is the maximum element in the lattice, while the minimum one is $[true]_\equiv$.

Query Checking for Finite Data Streams

In our work on LTL Query Checking [22], we were interested in solving LTL *queries* over Kripke structures. In this paper, we instead are interested in *Finite* LTL queries and normalized data streams obtained by observing the behavior of the system in question. This section defines this Finite LTL query-checking problem precisely and proves results used later in the paper. In what follows we restrict $\mathcal{AP}$ to be finite and non-empty.

Finite LTL queries correspond to Finite LTL formulas with a missing propositional subformula, which we denote **var**. It should be noted that **var** stands for an unknown *propositional formula*; it is *not* a (fresh) atomic proposition. The syntax of queries is as follows: $\phi := \mathbf{var} \mid a \in \mathcal{AP} \mid \neg\phi \mid \phi_1 \wedge \phi_2 \mid \mathbf{X}\phi \mid \phi_1 \mathbf{U} \phi_2$.

For notational and conceptual simplicity, in this paper we only consider the case of a single propositional unknown, although our definitions can be extended to multiple unknowns that range over arbitrary Finite LTL formulas. We often write $\phi[\mathbf{var}]$ for an LTL query containing unknown **var**, and $\phi[\gamma]$ for the LTL formula obtained by replacing all occurrences of **var** in $\phi[\mathbf{var}]$ by $\gamma \in \Gamma^{\mathcal{AP}}$. If $\gamma[\mathbf{var}]$ is a query containing no modalities then we call $\gamma[\mathbf{var}]$ a *propositional query*. We use $\Phi^{\mathcal{AP}}[\mathbf{var}]$ for the set of Finite LTL queries and $\Gamma^{\mathcal{AP}}[\mathbf{var}] \subsetneq \Phi^{\mathcal{AP}}[\mathbf{var}]$ for the set of propositional queries, omitting reference to $\mathcal{AP}$ when it is clear from context. We also lift the notion of logical equivalence, $\equiv$, to LTL queries as follows: $\phi_1[\mathbf{var}] \equiv \phi_2[\mathbf{var}]$ iff $\phi_1[\gamma] \equiv \phi_2[\gamma]$ for all $\gamma \in \Gamma$.

The query-checking problem $\mathrm{QC}(\Pi, \phi[\mathbf{var}])$ may be formulated as follows.

Given: Finite set Π of normalized data streams, Finite LTL query $\phi[\mathbf{var}]$
Compute: All propositional γ such that for all $\pi \in \Pi$, $\pi \models \phi[\gamma]$

If $\gamma \in \mathrm{QC}(\Pi, \phi[\mathbf{var}])$, then we call γ a *solution* for Π and $\phi[\mathbf{var}]$; if we have that $\mathrm{QC}(\Pi, \phi[\mathbf{var}]) \neq \emptyset$ then $\phi[\mathbf{var}]$ is called *solvable* for Π. Computing $\mathrm{QC}(\Pi, \phi[\mathbf{var}])$ for given Π and $\phi[\mathbf{var}]$ cannot be done explicitly in general, since the result may contain infinitely many formulas. However, if $\mathcal{AP}$ is finite then the result can be encoded finitely using equivalence classes of $\Gamma^{\mathcal{AP}}$.

As an example Finite LTL query, consider **G** var. A solution to this query is a formula that is invariant at every point in every data stream in Π. Another example query is **G** (var $\rightarrow$ **F** *err*). Assuming *err* is an atomic proposition representing the occurrence of an error condition, a solution to this query would give conditions guaranteed to trigger a future system error. Such information could be useful in subsequent root-cause analyses of why the error occurred.

4   From Finite LTL Queries to Automata

This section describes the basis for our query-checking approach for Finite LTL: a method for converting Finite LTL queries into special automata called *finite query automata* (FQAs). The section following then gives algorithms for solving query automata for a given finite, non-empty set of normalized data streams. Our technique for generating query automata relies on the tableau-based approach in [23] for producing variants of non-deterministic finite automata (NFAs), called *propositional NFAs* (PNFAs), from Finite LTL formulas. We first review the construction in [23], then describe how it can be adapted to produce FQAs.

4.1   From Finite LTL to PNFAs

The tableau construction in [23] works on Finite LTL formulas in *positive normal form* (PNF). A formula is in PNF if negation is only applied to atomic propositions; if Finite LTL is extended with the derived operators $\vee$, $\overline{\mathbf{X}}$ and $\mathbf{R}$ then any formula in this extended logic can be converted into PNF. We assume Finite LTL is extended in this way and recall the definition of PNFAs below.

Definition 5. *A propositional NFA (PNFA) is a tuple $(Q, \mathcal{AP}, q_I, \delta, F)$, where: Q is a finite set of states; $\mathcal{AP}$ is a finite non-empty set of atomic propositions; $q_I \in Q$ is the start state; $\delta \subseteq Q \times \Gamma^{\mathcal{AP}} \times Q$ is the transition relation; and $F \subseteq Q$ is the set of accepting states. If $M = (Q, \mathcal{AP}, q_I, \delta, F)$ is a PNFA, $q \in Q$, and $w \in (2^{\mathcal{AP}})^*$ is a sequence of subsets of $\mathcal{AP}$, then q accepts w in M iff:*

- *$w = \varepsilon$ and $q \in F$; or*
- *$w = Aw'$ for some $A \in 2^{\mathcal{AP}}$ and $w' \in (2^{\mathcal{AP}})^*$, and there exists $(q, \gamma, q') \in \delta$ such that $A \models \gamma$ and q' accepts w' in M.[2]*

The language of M, $L(M)$, is $L(M) = \{w \in (2^{\mathcal{AP}})^* \mid q_I$ accepts w in $M\}$.

PNFAs are like traditional NFAs, except that they are intended to accept/reject sequences in $(2^{\mathcal{AP}})^*$ (so $2^{\mathcal{AP}}$ is the alphabet rather than $\mathcal{AP}$), and their transitions are labeled by propositional formulas $\gamma \in \Gamma^{\mathcal{AP}}$ rather than elements of $2^{\mathcal{AP}}$. To process a sequence $w = A_0 \ldots A_{n-1}$ a PNFA begins in its start state, then successively consumes each $A_i \subseteq \mathcal{AP}$ of w by selecting transitions emanating from the current state and checking if A_i satisfies the

---

[2] Recall that $A \in 2^{\mathcal{AP}}$ is also a singleton data stream, and thus $A \models \gamma$ is defined.

propositional formula γ labeling the transition. If A_i indeed satisfies γ the transition may be taken, with A_i being consumed and the current state updated to the target state of the transition. If it is possible to reach an accepting state after processing the last element of w then the machine accepts w; otherwise, it rejects w. The following theorem is proven in [23], among other places.

Theorem 1. *Let ϕ be a Finite LTL formula. Then there exists PNFA $M_\phi = (Q, \mathcal{AP}, q_I, \delta, F)$ such that $[\![\phi]\!] = L(M_\phi)$.*

This theorem asserts that for any Finite LTL formula ϕ, there is a PNFA M_ϕ whose language consists of the data streams satisfying ϕ; thus M_ϕ is a PNFA characterizing $[\![\phi]\!]$. The proof in [23] for the theorem uses a tableau-based construction [33] to produce $M_\phi = (Q, \mathcal{AP}, q_I, \delta, F)$ from ϕ. Since we rely on this construction and the specific connections it makes between states in M_ϕ and subformulas of ϕ, we now give a brief overview of it. We begin by noting that since the alphabet of M_ϕ is $2^{\mathcal{AP}}$, it follows that $L(M_\phi)$ consists of sequences of subsets of $\mathcal{AP}$, which are just normalized data streams. The construction associates each state $q \in Q$ with a unique set of subformulas of ϕ – we sometimes write ϕ_q for the conjunction of all the formulas associated with q – and ensures that data streams accepted starting from state q in M_ϕ are exactly those that ϕ_q. The start state q_I has the single formula ϕ associated with it. F_ϕ, the set of accepting states, consists of states q with the property that $\varepsilon \models \phi_q$. The transition relation δ is defined so that the following hold.

– If $(q_1, \gamma, q_2) \in \delta$, $\pi \models \phi_{q_2}$, and $A \in 2^{\mathcal{AP}}$ is such that $A \models \gamma$, then $A\pi \models \phi_{q_1}$ ($A\pi$ is the normalized data stream obtained by prefixing A onto π).
– If $A\pi \models \phi_{q_1}$ then there exists $(q_1, \gamma, q_2) \in \delta$ with $A \models \gamma$ and $\pi \models \phi_{q_2}$.

These facts guarantee the desired correspondence between ϕ and M_ϕ [23].

Emptiness Checking for PNFAs. Our query-checking method relies on computing whether or not $L(M) = \emptyset$ for PNFA $M = (Q, \mathcal{AP}, q_I, \delta, F)$. This holds iff no accepting state $q' \in F$ is reachable via a sequence of *live* transitions from q_I, where a transition (q, γ, q') is live iff γ is satisfiable and *dead* otherwise. Computing whether or not $L(M) = \emptyset$ can be done using standard reachability techniques on a graph derived from M as follows: the nodes of the graph are elements of Q, and there is an edge $q \to q'$ in the graph iff there is a live transition $(q, \gamma, q') \in \delta$. Then $L(M_\phi) = \emptyset$ iff no accepting state is reachable from q_I in the graph.

4.2 From Finite LTL Queries to FQAs

Our query-checking methodology is automaton-based; it relies on converting queries into *Finite Query Automata* (FQAs). An FQA is like a PNFA except that the FQA's transition labels are propositional queries instead of formulas, and the acceptance information for states is encoded in propositional queries labeling each state. In the same way that instantiating a propositional unknown converts a query into a Finite LTL formula, instantiating an FQA's propositional unknown converts it into an appropriate PNFA.

Definition 6. *Let var be a proposition variable. Then a* Finite Query Automaton (FQA) *over var is a tuple* $M[var] = (Q, AP, q_I, \delta[var], F[var])$*, where:* Q *is a finite set of states;* AP *is a finite, non-empty set of atomic propositions;* $q_I \in Q$ *is the initial state;* $\delta[var] \subseteq Q \times \Gamma[var] \times Q$ *is the transition relation; and* $F[var] \in Q \to \Gamma[var]$ *is the* acceptance condition.

If $\gamma \in \Gamma$*, then the* instantiation $M[\gamma]$ *of* $M[var]$ *with respect to* γ *is the PNFA* $(Q, AP, q_I, \delta[\gamma], F[\gamma])$*, where* $\delta[\gamma] = \{(q, \gamma'[\gamma], q') \mid (q, \gamma'[var], q') \in \delta[var]\}$ *and* $F[\gamma] = \{q \in Q \mid \varepsilon \models (F[var](q))[\gamma]\}$.

An FQA $M[\text{var}]$ is intended to be the automaton analog of a Finite LTL query with unknown **var**. The instantiation $M[\gamma]$ of $M[\text{var}]$ with respect to γ is the PNFA obtained by replacing **var** by γ in the transition labels and in the propositional queries $F[\text{var}](q)$ associated with each state q. The latter are used to determine whether q is an accepting state in PNFA $M[\gamma]$ as follows: q is accepting iff the empty stream ε satisfies propositional formula $\gamma'[\gamma]$, where $\gamma' = F[\text{var}](q)$.[3] Note that the choice of γ can thus have two effects on the language of PNFA $M[\gamma]$: one via the transition relation, as some transitions may become dead, and the other via the accepting/non-accepting status of states, as determined by the effect γ has on the instantiation of the queries that $F[\text{var}]$ assigns to them.

Somewhat surprisingly, the definition implies that any instantiation $M[\gamma]$ of $M[\text{var}]$ can only have one of two possible sets of accepting states. To see why, define an equivalence relation $\sim_\varepsilon \subseteq \Gamma \times \Gamma$ as follows: $\gamma_1 \sim_\varepsilon \gamma_2$ if it is the case that $\varepsilon \models \gamma_1$ iff $\varepsilon \models \gamma_2$. It is easy to see that $\sim_\varepsilon$ induces two equivalence classes on Γ: $[true]_{\sim_\varepsilon}$, consisting of γ such that $\varepsilon \models \gamma$, and $[false]_{\sim_\varepsilon}$, consisting of γ' such that $\varepsilon \not\models \gamma'$. These equivalence classes have the following interval characterizations.

Lemma 1. $[true]_{\sim_\varepsilon} = [true, \bigwedge_{a \in AP} \neg a]$, *and* $[false]_{\sim_\varepsilon} = [\bigvee_{a \in AP} a, false]$.

We now have the following.

Lemma 2. *Let* $\gamma_1, \gamma_2 \in \Gamma$.

1. *If* $\gamma_1 \equiv \gamma_2$ *then* $\gamma_1 \sim_\varepsilon \gamma_2$.
2. *If* $\gamma_1 \sim_\varepsilon \gamma_2$ *then for any Finite LTL query* $\phi[var]$*,* $\varepsilon \models \phi[\gamma_1]$ *iff* $\varepsilon \models \phi[\gamma_2]$.

From this lemma, we observe that for any $\gamma \in \Gamma$, $M[\gamma]$ can have only one of two possible sets of accepting states: $F[true]$, when $\varepsilon \models \gamma$, or $F[false]$, when $\varepsilon \not\models \gamma$.

Shattering conditions for FQAs also play a major role in the following.

Definition 7. *Let* $M[var]$ *be a FQA. Then* γ *is a* shattering condition *for* $M[var]$ *iff* $L(M[\gamma]) = \emptyset$*. If a shattering condition exists for* $M[var]$ *we say that* $M[var]$ *is* shatterable.

---

[3] This definition of acceptance is purely for mathematical convenience.

Constructing FQAs from Finite LTL Queries. Our method for query solving involves constructing a semantically equivalent FQA $M_{\phi[\mathbf{var}]}[\mathbf{var}]$ from a Finite LTL query $\phi[\mathbf{var}]$. To compute $M_{\phi[\mathbf{var}]}[\mathbf{var}]$ we modify the tableau construction for PNFAs in [23] as follows. We begin by noting that any Finite LTL query $\phi[\mathbf{var}]$ is also a formula in Finite LTL with $\mathbf{var}$ added as an atomic proposition, and vice versa; more precisely, $\phi[\mathbf{var}] \in \Phi^{\mathcal{AP}}[\mathbf{var}]$ iff $\phi[\mathbf{var}] \in \Phi^{(\mathcal{AP}\cup\{\mathbf{var}\})}$. This means that any such $\phi[\mathbf{var}]$ can be put into PNF, where $\neg$ is only be applied to atomic propositions or $\mathbf{var}$. So assume that $\phi[\mathbf{var}]$ is in PNF; treating $\phi[\mathbf{var}]$ as a formula in $\Phi^{(\mathcal{AP}\cup\{\mathbf{var}\})}$ we may now apply the construction in [23] to obtain PNFA $M_{\phi[\mathbf{var}]} = (Q, \mathcal{AP} \cup \{\mathbf{var}\}, q_I, \delta, F)$. The construction ensures that each $q \in Q$ is associated with a set of Finite LTL formulas in $\Phi^{(\mathcal{AP}\cup\{\mathbf{var}\})}$ that are subformulas of $\phi[\mathbf{var}] \in \Phi^{(\mathcal{AP}\cup\{\mathbf{var}\})}$ (and hence are queries in $\Phi^{\mathcal{AP}}[\mathbf{var}]$), and each $(q, \gamma, q') \in \delta$ is such that $\gamma \in \Gamma^{(\mathcal{AP}\cup\{\mathbf{var}\})}$ is also a propositional query in $\Gamma^{\mathcal{AP}}[\mathbf{var}]$. Now define FQA $M_{\phi[\mathbf{var}]}[\mathbf{var}] = (Q, \mathcal{AP}, q_I, \delta[\mathbf{var}], F[\mathbf{var}])$, where $\delta[\mathbf{var}] = \delta$ and $F[\mathbf{var}](q)$ is a propositional query $\gamma_q[\mathbf{var}]$ with the property that for all $\gamma' \in \Gamma^{\mathcal{AP}}$, $\varepsilon \models \gamma_q[\gamma']$ iff $\varepsilon \models \bigwedge_{i=1}^n (\phi_i[\gamma'])$, where $\{\phi_1[\mathbf{var}], \ldots, \phi_n[\mathbf{var}]\}$ is the set of queries that the construction associates to q.[4] The next theorem establishes the semantic correspondence between $M_{\phi[\mathbf{var}]}[\mathbf{var}]$ and $\phi[\mathbf{var}]$.

Theorem 2. *Let $\phi[\mathbf{var}]$ be a PNF Finite LTL query, and let γ be a propositional formula. Then $L(M_{\phi[\mathbf{var}]}[\gamma]) = [\![\phi[\gamma]]\!]$.*

4.3 Composing PNFAs and FQAs

We now adapt the usual NFA language-intersection operation, $\otimes$, to PNFAs.

Definition 8. *Let M_i, $i \in \{1, 2\}$, be PNFAs $(Q_i, \mathcal{AP}, q_i, \delta_i, F_i)$. Then $M_1 \otimes M_2$ is PNFA $(Q_1 \times Q_2, \mathcal{AP}, (q_1, q_2), \delta_{1,2}, F_1 \times F_2)$ where:*

$$\delta_{1,2} = \{((q'_1, q'_2), \gamma_1 \wedge \gamma_2, (q''_1, q''_2)) \mid (q'_1, \gamma_1, q''_1) \in \delta_1 \text{ and } (q'_2, \gamma_2, q''_2) \in \delta_2\}.$$

Operation $\otimes$ can be extended to the case when one of the M_i is a FQA in an obvious manner. Without loss of generality assume M_1 is PNFA $(Q_1, \mathcal{AP}, q_1, \delta_1, F_1)$, and let $M_2[\mathbf{var}]$ be the FQA $(Q_2, \mathcal{AP}, q_2, \delta_2[\mathbf{var}], F_2[\mathbf{var}])$. Then $(M_1 \otimes M_2)[\mathbf{var}]$ is the FQA $(Q_1 \times Q_2, \mathcal{AP}, (q_1, q_2), \delta_{1,2}[\mathbf{var}], F_{1,2}[\mathbf{var}])$, where $\delta_{1,2}[\mathbf{var}]$ is defined as $\delta_{1,2}$ in Definition 8 and $F_{1,2}[\mathbf{var}]$ is defined as follows.

$$F_{1,2}[\mathbf{var}](q_1, q_2) = \begin{cases} F_2[\mathbf{var}](q_2) & \text{if } q_1 \in F_1 \\ false & \text{otherwise} \end{cases}$$

We have the following.

Theorem 3. *Let M_1 be a PNFA.*

1. *If M_2 is a PNFA then $L(M_1 \otimes M_2) = L(M_1) \cap L(M_2)$.*
2. *If $M_2[\mathbf{var}]$ is a FQA and $\gamma \in \Gamma$ then $L((M_1 \otimes M_2)[\gamma]) = L(M_1) \cap L(M_2[\gamma])$.*

---

[4] That such a $\gamma_q[\mathbf{var}]$ exists is a consequence of the fact that, as shown in [23], checking if $\varepsilon \models \phi$ for $\phi \in \Phi$ or not can be done by in effect ignoring the modal operators in ϕ.

5   Shattering FQAs

The basis for our query-checking procedure is the computation of shattering
conditions for specially constructed FQAs. In this section we give a procedure for
computing these conditions for general FQAs. The algorithm relies on computing
shattering intervals for propositional queries $\gamma[\text{var}]$. We first show how this is
done, then present our general FQA-shattering approach.

5.1   Shattering Propositional Queries

Our approach to shattering $M[\text{var}]$ relies on selecting γ so that some transitions in $M[\gamma]$ become dead because their labels, which are propositional queries
instantiated with γ, are unsatisfiable. If the combination of acceptance sets and
disabled transitions is such that no accepting state in $M[\gamma]$ is reachable, then γ
shatters $M[\text{var}]$. A key operation is the computation of all $\gamma' \in \Gamma$ for a given
propositional query $\gamma[\text{var}]$ such that $\gamma[\gamma']$ is unsatisfiable. We call such a γ' a
shattering condition for $\gamma[\text{var}]$. If $\gamma[\text{var}]$ indeed has a shattering condition (it
might not) we call $\gamma[\text{var}]$ *shatterable*. In this section we show that the shattering
conditions for shatterable $\gamma[\text{var}]$ can be represented as an interval $[\gamma_1, \gamma_2]$.

Definition 9. *Propositional query $\gamma[\text{var}]$ is in* shattering normal form (SNF)
iff it has form $\gamma_1 \vee (\text{var} \wedge \gamma_2) \vee ((\neg\text{var}) \wedge \gamma_3)$, where each $\gamma_i \in \Gamma$.

Lemma 3. *For every $\gamma[\text{var}] \in \Gamma[\text{var}]$ there is a $\gamma'[\text{var}] \in \Gamma[\text{var}]$ in SNF such
that $\gamma[\text{var}] \equiv \gamma'[\text{var}]$.*

Proof. Recall that $\gamma[\text{var}]$ can be treated as a propositional formula in
$\Phi(\mathcal{AP} \cup \{\text{var}\})$ and thus can be converted into *disjunctive normal form*, where every
clause has either no occurrences of var, or one occurrence of var, or one occur-
rence ¬var. We finish building $\gamma'[\text{var}]$ by grouping the clauses containing var
and then factoring out var, and similarly for ¬var.

Theorem 4. *Let $\gamma[\text{var}] = \gamma_1 \vee (\text{var} \wedge \gamma_2) \vee ((\neg\text{var}) \wedge \gamma_3)$ be in SNF.*

1. *$\gamma[\text{var}]$ is shatterable iff γ_1 is unsatisfiable and $\neg\gamma_2 \leq \gamma_3$.*
2. *If $\gamma[\text{var}]$ is shatterable then γ' shatters $\gamma[\text{var}]$ iff $\neg\gamma_2 \leq \gamma' \leq \gamma_3$.*

Proof. Follows from the definition of shatterability and that fact that if $\neg\gamma_2 \leq$
$\gamma' \leq \gamma_3$ then γ' shatters $(\text{var} \wedge \gamma_2) \vee ((\neg\text{var}) \wedge \gamma_3)$, and conversely.

As a consequence of this theorem and Lemma 3, we have that the set of shattering
formulas for any shatterable $\gamma[\text{var}]$ can be represented as a propositional interval
$[\gamma', \gamma'']$, which we refer to as a *shattering interval* for $\gamma[\text{var}]$.[5] Also note that when
var is positive in a shatterable $\gamma[\text{var}]$ (i.e. every occurrence of var is within an
even number of negations) then there is an SNF equivalent to $\gamma[\text{var}]$ of form
false $\vee$ (var $\wedge \gamma_2$) $\vee$ (¬var $\wedge$ *false*); thus $[\neg\gamma_2, \text{false}]$ is a shattering interval for

---

[5] Note that all shattering intervals for $\gamma[\text{var}]$ denote the same set of formulas.

$\gamma[\text{var}]$. Similarly, if var is negative (every occurrence of var is within an odd number of negations) then $[true, \gamma_3]$ is a shattering interval.

We finally note that a *joint shattering interval*, which shatters each $\gamma_i[\text{var}]$, can be computed for a finite set $\{\gamma_1[\text{var}], \ldots, \gamma_n[\text{var}]\}$ of shatterable propositional queries, based on the following lemma.

Lemma 4 (Based on [3]). *Let $[\gamma'_1, \gamma''_1]$ and $[\gamma'_2, \gamma''_2]$ be shattering intervals for $\gamma_1[\text{var}]$ and $\gamma_2[\text{var}]$, respectively. Then $[\gamma'_1 \wedge \gamma'_2, \gamma''_1 \vee \gamma''_2]$ is a shattering interval for query $\gamma_1[\text{var}] \wedge \gamma_2[\text{var}]$.*

In what follows we write $[\gamma'_1, \gamma''_1] \wedge [\gamma'_2, \gamma''_2]$ for $[\gamma'_1 \wedge \gamma'_2, \gamma''_1 \vee \gamma''_2]$, and $\bigwedge I = [\bigwedge \gamma'_i, \bigvee \gamma''_i]$ when $I = \{[\gamma'_1, \gamma''_1], \ldots, [\gamma'_n, \gamma''_n]\}$ is a finite set of shattering intervals.

5.2 Computing Shattering Conditions for FQAs

We now give an algorithm for computing the shattering conditions for FQA $M[\text{var}]$. The output consists of a set of shattering intervals S with the property that γ shatters $M[\text{var}]$ iff $\gamma' \leq \gamma \leq \gamma''$ for some $[\gamma', \gamma''] \in S$. The algorithm works by collecting all transition labels in $M[\text{var}]$, computing shattering conditions of each subset of the set of labels, then performing an emptiness check on the PNFAs (there may be two, since there can be two possible sets of accepting states) obtained by removing the shattered transitions. The algorithm also includes a preprocessing step that computes the shattering interval of each transition label in $M[\text{var}]$ and uses this information to eliminate transition labels, and transitions, that cannot affect subsequent emptiness checks. Specifically, it replaces the labels of transitions that are unshatterable (i.e. have empty shattering intervals) by *true*, and it eliminates dead transitions (i.e. transitions whose label has shattering interval $[true, false]$). Pseudocode for the procedure may be found in Algorithm 1. The following establishes the correctness of this algorithm.

Theorem 5. *Suppose $SC = ShatterFQA(M[\text{var}])$. Then $\gamma \in \Gamma^{\mathcal{AP}}$ shatters $M[\text{var}]$ iff $\gamma \in [\gamma', \gamma'']$ for some $[\gamma', \gamma''] \in SC$.*

Proof. It can be seen that $M'[\text{var}]$, as computed in Algorithm 1, has the property that for any γ, $L(M'[\gamma]) = \emptyset$ iff $L(M[\gamma]) = \emptyset$. It is also the case that for any $S \subseteq SL$ in the algorithm, if $L(M_t) = \emptyset$ then $L(M'[\gamma]) = \emptyset$ for any $\gamma \in I_S \cap [true]_{\sim\epsilon}$, and similarly for M_f and $I_S \cap [false]_{\sim\epsilon}$. Finally, we note that if S, I_S and $\gamma \in I_S \cap [true]_{\sim\epsilon}$ are such that $L(M[\gamma]) = \emptyset$ but $L(M_t) \neq \emptyset$, then there is an $S' \supseteq S$ such that $\gamma \in I_{S'} \cap [true]_{\sim\epsilon}$ and $L(M_t) = \emptyset$. A similar result holds for M_f, and therefore the theorem follows.

We now analyze the complexity of Algorithm *ShatterFQA* in terms of the number of conversions to DNF and propositional satisfiability checks required. We first note that for a given propositional query $\gamma[\text{var}]$, computing its shattering interval and shatterability requires one DNF conversion (to convert $\gamma[\text{var}]$ into SNF) and two satisfiability checks; thus $O(1)$ DNF conversions/satisfiability checks suffice. So the preprocessing step of the algorithm requires $O(|\delta[\text{var}]|)$ of these operations. Now consider the **foreach** loop in the main processing step. Each iteration requires two satisfiability checks to perform the tests in the first two **if** statements. Thus the total number of such operations required is $O(2^{|SL|})$, and as $|SL| \leq |\delta[\text{var}]|$, we get a complexity of $O(2^{|\delta[\text{var}]|})$ DNF conversions and satisfiability checks. (There are also $O(2^{|\delta[\text{var}]|})$ PNFA-emptiness checks.)

This complexity is quite high, but there are heuristics that can greatly reduce running time in practice. First, if $S \subseteq SL$ and I_S shatters $M[\text{var}]$, then so does $I_{S'}$ for every $S \subseteq S'$. Such S' thus do not require processing. The constructions of M_t and M_f can also exploit similar properties to enable incremental updates to the reachability analysis required for emptiness checking. Finally, the structure of transition labels in $M[\text{var}]$ can enable simpler satisfiability checks.

Algorithm 1: Algorithm for shattering FQAs

---

1 **Algorithm** *ShatterFQA* $(M[\text{var}])$
   Input   : FQA $M[\text{var}] = (Q, \mathcal{AP}, q_I, \delta[\text{var}], F[\text{var}])$
   Output: Set SC of shattering intervals
2 **Preprocessing step:**
3      $TL := \{\gamma[\text{var}] \mid \exists q, q' \in Q. (q, \gamma[\text{var}], q') \in \delta[\text{var}]\}$ // Transition labels
4   **foreach** $\gamma[var] \in TL$ **do** compute shattering interval $I_{\gamma[\text{var}]}$ of $\gamma[\text{var}]$
5      $UL := \{\gamma[\text{var}] \in TL \mid I_{\gamma[\text{var}]} = \emptyset\}$ // Unshatterable labels
6      $DL := \{\gamma[\text{var}] \in TL \mid I_{\gamma[\text{var}]} = [true, false]\}$ // Dead labels
7      $SL := TL - (UL \cup DL)$ // Surviving labels
8      $\delta'[\text{var}] := \{(q, \gamma[\text{var}], q') \in \delta[\text{var}] \mid \gamma[\text{var}] \in SL\}$
9      $\delta'[\text{var}] := \delta'[\text{var}] \cup \{(q, true, q') \mid \exists \gamma[\text{var}] \in UL. (q, \gamma[\text{var}], q') \in \delta[\text{var}]\}$
10      $M'[\text{var}] := (Q, \mathcal{AP}, q_I, \delta'[\text{var}], F[\text{var}])$ // $L(M'[\gamma]) = \emptyset$ iff $L(M[\gamma]) = \emptyset$
11 **Main:**
12      $SC := \emptyset$ // Shattering conditions for $M[\text{var}]$
13   **foreach** $S \subseteq SL$ **do**
14          $I_S := \bigwedge\{I_{\gamma[\text{var}]} \mid \gamma[\text{var}] \in S\}$
15          $PSC := \emptyset$
16          $\delta'' = \{(q, true, q') \mid (q, \gamma[\text{var}], q') \in \delta'[\text{var}] \text{ and } \gamma[\text{var}] \notin S\}$
17   **if** $I_S \cap [true]_{\sim\varepsilon} \neq \emptyset$ **then**
18              $M_t = (Q, \mathcal{AP}, q_I, \delta'', F[true])$ // PNFA with acc. set $F[true]$
19   **if** $L(M_t) = \emptyset$ **then** $PSC := \{I_S \cap [true]_{\sim\varepsilon}\}$
20   **if** $I_S \cap [false]_{\sim\varepsilon} \neq \emptyset$ **then**
21              $M_f = (Q, \mathcal{AP}, q_I, \delta'', F[false])$ // PNFA with acc. set $F[false]$
22   **if** $L(M_f) = \emptyset$ **then** $PSC := PSC \cup \{I_S \cap [true]_{\sim\varepsilon}\}$
23   **if** $|PSC| = 2$ **then** $SC := SC \cup \{I_S\}$ // Don't split I_S
24   **else** $SC := SC \cup PSC$
25   **end**
26   **return** (SC)

---

6   Solving $QC(\Pi, \phi[\text{var}])$

We now show how to solve the Finite LTL query-checking problem.

6.1   Query Checking Single Data Streams

In the single-stream query-checking problem $QC1(\pi, \phi[\text{var}]) = QC(\{\pi\}, \phi[\text{var}])$ we are given one normalized data stream π and a Finite LTL query $\phi[\text{var}]$ and asked to compute all propositional $\gamma \in \Gamma$ such that $\pi \models \phi[\gamma]$. We can convert this problem into an FQA-shattering problem as follows. To begin with, it is obviously the case that $\pi \models \phi$ for any Finite LTL formula ϕ if and only if $\pi \not\models \neg\phi$. Now suppose M_π is a PNFA such that $L(M_\pi) = \{\pi\}$. It immediately follows that $\pi \models \phi$ if and only if $L(M_\pi) \cap L(M_{\neg\phi}) = \emptyset$, where $M_{\neg\phi}$ is a PNFA such that $[\![\neg\phi]\!] = L(M_{\neg\phi})$ (see Theorem 1). Theorem 3 ensures that this in turn holds if and only if $L(M_\pi \otimes M_{\neg\phi}) = \emptyset$. The same theorem, together with Theorem 2, then guarantees that for query $\phi[\text{var}]$ and a given propositional formula γ, $\pi \models \phi[\gamma]$ if and only if $L(M_\pi \otimes M_{\neg(\phi[\gamma])}) = \emptyset$, or in other words, that γ shatters FQA $(M_\pi \otimes M_{\neg\phi[\text{var}]})[\text{var}]$, where the construction of $M_{\neg\phi[\text{var}]}$ is given in Sect. 4 immediately before Theorem 2.

Constructing M_π is easily done. Let $\pi = A_0 \ldots A_{n-1}$ and define $\langle A \rangle$, where $A \subseteq \mathcal{AP}$, to be the proposition $\bigwedge\{a : a \in A\} \wedge \bigwedge\{\neg b : b \in \mathcal{AP}, b \notin A\}$. Then $M_\pi = (\{q_0, \ldots, q_n\}, \mathcal{AP}, q_0, \delta_\pi, \{q_n\})$, where $\delta_\pi = \{(q_i, \langle A_i \rangle, q_{i+1}) : 0 \le i < n\}$.

We now give our method, $QC1$, for solving problem $QC1(\pi, \phi[\text{var}])$: (1) compute M_π, $M_{\neg\phi[\text{var}]}$ and $M_c[\text{var}] = M_\pi \otimes M_{\neg\phi[\text{var}]}$; (2) return $ShatterFQA(M_c[\text{var}])$.

Theorem 6. *Let $\pi \in \Pi^{\mathcal{AP}}$ and $\phi[\text{var}] \in \Phi[\text{var}]$, and let $SC = QC1(\pi, \phi[\text{var}])$. Then for any γ, $\pi \models \phi[\gamma]$ iff there exists $[\gamma_1, \gamma_2] \in SC$ such that $\gamma_1 \le \gamma \le \gamma_2$.*

Optimizing $QC1$. From the definition of $\otimes$ (Definition 8) it follows that transition labels in the $M_c[\text{var}]$ used in $QC1$ have form $\langle A \rangle \wedge \gamma'[\text{var}]$ for some $A \subseteq \mathcal{AP}$ and propositional query $\gamma'[\text{var}]$. This fact enables a simplification of the computation of shattering intervals for edge labels as performed in *ShatterFQA*. Recall that propositional queries $\gamma_1[\text{var}]$ and $\gamma_2[\text{var}]$ are logically equivalent if and only if for every propositional formula γ, $\gamma_1[\gamma] \equiv \gamma_2[\gamma]$. We have the following.

Lemma 5. *If propositional query $\gamma[\text{var}] = \langle A \rangle \wedge \gamma'[\text{var}]$, then $\gamma[\text{var}]$ is logically equivalent to one of the following: $\langle A \rangle$; false; $\langle A \rangle \wedge \text{var}$; or $\langle A \rangle \wedge \neg\text{var}$.*

Proof. $\langle A \rangle$ constraints the truth value for every $a \in \mathcal{AP}$ as follows: a is true if and only if $a \in A$. We may thus simplify $\gamma'[\text{var}]$: replace every $a \in \mathcal{AP}$ in $\gamma'[\text{var}]$ by *true* if $a \in A$, and *false* otherwise, then simplify the resulting expression.

This fact simplifies operations in *ShatterFQA*: a transition is dead iff its label reduces to *false*, and is shatterable iff it reduces to something other than $\langle A \rangle$. Also, all shatterable edge labels in $M_c[\text{var}]$ have shattering intervals of the form

$[\neg \langle A \rangle, false]$ (if the label simplifies to $\langle A \rangle \wedge \text{var}$) or $[true, \langle A \rangle]$ (if simplifies to $\langle A \rangle \wedge \neg \text{var}$). This obviates the need for conversions to SNF.

We remark on another optimization. *ShatterFQA* computes the joint shattering condition I_S for a set of transition labels (line 14 of Algorithm 1). In the case of M_c, each of individual shattering conditions has form either $[\neg \langle A \rangle, false]$ or $[true, \langle B \rangle]$. Applying Lemma 4 to types of shattering conditions yields an interval of form $I_S = [\neg \langle A_1 \rangle \wedge \cdots \wedge \neg \langle A_k \rangle, \langle B_1 \rangle \vee \cdots \vee \langle B_\ell \rangle]$. This interval may be represented as two sets, $\mathcal{E} = \{A_1, \ldots, A_k\}$ and $\mathcal{F} = \{B_1, \ldots, B_\ell\}$, with the property that for any $\gamma \in \Gamma$, $\gamma \in I_S$ iff $[\![\gamma]\!] \cap \mathcal{E} = \emptyset$ and $\mathcal{F} \subseteq [\![\gamma]\!]$. This implies that $\mathcal{I}_S = \emptyset$ iff $\mathcal{E} \cap \mathcal{F} \neq \emptyset$. Finally, Lemma 1 indicates that $[true]_{\sim_\varepsilon} = [true, \langle \emptyset \rangle]$, while $[false]_{\sim_\varepsilon} = [\neg \langle \emptyset \rangle, false]$. These facts can be used to implement efficiently the tests in lines 17 and 21 of Algorithm 1.

6.2   Query Checking Multiple Data Streams

We now briefly discuss query checking in the case of multiple data streams. Note that a solution to such a problem must be a solution for each of the single-stream problems formed by considering each data stream in isolation. This suggests a straightforward iterative strategy for the multi-stream case, in which QC1 is repeatedly called for each data stream in isolation and the results are conjoined with the running tally of previous data-stream results. Other approaches are possible, and left for future work.

7   Experimental Results

We have implemented our query-checking algorithms in C/C++ and evaluated it on a synthetic dataset from the Causality Workbench Benchmark [8] representing time series data for product sales. The Spot [15] platform (v.2.8.1) was used to handle the parsing of Finite LTL formulas, with an extension to support the $\overline{\mathbf{X}}$ (Weak Next) operator. Several Spot-provided automatic formula rewrites (such as $\mathbf{X}\, true \equiv true$) are based on standard LTL identities and do not hold for Finite LTL; these were disabled. The SymPy python package [27] was also used to manipulate propositional formulas when necessary. We present here an abridged summary of our findings, for a complete account of experimental results we refer to a longer version of this paper [24]. Experiments were carried out on a machine with an Intel Core i5-6600K, 32 GB RAM and a 64-bit version of GNU/Linux.

Our evaluation had two goals: (1) to establish that meaningful results are produced (2) to perform a "stress test" on the system's performance. The test dataset contains daily sales volumes for 100 different products over a three-year period, along with information about 1000 different promotional campaigns used to influence sales of different subsets of the products. The dataset also includes seasonal baselines for each product. To convert this data set into normalized data streams, 1100 atomic propositions were created: $prod_i$ for $i \in \{1, \ldots, 100\}$, and $promo_i$ for $i \in \{1, \ldots, 1000\}$. At time point t, $prod_i$ is true if product i's sale volume on day t was reported to be greater than the volume on day $t-1$, and false otherwise. Similarly, at time point t, $promo_i$ is true if and only if the promotion was active on day t. This construction yields a single data stream D of 1095 time points, with $|\mathcal{AP}| = 1100$. We also subdivided D into quarters to create a set of data streams D_{quarter} (12 in total, one for each quarter of a year). We did the same on a monthly basis to create D_{month} (36 data streams). For a subset $A \subseteq \mathcal{AP}$, we denote by $D[A]$ ($D_{\text{quarter}}[A]$, $D_{\text{month}}[A]$) the data stream(s) in which we consider only the restricted set of atomic propositions A.

Two distinct query classes are explored, the first of which is as follows.

$$\Phi_1[\text{var}] = \{\mathbf{G}(prod_i \rightarrow \mathbf{F}(\text{var} \wedge \mathbf{X}\ true))\}$$

Instances of this class relate an increase in $prod_i$'s sales to a future condition captured by var. Instances of the second class

$$\Phi_2[\text{var}] = \{\mathbf{G}((promo_i \wedge prod_j) \rightarrow \mathbf{F}(\text{var} \wedge \mathbf{X}\ true))\}$$

restrict the first class by only considering time points where a promotion is also active. This second class could be useful when planning a promotional strategy, as it establishes a future condition that is triggered were a promotion to be activated while a product is selling well.

Our first goal was to evaluate our methodology's ability to produce "meaningful" solutions that convey interesting information about the relationships between the increase of sales in one product, potentially coupled with a promotion, and its future effect on the sales volumes of other products. Subsets $A \subset \mathcal{AP}$ were chosen based on correlation data provided with the data set, and query checking was performed on streams restricted by A. Meaningful solutions were found for a number of the query-checking problems considered. Due to space limitations we omit the details; we refer the reader to [24] for these.

Our second goal was to evaluate overall performance for different sets of data streams and atomic propositions. The general form of these experiments was as follows. Given n, an appropriate set $A \subseteq \mathcal{AP}$ of size n was randomly chosen based on the query class. Then $D[A]$, $D_{\text{quarter}}[A]$ and $D_{\text{month}}[A]$ were computed. An instance $\phi_1[\text{var}] \in \Phi_1[\text{var}]$ was chosen by randomly selecting $prop_i \in A$; similarly, an instance $\phi_2[\text{var}] \in \Phi_2[\text{var}]$ is chosen by selecting $prod_i, promo_j \in A$.

Performance results were then collected for computing the single-stream query-checking problems $QC1(D[A], \phi[\text{var}])$, for $\phi[\text{var}] \in \{\phi_1[\text{var}], \phi_2[\text{var}]\}$. Experiments were repeated by re-sampling A, with statistical averages reported for the set of trials. This was similarly done for the monthly and quarterly streams by randomly selecting a specific data stream $\pi \in D_{\text{month}}[A]$ and $\pi \in D_{\text{quarter}}[A]$, accordingly, and then computing $QC1(\pi, \phi[\text{var}])$. Figures 1a–c show the results for $QC1(D[A], \phi[\text{var}])$, $QC1(\pi \in D_{\text{quarter}}[A], \phi[\text{var}])$, and $QC1(\pi \in D_{\text{month}}[A], \phi[\text{var}])$. Average computation time is reported, along with the number of shatterable edges and distinct shatterable labels in the composed FQA produced during query checking. Individual invocations of $QC1(\cdot; \cdot)$ that ran for over 1 h were terminated, and aggregates affected are reported as "t/o."

It can be observed that the time cost of query checking scales with both the number of atomic propositions considered ($|A|$) and the length of the data stream. The number of shatterable edges present in the composed FQA also is correlated with data-stream length. The number of shatterable labels (i.e. $|SL|$ from Algorithm 1) has in the worse case an exponential relationship with runtime and so efforts to lower it (primarily by restricting $|A|$) will afford runtime savings.

# products	# promotions	ϕ_1[var] time	shatterable edges	shatterable labels
2	0	2.23 ± 0.05	1642.46 ± 10.74	4.00 ± 0.00
3	0	3.46 ± 0.42	1640.45 ± 8.34	8.00 ± 0.00
4	0	17.35 ± 6.01	1640.44 ± 8.28	16.00 ± 0.00
5	0	t/o	t/o	t/o
# products	# promotions	ϕ_2[var] time	shatterable edges	shatterable labels
2	1	2.74 ± 0.44	1326.17 ± 253.70	7.76 ± 0.87
3	1	8.51 ± 5.73	1379.36 ± 205.88	15.28 ± 2.13
4	1	t/o	t/o	t/o

(a) $D[A]$. Data stream is of length 1095. Averages taken over 100 trials.

# products	# promotions	ϕ_1[var] time	shatterable edges	shatterable labels
2	0	0.49 ± 0.03	135.08 ± 3.61	4.00 ± 0.00
3	0	0.55 ± 0.03	135.28 ± 3.79	8.00 ± 0.00
4	0	1.25 ± 0.28	135.15 ± 3.57	15.95 ± 0.23
5	0	t/o	t/o	t/o
# products	# promotions	ϕ_2[var] time	shatterable edges	shatterable labels
2	1	0.52 ± 0.06	113.04 ± 30.54	6.37 ± 1.66
3	1	0.76 ± 0.23	111.17 ± 30.62	12.39 ± 3.24
4	1	t/o	t/o	t/o

(b) $D_{\text{quarter}}[A]$. Streams are of length 91 or 92. Averages taken over 100 trials.

# products	# promotions	ϕ_1[var] time	shatterable edges	shatterable labels
4	0	0.50 ± 0.22	43.74 ± 2.34	13.85 ± 1.16
5	0	5.56 ± 9.28	43.91 ± 2.34	19.85 ± 1.76
6	0	110.75 ± 146.24	43.75 ± 2.08	24.12 ± 2.51
7	0	t/o	t/o	t/o
# products	# promotions	ϕ_2[var] time	shatterable edges	shatterable labels
4	1	4.07 ± 9.69	38.66 ± 9.95	16.34 ± 4.43
5	1	134.10 ± 395.66	39.58 ± 10.66	23.00 ± 6.51
6	1	t/o	t/o	t/o

(c) $D_{\text{month}}[A]$. Streams are of length 30 or 31. Averages taken over 50 trials.

Fig. 1. Performance results of QC1. All times in seconds.

8   Conclusions and Future Work

We have presented an automaton-theoretic approach to solving Finite LTL queries over normalized finite data streams. We showed how to compute finite query automata (FQAs), which also contain a propositional unknown, from such queries and compose them with finite data streams; solutions to the queries were computed from these composite automata. A prototype implementation of our algorithm was also evaluated on a synthetic data set from the literature.

As future work, more experimentation with our approach would yield further insight into the scope of problems to which it may be applied. Comparing our technique to traditional sequential data-mining approaches [2,18], which target time-series data but are not query-based, would open up new and interesting avenues for exploration, as would the study of query languages that are tolerant of the *noise* typically found in many experimental data sets. We also wish to investigate query checking for temporal logics that incorporate reasoning about discrete time, such as a discrete-time version of MITL [4], as well as other linear-time logics such as Linear Dynamic Logic [14], the modal mu-calculus [25] over finite sequences, and Allen Linear Temporal Logic [30].

References

1. Ackermann, C., Cleaveland, R., Huang, S., Ray, A., Shelton, C., Latronico, E.: Automatic requirement extraction from test cases. In: Barringer, H., Falcone, Y., Finkbeiner, B., Havelund, K., Lee, I., Pace, G., Roşu, G., Sokolsky, O., Tillmann, N. (eds.) RV 2010. LNCS, vol. 6418, pp. 1–15. Springer, Heidelberg (2010). https://doi.org/10.1007/978-3-642-16612-9_1

2. Agrawal, R., Srikant, R.: Mining sequential patterns. In: Proceedings of the Eleventh International Conference on Data Engineering, pp. 3–14. IEEE Computer Society, Washington, DC (1995)

3. Ahlswede, R., Cai, N.: Incomparability and intersection properties of Boolean interval lattices and chain posets. Eur. J. Comb. **17**(8), 677–687 (1996). https://doi.org/10.1006/eujc.1996.0059

4. Alur, R., Feder, T., Henzinger, T.A.: The benefits of relaxing punctuality. J. ACM (JACM) **43**(1), 116–146 (1996)

5. Baier, C., Katoen, J.P.: Principles of Model Checking. MIT Press, Cambridge (2008)

6. Browne, M., Clarke, E., Grumberg, O.: Characterizing finite Kripke structures in propositional temporal logic. Theor. Comput. Sci. **59**(1), 115–131 (1988). https://doi.org/10.1016/0304-3975(88)90098-9

7. Bruns, G., Godefroid, P.: Temporal logic query checking. In: Proceedings 16th Annual IEEE Symposium on Logic in Computer Science, pp. 409–417, June 2001. https://doi.org/10.1109/LICS.2001.932516

8. Causality workbench team: PROMO: simple causal effects in time series, August 2008. https://data.world/data-society/causal-effects-in-time-series

9. Chan, W.: Temporal-logic queries. In: Emerson, E.A., Sistla, A.P. (eds.) CAV 2000. LNCS, vol. 1855, pp. 450–463. Springer, Heidelberg (2000). https://doi.org/10.1007/10722167_34

10. Chockler, H., Gurfinkel, A., Strichman, O.: Variants of LTL query checking. In: Barner, S., Harris, I., Kroening, D., Raz, O. (eds.) HVC 2010. LNCS, vol. 6504, pp. 76–92. Springer, Heidelberg (2011). https://doi.org/10.1007/978-3-642-19583-9_11

11. Clarke, E.M., Emerson, E.A.: Design and synthesis of synchronization skeletons using branching time temporal logic. In: Kozen, D. (ed.) Logic of Programs 1981. LNCS, vol. 131, pp. 52–71. Springer, Heidelberg (1982). https://doi.org/10.1007/BFb0025774

12. Clarke, E.M., Henzinger, T.A., Veith, H., Bloem, R.: Handbook of Model Checking. Springer, Heidelberg (2018). https://doi.org/10.1007/978-3-319-10575-8

13. De Giacomo, G., De Masellis, R., Montali, M.: Reasoning on LTL on finite traces: insensitivity to infiniteness. In: Proceedings of the Twenty-Eighth AAAI Conference on Artificial Intelligence, AAAI 2014, Québec City, Québec, Canada , pp. 1027–1033. AAAI Press (2014)

14. De Giacomo, G., Vardi, M.Y.: Linear temporal logic and linear dynamic logic on finite traces. In: Proceedings of the Twenty-Third International Joint Conference on Artificial Intelligence, IJCAI 2013, Beijing, China, pp. 854–860. AAAI Press (2013)

15. Duret-Lutz, A., Lewkowicz, A., Fauchille, A., Michaud, T., Renault, É., Xu, L.: Spot 2.0 — a framework for LTL and ω-automata manipulation. In: Artho, C., Legay, A., Peled, D. (eds.) ATVA 2016. LNCS, vol. 9938, pp. 122–129. Springer, Cham (2016). https://doi.org/10.1007/978-3-319-46520-3_8

16. Eisner, C., Fisman, D.: Functional specification of hardware via temporal logic. In: Clarke, E., Henzinger, T., Veith, H., Bloem, R. (eds.) Handbook of Model Checking, pp. 795–829. Springer, Cham (2018). https://doi.org/10.1007/978-3-319-10575-8_24

17. Fionda, V., Greco, G.: The complexity of LTL on finite traces: hard and easy fragments. In: Proceedings of the Thirtieth AAAI Conference on Artificial Intelligence, AAAI 2016, Phoenix, Arizona, pp. 971–977. AAAI Press (2016)

18. Fradkin, D., Mörchen, F.: Mining sequential patterns for classification. Knowl. Inf. Syst. **45**(3), 731–749 (2015). https://doi.org/10.1007/s10115-014-0817-0

19. Georgala, K., Sherif, M.A., Ngomo, A.C.N.: An efficient approach for the generation of Allen relations. In: Proceedings of the Twenty-Second European Conference on Artificial Intelligence, ECAI 2016, The Hague, The Netherlands, pp. 948–956. IOS Press (2016). https://doi.org/10.3233/978-1-61499-672-9-948

20. Gurfinkel, A., Chechik, M., Devereux, B.: Temporal logic query checking: a tool for model exploration. IEEE Trans. Softw. Eng. **29**(10), 898–914 (2003). https://doi.org/10.1109/TSE.2003.1237171

21. Holzmann, G.J.: The SPIN Model Checker: Primer and Reference Manual, vol. 1003. Addison-Wesley, Reading (2004)

22. Huang, S., Cleaveland, R.: Query checking for linear temporal logic. In: Petrucci, L., Seceleanu, C., Cavalcanti, A. (eds.) FMICS/AVoCS -2017. LNCS, vol. 10471, pp. 34–48. Springer, Cham (2017). https://doi.org/10.1007/978-3-319-67113-0_3

23. Huang, S., Cleaveland, R.: A tableau construction for finite linear-time temporal logic. arXiv preprint arXiv:1910.09339 (2019)

24. Huang, S., Cleaveland, R.: Temporal-logic query checking over finite data streams. arXiv preprint arXiv:2006.03751 (2020)

25. Kozen, D.: Results on the propositional μ-calculus. Theor. Comput. Sci. **27**(3), 333–354 (1983)

26. Leucker, M.: Runtime verification for linear-time temporal logic. In: Bowen, J.P., Liu, Z., Zhang, Z. (eds.) SETSS 2016. LNCS, vol. 10215, pp. 151–194. Springer, Cham (2017). https://doi.org/10.1007/978-3-319-56841-6_5

27. Meurer, A., Smith, C.P., et al.: SymPy: symbolic computing in Python. PeerJ Comput. Sci. **3**, e103 (2017). https://doi.org/10.7717/peerj-cs.103

28. Pnueli, A.: The temporal logic of programs. In: 18th Annual Symposium on Foundations of Computer Science, pp. 46–57, October 1977. https://doi.org/10.1109/SFCS.1977.32
29. Roşu, G.: Finite-trace linear temporal logic: coinductive completeness. In: Falcone, Y., Sánchez, C. (eds.) RV 2016. LNCS, vol. 10012, pp. 333–350. Springer, Cham (2016). https://doi.org/10.1007/978-3-319-46982-9_21
30. Roşu, G., Bensalem, S.: Allen linear (interval) temporal logic – translation to LTL and monitor synthesis. In: Ball, T., Jones, R.B. (eds.) CAV 2006. LNCS, vol. 4144, pp. 263–277. Springer, Heidelberg (2006). https://doi.org/10.1007/11817963_25
31. Sistla, A.P., Clarke, E.M.: The complexity of propositional linear temporal logics. J. ACM (JACM) 32(3), 733–749 (1985)
32. Vardi, M.Y., Wolper, P.: An automata-theoretic approach to automatic program verification. In: Proceedings of the First Symposium on Logic in Computer Science, pp. 322–331. IEEE Computer Society (1986)
33. Wolper, P.: The tableau method for temporal logic: an overview. Logique Et Analyse 28(110–111), 119–136 (1985)

Verification of a Failure Management Protocol for Stateful IoT Applications

Umar Ozeer[1], Gwen Salaün[2]($\boxtimes$), Loïc Letondeur[1], François-Gaël Ottogalli[1], and Jean-Marc Vincent[2]

[1] Orange Labs, Meylan, France
[2] University of Grenoble Alpes, LIG, CNRS, Inria, Grenoble, France
gwen.salaun@inria.fr

Abstract. Fog computing provides computing, storage and communication resources at the edge of the network, near the physical world. Devices deployed in the Fog have interesting properties such as short delays, responsiveness, optimised communications and privacy. However, these devices have low stability and are prone to failures. Thus, there is a need for management protocols to tolerate failures of IoT applications in the Fog. We propose a failure management protocol which recovers from failures of devices and software elements involved in an IoT application. Designing such highly distributed management protocols is a difficult and error-prone task. Therefore, the main contribution of this paper is the formal specification and verification of this failure management protocol. Formal specification is achieved using a process algebraic language. The corresponding formal model was used to carry out extensive analysis of the protocol to ensure that it preserves important architectural invariants and functional properties. The verification step was performed using model checking techniques. The analysis of the protocol was a success because it allowed us to detect and correct several issues in the protocol.

1 Introduction

Fog Computing provides computing, storage and communication resources at the edge of the network, in proximity to the physical world. The Fog thus meets the latencies, privacy, QoS and geographical requirements of IoT applications that the cloud fails to resolve. For this reason, the deployment of IoT applications in the Fog has become increasingly popular and finds application in a wide range of sectors such as smart cities, agriculture, mining, healthcare or transportation.

There is a need of resilient IoT applications because devices in the Fog are unstable and prone to many types of failures like power failure (accidental unplugging, battery drain), hardware failures (due to external environmental conditions or wear-out), or software failures. These devices are also often connected through wireless networks which can be volatile and unstable because of connectivity issues. However, the design of a failure management protocols for IoT applications in the Fog is difficult because of the main characteristics of this environment, which is dynamic with entities joining and leaving the application, and heterogeneous in terms of hardware, software, network and communication models. Moreover, since IoT applications are geographically distributed and large-scale, a distributed management protocol is required.

© Springer Nature Switzerland AG 2020
M. H. ter Beek and D. Ničković (Eds.): FMICS 2020, LNCS 12327, pp. 272–287, 2020.
https://doi.org/10.1007/978-3-030-58298-2_12

This paper first introduces a failure management protocol for IoT applications. An IoT application consists of interacting appliances (i.e., sensors and actuators) and software elements hosted on Fog Nodes. This protocol provides a software solution to monitor the application and react to occurring failures in order to repair and restore a consistent pre-failure state of the application. It is worth noting that we focus on stateful IoT applications here, that is, applications involving devices and software that have internal states characterised by execution conditions, input parameters, environment variables and stored data resulting from computations and external interactions. These must be taken into account to restore the state of the application. Several managers are required to implement this protocol: a Stable Storage that keeps track of the state of the distributed elements of the application, a Global Manager which is notified in case of failure and that guides the recovery process, and Fog agents associated to Fog Nodes and appliances that are locally in charge of detecting and propagating failures as well as applying local recovery strategy to repair a failed entity.

Designing this protocol is very difficult particularly due to its distributed nature. Moreover, this protocol must respect important correctness properties (e.g., a failed software entity must eventually be restarted and restored, when a failure occurs every dependent entity must be paused until the failed entity has recovered, the state of a failed entity after restoration should be identical to its pre-failure state, etc). Thus, we decided to use formal techniques and tools to ensure that the protocol works as expected and respects the aforementioned properties. We chose to use LNT [5], a modern language for formally specifying concurrent systems, and model checking techniques [12] for analysing the specification with respect to the temporal properties to be preserved. These specification and verification steps were very useful for clarifying several questions as well as identifying and correcting some issues in the protocol. The main contribution of this paper is to report on the specification and analysis of the protocol using formal modelling languages and model checking techniques. The verification of the protocol allowed us to detect several issues and correct them in its implementation developed by Orange Labs.

The rest of this paper is organised as follows. Section 2 introduces the failure management protocol with a focus on the recovery phase. Section 3 presents the LNT specification of the protocol, the properties to be satisfied by the protocol, and the results of the verification including the detected issues. Section 4 compares our approach to related work and Sect. 5 concludes the paper.

2   Failure Management Protocol

This section presents successively the model for describing an IoT application, the managers implementing the failure management protocol, the four phases of the protocol in a nutshell, and the recovery phase in more details. Since the recovery phase is the most important and complex phase of the protocol, we decided to focus the specification and verification effort (Sect. 3) on that phase. The whole framework is called F^3ARIoT, and has been developed as a research prototype at Orange Labs. More details about the description of the protocol can be found in [20].

2.1   Application Model

An *IoT application* (application for short) is composed of the following constituents:

- *Software Elements* (SEs) are units of software to be executed. They participate in the execution of the application through their corresponding functions. A software element has an internal state and exposes a set of functional interfaces as well as non-functional interfaces for its administration.
- *Appliances* correspond to physical objects (e.g., switch, light, sensor, etc.) with no hosting capabilities. They are only accessible through their exposed API.
- *Fog Nodes* host the software elements, that is, they give access to physical resources and provide the runtime environment for the execution of software elements. Physical resources are usually restrained (e.g., Raspberry Pi or Arduino).
- *Logical Bindings* are abstractions of the communication models, which allow a couple of software elements or a software element and an appliance to interact together (two appliances cannot depend one of another).

An Application is modelled as a directed acyclic graph where each vertex represents a software element or an appliance, and each edge represents a binding. The direction of an edge gives the functional dependency between two vertices. If a vertex v_1 depends on a vertex v_2, then v_1 requires v_2 to be functional.

Note that we assume that all elements are uniquely identified and that applicative entities (software elements and appliances) are described using a behavioural model. Such a model defines the operations possible on that software or device as well as the order in which these operations must be triggered. As an example, a light can be turned on and off infinitely. In this work, we use Labelled Transition System for describing behavioural models. An LTS is a tuple (S, A, T, s_0), where S is a set of states, A is a set of operations associated to transitions, $T \subseteq S \times A \times D \times S$ is the transition relation, and $s_0 \in S$ is the initial state. A transition is defined by a tuple $(s_s, op, dir, s_t) \in T$ where s_s is the source state, op is the operation name, dir is the direction (either send operation with "!" or receive operation with "?"), and s_t is the target state.

Failures. As far as failures of the application are concerned, we consider in this work crash failures of software elements, appliances, and Fog Nodes. Therefore, a software element and an appliance can be in three different states in its lifecycle:

- Running: It executes its behaviour according to its behavioural model.
- Failed: It deviates from its correct behaviour and crashes. It stops sending and receiving messages as well as performing computations.
- Paused: The execution of its behaviour is temporarily stopped by the management protocol. It can later resume its activities when indicated.

The failure of a software element is different from that of an appliance in the sense that the former can always be restarted which is not the case for the latter. If the appliance has permanently failed and cannot be rebooted, it should be replaced by a functionally equivalent one. If no such appliance exists, the application can work in degraded mode, providing only a partial service. Note that the failure of a Fog Node induces the failure of all software elements hosted on the Fog Node.

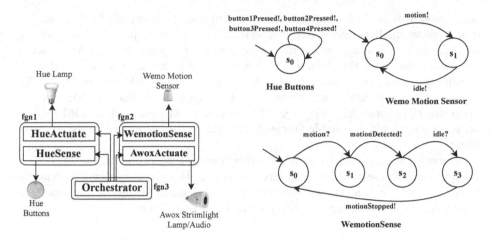

Fig. 1. Smart home application   **Fig. 2.** Behavioural models

Application Example. Figure 1 introduces a simplified version of a smart home application for light automation and physical intrusion detection developed at Orange Labs. It is composed of four appliances, three Fog Nodes (fgn1, fgn2, fgn3) on which the software elements are executed, and eight bindings. The appliance Hue Buttons controls the Hue Lamp. The Hue Buttons are also used to set an alarm for intrusion detection. If a motion is detected by the Wemo Motion Sensor after setting the alarm, a warning sound is triggered on the Awox Striimlight and all the lamps are turned on. The Orchestrator triggers these scenarios based on the sensed events from the software elements HueSense and WemotionSense. Events are then pushed to the software elements AwoxActuate and HueActuate according to the defined scenarios.

Figure 2 shows the behavioural models of two appliances, Hue Buttons and Wemo Motion Sensor, and of the software element WemotionSense. The Hue Buttons device sends an event corresponding to the button pressed (four possible buttons). There is no specific state for that appliance and all four events are possible at any time. This explains why the behavioural model consists of a single state. In contrast, the Wemo Motion Sensor has two states to distinguish when motion is detected and then stopped. The software element WemotionSense has four states: It receives motion events and forwards them to the Orchestrator. Software elements may exhibit more complex behaviours. The behavioural model of the Orchestrator for instance consists of ten states and fifteen transitions as it synchronises with all the other software elements.

2.2 Protocol Managers

This section describes the managers that compose the failure management protocol. A *Stable Storage* (SS) is used for persisting data of all entities involved in an application. We assume that this storage is unaffected by applicative failures and its implementation can take various forms such as replicated or redundant file systems [17]. A *Global Manager* (GM) is a control and decision making entity that has a global view on the application. It is notified when failures occur and it keeps a record of failed entities. It also guides the Fog Agents (see below) during the recovery process. The GM can also request available appliances from a device/object registry in order to replace a failed appliance. Each Fog Node and each appliance is managed by a *Fog Agent* (FA). This local manager provides an entry point for managing the lifecycle of the locally hosted software elements and appliances. A Fog Agent is in charge of local failure management. In particular, a Fog Agent detects failures, interacts with the GM for failure recovery and with the Stable Storage to retrieve the data necessary for the recovery phase.

Figure 3 gives an overview of the aforementioned managers and the way they interact together. We use a different syntax for distinguishing communication channels between Fog Agents and Global Manager/Stable Storage. In the rest of this paper, we assume all managers interact using synchronous communication.

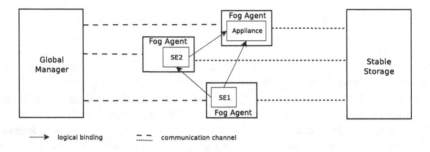

Fig. 3. Overview of protocol managers

2.3   Failure Management Protocol

The failure management protocol consists of four functional steps, which are carried out by the managers presented in the previous section: (i) state saving, (ii) monitoring and failure detection, (iii) failure notification, and (iv) decision and recovery. The first step aims at saving the local data that represents the state of execution of each entity of the application on the Stable Storage. The state saving step is policy-based to cope with the heterogeneous nature of the environment. A state saving policy defines for each applicative entity the data to be saved as well as the technique of saving. The techniques are based on checkpoint, message logging and function call record [8]. These techniques are chosen depending on the local storage and reliability assumptions made at the local Fog Node. The second step involves the monitoring of the application for failure detection. Monitoring can be achieved by Fog Agents through the following techniques: heartbeat, ping-acks, applicative message observation and local system observation. A failure detection triggers the third step in which failure notifications are propagated to Fog Agents of dependent entities so as to functionally pause the part of the application impacted by the failure. Concretely, when a failure occurs, the GM notifies the Fog Agents of the direct dependent entities of this failure. These Fog Agents pause the functional behaviour of these applicative entities and propagate the failure notification by sending similar messages to the Fog Agents of the entities depending on them. In the worst case, all entities are paused. The final recovery phase aims at repairing and restoring the state of the application in order to bring back the application to a consistent state. In the case of a failed software element, it is restarted before restoring its state. If a Fog Node fails, a new placement for the hosted software elements is computed before redeploying them onto failure-free Fog Nodes and restoring their states. When an appliance fails, it is replaced by another functionally equivalent appliance. When recovery is completed, the GM initiates the sending of recovery notifications that are propagated by the Fog Agents to all dependent entities.

2.4 Recovery Phase

In this subsection, we present the final phase of the failure management protocol with more details. This recovery phase aims at repairing and restoring the application into a consistent state upon occurrence of a failure.

Global Manager. When a failure occurs, the GM is notified by the Fog Agent that monitors the failed entity. The notification includes the identifier of the failed entity. The GM warns the Fog Agents of the entities having dependencies on the failed one that this failure has occurred. To do so, the GM relies on the architectural description of the application and sends a message to all Fog Agents of depending entities to let them know of the failure. We will see how Fog Agents react to those messages later on in this section. The GM then decides the steps for recovery depending on the type of entity that has failed. In the case of a software element or a Fog Node, it is assumed that there are enough resources to restart a software element or to find another Fog Node. If the failed entity is an appliance, the GM checks in the set of available appliances if there is an appliance that can replace the failed one. An appliance can act as a replacement if it has a similar behaviour to the failed one (checked using strong behavioural equivalence [19]). If there is one functionally equivalent appliance, the state of the failed appliance is restored on the replacement one. If this is not the case, the application cannot be restored and continues its execution with less features in a degraded mode.

The GM awaits for a notification from the Fog Agent confirming that the restoration has been completed (this notification is not necessary in degraded mode). Upon reception of this message, the GM sends a message to all Fog Agents of the depending entities (that have been previously warned of the failure) to let them know that the corresponding entities can resume their activity. The GM finally starts over and can handle a second failure. Note that in the current version of the protocol, the GM handles failures in sequence. In practice, the simultaneous occurrence of two failures hardly ever happens. Moreover, the recovery time is very low, less than a second according to the experiments we made with the protocol implementation. Figure 4 summarises the behaviour of the Global Manager.

Fog Agent. A Fog Agent (FA) is in charge of handling software element failures on the local Fog Node and neighbouring appliances. When a failure occurs the FA first notifies the GM and waits for its decision with respect to that failure. If the failure is confirmed and restoration initiated, the FA retrieves the former state of the failed entity

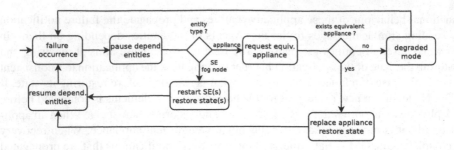

Fig. 4. Global manager behaviour

from the Stable Storage. It restores the state of the entity and resumes the execution of its functional behaviour from that state.

Another role of the FA is to propagate start/pause messages when a failure occurs in one of the neighbouring entities. In that case, the FA can receive a message directly from the GM or from one of the FAs of the neighbouring entities. Upon reception of this message, the FA interrupts the functional behaviour of its entities and propagates the message to all FAs of depending entities. In this way, all the entities that are impacted by the failure pause their functional behaviour. When the failure has been handled and the failed entity restored, each FA receives a message indicating it to start the paused entities again. This decision is propagated in the same way that failure notifications are propagated so that the application becomes fully functional again.

3 Model Checking

In this section, we first introduce the LNT specification for the failure notification and recovery phases of the failure management protocol (phases (iii) and (iv) in Sect. 2.3). Then, we present the properties of interest that must be preserved by the protocol. Finally, verification is described with some experimental results and a presentation of the issues detected and corrected in the protocol.

3.1 Specification

We chose LNT [5] as specification language because it is expressive enough and adequate for formally describing communication protocols as the failure management protocol presented beforehand in this paper. Moreover, it is equipped with CADP [12], a rich toolbox for analysing LNT specifications using model checking techniques.

LNT is an extension of LOTOS [14], an ISO standardised process algebra, which allows the definition of data types, functions, and processes. Table 1 provides an excerpt of the behavioural fragment of LNT syntax. B stands for a LNT term, A for an action, E for a Boolean expression, x for a variable, T for a type, and P for a process name. The syntax fragment presented in this table contains the termination construct (**stop**) and actions (A). LNT processes are then built using several operators: sequential composition (**;**), conditional statement (**if**), non-deterministic choice (**select**), parallel composition (**par**) where the communication between the involved processes is carried out by rendezvous on a list of synchronised actions, looping behaviours described using process calls or explicit operators (**while**), and assignment (**:=**) where the variable should be defined beforehand (**var**). LNT is formally defined using operational semantics based on Labelled Transition Systems.

Table 1. Excerpt of LNT syntax (behaviour part)

$B ::= $ **stop** | A $(!E, ?x)$ | $B_1; B_2$

     | **if** E **then** B_1 **else** B_2 **end if** | **select** B_1 **[]** ... **[]** B_n **end select**

     | **par** $A_1, ..., A_m$ **in** $B_1 \| ... \| B_n$ **end par** | $P[A_1, ..., A_m](E_1, ..., E_n)$

     | **while** E **loop** B **end loop** | **var** $x{:}T$ **in** $x := E$; B **end var**

The specification for the failure management protocol consists of three parts: *data types* (~100 lines), *functions* (~600 lines), and *processes* (>800 lines). A large part of the specification depends on the input application model (involved applicative entities and their dependencies), and is therefore automatically generated from a Python program (~1,500 lines) we implemented. For instance, the application used as example in Sect. 2.1 (consisting of nine software elements/appliances) results in about 2,500 lines of LNT specification that are generated automatically from the Python program.

Data types are used to describe mainly the application model (Fog Nodes, software elements, appliances, dependencies, behavioural models). As an example, an application consists of a set of Fog Nodes, a set of appliances and a set of logical bindings. *Functions* apply to data expressions and are necessary for several kinds of computation: extracting information from the application such as dependent entities, checking if two appliances have equivalent behavioural models, checking whether the application respects some specific invariants (absence of cycles, no disconnected entity, etc.), computing the target state in case of recovery of an entity, etc. *Processes* are used to specify the different managers of the failure management approach, namely the behaviour of the Stable Storage, of the Global Manager and of the Fog Agents. Note that we also use Fog Agents in this specification to model the functional part of the application, that is, the operations executed and exchanged among applicative entities. Another process, called simulator, is used to make the application execute functional operations and inject failures to the system. This simulator process is parameterised by the length of the execution (the max number of functional operations) and the max number of failures.

Figure 5 shows the four LNT modules used to specify the protocol where boxes correspond to LNT modules (generated code with dashed boxes). When a module is inside another one, it means that the external one includes the inner one. The DATATYPES module defines data types and functions. The APPLI module describes the application model. The GM module defines the behaviour of the Global Manager, which is independent of the application, so written once and for all. The MAIN module defines all other processes for the Stable Storage, Fog Agents and the main behaviour of the protocol.

For illustration purposes, we give in Fig. 6 one instance of the simulator process, which is an example of processes. One can see that this process can either make the application evolved (top part) illustrating by the way why a part of the specification

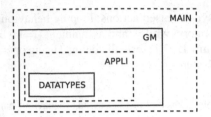

Fig. 5. Overview of the specification structure

depends on the application, or can inject different types of failures to the application. The process keeps track of the number of occurred operations (functional or failure) in order to terminate (correctly) when the simulation has reached the max number of execution steps. As illustrated in Fig. 6, we use actions for modelling functional operations (e.g., initiate, on, off) or for identifying the occurrence of specific events in the protocol (e.g., failureSE, failureAppliance, failureFogNode).

```
1  process simulator [ initiate:any, on:any, off:any, failureSE: any,
      failureAppliance: any, failureFogNode: any, finish: any]
      (nbFuncOperationsMax: Nat, nbFailureMax: Nat) is
2  var x, y: ID, sender: ID, receiver: ID, nbFuncOperations: Nat, senderTargetState:
      ID, receiverTargetState: ID, nbFailure: Nat in
3    nbFuncOperations := nbFuncOperationsMax ;   -- to count the size of the trace
4    nbFailure := 0 ;                  -- to count the number of effective failures
5    while (nbFuncOperations > 0) loop
6      select  -- functional behaviour
7        initiate (?sender of ID, ?receiver of ID, ?senderTargetState of ID,
            ?receiverTargetState of ID)
8      []
9        on (?sender of ID, ?receiver of ID, ?senderTargetState of ID,
            ?receiverTargetState of ID)
10     []
11       off (?sender of ID, ?receiver of ID, ?senderTargetState of ID,
            ?receiverTargetState of ID)
12     [] -- failure injector (3 kinds of failures)
13       if (nbFailure < nbFailureMax) then
14         select
15           failureSE (?x of ID, ?y of ID)
16         []
17           failureAppliance (?x of ID, ?y of ID)
18         []
19           failureFogNode (?x of ID)
20         end select;
21         nbFailure := nbFailure + 1            -- updating the number of failures
22       end if
23     end select;
24     nbFuncOperations := nbFuncOperations - 1  -- updating the number of operations
25   end loop;
26   finish  -- correct termination
27 end var
28 end process
```

Fig. 6. Example of simulator process

Finally, the main process is generated and represents all processes (simulator, Stable Storage, Global Manager, Fog Agents for SEs and appliances) in parallel as well as the way they interact together as depicted previously in Fig. 3.

3.2 Properties

We identified 12 properties that must be respected by the protocol. These properties can be organised in three different groups: (i) architectural invariants (prop. 1, 2, 3 below), (ii) final objective of the protocol (prop. 4 below), and (iii) additional functional properties (prop. 5–12 below). For some of these properties, we also give their formulation in the MCL language [18], the temporal logic used in CADP. MCL is an extension of alternation-free μ-calculus with regular expressions, data-based constructs, and fairness operators. Note that, since some of these properties depend on the functional actions used in the application (prop. 6, 7, 9), they are generated automatically using our Python program at the same time as the LNT specification. Note that we could verify additional properties, but the following 12 properties are the most important ones.

(i) Architectural invariants:
  1. There are no cycles in the application through dependencies.
  2. There are no disconnected entities in the application.
  3. Appliances have no dependencies on other appliances.
(ii) Final Objective:
  4. The state of a failed SE (or appliance if there is an equivalent appliance available) after restoration is identical to its state before the failure.
(iii) Functional properties:
  5. When a failure occurs, the failed entity eventually recovers. This is true for appliance only if there is an equivalent one available.

```
library actl.mcl end library
[ true* . '{FAILURESE ?se:String ?state:String}' ]
            AU_A_A(true, not '{FAILURESE !se !.*}',
                   '{RESTORESECOMPLETED !se !.*}', true)
```

  This property is formalised making use of action CTL patterns [7].
  6. When a SE/Fog Node is paused, it eventually starts again. This is not always true for appliances because they cannot always be replaced.
  7. When a failure occurs, every dependent SE/appliance is paused.
  8. A sequence exists resulting in the application execution with no failure.
  9. A SE/appliance cannot execute its functional behaviour when paused or failed.
  10. The managers implementing the protocol (Global Manager, Stable Storage and Fog Agents) can always terminate correctly.

  mu X . (< **true** > **true** **and** [not FINISH] X)

  11. The application is fully operational except when operating in degraded mode.

12. There is no sequence of two failures without a restore in between (illustrated on
    SEs below).

```
(
    [ true* . ' FAILURESE ?se:String ?state:String ' .
      not (' RESTORESECOMPLETED !se !.* ') .
      ' FAILURESE !se !.* '
    ] false
)
```

All the properties verified on the example introduced in Sect. 2.1 consists of about
600 lines of MCL. Half of the code corresponds to property 9, since in that case we
generate one property for each possible functional operation for each entity in the application. Property 9 consists of the conjunction of all these atomic properties.

3.3 Experiments

To verify the protocol, we use as input a set of applications. For each application, we
generate the part of the LNT specification depending on the application, and then we
call CADP exploration tools for generating an LTS describing all the possible executions of the protocol for that application. In this LTS, transitions are labelled with the
actions introduced previously in the specification, and we use these actions in the properties to check that the protocol works as expected.

The analysis of the protocol was run on a macOS Mojave machine with a 2.8 GHz
Intel Core i7 processor, 16 GB of DDR3 RAM and 256 GB PCIe-based flash storage.
In these experiments, we rely on a set of realistic smart home applications exhibiting
various architectures, and involving different entities (Fog Node, SE, appliance) and
logical dependencies. The two other parameters of these experiments are the length of
the execution, that is, the max number of functional operations executed by the application, and the max number of failures. It is worth noting that since we use enumerative
techniques here, there is no need to experiment with large applications, long executions
or a high number of failures in order to find issues in the protocol. In contrast, most
problems are usually detected on small applications and scenarios.

Table 2 summarises some of the experiments we carried out during the verification
phase. The first column identifies the example. The next four columns characterise the
size of the application (number of Fog Nodes, of software elements, of appliances and of
dependencies). The following columns characterise the scenario in terms of execution
length and number of failures, the size of the raw LTS (number of states and transitions), and the time in seconds for generating the LTS and for verifying all temporal
properties. Those properties are analysed on a minimised version of the LTS (reduced
wrt. strong bisimulation). It takes a few seconds to obtain that minimised version, which
is computed using CADP reduction tools. The minimised version is about the half in
average in terms of states and transitions compared to the raw version.

We now comment on the results presented in this table. Example 4 corresponds to
the application introduced in Fig. 1. These results show that the larger the application
is (in terms of entities), the longer it takes to generate the corresponding LTS model

Table 2. Experimental results

Ident	Appli. model				Simul.		LTS (raw)		Time (sec.)	
	|FG|	|SE|	|APP|	|DEP|	|E|	|F|	|S|	|T|	Gen.	Verif.
1a	3	3	2	4	10	1	56,416	193,025	11	179
1b	3	3	2	4	10	2	156,432	517,758	12	535
1c	3	3	2	4	10	3	236,871	713,535	12	783
1d	3	3	2	4	10	4	281,549	756,433	12	1,285
1e	3	3	2	4	10	5	296,946	716,387	12	4,469
2a	3	4	3	7	5	1	3,815	13,045	15	64
2b	3	4	3	7	5	2	16,081	52,582	16	163
2c	3	4	3	7	7	2	52,207	198,247	16	338
2d	3	4	3	7	7	3	105,550	358,924	17	397
2e	3	4	3	7	10	3	489,778	2,096,701	25	1,012
3a	4	5	3	11	5	2	29,779	112,377	102	365
3b	4	5	3	11	10	3	314,349	2,077,252	109	992
4	3	5	4	8	5	2	22,709	58,177	2,403	111
5	5	6	4	11	5	2	33,444	121,254	327	371
6	5	8	4	15	5	2	53,973	212,742	9,392	16,764

(see row 6 for example). Second, the main factor impacting the size of the LTS is the simulation parameters. Since we rely on enumerative techniques, one more functional action or one more failure generates many more executions since this action/failure may occur at any moment during the application execution and this results in additional interleavings of actions (see rows 1a–e and 2a–e in the table). The time for model checking all properties is much longer than the generation time for applications with up to 8 entities, but becomes smaller for larger applications (see rows 4 and 6). More generally, the verification time linearly increases with the size of the LTS whereas the generation time tends to explode when the application size increases. We use rather small applications for verification purposes (up to 12 entities for example 6 in the table) because this is not necessary to use large applications for finding issues, and contrarily, most problems are usually found on small yet pathological applications.

3.4 Detected Issues

The specification and verification helped to refine our understanding of the finer points of the procotol. In this section, we focus on three points of interest, which were identified or confirmed using model checking.

First, it is worth reminding that, although the protocol is always able to work and terminate correctly, this is not the case of the application. Indeed, in case of appliance failure, if there is no functionally equivalent appliance available, the application cannot be restored and the application keeps working in degraded mode. This was confirmed using verification techniques. During our experiments, when there were no additional equivalent appliance for replacing failed ones, the first part of property 11 in Sect. 3.2 *"the application is fully operational"* was violated because, in that case, an appliance has failed and cannot be replaced.

Another problem comes from the propagation of notifications in case of failure in an application with multiple dependencies. Suppose there is an application with four entities and dependencies among them looking like a diamond (for instance e_2 depends on e_1, e_3 depends on e_1 and e_4 depends on both e_2 and e_3). If e_1 fails, the Fog Agents of e_2 and e_3 are notified of that failure and send a notification to all Fog Agents depending on them. In that case, both e_2 and e_3 Fog Agents actually send a notification to e_4 Fog Agent, so the Fog Agent of e_4 is supposed to receive two notifications in that case. If those messages are not consumed, this can induce a deadlock (correct termination of the protocol is not possible, prop. 10) because one of the Fog Agents of e_2 and e_3 is not able to propagate its notification, resulting in an erroneous situation in the protocol. This can be corrected by either receiving as many notifications as supposed with respect to the failed entity and the structure of the application, or by accepting the first notification message and discarding the forthcoming similar ones.

Another interesting issue concerns multiple simultaneous failures. The protocol was originally supposed to support such failures, but the design of the protocol was more complicated and several properties were violated. This is due to the fact than when trying to handle several failures at the same time, some contradictory messages can be exchanged among Fog Agents (e.g., one message saying to restart an entity whereas another failure has occurred so a contradictory message asking to pause is also received). As a consequence, in the first version of the protocol, we decided to treat failures one after the other, which is reasonable since the occurrence of multiple failures is scarce and the implementation of the failure management protocol on a realistic testbed shows that the time taken to recover from failures is less than one second.

To conclude, it is worth saying that all properties were satisfied for all the examples of our dataset of applications used for verification purposes. In addition, the existing implementation of this industrial protocol developed by Orange Labs was modified in order to integrate all the feedback and issues discovered during the analysis of the protocol.

4 Related Work

In this section, we first compare the protocol presented in this paper with respect to similar protocols for failure management proposed in cloud computing or Fog computing/IoT. In a second step, we have a specific focus on similar protocols, which also make use of formal methods for verification purposes.

Failure Management. [11] proposes a self-healing approach to handle exceptions in service-based processes and to repair the faulty activities with a model-based approach. More precisely, a set of repair actions is defined in the process model, and repairability of the process is assessed by analysing the process structure and the available repair actions. When an exception arises during execution, repair plans are generated by taking into account constraints coming from the process structure, dependencies among data, and available repair actions. In [4], the authors present fault-aware management protocols, which permit to model the management behaviour of composite cloud applications, by taking into account the possible occurrence of faults suddenly occurring and misbehaving components. This approach also proposes to generate plans for changing the actual configuration of an application for, e.g., recovering an application that is stuck because of a faulted node. A few recent papers have focused on fault tolerance of IoT applications. [23] provides a fault tolerant approach through virtual service composition. Single service and single device failures are supported by using IoT devices of different modalities as fault tolerant backups for each other. [22] discusses the challenges of fault tolerance in IoT and proposes some potential solutions to consider. It suggests that natural redundancy of functionality across devices within the home, as well as usage scenarios, should be exploited to provide fault tolerance and also discusses the issues of this approach, like incorrect context sensing and actuating of devices. [1] proposes a fault tolerant platform for smart home applications. It provides fault tolerant delivery of sensor events and actuation commands in the presence of link loss and network partitions. [13] proposes an IoT-based architecture supporting fault tolerance for healthcare environment. The approach focuses on network fault tolerance which is achieved by backup routing between nodes and advanced service mechanisms to maintain connectivity in case of failing connections. Compared to these approaches, the main difference is that our approach focuses on stateful applications and allows the end-to-end management of a failure from detection to recovery of a consistent state of the application. The proposed protocol also takes into account the specificities of the environment such as heterogeneity and dynamicity.

Protocol Verification. In [2,3], the authors present a reconfiguration protocol applying changes to a set of connected components for transforming a current assembly to a target one given as input. Reconfiguration steps aim at (dis)connecting ports and changing component states (stopped or started). This protocol supports failures and preserves a number of architectural invariants. This was proved using the Coq theorem prover. We preferred model checking techniques here, because they are convenient at design time in order to detect possible issues. Theorem proving is interesting when the developers have already at their disposal a stable version of a protocol, and they ultimately want to prove its correctness. In [9,10,21], the authors present a self-deployment protocol that was designed to automatically configure cloud applications consisting of a set of software elements to be deployed on different virtual machines. This protocol works in a decentralized way, i.e., there is no need for a centralized server. It also starts the software elements in a certain order, respecting important architectural invariants. This protocol supports virtual machine and network failures, and always succeeds in deploying an application when faced with a finite number of failures. A formal specification of the protocol allowed the successful verification of important properties to be preserved. [15,16] propose verification of IoT applications before deployment using model checking techniques. [6] applies infinite-state model checking to formally verify IoT protocols such as the Pub/Sub consistency protocol adopted by the REDIS distributed file system. The verification method is based on a combination of SMT solvers and overapproximations as those implemented in the Cubicle verification tool. Since these protocols involve infinite data structures, the authors chose to use analysis techniques capable of reasoning on infinite state spaces.

5 Concluding Remarks

In this paper, we focus on a failure management protocol, which allows the supervision of IoT applications and the management of failures. This protocol targets stateful IoT applications in the sense that those applications handle and store data during their execution. When a failure occurs, the protocol detects the failure and restores a consistent pre-failure state of the application to make it functional again. Since designing such distributed protocol is error-prone, we decided to rely on formal specification techniques and verification tools in order to ensure that the protocol respects some important properties. We used a process algebraic specification language and model checking techniques for verifying these properties. These analysis steps helped to detect several issues and clarify some subtle parts of the protocol. This information was used to correct and revise the implementation of the protocol developed by Orange Labs.

As for future work, the first perspective is to extend the protocol specification to support asynchronous communication (communication via message buffers). Another perspective is to revise the protocol in order to support simultaneous failures. An idea in that direction is to distribute the behaviour of the Global Manager locally on Fog Agents in order to have a fully decentralised version of the protocol, which will make it more amenable to support multiple failures.

References

1. Ardekani, M.S., Singh, R.P., Agrawal, N., Terry, D.B., Suminto, R.O.: Rivulet: a fault-tolerant platform for smart-home applications. In: Proceedings of Middleware 2017, pp. 41–54. ACM (2017)
2. Boyer, F., Gruber, O., Pous, D.: Robust reconfigurations of component assemblies. In: Proceedings of ICSE 2013, pp. 13–22. IEEE Press (2013)
3. Boyer, F., Gruber, O., Salaün, G.: Specifying and verifying the SYNERGY reconfiguration protocol with LOTOS NT and CADP. In: Butler, M., Schulte, W. (eds.) FM 2011. LNCS, vol. 6664, pp. 103–117. Springer, Heidelberg (2011). https://doi.org/10.1007/978-3-642-21437-0_10
4. Brogi, A., Canciani, A., Soldani, J.: Fault-aware management protocols for multi-component applications. J. Syst. Softw. **139**, 189–210 (2018)
5. Champelovier, D., et al.: Reference manual of the LNT to LOTOS translator, version 6.7. Inria (2018)
6. Delzanno, G.: Formal verification of internet of things protocols. In: Proceedings of FRIDA 2018 (2018)
7. Dwyer, M.B., Avrunin, G.S., Corbett, J.C.: Patterns in property specifications for finite-state verification. In: Proceedings of ICSE 1999, pp. 411–420. ACM (1999)
8. Elnozahy, E.N.M., Alvisi, L., Wang, Y.-M., Johnson, D.B.: A survey of rollback-recovery protocols in message-passing systems. ACM Comput. Surv. **34**(3), 375–408 (2002)
9. Etchevers, X., Salaün, G., Boyer, F., Coupaye, T., Palma, N.D.: Reliable self-deployment of cloud applications. In: Proceedings of SAC 2014, pp. 1331–1338. ACM (2014)

10. Etchevers, X., Salaün, G., Boyer, F., Coupaye, T., Palma, N.D.: Reliable self-deployment of distributed cloud applications. Softw. Pract. Exp. **47**(1), 3–20 (2017)
11. Friedrich, G., Fugini, M., Mussi, E., Pernici, B., Tagni, G.: Exception handling for repair in service-based processes. IEEE Trans. Softw. Eng. **36**(2), 198–215 (2010)
12. Garavel, H., Lang, F., Mateescu, R., Serwe, W.: CADP 2011: a toolbox for the construction and analysis of distributed processes. STTT **2**(15), 89–107 (2013)
13. Gia, T.N., Rahmani, A.-M., Westerlund, T., Liljeberg, P., Tenhunen, H.: Fault tolerant and scalable IoT-based architecture for health monitoring. In: Processing of SAS 2015. IEEE (2015)
14. ISO: LOTOS – A formal description technique based on the temporal ordering of observational behaviour. Technical report 8807, ISO (1989)
15. Krishna, A., Pallec, M.L., Mateescu, R., Noirie, L., Salaün, G.: IoT composer: composition and deployment of IoT applications. In: Proceedings of ICSE 2019, pp. 19–22. IEEE/ACM (2019)
16. Krishna, A., Pallec, M.L., Mateescu, R., Noirie, L., Salaün, G.: Rigorous design and deployment of IoT applications. In: Proceedings of FormaliSE 2019, pp. 21–30 (2019)
17. Lampson, B., Sturgis, H.E.: Crash recovery in a distributed data storage system. Technical report, Xerox Palo Alto Research Center (1979)
18. Mateescu, R., Thivolle, D.: A model checking language for concurrent value-passing systems. In: Cuellar, J., Maibaum, T., Sere, K. (eds.) FM 2008. LNCS, vol. 5014, pp. 148–164. Springer, Heidelberg (2008). https://doi.org/10.1007/978-3-540-68237-0_12
19. Milner, R.: Communication and Concurrency. Prentice Hall, Upper Saddle River (1989)
20. Ozeer, U., Etchevers, X., Letondeur, L., Ottogalli, F.-G., Salaün, G., Vincent, J.-M.: Resilience of stateful IoT applications in a dynamic fog environment. In: Proceedings of MobiQuitous 2018, pp. 332–341. ACM (2018)
21. Salaün, G., Etchevers, X., De Palma, N., Boyer, F., Coupaye, T.: Verification of a self-configuration protocol for distributed applications in the cloud. In: Cámara, J., de Lemos, R., Ghezzi, C., Lopes, A. (eds.) Assurances for Self-Adaptive Systems. LNCS, vol. 7740, pp. 60–79. Springer, Heidelberg (2013). https://doi.org/10.1007/978-3-642-36249-1_3
22. Terry, D.: Toward a new approach to IoT fault tolerance. Computer **49**(8), 80–83 (2016)
23. Zhou, S., Lin, K.-J., Na, J., Chuang, C.-C., Shih, C.-S.: Supporting service adaptation in fault tolerant internet of things. In: Proceedings of SOCA 2015, pp. 65–72. IEEE (2015)

Correction to: Formally Verified Timing Computation for Non-deterministic Horizontal Turns During Aircraft Collision Avoidance Maneuvers

Yanni Kouskoulas, T. J. Machado, and Daniel Genin

Correction to:
Chapter "Formally Verified Timing Computation
for Non-deterministic Horizontal Turns During Aircraft
Collision Avoidance Maneuvers" in: M. H. ter Beek
and D. Ničković (Eds.): *Formal Methods for Industrial*
Critical Systems, **LNCS 12327,**
https://doi.org/10.1007/978-3-030-58298-2_4

In the originally published version of chapter 4 Equations 29 and 30 had the wrong guard expressions. This has now been corrected.

The updated version of this chapter can be found at
https://doi.org/10.1007/978-3-030-58298-2_4

Correction to: The 2020 Expert Survey on Formal Methods

Hubert Garavel, Maurice H. ter Beek, and Jaco van de Pol

Correction to:
Chapter 1 in: M. H. ter Beek and D. Ničković (Eds.):
Formal Methods for Industrial Critical Systems, **LNCS 12327,**
https://doi.org/10.1007/978-3-030-58298-2_1

In the originally published version of chapter 1, the particle in the author names have been structured incorrectly. This has been corrected.

The updated version of this chapter can be found at
https://doi.org/10.1007/978-3-030-58298-2_1

Author Index

Printed in the United States
by Baker & Taylor Publisher Services